COOPERATION AND

HELPING BEHAVIOR

Theories and Research

COOPERATION AND
HELPING BEHAVIOR
Theories and Research

Edited by

Valerian J. Derlega

Department of Psychology
Old Dominion University
Norfolk, Virginia

Janusz Grzelak

Institute of Psychology
University of Warsaw
Warsaw, Poland

ACADEMIC PRESS

A Subsidiary of Harcourt Brace Jovanovich, Publishers

New York   London   Toronto   Sydney   San Francisco

ACADEMIC PRESS, INC.
111 Fifth Avenue, New York, New York 10003

United Kingdom Edition published by
ACADEMIC PRESS, INC. (LONDON) LTD.
24/28 Oval Road, London NW1 7DX

Library of Congress Cataloging in Publication Data

Main entry under title:

Cooperation and helping behavior

     Bibliography: p.
     Includes index.
     1. Helping behavior. 2. Cooperativeness. 3. Altruism.
I. Derlega, Valerian J. II. Grzelak, Janusz.   [DNLM:
1. Cooperative behavior. 2. Helping behavior.   HM 132
D434c]
BF637.H4C66   158'.2   81-19130
ISBN 0-12-210820-5   AACR2

To the memory of my mother, Tekla Baran Derlega
—**VJD**

In honor of my parents, Regina and Czeslaw Grzelak
—**JG**

Contents

Chapter 3
Social Values and Rules of Fairness: A Theoretical Perspective

CHARLES G. McCLINTOCK and EDDY VAN AVERMAET

Chapter 4
Cognitive Processes Underlying Cooperation: The Theory of Social Representation

JEAN CLAUDE ABRIC

Chapter 5
Preferences and Cognitive Processes in Interdependence Situations: A Theoretical Analysis of Cooperation

JANUSZ L. GRZELAK

Chapter 6
The Effects of Intergroup Competition and Cooperation on Intragroup and Intergroup Relationships

JACOB M RABBIE

Chapter 7
The Development of Integrative Agreements
DEAN G. PRUITT and PETER J. D. CARNEVALE

Chapter 8
Social Trap Analogs: The Tragedy of the Commons in the Laboratory
DARWYN E. LINDER

Chapter 9
Altruism and the Problem of Collective Action
GERALD MARWELL

Part II
HELPING BEHAVIOR

Chapter 10
Promotive Tension: Theory and Research
HARVEY A. HORNSTEIN

Chapter 11
The Justice Motive in Human Relations and the Economic Model of Man: A Radical Analysis of Facts and Fictions
MELVIN J. LERNER

Chapter 12
Responsive Bystanders: The Process of Intervention
JANE A. PILIAVIN, JOHN F. DOVIDIO, SAMUEL L. GAERTNER, and RUSSELL D. CLARK, III

Chapter 13
The Help-Seeking Process
ALAN E. GROSS and PEG A. McMULLEN

Chapter 18
Altruism, Envy, Competitiveness, and the Common Good
ROBERT B. ZAJONC

List of Contributors

Numbers in parentheses indicate the pages on which the authors' contributions begin.

JEAN CLAUDE ABRIC (73), Department de Psychologie, Universite de Provence, Aix-en-Provence, France

EDDY VAN AVERMAET (43), Laboratorium voor Experimentele Sociale Psychologie, Katholieke Universiteit Leuven, Tiensestraat 102, B-3000 Leuven, Belgium

DANIEL BAR-TAL (377), School of Education, Tel-Aviv University, Tel-Aviv, Israel

PETER J. D. CARNEVALE (151), Department of Psychology, State University of New York at Buffalo, Buffalo, New York 14226

RUSSELL D. CLARK, III (279), Department of Psychology, Florida State University, Tallahassee, Florida 32306

VALERIAN J. DERLEGA (1), Department of Psychology, Old Dominion University, Norfolk, Virginia 23508

MORTON DEUTSCH (15), Department of Psychology, Program in Social Psychology, Teachers College, Columbia University, New York, New York 10027

JOHN F. DOVIDIO (279), Department of Psychology, Colgate University, Hamilton, New York 13346

SAMUEL L. GAERTNER (279), Department of Psychology, University of Delaware, Newark, Delaware 19711

ALAN E. GROSS (305), Department of Psychology, University of Maryland, College Park, Maryland 20742

JANUSZ GRZELAK (1, 95), Institute of Psychology, University of Warsaw, ul. Stawki 5/7, 00-183 Warsaw, Poland

HARVEY A. HORNSTEIN (229), Department of Psychology, Program in Social Psychology, Teachers College, Columbia University, New york, New York 10027

JUDITH A. HOWARD (327), Department of Sociology, University of Wisconsin—Madison, Madison, Wisconsin 53706

JERZY KARYLOWSKI (397), Department of Psychology, Polish Academy of Sciences, Pl. Malachowskiego 00-063, Warsaw, Poland

MELVIN J. LERNER (249), Department of Psychology, University of Waterloo, Waterloo, Ontario, Canada N2L 3G1

DARWYN E. LINDER (183), Department of Psychology, Arizona State University, Tempe, Arizona 85281

GERALD MARWELL (207), Department of Sociology, University of Wisconsin—Madison, Madison, Wisconsin 53706

CHARLES G. McCLINTOCK (43), Department of Psychology, University of California, Santa Barbara, Santa Barbara, California 93106

PEG A. McMULLEN (305), Counseling Service, Washington University, St. Louis, Missouri 63105

JANE ALLYN PILIAVIN (279), Department of Sociology, University of Wisconsin—Madison, Madison, Wisconsin 53703

DEAN G. PRUITT (151), Department of Psychology, State University of New York at Buffalo, Buffalo, New York 14226

JACOB M. RABBIE (123), Institute of Social Psychology, University of Utrecht, St. Jacobsstraat 14, 3511 BS Utrecht, Netherlands

AMIRAM RAVIV (377), Department of Psychology, Tel-Aviv University, Tel-Aviv, Israel

JANUSZ REYKOWSKI (355), Department of Psychology, Polish Academy of Sciences, Pl. Malachowskiego 00-063, Warsaw, Poland

SHALOM H. SCHWARTZ[1] (327), Department of Sociology, University of Wisconsin—Madison, Madison, Wisconsin 53706

RUTH SHARABANY (377), Department of Psychology, University of Haifa, Haifa, Israel, and Department of Psychology, Tel Aviv University, Tel Aviv, Israel

ROBERT B. ZAJONC (417), Institute for Social Research, University of Michigan, Ann Arbor, Michigan 48104

[1] *Present address:* Department of Psychology, The Hebrew University, Givat Ram Campus, Jerusalem, Israel.

Preface

Several thousand years of civilization have brought about amazing economic and technological progress. We have learned how to control nuclear power and how to send men and women into space. At the same time, our technology in solving human problems remains at about the same level as it was centuries ago. We daily confront dramatic social problems of aggression, delinquency, brutal competition, and social apathy, and we still do not really know how to cope with these problems.

Relationships with other people are a critical aspect of human experience. Our lives are spent in interaction with others. The nature of these interrelationships varies, but a major component involves the coordination of social interaction to facilitate the fulfillment of important, socially mediated goals. People contribute to each other's attainment—a close friend listens sympathetically to one's personal problems, a mother nurses her child, drivers use less fuel to maintain an adequate supply of gasoline, a bystander offers aid after seeing a severe accident occur. Understanding how to live with other people is an important problem that confronts individuals, governments, and social scientists. Survival literally depends on how individuals and groups coordinate their activities.

The goals that relationships fulfill for individuals take many forms. For instance, such goals extend to the satisfaction of others' needs as well as our own or may be limited to our own, purely personal satisfaction. Technological progress is based on theoretical developments in physics, chemistry, and mathematics. Similarly, any progress in the technology of solving human problems requires theoretical progress in the social sciences. Thus this book places heavy emphasis on theory and research with respect to how individuals pursue goals contributing to others', as well as their own, need satisfaction. "Positive forms of social behavior" is a label that has been used to describe this overall field of study.

Two major traditions of theory and research on positive forms of social behavior are represented in this book: cooperation and helping behavior. Cooperative behavior leads to maximum joint profit for all involved parties (i.e., individuals, groups, or organizations) in a situation in which all the parties are interdependent (the actions of each influence others' gains or losses). Helping behavior involves providing aid or benefit to others, usually without direct evidence of benefit to the giver. Our book, we hope will contribute to theory development and the integration of ideas in these areas of study. Each chapter represents the most recent statement of its author's or co-authors' theoretical positions.

Our introduction and the postscript by Robert Zajonc provide a perspective and brief discussion of theories and research on cooperation and helping behavior. Part I of the book includes chapters by researchers who have been actively engaged in the study of cooperation. The first chapter in this part is by Morton Deutsch, who places the problem of interdependence in a larger context of interpersonal relations and analyzes types of interdependence and individuals' psychological orientations. In subsequent chapters Charles McClintock and Eddy Van Avermaet present a theory of values, Jean Claude Abric discusses cognitive processes affecting cooperation, Janusz Grzelak explores motivational and cognitive antecedents of cooperation, Jacob Rabbie examines the effects of intergroup competition and cooperation on intragroup and intergroup relationships, Dean G. Pruitt and Peter J. D. Carnevale discuss the opportunities for gaining satisfactory solutions to conflict through negotiation, Darwyn Linder examines social trap analogs of social dilemmas such as the energy crisis and overpopulation, and Gerald Marwell offers a socioeconomic analysis of altruism and the problem of collective action.

Part II includes chapters by researchers who are active in the study of helping behavior. Harvey Hornstein looks at psychological tension and helping behavior: Melvin Lerner considers justice-motive theory; Jane Allyn Piliavin, John F. Dovidio, Samuel Gaertner, and Russell D. Clark, III, offer an arousal and cost–reward theory of bystander intervention; Alan Gross and Peg A. McMullen discuss the psychological aspects of receiving help; Shalom

Schwartz and Judith Howard present a self-based motivational model; Janusz Reykowski explores cognitive motivational theory; Daniel Bar-Tal, Ruth Sharabany, and Amiran Raviv offer a developmental stage theory of helping behavior; and finally, Jerzy Karylowski discusses types of psychological mechanisms underlying prosocial behavior and its development.

Our contributors work and live in different countries—Belgium, Canada, France, Israel, the Netherlands, Poland, and the United States. This diverse group of contributors reveals the richness of theory and research that has developed in various cultural settings. A major goal of this book was to facilitate an international exchange of ideas, and we hope we have accomplished such an exchange through this enterprise.

Many individuals and organizations contributed to the book's successful completion. We are indebted to the authors for their thought-provoking essays as well as for their patience during the 2½-year evolution of this book. We thank the staff of Academic Press for their enthusiasm and support. The Institute of Psychology at Warsaw University, Poland, and the Department of Psychology at Old Dominion University, Norfolk, Virginia, steadfastly supported us with their generosity and encouragement. We especially owe thanks to Jan Strelau at Warsaw University and Raymond Kirby and President Alfred Rollins at Old Dominion University. The book was greatly facilitated by financial support from the International Research and Exchanges Board (IREX) and the Kosciuszko Foundation. Thanks are also due to Monica Presser, who typed a substantial portion of the manuscript and to Barbara Z. Derlega, who prepared the index and gave valuable editorial advice for several chapters. We were fortunate in having the patience and emotional support of our families, Barbara and John Derlega and Barbara and Simon Grzelak. We gratefully acknowledge their encouragement and aid.

Chapter 1

Cooperation

and Helping Behavior:

An Introduction

JANUSZ GRZELAK

VALERIAN J. DERLEGA

Imagine the following situations:

1. North America experienced a scorching heat wave during July and August. Temperatures frequently rose above 100°F. People who were lucky enough to have access to swimming pools spent their time cooling off in the water. At the same time a tremendous burden was placed on utility companies, which attempted to meet the heightened energy demand for air conditioning. A plea went out in many communities for consumers to conserve energy and to reduce their use of electrical appliances. Many companies raised the thermostats on air conditioners and dimmed hall lights. Many households chose not to run washing machines and dryers during the periods of peak energy demand. Individuals and organizations thus cooperated to avoid a "blackout" from excess energy demands. All people felt obligated to reduce their energy consumption lest they risk an energy disaster.

2. Paul Novak was in Grand Central Station in New York City. He wanted to buy a ticket to Buffalo, New York, to visit his parents. While examining the train timetable, he noticed a man and woman who were speaking French and who looked lost. Paul felt some personal responsibility to help. He certainly had no expectation of reward. He experienced a great deal of

1

Copyright © 1982 by Academic Press, Inc.
All rights of reproduction in any form reserved.
ISBN 0-12-210820-5

sympathy for the couple, and felt good inside as he helped them go to the Traveler's Aid office, where someone understood French and could help them. Paul left before anyone could thank him.

3. Joan Rader had just heard that her supervisor's father was gravely ill. Her supervisor, Karin, asked Joan to give blood at a local hospital. Joan was reluctant to give blood, since she had never done that before. Joan was concerned about her position at the office, and she decided to give blood so that her supervisor would have no reason to take any action against her in the future.

Cooperation and Helping Behavior: Similarities and Dissimilarities in the Domains of Research

What is the difference between cooperation and helping behavior? A great deal of confusion surrounds this question. There are some important differences between these two phenomena that reflect differences in research and theory. In this chapter, though, we want to suggest that the traditional distinctions between cooperation and helping may be somewhat artificial. These distinctions seem to derive from an exaggerated emphasis on minor differences in the nature of each behavior and in varying theoretical approaches to each that focus on different facets of prosocial behavior.

Some major similarities between cooperation and helping behavior should be noted first. Both behaviors fall under the general category of positive social behavior (see, e.g., Staub, 1980; Wispé, 1972). Both types of behavior increase other persons' positive outcomes. Consider, for instance, the first two illustrations at the beginning of this chapter: Individuals who did not run energy-consuming appliances during peak periods increased others' as well as their own future well-being; Paul helped the French-speaking couple escape from a difficult situation, presumably making them feel better. These particular examples also reflect some real dissimilarities between cooperation and helping behavior that have traditionally been emphasized: the structure of interdependence in the social situation and the choice of a situational versus personality-oriented approach to research and theory construction.

Structure of Interdependence in Social Situations

The interests of energy consumers in a given district are interrelated. An action taken by one individual (such as the decision either to save energy or to overuse it) affects others' interests and, at the same time, others' actions influence the individual. This situation involves social interdependence, or mutual control over outcomes. In some interdependence situations the interests of the involved parties are correspondent (an individual's most preferred action brings about the most preferred outcome, not only for the individual but for others). In other situations, interests are at least partially noncorrespondent, or in conflict. What is best for one individual is not best for other people (see Kelley & Thibaut, 1978; Rapoport, 1966). Cooperative behavior is simply behavior that maximizes both the individual's and others' interests whether the situation involves correspondent or noncorrespondent interests.

To return to our illustration, Paul Novak had never seen the French couple before and had no subsequent contact with them. The couple did not expect him to help them and did not reward him for his behavior. Their interests and his interests were not interrelated in any apparent way. His help represented a single act with no expectations of future reward. Consider the following example, fundamentally similar to that of Paul Novak: The pilot of a jet aircraft realizes that the jet's engine has malfunctioned and that a crash is inevitable. If the pilot decides to eject from the aircraft immediately, he will save his own life but the jet may crash in a heavily populated area. Rather than risk the death of other people, the pilot decides to stay with the aircraft, and he steers a course over water. Soon, out of control, the plane falls into the ocean, killing the pilot. (Exactly this situation occurred in Virginia Beach, Virginia, in the early 1970s.) This heroic action has occurred without any kind of mutual control: The pilot alone predicted the effects of his actions on himself and on others; the other people had no influence on him. Thus, this situation and that of Paul Novak exemplify unilateral control: One person's actions affect outcomes both for him or her and for others, but others' actions do not affect the person.

The examples of Paul Novak and the pilot show that some extreme situations exist in which no apparent interdependence exists. However, it is necessary to emphasize (as Schwartz and Howard do in Chapter 14) that many if not most helping acts occur in situations where at least some actual and/or anticipated interdependence exists. In our third illustration, Joan Rader helped because of her involvement in an interdependence situation. Also, a husband who helps his wife in the kitchen with the cooking can be considered to be in an interdependence situation: Both people are involved in numerous exchanges that affect both of them. Even such a classic example of apparently altruistic behavior as donating blood can be put into a broader social context that emphasizes social interdependence. If I give blood I increase the probability (I hope, by setting a good example) that someone else will give her or his blood when I am in need of help. Despite the social aspects of helping behavior, people may not consciously perceive that their behavior is part of social interdependence. (On the other hand, people may believe that their actions are interdependent even when interdependence is actually very small or nonexistent.) Thus, in many cases both unilateral and mutual control perspectives are probably necessary to understand an individual's cooperative and helping behavior.

Situational versus Personality-Oriented Approaches

As Karylowski notes in Chapter 17, sources of prosocial behavior can be grouped into two broad classes—exocentric motivation and endocentric motivation. *Exocentric motivation* is the basis for a person's helping because of actual or expected external rewards; *endocentric motivation* is the basis for a person's acting for others' benefit without any visible external reinforcement.

An important feature of any interdependence situation is the exchange of rewards, that is, reciprocal give and take. Thus, it is not surprising that, for many years, analysis of motivational sources of cooperation focused more on the external, situational structure than on the internal, motivational structure of people's interests.

The fact that research on cooperation has been dominated by theories of decision making, and particularly by game theory, has affected the development of research in the field in at least three ways. First, decisional analyses of interdependence emphasized distinctive features of situations, such as the outcome structure (or relationships between outcomes). Second, game theory was designed to help solve economic problems. As a result, along with the theory, psychologists inherited its underlying ideology of *economic man*, which was often presented in an oversimplified way. In other words, psychologists have assumed that people seek to maximize their interests (that is, the value for them of their own actions and the consequences of those actions); however, these interests have usually been reduced to external, material goods. Third, the methods used to investigate cooperation—that is, experimental games—focused undue attention on external, monetary rewards at the expense of the internal, cognitive and emotional processes that underlie choice behavior. Thus, partly because of game theory itself, but mostly because of the theory's simplified psychological interpretation, research on cooperation and interdependence has in general focused on situational factors rather than take the "personality oriented" approach characteristic of many psychologists who have studied helping behavior.

It was not long ago (beginning in the late 1960s and early 1970s) that researchers began to reinterpret the nature of interdependence. The current view is that what constitutes psychological interdependence is not the external, outcome structure but the subjective value of these outcomes and the individual's perception of the situation. Kelley and Thibaut (1978) clearly show how the external situation (that is, the *given matrix*) is transformed through various mental processes into the final subjective image of the situation (the *effective matrix*). The chapters on cooperation presented in the first section of the book represent this more "psychological" and "subjective" approach.

If we agree that interdependence should be defined by the subjective evaluation of outcomes, the individual's perception of the interrelations among outcomes, his or her perceptions about a partner's characteristics, and so forth, we have the same type of psychological analysis in studying cooperation as we have in the investigation of other types of prosocial behavior. When McClintock and Van Avermaet (see Chapter 3) and Grzelak (see Chapter 5) discuss concepts such as *social values* or *system of preferences*, it is clear that these internal psychological factors should operate just as well in settings other than interdependent social interactions, including classic examples of helping. On the other hand, do such sources of motivation as promotive tension (see Chapter 10, by Hornstein), beliefs in a just world (see Chapter 11, by Lerner), discrepancies between observed and ideal representations of objects (see Chapter 15, by Reykowski), arousal (see Chapter 12, by Piliavin, Dovidio, Gaertner, and Clark), personal norms (see Chapter 14, by Schwartz and Howard) operate only in helping situations? Of course not. In fact, most of the authors who have developed theories of helping assume that these motivating factors underly most kinds of prosocial behavior. In sum, what has been considered to be a major difference of theoretical approach in studying cooperation and helping (i.e., the situational versus personality dimension) may not be so critical. This book, we hope, will show that a joint emphasis on situational and personality (i.e., internal psychological) factors is necessary to explain any kind of prosocial behavior.

In sum, the research domains of cooperation and helping behavior overlap greatly. The theoretical perspectives of the researcher may not reflect the actual properties of a situation so much as his or her theoretical bias and research background. These perspectives—originally very different in the two fields—gradually converge, at least with respect to general assumptions about the nature of the investigated phenomena and about the importance of both subjective and situational antecedents of cooperation and helping behavior. First, there is an increasing recognition that most prosocial behaviors take place in interactional settings, that is, when at least some interdependence occurs. Second, even among most situationally oriented researchers investigating cooperation, there is an increasing concern with personality-oriented variables, such as systems of values and cognitive processes.

Problems in Theoretical Integration

The examination of the similarities between cooperation and helping behavior provides a basis for dialogue and eventual integration. However, discussing theoretical similarities at such a high level of generality does not mean that the theories presented in the book can already be compared directly and integrated. A valuable effort to create a linkage between co-operation and helping behavior, as well as among different theories of helping behavior, is illustrated by Schwartz and Howard's chapter (see Chapter 14). However, that chapter also shows that different theories are in fact not easily translatable and cannot be directly reduced into a single theoretical model. Even if we try to compare and reconcile different ap-proaches, it is possible to compare only the most general ideas in different theories. We are not even certain to what degree theoretical terms keep the same meaning when they are analyzed in the context of another theory. Hence, there are a number of reasons why it is difficult to effect a successful integration of different theoretical approaches at the present time. We will mention some of them.

Complexity of the Phenomenon
of Positive Social Behavior

A problem in developing a theory of cooperation and helping behavior (that is, positive social behavior) is the complexity of the phenomenon to be explained. Although we think of positive forms of social behavior as benefiting other persons, motivational sources of those kinds of behavior may be difficult to define. As an extreme example, the decision to cooperate with someone may in the short term be intended as an ingratiatory tactic. Ultimately, the person may intend to create a trusting atmosphere and then to exploit or dominate the other. Thus, a wide range of intentions (or personal goals) may underlie the positive social behavior (see Chapter 3, by McClintock and Van Avermaet).

As Reykowski (see Chapter 15) points out, the complexity of positive social behavior raises the issue of whether a single theory can encompass the phenomenon. A theory of positive social behavior has to incorporate many different internal factors (e.g., arousal, emotions, cognitions) and external factors (e.g., characteristics of the other person, social norms, clarity of the situation). Theories that emphasize mainly the role of single variables (e.g., personal norms, arousal) seem able to explain only a facet of the phenomenon. A problem emerges, though, in attempting to synthesize various theoretical concepts. Assuming that a single factor cannot explain a substantial portion of the variance in positive social behavior, how can the various factors be combined into a single theory? Schwartz and Howard's work (Chapter 14) is a notable contribution toward such an integration. Their decision-making model shows how social and personal norms influence altruistic and helping behavior through the influence of general values. However, their decision-making model operates at such a general level that it is hard to imagine how behavior might be predicted in a variety of settings.

Theorists most often deal with this problem of complexity by studying a simplified version of the phenomenon, focusing on only some of the factors that affect prosocial behavior. We have theories that deal with situational factors, cognitive representations of objects, systems of values, personal norms, physiological arousal, and decisional processes. It may be that these theories account for different aspects of the phenomenon of prosocial behavior and that a single explanation cannot account for all aspects of the phenomenon. For instance, the work of Piliavin and her colleagues (see Chapter 12) shows the value of having more than one explanation: These researchers suggest that physiological arousal is the main determinant of impulsive, automatic behavior in an emergency but that in other situations, when action is taken deliberately, other factors (such as a decisional analysis) become more important.

A major effort at theoretical synthesis in psychology derives from the attempt to combine personality-oriented and situational approaches (see, e.g., Magnusson & Endler, 1977; Pervin & Lewis, 1978; Staub, 1980). According to Staub (1980),

a major concern we must have is not the relative influence of persons versus situations—to what *degree* it is the characteristics of the person and to what *degree* it is the situation that determines behavior. Instead, we must be concerned with how personal characteristics and situations *join*, how they each enter, and how they combine. What will result from particular personality environment combinations, and why? [p. 243].

Theoretical attention must be given to how this interaction between personality and environment operates to influence cooperation and helping. Important contributions in this direction are found in many chapters of the book, among them those by Bar-Tal, Sharabany, and Raviv (Chapter 16), Piliavin, Dovidio, Gaertner, and Clark (Chapter 12) and Schwartz and Howard (Chapter 14). Fruitful interactionist approaches include those that emphasize cognitive components of personality structure, such as internalized values and perceptions of similarity with others (see, e.g., the chapters by McClintock and Van Avermaet, Grzelak, and Bar-Tal *et al.*).

Conceptual Similarities and Differences

Although different theories emphasize the roles of different factors and/ or focus on different facets of the prosocial behavior phenomena, many also seem to have important conceptual similarities with other approaches. For instance, various arousal models of helping have been presented to account for intervention in emergencies. The Piliavin model (see Chapter 12) assumes that seeing an emergency arouses the observer physiologically, depending on such factors as the emergency's severity, perceived similarity between victim and observer, and so forth. In Hornstein's model (see Chapter 10), psychological arousal (*promotive tension*) occurs when someone with whom we identify is seeking to reach a goal that we value ourselves. The other's need state arouses an aversive psychological state in the observer. In Reykowski's approach (see Chapter 15), awareness of similarity between oneself and someone else is an important factor in helping behavior also. Individuals presumably have cognitive representations of other people, that is, as external social objects that are different from oneself. Cognitive inconsistency occurs when a discrepancy exists between the other's current situation and an expected or ideal state. This inconsistency motivates behavior to reduce the discrepancy, resulting in helping behavior. Despite significant overlap in these approaches, based on a discrepancy between an ideal and real state of affairs that exists for the other person, theoretical effort at synthesis is still at an early stage. (See the chapters by Schwartz and Howard and by Karylowski.)

Difficulty in achieving theoretical synthesis derives in part from the fact that only a few theorists make intergrative efforts and in part from objective difficulties. Even the major concepts used in theories of prosocial behavior are often not well defined. As in many other domains of psychology, theoretical concepts may be defined partly in terms of intuitive beliefs and/or common sense notions that are not well articulated. Thus, in many cases, terms from one theory are not easily transferable to another (which is demonstrated in the last section of Schwartz and Howard's chapter). We use different languages, and some concepts may not be reducible to others at all. For instance, one could raise a question whether the arousal concept is really comparable with concepts used in other theories since it comes from biology and describes physiological rather than psychological phenomena. Also, from the work of Piliavin *et al.* we know that a high level of arousal is associated with many prosocial behaviors, but that does not mean that other, basically psychological mechanisms (described in other theories) do not take place even in emergency situations. Another difficulty is at the level of generality of theories. For instance, Reykowski's explanation of prosocial behavior (Chapter 15) is based on a very general conception of personality, its structure, and functioning, whereas Lerner's theory (Chapter 11) is based on much more specific factors (that is, on a set of beliefs about social justice). Can Lerner's theory somehow be incorporated into a more general theory such as Reykowski's?

These questions about which theories and concepts are reducible to one another, which are concurrent, and which are complementary require a great deal of conceptual and methodological analysis in which the first step has to be an increase in the clarity and consistency with which each theory is framed.

Individualistic Motivation Underlying Research on Prosocial Behavior

Despite the inherent conceptual difficulties in achieving theoretical syntheses, additional difficulties in pursuing this goal may exist in the "psychology of psychologists." Many psychologists display great concern for the development of their own unique theoretical models and for the collection of data that, they hope, will confirm that model. At the same time, they show little concern for testing whether the same data confirm or disconfirm hypotheses derived from other models and for creating (from the beginning of a research program) experiments that would test the validity of different hypotheses. Unfortunately, developing one's own unique theoretical language discourages tests of other, different theories and, occasionally, permits some theories to survive without being subject to rigorous challenge in the scientific marketplace of ideas.

Problem of Evaluative Bias: Does Prosocial Equal Good?

An unquestioned assumption in theory and research is that cooperative and helping behaviors actually benefit another person. By definition, cooperation and helping are aimed at increasing another's positive outcomes (as well as one's own, in the case of cooperation). We would like to raise the issue whether these "positive forms of social behavior" actually are good for the other person. There are numerous examples in the literature of how individuals who pursue their own personal advantage or self-interest inevitably create problems for others. Thus people who have many children contribute to overpopulation, drivers of big cars deplete energy resources, entrepreneurs exploit workers, and passing by someone in trouble indicates one's callousness. In fact, a collectivist ethic seems to pervade the social sciences as well as politics, emphasizing the value of coordinating one's interests with others and foregoing the pursuit of private (usually translated to mean "selfish") self-interest.

The social theorist Adam Smith (1776) dealt with situations in which individuals who worked for their private self-interest actually contributed to the general good in a laissez-faire, capitalistic society. We do not want to become entangled in a discussion of the relative merits of capitalism versus other economic systems. However, Smith's analysis at least suggests in theory how an individual who tries to pursue private benefits may have a positive effect on society (cf. Dawes, 1980).

Clearly, there are situations in which individuals who pursue their own self-interest increase not only their own benefits but (either directly or indirectly) others' benefits as well. For instance, Pruitt and Carnevale (see Chapter 7) show how high joint benefit may emerge from social conflict. They note that "social conflict is often necessary for the emergence of high joint benefit. Each party must make demands on the other while resisting the other's demands, which is the essence of conflict [p. 26]." Pruitt and Carnevale note perceptibly the paradoxical nature of conflict, which can either undermine problem solving or help achieve high joint benefit. It is to be hoped that other researchers will examine the relative merits (or "positiveness") of different kinds of social behavior rather than simply assume that cooperation and helping are intrinsically more prosocial than the pursuit of one's private self-interests. Whether cooperation and helping are in fact "positive forms of social behavior" is an empirical question. The answer may depend on the nature of the situation, the interactants, criteria of what is positive behavior, and so forth.

In conclusion, this book illustrates the variety of approaches that currently exist in the study of cooperation and helping behavior. This diversity illustrates the richness of theory and research that has accumulated over the last 20 years. Ironically, this diversity also presents a major problem of integration. A dialogue among theorists is needed to make further progress in these fields. We hope that this book will facilitate such discussions.

References

Dawes, R. M. Social dilemmas. *Annual Review of Psychology*, 1980, *31*, 169–193.
Kelley, H. H., & Thibaut, J. W. *Interpersonal relations: A theory of interdependence.* New York: Wiley-Interscience, 1978.

Magnusson, D., & Endler, N. S. (Eds.), *Personality at the crossroads: Current issues in interactional psychology*. Hillsdale, N. J.: Lawrence Erlbaum Associates, 1977.

Pervin, L. A., & Lewis, M. (Eds.), *Perspectives in interactional psychology*. New York: Plenum, 1978.

Rapoport, A. *Two-person game theory: The essential ideas*. Ann Arbor, Michigan: Michigan University Press, 1966.

Smith, A. *The wealth of nations*. 1776. Reprint. Chicago: University of Chicago Press, 1976.

Staub, E. Social and prosocial behavior: Personal and situational influences and their interactions. In E. Staub (Ed.), *Personality: Basic aspects and current research*. Englewood Cliffs, N. J.: Prentice-Hall, 1980.

Wispé, L. G. Positive forms of social behavior: An overview. *Journal of Social Issues*, 1972, *28*, (3), 1–19.

Part I

COOPERATION

Chapter 2

Interdependence

and Psychological

Orientation[1]

MORTON DEUTSCH

In this chapter, I shall examine the relations between types of psychological interdependence and psychological orientations. I shall employ the term *psychological orientation* to refer to a more or less consistent complex of cognitive, motivational, and moral orientations to a given situation that serve to guide one's behavior and responses in that situation. In brief, my theoretical analysis posits that distinctive psychological orientations are associated with the distinctive types of interdependence. I also assume that the causal arrow connecting psychological orientations and types of interdependence is bidirectional: A psychological orientation can induce or be induced by a given type of interdependence. Implicit in this view is the further assumption that each person has the capability to utilize the various psychological orientations and their associated cognitive, motivational, and moral orientations. Although individuals may differ in their readiness and ability to use the different orientations as a result of their cultural backgrounds, their personal histories, and their genetic endowments, people participate in diverse social relations in complex societies; and these varied

[1] The writing of this paper has been supported, in part, by a National Science Foundation Grant, BNS 77-16017.

COOPERATION AND HELPING BEHAVIOR
Theories and Research

social relations require and, hence, induce different psychological orientations. Thus, my basic assumption is an evolutionary one: Namely, to cope with the psychological requirements of assorted types of social relations, people have developed the capacity to utilize psychological orientations as they are necessary in different situations.

This chapter is structured into four sections: (*a*) a discussion of types of interdependence; (*b*) a characterization of psychological orientations; (*c*) a discussion of the relationship between types of interdependence and psychological orientations; and (*d*) a brief consideration of some relevant research. At the outset, I give notice to the reader that my chapter is not so ambitious as it may appear. I shall not attempt to discuss the full range of types of interdependence or psychological orientations. My aim is the more modest one of illustrating the potential fruitfulness of an idea that is still in the process of being formed in the hope that doing so will stimulate other investigators to contribute to its development.

Types of Interdependence

Several years ago, I collaborated with Wish and Kaplan (Wish, Deutsch, & Kaplan, 1976) in research that sought to identify the fundamental dimensions of interpersonal relations.[2] Based on this research, as well as earlier research by Triandis (1972) and Marwell and Hage (1970) and later research by Wish and Kaplan (1977), it seems reasonable to assert that the fundamental dimensions of interpersonal relations include the following:

1. *Cooperation–competition.* This dimension is referred to variously in the social psychological literature. I have characterized it as *promotive versus contrient interdependence* (Deutsch, 1949a) or as a *pro–con* dimension (Deutsch, 1962). Triandis (1972) referred to it as *association–disassociation;* Kelley and Thibaut (1978) used the term *correspondence–noncorrespondence;* and it has been labeled *love–hate, evaluative, positive–negative interpersonal disposition, friendly–hostile,* etc. by other investigators. In the Wish, Deutsch, and Kaplan (1976) study, scales of the following sort were strongly weighted on this dimension: "Always harmonious versus always clashing," "very cooperative versus very competitive," "very friendly versus very hostile," "have compatible versus incompatible goals and desires," "very productive versus very destructive," "find it easy versus difficult to resolve conflicts with each other," "very altruistic versus very selfish," "very fair versus very unfair."

---

[2] Although this research studied the *perceptions* of interpersonal relations, I see no reason to doubt that the identified dimensions are fundamental aspects of interpersonal relations.

Such interpersonal relations as "close friends," "teammates," and "co-workers" are at the cooperative end of the dimension, whereas "political opponents," "personal enemies," "divorced couple," and "guard and prisoner" are toward the competitive end. The social psychological processes and consequences associated with this dimension have been extensively investigated in my theorizing and research (Deutsch, 1949a, 1949b, 1962, 1973).

2. *Power distribution ("equal" versus "unequal").* This dimension has been given various labels: Triandis (1972) characterized it as *superordination–subordination,* Kelley (1979) described it in terms of *mutuality of interdependence,* and others have used such terms as *dominance–submission, potency,* and *autonomy–control.* Such scales as the following are strongly weighted on this dimension: "exactly equal versus extremely unequal power," "very similar versus very different roles and behaviors," and "very democratic versus very autocratic attitudes." "Business partners," "close friends," and "business rivals" are at the "equal" end; "master and servant," "teacher and pupil," "parent and child," and "guard and prisoner" are at the "unequal" end. The social psychological processes and consequences associated with this dimension are reviewed in Cartwright and Zander (1968).

3. *Task-oriented versus social–emotional.* This dimension has been labeled *intimacy* by Triandis (1972) and Marwell and Hage (1970) and *personal* by Kelley (1979). Others have identified it as *personal–impersonal, subjective versus objective, particularistic versus universalistic,* or *emotionally involved versus emotionally detached.* The two following scales are strongly weighted on this dimension: "pleasure-oriented versus work-oriented," and "emotional versus intellectual." Such interpersonal relations as "close friends," "husband and wife," "siblings" are at the social–emotional end of the dimension; "interviewer and job applicant," "opposing negotiators," "supervisors and employees," and "business rivals" are at the task-oriented end. Bales's (1958) distinction between social–emotional and task-oriented leaders of groups is relevant; the former focuses on the solidarity relations among group members, and the latter focuses on the external task and problem-solving activities of the group. Earlier, I made a similar distinction between *task functions* and *group maintenance functions* (Deutsch, 1949a, 1949b), which was elaborated in a paper by Benne and Sheats (1948). The sociological distinction between *gemeinschaft* and *gesellschaft* groups also reflects this basic dimension of social relations.

4. *Formal versus informal.* Wish and Kaplan (1977) have shown that this dimension can be separated from the preceding one. It appears to be the same as the dimension of *regulation* identified by Marwell and Hage (1970).

In an informal relationship the definition of the activities, times, and locations involved in the relationship are left largely to the participants; in a formal or regulated relationship, social rules and norms largely determine the interactions among those involved. Such scales as "very formal versus very informal" and "very flexible versus very rigid" reflect this dimension. Relations within a bureaucracy tend to be formal, whereas relations within a social club tend to be informal; also, relations between equals are more likely to be informal than relations between unequals. Formal, bureaucratic relationships have been the subject of extensive discussions by such sociological theorists as Weber (1957) and Merton (1957).

5. *Intensity or importance.* This dimension has to do with the intensity or superficiality of the relationship. Kelley (1979) suggests that it reflects the degree of interdependence (or dependence) in the relationship. Such scales as the following are strongly weighted on it: "very active versus very inactive," "have intense versus superficial interactions with each other," "have intense versus superficial feelings toward each other," and "important versus unimportant to the individuals involved." "Casual acquaintances," "second cousins," and "salesman and customer" are at the superficial end of this dimension; "parent and child," "husband and wife," "psychotherapist and patient" are at the intense end.

Several other dimensions of interpersonal relations have been identified, including the enduring or temporary nature of the relationship; its voluntary or involuntary character; its public versus private nature; its licit or illicit quality; and the number of people involved in the relationship. It is beyond the scope of this paper to consider these other dimensions.

Table 2.1 presents the first four dimensions in dichotomous form and provides illustrations of the types of interpersonal relations and types of interpersonal activities that could occur in each of the 16 regions of this four-dimensional space. (I have selected illustrations from the "more intense" rather than "less intense" end of the intensity dimension.) It is, of course, an oversimplification to dichotomize each of the dimensions, but it is a reasonable place to start. If the reader were to blank out the illustrations in Table 2.1 and attempt to provide other examples, he or she would probably discover that the dimensions are correlated. It is easier to find illustrations for some of the 16 regions than others; some of the regions are undoubtedly more heavily populated than others.

Thus, social–emotional relations or activities are more likely to be informal than the task-oriented ones, especially if there are relatively more people involved in the task-oriented ones. Also, there appears to be a positive linkage between the informality of the relation or activity and its equality so that it is more difficult to find unequal, informal relations and activities

Table 2.1
Sixteen Types of Social Relations

	Social–Emotional		Task-Oriented	
	Informal	Formal	Informal	Formal
Cooperative Equal	**1** Intimate Lovers Love-making	**5** Fraternal Club members Social party	**9** Problem-solving Colleagues Staff meeting	**13** Organized cooperation Task force members Working together with differentiated responsibilities to solve problem
Unequal	**2** Caring Mother–child Nursing	**6** Protecting Police officer–child Helping	**10** Educational Professor–graduate student Working together informally on research project under professor's direction	**14** Hierarchical organization Supervisor–employee Supervisor assigning employee to do certain task
Competitive Equal	**3** Antagonistic Personal enemies Fighting	**7** Rivalrous Divorced couple Custody suit	**11** Competitive Contestants in informal game Trying to score points against the other	**15** Regulated competition Business rivals Bidding against one another for a contract
Unequal	**4** Sadomasochistic Bully–victim Tormenting	**8** Dominating Expert–novice Intimidating	**12** Power struggle Authority–rebel Guerilla warfare	**16** Regulated power struggle Guard–prisoner Ordering prisoner to keep in step

Note: Each cell characterizes a type of social relation by labeling the relation (first entry), naming people who might be in such a relationship (second entry), and describing an activity that might occur in such a relationship (third entry).

than equal, informal ones. Moreover, there is evidently a positive association between the cooperativeness and informality of a relation or activity. Similarly, there appears to be a positive connection between the equality of an activity or relation and its cooperativeness. Additionally, there is likely to be a positive association between the social–emotional nature of a relation or activity and its cooperativeness. Further, one can expect that social–emotional relations and activities will more frequently be intense than task-oriented ones. And also that interpersonal relations or activities that are extremely cooperative or competitive rather than moderately so will be more intense.

The foregoing, hypothesized correlations among the dimensions suggest which regions of the interpersonal space will be heavily populated and which will not.[3] (See Wish and Kaplan, 1977, for some support for the hypothesized correlations.) Thus, one would expect more interpersonal relations and activities (particularly, if they are stable and enduring) to be clustered in the cooperative, equal, informal, and social–emotional region (Cell 1 in Table 2.1), which I shall label the *intimacy* region, than in the competitive, equal, informal, and social-emotional region (Cell 3), which I shall label the *antagonistic* region. Intense competitive relations or activities are more likely to be stable and enduring if they are regulated or formal rather than unregulated. Thus, one would expect Cell 7 ("rivalry") to be more populated than Cell 3 ("antagonism"); similarly, for Cell 8 ("sado-masochism") and for Cells 15 ("regulated competition") and 16 ("regulated power struggle") compared to their respective unregulated cells.

Intense, cooperative, task-oriented relations or activities are more apt to be equal and informal than otherwise unless there are clear status differences among the people involved (i.e., to be located in Cell 9 rather than in Cell 10, 13, or 14). However, the demands of large-scale cooperative tasks involving more than small numbers of people are apt to require a formal, hierarchical (i.e., unequal) organization for the tasks to be worked on effectively and efficiently. Thus, one could expect many hierarchically organized cooperative relations and activities to be found in Cell 14 ("hierarchical organization"). Yet the nature of such unequal relations as superordinate–subordinate ones in organizations, especially when they are not strongly legitimated for those in the subordinate position, is such as to produce conflict over the power differences. Hence, this type of relation is rarely free of strong competitive elements. It follows, then, that some superordinate–subordinate relations in hierarchically organized systems will

---

[3] *INDSCAL*, the multidimensional scale analysis procedure used in the Wish, Deutsch, and Kaplan (1976) and the Wish and Kaplan (1977) studies does not force the identified dimensions to be orthogonal.

have the character of power struggles, and these would be more appropriately classified as belonging to Cell 16.

Psychological Orientations

In writing an earlier draft of this chapter, I entitled this section "Modes of Thought." This earlier title did not seem to be a sufficiently inclusive label. It appeared to me evident that cognitive processes differ in different types of social relations, and I wanted to sketch out the nature of some of these differences. However, I also thought that the psychological differences among the different types of social relations were not confined to the cognitive processes: Different motivational and moral predispositions were also involved. It has been customary to consider these latter predispositions as more enduring characteristics of the individual and to label them "personality traits" or "character orientations." Since my emphasis is on the situationally induced nature and, hence, temporariness of such predispositions, such labels also did not seem fitting for the material in this section. I have used the term *psychological orientation* to capture the basic theme of this section: People orient themselves differently to different types of social relations, and different orientations reflect and are reflected in different cognitive processes, motivational tendencies, and moral dispositions.

The Cyclical Relation between Psychological Orientations and Social Relations

Figure 2.1 depicts in schematic form my view of this association between psychological orientations and social relationships, as well as some other factors influencing both of them. It was stimulated by Neisser's (1976) conception of the perceptual cycle but is a radical modification of it. My emphasis, like Neisser's, is on the cyclical and active process involved in the connection among the elements. In characterizing this cyclical, active process one can start at any point in the cycle. In practice where one starts will usually be determined by what one manipulates as one's independent variable. The nonmanipulated variables will be considered to be the dependent ones.

Let us suppose, for example, that, as an experimenter, I lead a subject to have the psychological orientation toward another typical of a mutually promotive, interdependent relationship. This, in turn, will lead the subject to have some characteristic interactions with the other and these, in turn, will have some effects upon both the subject and the other that will provide evidence as to the type of relationship that exists between them. Finally,

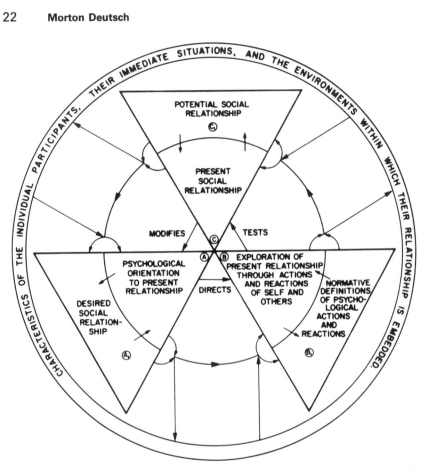

Figure 2.1. The circular relation between an individual's psychological orientation and the type of social relationship in which he or she is involved.

this will validate as appropriate or invalidate as inappropriate the subject's psychological orientation and require its modification. Here the cycle is A→B→C→A. Or, I might begin at a different point, C, inducing the subject to believe that he was in a mutually promotive, interdependent relation. This would, in turn, lead the subject to have a psychological orientation toward the relationship that has specifiable characteristics and this, in turn, would lead to certain interactions with the other, etc. Here the cycle is C→A→B→C. Or, I might commence by leading the subject to interact with the other in specified ways that, in turn, would produce certain consequences that, in turn, would produce evidence as to what kind of relationship the subject was in, etc. Here the starting point is B and the cycle goes on to C, etc.

Several other features of Figure 2.1 merit comment. I assume that the two parts of each triangle can affect one another:

1. One's psychological orientation to one's present social relationship can be affected by and can also affect one's desires with regard to that relationship. Thus, if one has a desire for a cooperative relationship but a contrient orientation to the other, one may change either one's desire or one's orientation, depending on which is less strongly rooted.

2. One's present social relations with another can influence or be influenced by the potential one sees for the development of the relationship. If I experience the present relationship as a destructive one, I might not see it as having a future; on the other hand, if I see the potential of developing a warm, loving relationship, I might be more positive toward an initially difficult relationship than I might otherwise be.

3. The nature of one's actions and reactions in a relationship can affect as well as be affected by the normative definitions that exist regarding interactions in a given social relationship. Although early in a relationship, culturally determined, normative definitions often govern the meanings of social interactions, relations tend to build up their own idiosyncratic normative definitions as a result of repeated interactions that may be peculiar to the particular relationship.

There is, of course, a tendency for the two parts of each triangle to be consistent with one another. When they are not, one can expect a more complex psychological structure than the one depicted in Figure 2.1. For example, if the present and future characteristics of the social relationship are perceived to be inconsistent with one another, the time perspective dimension of the relationship will be very prominent. If there is an inconsistency between the desired social relationship and the present psychological orientation, the reality dimension will be very prominent. It is beyond the scope of the present paper to consider these important psychological aspects of social relations; Lewin (1951) makes suggestive remarks about these dimensions of the life space in his writings.

Surrounding the triangles of Figure 2.1 is the "objective" world of the participants; this includes the characteristics of the individual participants, their immediate situations, and the environment within which their relationship is embedded. I have characterized this objective world as sending causal arrows to all of the elements involved in the psychological orientation–social relations cycle and also as receiving causal arrows from these elements. The nature of the participants and their immediate situations as well as their environment affect their social relations, their psychological orientation, and their interactions; and these phenomena, in turn, affect the participants and the realities confronting them. In this larger cycle, it is the variables that one considers independent that one manipulates.

The Nature of Psychological Orientations

COGNITIVE ORIENTATIONS

In recent years, scholars in a number of different disciplines—cognitive psychology, social psychology, sociology, linguistics, anthropology, and artificial intelligence—have utilized such terms as *schema, script,* and *frame* to refer to the *structures of expectations* that help orient the individual cognitively to the situation confronting him. I shall employ the term *cognitive orientation* as being essentially the same as these terms. In the view being presented here, the person's cognitive orientation to his situation is only one aspect of his psychological orientation to a social relationship. Other aspects include his motivational orientation and his moral orientation.

The term *schema* goes back to Bartlett (1932) who, much influenced by the work of the neurologist Sir Henry Head (1920), emphasized the constructive and organized features of memory as opposed to the notion of memory as passive storage. The term *script* derives from the work of Abelson (1975, 1976) and Schanck and Abelson (1977) who also stress that people have organized knowledge of a stereotypic form about most recurrent situations they encounter. Abelson (1975) defines a script as a "coherent sequence of events expected by the individual, involving him either as a participant or as an observer [p. 33]." He goes on to postulate that "cognitively mediated social behavior depends on the joint occurrence of two processes: (*a*) the selection of a particular script to represent the given social situation and (*b*) the taking of a participant role within that script [pp. 42–43]." The term *frame* was introduced by Bateson (1955) to explain how individuals exchange signals that allow them to agree on the level of abstraction at which any message is intended—for example, whether the message is intended as serious or playful. Goffman (1974) has generalized Bateson's discussion of frames in an extended analysis of how individuals, as they attend to any current situation, face the question, "What is it that's going on here?"

Underlying the concepts of schema, script, and frame is the shared view that people approach their social world actively, with structured expectations about themselves and their social environments that reflect their organized beliefs about different social situations and different people. Our structured expectations make it possible for us to interpret and respond quickly to what is going on in specific situations. If our expectations lead us to inappropriate interpretations and responses, then they are likely to be revised on the basis of our experiences in the situation. Or if the circumstance confronting us is sufficiently malleable, our interpretations and responses to it may help to shape its form.

Schemas, scripts, or frames may be very concrete and specific—for example, how to work together with a particular person on a given task—or they may be rather abstract and general—for example, what is involved in a competitive as compared to a cooperative relation. In any society that provides a variety of situations in which different areas in the multidimensional space of social relations (the space being composed from the dimensions that were described in the first major section of this chapter) are well-represented, it is likely that rather abstract schemas or scripts will develop to characterize the types of relations depicted in Table 2.1. Such scripts, or cognitive orientations, are a central component of what I am here terming psychological orientations.

It is important for the participants in a particular social relationship to know "what's going on here"—to know the actors, the roles they are to perform, the relations among the different roles, the props and settings, the scenes, and the themes of the social interaction. However, everyday social relations are rarely as completely specified by well-articulated scripts as is social interaction in a play in the traditional theatre; ordinary social interactions have more the qualities of improvisational theatre in which only the nature of the characters involved in the situation is well-specified and the characters are largely free to develop the details of the skeletonized script as they interact with one another.

The improvisational nature of most social relations—the fact that given types of social relations occur in widely different contexts and with many different kinds of actors—makes it likely that relatively abstract or generalized cognitive orientations, schemas, or scripts will develop for the different types of social relations. I assume that people are implicit social psychological theorists and, as a result of their experience, have developed cognitive schemas of the different types of social relations that, though usually not articulated, are similar to those articulated by theorists in social psychology and the other social sciences. Undoubtedly, at this early stage of the development of social science theory, the unarticulated conceptions of the average person are apt to be more sophisticated than the articulated ones of the social scientists.

MOTIVATIONAL ORIENTATIONS

Just as different cognitive orientations are associated with the different types of social relations, so also are different motivational orientations. A motivational orientation toward a given social relationship orients one to the possibilities of gratification or frustration of certain types of needs in the given relationship. To the cognitive characterization of the relationship, the motivational orientation adds the personal, subjective features arising from one's situationally relevant motives or need-dispositions.

The motivational orientation gives rise to the cathexis of certain regions of the cognitive landscape, making them positively or negatively valent, and highlights the pathways to and from valent regions. It gives the cognitive map a dynamic character. It predisposes one to certain kinds of fantasies (or nightmares) and to certain kinds of emotions. It orients one to such questions as "What is to be valued in this relationship?" and "What do I want here and how do I get it?"

It is evident that different types of social relations offer different possibilities of need gratification. It would be unreasonable, for example, to expect one's need for affection to be gratified in a business transaction and inappropriate to expect one's financial needs to be fulfilled in an intimate relationship. In the third section of the chapter I shall attempt to characterize briefly the motivational orientations associated with the polar ends of the different dimensions of interpersonal relations.

MORAL ORIENTATIONS

A moral orientation toward a given social relationship orients one to the mutual obligations, rights, and entitlements of the people involved in the given relationship. It adds an "ought to," "should," or obligatory quality to a psychological orientation. The moral orientation implies that one experiences one's relationship not only from a personal perspective but also from a social perspective that includes the perspective of the others in the relationship. A moral orientation makes the experience of injustice more than a personal experience. Not only is one personally affected; so are the other participants in the relationship, because its value underpinnings are being undermined. The various participants in a relationship have the mutual obligation to respect and protect the framework of social norms that define what is to be considered as fair or unfair in the interactions and outcomes of the participants. One can expect that the moral orientation, and hence what is considered fair, will differ in the different types of social relations.

The Relationship between Types of Interdependence and Psychological Orientations

In this section, I shall characterize the psychological orientations that are associated with the dimensions of cooperation–competition, power, task-oriented versus social–emotional, and formal versus informal. For each of the four dimensions depicted in Table 2.1, I shall describe the cognitive, motivational, and moral orientations that typify the dimension.

Cooperation–Competition

COGNITIVE ORIENTATION

The cooperative–competitive dimension seems so fundamental to social life that one would assume a well-developed innate predisposition to develop abstract cognitive orientations to help an individual define quickly whether "what's going on here?" is "good" for him or "bad" for him. With additional experience and further psychological differentiation and integration, the basic cognitive schema of cooperation–competition should emerge: We are "for" one another or "against" one another; we are linked together so that we both gain or lose together or we are linked together so that if one gains, the other loses. This basic schema has many implications (see Deutsch 1949a, 1949b, 1962, 1973, 1979 for an elaboration of these implications). It leads an individual holding it to expect that in a cooperative relation, the other will be pleased by the individual's effective actions and ready to help him or her achieve success; the individual will expect the opposite to be true in a competitive relationship. If one believes one is in a cooperative relationship and the other is displeased by one's effective actions, one will wonder, "What is going on here?" "Am I in the kind of relation that I think I am in?" "What can I do to find out what is going on here?"

MOTIVATIONAL ORIENTATION

In a cooperative relation, one is predisposed to cathect the other positively; to have a trusting and benevolent attitude toward the other; to be psychologically open to the other; to be giving as well as receptive to the other; to have a sense of responsibility toward the other and toward the mutual process of cooperation; to see the other as similar to oneself; etc. One is also predisposed to expect the other to have a similar orientation toward oneself. Murray's (1938, pp. 175–177) description of the *need for affiliation* captures much of the essence of this motivational orientation. It is clear that the specific quality of this orientation will be very much influenced by what type of cooperative relation is involved: social–emotional or task-oriented, equal or unequal, formal or informal, intense or superficial.

In a competitive relation, one is predisposed to cathect the other negatively; to have a suspicious and hostile, exploitative attitude toward the other; to be psychologically closed to the other; to be aggressive and defensive toward the other; to seek advantage and superiority for the self and disadvantage and inferiority for the other; to see the other as opposed to oneself and basically different; etc. One is also predisposed to expect the other to have the same orientation. Murray's (1938) description of the *need for aggression* (pp. 159–161) and "need for defendance" (pp. 194–195) as well as the associated needs for "infavoidance" (pp. 192–193) and "counteraction" (pp. 195–197) seem to characterize many of the basic features of this motivational orientation. The specific quality of this motivational orientation will be determined by the type of competitive situation: task-oriented or social–emotional, equal or unequal, formal or informal, intense or superficial. In addition, it will be colored by one's conception of one's chances of winning or losing.

MORAL ORIENTATION

Although the specific character of the moral orientations associated with cooperation and competition will also depend on other features of the social relationship, it seems evident that cooperation and competition elicit different types of moral orientations. The moral orientation linked with cooperation is a tendency toward egalitarianism. This tendency underlies a general conception of justice that Rawls (1972) has expressed as follows: "All social values—liberty and opportunity, income and wealth, and the bases of self-respect—are to be distributed equally unless an unequal distribution of any, or all, of these values is to everyone's advantage [p. 62]." The moral orientation connected with cooperation fosters mutual respect and self-respect and favors equality as a guiding value to be breached only when inequality brings greater benefits and advantages to those less fortunate than they would otherwise have been if all were treated equally. Given this moral orientation, as Rawls (1972) points out, "Injustice, then, is simply inequalities that are not to the benefit of all [p. 62]."

In contrast, the moral orientation linked with competition sanctions inequality and legitimates a win–lose struggle to determine who will have superior and who will have inferior outcomes in a competitive relationship. Depending on other features of the relationship, the struggle may be regulated so that the competition takes place under fair rules (as in a duel of honor) and one's moral orientation will include an obligation to obey the rules, or the struggle may be a "no-holds-barred" one in which any means to defeat the other can be employed. An active state of competition implies that the competitors do not mutually perceive and accept a superior–inferior relationship between them: If they do, and they continue to wage competition, then they are violating the moral imperatives of competitive justice. Thus, it is part of the moral orientation of competition for a victor to accept the defeat of someone who acknowledges being vanquished without continuing to beat the defeated one.

Power ("Equality" versus "Inequality")

COGNITIVE ORIENTATION

The basic schema of "relationship power" (Deutsch, 1973) has to do with the relative power of the participants in a relationship to benefit or harm or persuade one another and, hence, their relative power to influence one another. In a relationship of unequal power, it is expected that the more powerful member will be advantaged and the less powerful one will be disadvantaged whenever their interests are opposed: Hence, it is considered better to be in the more- rather than the less-powerful position in a competitive relationship. The competitive branch of the unequal power schema highlights the roles of "victor" and "vanquished"; the equal power schema orients more to continuing struggle. In both competitive branches, the use of tactics of coercion, intimidation, and power bluffs are made salient. Even in a situation where the more- and less-powerful members have congruent interests, the less-powerful member is expected to be more dependent on the other and, hence, more likely to engage in ingratiating behavior. The cooperative branch of the unequal power schema emphasizes the orientation toward responsibility in the high power position and of respectful compliance from the low power position; the equal power schema orients more toward mutual responsibility and respect. Both cooperative branches make salient the use of the more positive forms of power: persuasion rather than coercion, benefits rather than harms, legitimate rather than illegitimate power, etc.

MOTIVATIONAL ORIENTATION

In an equality relation, one is predisposed to consider that the other is entitled to the same esteem and respect as oneself. The equality of power is likely to signify that the different participants in a relationship have the same value. Respect and esteem are more valuable if they are received from those whom one respects; equal status relations represent the optimum distribution for the mutual support of self-esteem. The need-dispositions related to self-esteem and self-respect seem to underlie this motivational orientation. The need for self-esteem involves the need to have a sense of the worthiness of one's goals and a sense of confidence in one's ability to fulfill one's intentions; the need for self-respect involves the need to have a sense of one's moral worth, of one's equal right to justice and fair treatment. It undermines one's sense of belonging to a moral community to be treated more fairly or less fairly than others and this, in turn, weakens the foundations of self-respect. Hence, one's self-respect is more firmly grounded in relationships where one can feel the others are also entitled to respect.

Similarly, the confidence in oneself that is connected with a secure self-esteem is fostered by association and comparison with people who are similar in status rather than with those who are higher or lower.

In an unequal relationship, one is predisposed either to take a more dominant or a more subordinate role or to resist the inequality. Murray (1938) has characterized the different aspects of the *need for dominance*. It is manifest in the desire to control, influence, direct, command, induce, dictate, supervise, instruct, or lead. In a competitive situation, the need for dominance will often be fused with the need for aggression and will lead to attempts to coerce and force the other to comply with one's desires. In a cooperative situation, it will often be fused with the need for nurturance and will lead to a protective, guiding, and caring orientation toward the other. Different needs are associated with the submissive role, depending on whether it occurs in a cooperative or competitive context. In a cooperative context, Murray's (1938, pp. 154–156) description of the *need for deference* seems appropriate. It involves a readiness to follow, to comply, to emulate, to conform, to obey, to defer, to admire, to revere, to be suggestible, to heed advice, and otherwise to accept the superior authority of the other. In a competitive relationship, the need-disposition associated with the acceptance of the inferior role is well characterized in Murray's (1938, pp. 161–164) description of the *need for abasement*. This disposition is reflected in the tendency to submit passively, to accept blame, to surrender, to seek punishment or pain, to be servile, to be resigned, to acquiesce, to be timorous, to give in, and to allow oneself to be bullied. It is evident that the subordinate role in an unequal relationship may be difficult to accept and may be resisted. The resistance to an unequal relationship will be evidenced in aspects of what Murray has termed the *need for autonomy* (pp. 156–159) and the *need for rejection* (pp. 177–180). The need for autonomy is characterized by the tendency to resist coercion and restraint, to be defiant and rebellious in relation to arbitrary authority, to be independent of social ties, and to be a nonconformist. The need for rejection is reflected in the tendency to separate oneself from a negatively cathected other; to reject a disliked superior other; to out-snub a snob; to exclude, abandon, expel or remain indifferent to an inferior other.

MORAL ORIENTATION

As the preceding discussion of motivational orientations would suggest, there are a number of different moral orientations connected with equality and inequality: Other features of the relationship, in addition to the distribution of power within it, will determine the nature of the moral orientation that will be elicited. Thus, in a cooperative, equal relationship one would expect the kind of egalitarian relationship described in the section on the moral orientation associated with cooperation–competition. In a cooperative, unequal relationship, the moral orientation obligates the more powerful person to employ his power in such a way as to benefit the less powerful one, not merely himself. In such a relationship, the less powerful one has the obligation to show appreciation, to defer to, and honor the more powerful person. These obligations may be rather specific and limited if the relationship is task-oriented or they may be diffuse and general if the relationship is a social–emotional one.

In an equal, competitive relationship, one's moral orientation is toward the value of initial equality among the competitors and the subsequent striving to achieve superiority over the others. This orientation favors "equal opportunity" but not "equal outcomes": The competitors start the contest with equal chances to win, but some win and some lose. In an unequal, competitive relationship the moral orientations of the strong and the weak support an exploitative relationship. The strong are likely to adopt the view that the rich and powerful are biologically and, hence, morally superior; they have achieved their superior positions as a result of natural selection; it would be against nature to interfere with the inequality and suffering of the poor and weak; and it is the manifest destiny of superior people to lead inferior peoples. The beatitude of those in powerful positions who exploit those in weaker positions appears to be, "Blessed are the strong, for they shall prey upon the weak" (Banton, 1967, p. 48). In an unequal, competitive relationship, the weak are apt to *identify with the aggressor* (A. Freud, 1937) and adopt the moral orientation of the more powerful and to feel that their inferior outcomes are deserved. Or, they may feel victimized. If so, they may either develop a revolutionary moral orientation directed toward changing the nature of the existing relationship or they may develop the moral orientation of being a victim. The latter orientation seeks to obtain secondary gratification from being morally superior to the victimizer: "It's better to be sinned against than to sin"; "the meek shall inherit the earth."

Task-Oriented versus Social–Emotional

COGNITIVE ORIENTATION

The basic schema here has to do with the focus of involvement. In a task-oriented relationship, one expects the attention and the activities of the participants to be directed toward something external to their relationship, whereas in a social–emotional relationship one expects much of the involvement to be centered on the relationship and the specific persons in the relationship. This difference in focus leads one to expect a relationship that is primarily task-oriented to be impersonal in the sense that the actual accomplishment of the task is more important than the identity of the persons involved in accomplishing it and the nature of their personal relationships. In a task-oriented relationship, people who can perform equally well on the task are substitutable for one another. The personal identity and the unique individuality of the performer have little significance in such a relationship.

In contrast, in a social–emotional relationship, the personal qualities and identity of the individuals involved are of paramount importance. People are not readily substitutable for one another. Using Parsonian terminology, in a task-oriented relation people are oriented to one another as *complexes of performances*—that is, in terms of what each *does;* in a social–emotional relationship people are oriented to each other as *complexes of qualities*— that is, in terms of what each *is.* Also, in a task-oriented relationship, one's orientation toward the other is universalistic—that is, one applies general standards that are independent of one's particular relationship with the other; in a social–emotional relationship, one's orientation is particularistic—that is, one's responses to the other are determined by the particular relatedness that exists between oneself and the other.

In a task-oriented relationship one is oriented to making decisions about which means are most efficient in achieving given ends.[4] This orientation requires an abstract, analytic, quantifying, calculating, comparative mode of thought in which one is able to adopt an affectively neutral, external attitude toward different means in order to be able to make a precise appraisal of their comparative merit in achieving one's ends. One orients to other people as instrumental means and evaluates them in comparison or competition with other means. In contrast, in a social–emotional relationship one is oriented to the attitudes, feelings, and psychological states of the other as ends. This orientation requires a more holistic, concrete, intuitive, qualitative, appreciative–aesthetic mode of thought in which one's own affective reactions help one to apprehend the other from the "inside." Other people are oriented to as unique persons rather than as instruments in which aspects of the person are useful for particular purposes.

MOTIVATIONAL ORIENTATION

A task-oriented relationship tends to evoke achievement-oriented motivations. Achievement motivation has been discussed extensively by Murray

---

[4] I caution the reader not to conclude from this sentence or from anything else in this chapter that relationships that are exclusively task-oriented will be more productive than those that have a mixture of task-orientedness and social–emotional orientedness. Effective group functioning on tasks, for example, requires attention to "group maintenance" as well as to "task functions" (Deutsch, 1949b).

(1938), McClelland, Atkinson, Clark, and Lowell (1953), Atkinson and Feather (1966), and Weiner (1974). Here I wish merely to indicate that it consists not only of the egoistic motivations to achieve success and to avoid failure; motivations related to using one's capabilities in worthwhile activities may also be involved. Additionally, since achievement motivation is often instrumentally oriented to serve an adaptive function in relation to the external environment characterized by a scarcity rather than abundance of resources, it usually contains an element of motivation that is oriented toward rational, efficient accomplishment of the task. Further, since task-oriented relationships are primarily instrumental rather than consummatory in character, they require a motivational orientation that accepts delay-in-gratification and that obtains satisfaction from disciplined activity oriented toward future gratification.

A number of different motivational orientations are likely to be elicited in social–emotional relationships: affiliation, affection, esteem, play, sentience, eroticism, and nurturance–succorance. The primary feature of these different need-dispositions as they are manifested in social–emotional relationships is that they are focused on the nature of the person-to-person (or person-to-group) relationship: They are oriented toward giving and receiving cathexes; toward the attitudes and emotions of the people involved in the relationship; toward the pleasures and frustrations arising from the interaction with the particular others in the given relationship. Although past experiences and future expectations may affect how one acts toward others and how one interprets the actions of others in a social–emotional relationship, such a relationship—if it is a genuine one—is not instrumental to other, future goals; it is an end in itself. In this sense, the need-dispositions in a social–emotional relationship are oriented toward current rather than delayed gratification.

MORAL ORIENTATION

The moral orientation in a task-oriented relationship is that of utilitarianism. Its root value is maximization: People should try to get the most out of situations. Good is viewed as essentially quantitative, as something that can be increased or decreased without limit (Diesing, 1962, p. 35). A second element in this moral orientation is the means-end schema, in which efficient allocation of means to achieve alternative ends becomes a salient value. A third element is impartiality in the comparison of means, so that means can be compared on the basis of their merit in achieving given ends rather than on the basis of considerations irrelevant to the means–end relationship. In Parsonian terms, the moral-orientation in task-oriented relations are characterized by the values of universalism, affective neutrality, and achievement. In contrast, the moral orientation of social–emotional relations are characterized by the values of particularism, affectivity, and ascription (Diesing, 1962, p. 90). Obligations to other people in a social–emotional relationship are based on their particular relationship to oneself rather than on general principles: They are strongest when relations are close and weakest when relations are distant. In a task-oriented relation, one strives to detach oneself from the objects of one's actions and to treat them all as equal, separate interchangeable entities; in a social–emotional relationship one is the focal point of myriad relationships that one strives to maintain and extend, since action takes place only within relationships (Diesing, 1962, p. 91). Ascription is the opposite of the achievement value: It means that one's actions and obligations toward people spring solely from their relationship to oneself rather than as a response to something they have done.

Formal versus Informal

COGNITIVE ORIENTATION

The basic element in the schema related to this dimension has to do with whether one expects the people involved in the social situation to let their activities, forms of relationship, demeanor, and the like be determined and regulated largely by social rules and conventions or whether one expects such people to have the freedom to make and break their own rules as suit their individual and collective inclinations. In a formal relationship, one expects that the latitude for deviation from conventional forms of behavior is small and that when one violates the rules, others will react negatively and one will be embarrassed (if the violation is unwitting). Since the rules are usually well-known and well-articulated in a formal relationship, it is apt to be characterized by more predictability and less surprise than an informal one. Hostile rather than friendly relations, unequal rather than equal ones, and impersonal rather than formal ones are more likely to be regulated than informal.

MOTIVATIONAL ORIENTATION

Formal social relations appear to be related to a cluster of psychological tendencies. Murray (1938, pp. 200–204) has described various elements of this cluster: the *need for order*, subsuming conjunctivity, sameness, deliberateness, and placidity. Although Murray's emphasis is on the enduring character of these psychological predispositions, it seems likely that the psychological tendencies underlying the *bureaucratic personality* (Merton, 1957) can be elicited by bureaucratic structures. These tendencies have been well described by Merton in his classic paper on bureaucratic structure and personality and amply characterized in the literature on the obsessive–compulsive personality. The emphasis here is on how "formal" situations can temporarily induce in otherwise nonbureaucratic and nonobsessive personalities psychological predispositions to value order, regulation, predictability, sameness, lack of surprise, and the like.

Informal relations tend to be more open, more particularistic, more frank, more flexible, more emotional, and more personal than formal ones. They have a more relaxed, improvisational character in which quickly formed, intuitive and impressionistic reactions to the specific other in the particular situation largely determine one's behavior. In an informal relation, one's motivational orientation is more directed toward persons, whereas in a formal relation it is more directed toward rules and authority. Emotion and conflict is more apt to be openly expressed in informal relations and avoided in formal ones. The more enduring psychological predispositions that are characteristic of the so-called hysterical personality and the field dependent person, resemble the situationally induced motivational orientations to be found in informal relations.

MORAL ORIENTATION

In many respects, the moral orientations to task-oriented and formal relations are similar; this is also the case for social–emotional and informal relations. Formal relations go beyond the values of universalism and affective neutrality or impartiality to include a moral orientation to the rules and conventions that guide social relations. One has an obligation to respect them and to conform to them. One's obligation is to the form of the relationship rather than to its spirit. In contrast, in an informal relationship one is morally oriented to the spirit rather than the form of the relationship. It is the relationship to which one is obligated rather than to the rules that are supposed to regulate it.

In the preceding pages, for brevity's sake, I have discussed the psychological orientations characterizing each of the four dimensions of interpersonal relations as though the dimensions existed in isolation from one another. Of course, in doing so, I have not adequately characterized the psychological orientations characterizing the different types of interpersonal relations: Each type reflects a combination of different dimensions. The psychological orientation associated, for example, with an intimate relation fuses the orientation connected with the particular positions on the cooperative, social–emotional, equal, informal, and intense dimensions. Here, the psychological orientations arising from the different dimensions of the relationship are all concordant with one another. A threat to an intimate relationship might arise from a discordance on any of the dimensions: for

example, from a competitive orientation rather than a cooperative one
("I am more giving than you are"); from a task-oriented rather than a
social–emotional one ("You don't accomplish enough"); from a dependent
rather than an equal one ("I need you to protect me and to take care of
me"); or from a formal rather than informal one ("I get upset in a relationship unless I always know what is expected, unless it has no surprises,
unless it is always orderly and predictable").

From our discussion of the correlations among the different dimensions
in the first section of this chapter, it is evident that there is more or less
discordance among the psychological orientations related to the different
dimensions in the different types of social relations. Thus, the psychological
orientation associated with cooperation is more concordant with the psychological orientations associated with equality, informality, and
social–emotional activities than with the orientations associated with inequality, formality, and task-oriented activities. However, many cooperative
relations are task-oriented and/or unequal and/or formal. Where there is
discordance among the different dimensions characterizing a relationship,
it seems likely that the relative weights or importance of the different
dimensions in the given type of relationship will determine the relative
weights of their associated psychological orientations. That is, if the task-
oriented character of the relationship has stronger weight than the cooperative aspects, it will have more influence in determining the governing
psychological orientation. It also seems likely that the more extreme is the
location on a given dimension, the more apt is that dimension to have the
key role in determining the nature of the psychological orientation: In a
situation that is extremely formal and only slightly cooperative, the psychological orientation will be determined more by the situation's formality
than by its cooperativeness.

Some Relevant Research

In the opening paragraph of this chapter, I stated that the causal arrow
connecting psychological orientations and types of interdependence is bidirectional: A psychological orientation can induce or be induced by a given
type of interdependence. Here, I would go further and indicate that the
cognitive, motivational, and moral components of a psychological orientation can each induce one another—hence, they are likely to be found
together—and each of the components can induce or be induced by a given
type of interdependence. The foregoing assumptions proliferate into a great
number of testable, specific hypotheses that I do not have the space to
elaborate in this chapter. To illustrate, however, these hypotheses would

predict a two-way causal arrow between specific modes of thought and specific types of social relations. Thus, a "bureaucratic" social situation will tend to induce "obsessive–compulsive" modes of thought and obsessive–compulsive modes of thought will tend to "bureaucratize" a social relationship. They would also predict that a competitive social relationship will tend to increase the psychological weight or importance of the differences in values between oneself and one's competitors, whereas a cooperative relationship will tend to increase the psychological importance of the similarities in values between oneself and one's fellow cooperators. We would also hypothesize that a tendency to accentuate the differences in values between oneself and others is apt to induce a competitive relationship, whereas a tendency to accentuate the similarities is likely to induce a cooperative relationship. Further, it can be predicted that different principles of distributive justice will be associated with different types of social relations: A fraternal relationship will be connected with the principle of equality; a caring relationship with the principle of need; a hierarchical organization with the principle of equity; a power struggle with the principle of "winner-take-all." Each of these different principles can induce different modes of thought and different types of social relations when experimentally introduced into an otherwise unstructured social situation. For all of the various hypotheses that entail two-way causal arrows, from an experimental point of view, the independent variables are the ones that are manipulated by the experimenter and the dependent variables are the ones that are affected by the manipulated variables.

Some of the hypotheses suggested by the theoretical ideas presented in this chapter have been tested in my laboratory (Deutsch, 1973) and by many other researchers working in a variety of areas in social psychology. However, many of these ideas have not yet been systematically investigated. Here, I wish to describe briefly two dissertation studies. One has recently been published (Judd, 1978); data for the other are now being analyzed. Both were conducted in our laboratory and reflect our interests in the relation between types of interdependence and modes of thought.

In the first of these studies, Judd (1978) argues that competitive processes in attitude conflicts are characterized by a tendency to accentuate the evaluative differences between one's own position and the position of the person one is arguing with. One of the ways in which this might be done is by emphasizing those conceptual dimensions along which there are larger differences. Hence, Judd hypothesized that in a competitive attitude conflict, the conflicting parties will come to see their positions as being relatively dissimilar and this will be accomplished by heightening the evaluative centrality of those conceptual dimensions that best distinguish between the positions.

For cooperative processes, he argued that parties have the mutual goal of learning more about the issue under dispute. An emphasis on conceptual dimensions along which positions differ significantly may well lead to a more competitive conflict; therefore, Judd hypothesized that a cooperative orientation will motivate individuals to deemphasize those dimensions that best discriminate between the positions and to emphasize dimensions along which there is less of a difference. Thus, a cooperative orientation between conflicting parties will lead to the heightened perception of position similarity as a result of lowered evaluative centrality of the most discriminating dimensions and heightened evaluative centrality of less discriminating dimensions.

Judd came to the interesting conclusion that the perceptions of the similarity–dissimilarity of positions induced by one's orientation (competitive or cooperative) to a conflict will be mediated by *conceptual* changes in the way we look at the issue under dispute. We will come to place more evaluative emphasis on some dimensions and less on others, and these changes may be relatively long-lasting.

Judd's research was designed to test this hypothesis. Pairs of subjects were assigned positions on how National Health Insurance should be organized, an issue about which they did not have strong opinions. These positions differed along three attribute dimensions, positions of pairs being highly distant on one dimension, less distant on a second, and identical on the third. Distance positions along dimensions and content of dimensions were varied independently so that Judd's hypothesis could be tested independently of dimension content. Subjects were asked to either discuss or debate the issue under either a cooperative or competitive orientation. Following this, judgments of similarity of positions were gathered and dimensional evaluative centrality was measured in order to test the hypothesis under investigation.

The results of the experiment strongly confirmed its underlying hypothesis: Competition led to decreased perceived similarity between the positions, and the dimension on which positions differed most was most evaluatively central; cooperation had opposite effects. In other words, the competitive orientation led the competitors to develop conceptual structures, related to the issue under dispute, that accentuated the differences between them and made these differences more attitudinally significant to them; in contrast, the cooperative orientation led the disputants to develop conceptual structures that emphasized the similarities in their positions and made the similarities more emotionally important to them.

An experiment by William A. Wenck, now in progress in our laboratory is also concerned with the relation between types of interdependence and modes of thought. In his study, Wenck is investigating the effects on modes of thought and types of social relations of three different distributive systems: (a) *winner-take-all*, where whoever contributes the most to the group receives the total outcome or reward received by the group; (b) *equity*, where the group's outcome is distributed to the individuals in proportion to their respective contributions to the group; and (c) *equality*, where the group's outcome is shared equally by all its members.

Wenck's investigation of the correlates of these three distributive systems derives from my (Deutsch, 1976) characterization of them:

1. The *winner-take-all* system is associated with a "macho," power-oriented mentality; it also is associated with a high risk-taking, gambling orientation. This mode of thought is much more prevalent in men than in women. It is common in social conditions of disorder, intense competition, widespread illegality, violence, or poverty. It is common in frontier societies, in societies lacking a middle class, in illegal organizations, in adolescent male gangs, in warring groups, etc. It can be elicited by challenge to basic values, by unregulated competition, by an atmosphere of violence and illegality, by anything that stimulates greed or desperation.

2. The *equity* system is associated with an economic mode of thought that is characterized by quantification, measurement, calculation, comparison, evaluation, impersonality, and conversion of unique values to a common currency. It is a cool, detached, future-oriented, analytic, tough-minded mode of thought that appeals to universalistic values, logical reasoning, and objective reality rather than particularistic values, intuition, emotion, and subjective considerations. It is more prevalent in men than women. It is common in societies characterized by a stable hierarchical order, regulated competition, a developed economy, technological advancement, and a large middle class who are neither poor nor rich. It is elicited by conditions that stress productivity, efficiency, objectivity, impersonality, detachment, individualism, and instrumentalism.

3. The *equality* system is associated with a particularistic, social–emotional orientation that is characterized by reliance on intuition, empathy, and personal feeling as a guide to reality. It is a holistic, involved, related, present-oriented "soft" mode of thought in which the reality of others is apprehended from their inside rather than from the outside. Unlike the equity orientation, it is more prevalent in women than men. It is common in fraternal societies and in small cohesive groups that stress friendship, intimacy, loyalty, personal attachments, mutual respect, individual dignity, and cooperation. It is elicited by conditions that emphasize the bonds with others and the symmetrical–reciprocal character of these bonds.

Wenck's study employs a very involving, three-person task in which the group's outcome is determined by the activities of all three persons. The group outcome is distributed to the individuals according to one of the three distributive principles described earlier. The task permits a variety of individual behaviors: The participants can work independently, they can help one another, they can harm one another. After working on the task for 30 minutes, the subjects are interrupted, and are administered a number of different instruments to obtain the dependent measures. Several questionnaires get at subjects' strategy in the task, their self-concepts as they worked on the task, their orientation toward other subjects, and their perception of others' orientation toward them as they all worked on the task. Adjective checklists elicit the motives and emotions that were activated during work on the task. In addition, projective techniques are employed to obtain the subjects' views of the group and of themselves as they worked in the group.

At this writing, the data have been collected and not yet completely analyzed. However, preliminary analyses show the following significant results: The "equality" groups were more productive than the "equity groups" who were in turn more productive than the "winner-take-all" groups; the "autobiographies" composed by the subjects for the roles they developed in the three experimental conditions differed from one another in expected ways; "winner-take-all" subjects characterized their thoughts and feelings as being more "aggressive," "risk-taking," "ruthless," "selfish," "rougher," "unsharing," and "changeable" than did the subjects in the other two conditions; the subjects in the "equality" condition described themselves as more "nurturant," "affiliative" "cooperative," and "altruistic" than did those in the other two conditions; self-characterization of the subjects in the "equity" condition fell in between the "winner-take-all" and "equality" conditions. It is apparent that the results which have been analyzed so far are in accord with the basic ideas underlying the experiment.

Concluding Comments

In this chapter, I have advanced several theses. First, different types of social relations can be characterized in terms of their positions on a number of basic dimensions of interpersonal relations. Second, each of the different types of social relations have associated with them distinctive psychological orientations. A psychological orientation is a complex consisting of interrelated cognitive, motivational, and moral orientations. Third, the causal arrow connecting psychological orientations and types of social relations is bidirectional: A psychological orientation can induce or be induced by a given type of social relationship. And, fourth, the various elements (cognitive, motivational, and moral) of a psychological orientation tend to be consistent with one another.

My argument is not that social relations determine psychological orientations without regard to the personalities of the individual participants nor is it that psychological orientations induce distinctive social relations without regard to the nature of the social situation confronting them. My thesis is rather that there is a tendency for consistency between psychological orientations and social relations that will lead to change in one or both until congruence between the two has been largely achieved. In some circumstances, it will be easier to change psychological orientations; in others, social relations can be more readily altered. I have not addressed the problem of what determines how a conflict between one's psychological orientation to a relationship and the nature of that relationship will be resolved. This is an important problem for future work.

One final comment: My discussion throughout this paper has been of "ideal types" of social relations. Actual social relations are inevitably more complex than my discussion would suggest. An intimate, love relationship, for example, is often characterized by considerable ambivalence: There are not only strong positive elements manifest in the relations but also intense anxieties latent within it; there are quarrels as well as embraces. In addition, it must be recognized that relationships develop and change. Apart from my brief discussion of Figure 2.1, I have not attempted to characterize the dynamics of relationships. This, too, is an important problem for future work.

References

Abelson, R. P. Representing mundane reality in plans. In D. G. Bobrow & A. M. Collins (Eds.), *Representation and understanding.* New York: Academic Press, 1975.

Abelson, R. P. Script processing in attitude formation and decision-making. In J. S. Carroll & J. W. Payne (Eds.), *Cognition and social behavior.* Hillsdale, N.J.: Lawrence Erlbaum Associates, 1976.

Atkinson, J. W., & Feather, N. T. (Eds.), *A theory of achievement motivation.* New York: John Wiley & Sons, 1966.

Bales, R. F. Task roles and social role in problem-solving groups. In E. E. Maccoby, T. M. Newcomb, & E. L. Hartley (Eds.), *Reading in social psychology.* (3rd ed.). New York: Henry Holt and Co., 1958.

Banton, M. *Race relations.* New York: Basic Books, 1967.

Bartlett, F. C. *Remembering.* Cambridge, England: Cambridge University Press, 1932.

Bateson, G. A theory of play and fantasy. *Psychiatric Research Reports 2*, 1955, 39–51.

Benne, K. D., & Sheats, P. Functional roles and group members. *Journal of Social Issues*, 1948, 4, 41–49.

Cartwright, D. P. & Zander, A. F. (Eds.), *Group dynamics: Research and theory.* New York: Harper & Row, 1968.

Deutsch, M. A theory of cooperation and competition. *Human Relations,* 1949, 2, 129–152. (a)

Deutsch, M. An experimental study of the effects of cooperation and competition upon group processes. *Human Relations,* 1949, 2, 199–232. (b)

Deutsch, M. Cooperation and trust: Some theoretical notes. In M. R. Jones (Ed.), *Nebraska Symposium on Motivation. Vol. X.* Lincoln: University of Nebraska Press, 1962.

Deutsch, M. *The resolution of conflict: Constructive and destructive processes.* New Haven: Yale University Press, 1973.

Deutsch, M. Education and distributive justice: Some reflections on grading systems. *American Psychologist,* 1979, 34, 391–401.

Diesing, P. *Reason in society.* Urbana, Illinois: University of Illinois Press, 1962.

Freud, A. *The ego and the mechanisms of defence.* London: Hogarth Press, 1937.

Goffman, E. F. *Frame analysis.* New York: Harper & Row, 1974.

Head, Sir Henry. *Studies in neurology.* Oxford: Oxford University Press, 1920.

Judd, C. M. Cognitive effects of attitude and conflict resolution. *Journal of Conflict Resolution,* 1978, 22, 483–498.

Kelley, H. H., & Thibaut, J. W. *Interpersonal relations: A theory of interdependence.* New York: John Wiley & Sons, 1978.

Kelley, H. H. *Personal relationships: Their structure and processes.* Hillsdale, N.J.: Lawrence Erlbaum Associates, 1979.

Lewin, K. *Field theory in social science.* New York: Harper & Brothers, 1951.

Marwell, G., & Hage, J. The organization of role relationships: A systematic description. *American Sociological Review,* 1970, 35, 884–900.

McClelland, D. C., Atkinson, J. W., Clark, R. A., & Lowell, E. L. *The achievement motive.* New York: Appleton-Century-Crofts, 1953.

Merton, R. K. *Social theory and social structure.* (Revised and enlarged edition.) Glencoe, Illinois: Free Press, 1957.

Murray, H. A. *Explorations in personality: A clinical and experimental study of fifty men of college age.* New York; Oxford University Press, 1938.

Neisser, U. *Cognition and reality.* San Francisco: W. H. Freeman & Co., 1976.

Rawls, J. A. *A theory of justice.* Cambridge: Harvard University Press, 1972.

Schank, R. C., & Abelson, R. P. *Scripts, plans, goals, and understanding: An inquiry into human knowledge structures.* Hillsdale, N.J.: Lawrence Erlbaum Associates, 1977.

Triandis, H. C. *The analysis of subjective culture.* New York: Wiley Interscience, 1972.

Weber, M. *The theory of social and economic organization.* A. M. Henderson & Talcott Parsons, trans. and eds. Glencoe, Illinois: Free Press, 1957.

Weiner, B. *Achievement motivation and attribution theory.* Morristown, New Jersey: General Learning Press, 1974.

Wish, M., Deutsch, M., & Kaplan, S. J. Perceived dimensions of interpersonal relations. *Journal of Personality and Social Psychology,* 1976, 33, 409–420.

Wish, M., & Kaplan, S. J. Toward an implicit theory of interpersonal communication. *Sociometry,* 1977, 40, 234–246.

Chapter 3

Social Values and

Rules of Fairness:

A Theoretical

Perspective

CHARLES G. McCLINTOCK

EDDY VAN AVERMAET

In this chapter we will briefly describe two theoretical paradigms that have been developed to explain how interdependent actors make decisions regarding the distributions of outcomes between themselves and others. In doing this, we will first set forth a set of assumptions that are common to most decision theoretical explanations of human preference behavior. Next, we will describe a general taxonomic model of social values, briefly reviewing some of the more important efforts that have been made to assess such values. Subsequently, we will describe a second area that focuses on actors' use of equity and other rules of fairness to define appropriate distributions of resources between themselves and others or, if actors are third parties, between others. Finally, we will consider whether and how equity and other rules of fairness can be represented in the taxonomic model described initially. In doing so, we will simultaneously be concerned with the ways in which social values and fairness rules may be similar or different, as well as how they might interact to influence actors' expressions of preference for varying distributions of such valued resources as money, S&H Green Stamps, affection, sexual favors, and status.

COOPERATION AND HELPING BEHAVIOR
Theories and Research

Social Values

By *social values* we mean simply actors' preferences for differing distributions of their own and others' outcomes. We assume that such values can be assessed by ascertaining an actor's choices between various distributions of valued resources for self and others. Such value preferences are further assumed to be composed of two functional components: a goal or motivational component, and a strategic or instrumental one.

Goals are end-states that an actor wishes to achieve. Strategies, on the other hand, are instrumental forms of action that an actor follows to increase the likelihood of ultimately reaching a preferred distribution of resources. Interpersonal strategies are directed toward influencing the behavior of one or more others with whom one shares interdependence. Such strategies may employ overt or covert means to increase the likelihood that an actor will obtain a particular end-state. For example, actors may make cooperative choices because they wish to maximize both own and others' short-term and long-term outcomes. On the other hand, such cooperative choices may represent ploys to encourage others with more resources to behave subsequently in a generous way toward the actors. In effect, what appear to be choices consistent with a cooperative goal may actually reflect a strategy of ingratiation pursued for the purpose of maximizing an actor's ultimate own gain. Alternatively, actors may maintain a cooperative posture over a few behavioral episodes in order to elicit cooperation from the other. Once the cooperative pattern is established, the actor may begin to exploit the other party. Such a strategy of "double cross" may serve such social goals as individualism, competition, or aggression.

A Purposive View of Behavior

The social value approach to understanding human behavior focuses primarily on actors who are outcome interdependent and derives primarily from decision and game theoretical models of human action. It attempts to define rational, economic models of human behavior in more social terms. It should be noted from the very outset, however, that we do not contend that human action, whether individual or social, is necessarily purposive or rational. There are obviously numerous acts that are irrationally pursued or explained after-the-fact. Further, much human behavior, because it is governed by habits, occurs more or less routinely, and there is every reason to believe that this obtains for stereotyped patterns of interpersonal as well as individual behaviors. For example, Abelson's (1976) recent work on cognitive scripts indicates that decision making may in certain instances reflect overlearned, coherent patterns of role behaviors. And finally, there are instances where the normative constraints of one's peer group or society are sufficiently strong to leave little room for behavioral variability based on more purposive deliberations. But after one has subtracted out these various alternative explanations of human behavior, there remains a substantial amount of interpersonal activity that is purposive or planned and more or less rational in design. Such activity seems particularly likely to obtain when an actor is confronted with new and novel tasks, with settings where the social outcomes are particularly important to the values of an actor, or when conflict has emerged between two or more actors.

The fundamental and very simple assumption made in value models of human action is that actors rank order and choose among the alternatives available to them in terms of some internal criteria of goodness. The etiology and the nature of the alternatives available may vary markedly between actors and settings, and so may the way in which actors order them. No listing or ranking of alternatives is assumed to be more rational than any other. Rather, rationality in value models refers to the effectiveness of the procedures employed to obtain preferred outcomes. Thus, a preference for suicide is assumed to be neither rational nor irrational. However, one can, of course, be more or less effective (rational) in pursuing this act given various environmental contingencies. Further, suicide—particularly the threat of such—can be employed not as a goal but as an interpersonal strategy designed to influence others. Whether the threat of suicide is strategically a rational act depends on whether it produces the intended effect on other's behavior, thereby enabling actor to achieve some preferred goal or outcome state. The need to exercise influence on other's behavior is, of course, particularly important in social settings where two or more actors are dependent on each other for achieving valued outcomes.

Riskless Choice

In situations where no uncertainties are associated with obtaining the outcomes that one values—settings of *riskless choice*—economists have extended and enriched the preceding simple principle of value maximization by assuming that actors can and do rank order preferences for combinations of varying amounts of two or more valued commodities (Heath, 1976). For example, they assume that an actor can rank order his or her preferences for various combinations of bottles of red and white wine. The possibility of such rankings enables one to describe a preference structure (MacCrimmon & Messick, 1976) for an individual decision maker in terms of a two-dimensional commodity or outcome space, formed in this instance by preferences for various combinations of bottles of red and white wine.

The preference structures of actors in such a two-dimensional outcome space can be theoretically defined on an a priori basis or empirically inferred by observing actors' actual choices. To illustrate such a preference structure, imagine a two-dimensional space with the number of bottles of red wine on the horizontal axis and the number of bottles of white wine on the vertical so that any point in the space represents some "bundle" of bottles of red and white wine. Suppose an actor likes only red wine and suppose further that he or she has an option of receiving two bottles of red wine and two bottles of white. Hypothetically, we can pair this "bundle" with all others, that is, 4 red, 1 white, or 0 red and 12 white and observe, for each pair of bundles, whether our actor would prefer the "standard," two of each, or the other option. In this way the space is partitioned into the set of points that is preferred to the standard and the set to which the standard is preferred. The boundary between these two sets is called a preference boundary for the point two red, two white. The preference boundary for our actor who likes only red wine would be a vertical line passing through the point two red, two white since the actor would, we presume, prefer any bundle that yielded three or more bottles of red wine to the standard but would prefer the standard to any bundle that yielded fewer than two bottles of red.

In contrast, imagine someone who likes red and white wine equally well and who would prefer to get as many bottles as possible regardless of color. Since the number of bottles this actor receives with the standard is 4, he or she would prefer any combination that would yield more than 4 and would prefer the standard to any bundle that yielded less than 4. Thus the preference boundary for this person would be a line with slope -1 passing through the standard.

One can add to MacCrimmon and Messick's (1976) definition of preference boundary the construct of indifference curves as defined by economists working on models of individual decision making. An indifference curve is defined by joining a series of points representing combinations of two commodities (e.g., combinations of bottles of red and white wine) between which an actor is indifferent. In economics, a knowledge of such curves has several important functions. For example, if one knows the resources an actor has to expend on wine, the actor's indifference structure, and the unit costs of the two kinds of wine, one can then order an actor's choices between various combinations of wines. More important, one can also predict how an actor's choices will vary given various levels of resources available to the actor, or given changes in the unit costs of one or both of the commodities.

We have very briefly introduced the constructs of preference boundaries and indifference curves because they are useful in defining social values and in suggesting ways to develop and test more rigorous models of social choice behavior. In social value theory, of course, the two commodities that one maps into a two-dimensional outcome or commodity space are actor's own and other's outcomes. Given these commodities and a two-dimensional own and other outcome space, one can go on to describe the particular preference boundaries that define various actor orientations toward self and others, as well as to depict indifference curves that are consistent with the various value orientations.

Beyond Riskless Choice

Before attempting to define those social values that we believe to be of central importance in social behavior, particularly in settings of outcome interdependence, we would like to make two additional observations regarding the relationship between economic models of choice and a theory of social value. First, the preceding preference analysis, as we noted, is particularly relevant to instances where actors are making choices between alternatives whose outcomes, given a choice, are relatively certain to obtain. There are, of course, many instances where choosing a particular alternative does not assure one of achieving a particular outcome. Rather, there is some probability of risk attached to whether the choice will produce the desired effect. Gambling is an obvious example. And such uncertainty underlies many economic and social decisions as well. For this reason, much of the work on individual and interdependent decision making in economics contains assumptions about how one should choose when alternatives have a risk component. The most basic assumption made, of course, is that actors should maximize their expected value. Namely, a rational decision maker is advised to select that alternative for which the highest value obtains when one multiplies the goodness of the possible outcomes (their utilities to the actor) by the likelihood of the outcome occurring (its probability). One can go on, of course, to define instances of riskless choice in terms of expected value theory where the likelihood that a particular outcome will follow from a particular choice approximates certainty, that is, a probability of 1.

The second observation is that one can define two kinds of settings in which actors make decisions regarding own and other's outcomes (Eckhoff, 1974). The first setting is one of *allocation*, where a given actor has unilateral responsibility for distributing outcomes between self and other, or two others. The second kind of setting involves *reciprocation* or *exchange*, where two or more actors have partial control over both their own and others' outcomes. Obviously, a theory of riskless choice is more appropriate to settings of allocation insofar as one actor exercises unilateral outcome control. And as will become apparent from the research to be reviewed subsequently, most recent attempts to assess social values and to develop and test value models of social choice have been undertaken in such "riskless" settings.

In contrast, theoretical and empirical studies of social choice in settings of reciprocation make assumptions concerning decision making under conditions of uncertainty and risk, assumptions that generally derive directly from the theory of games developed by Von Neumann and Morgenstern (1944). In decision theories of individual choice behavior, risk by convention refers to instances where a decision maker knows the likelihoods of outcomes and hence can assign specific numerical probabilities to them. Uncertainty refers to instances where likelihood cannot be specifically enumerated by the decision maker. In both instances, it is nature that generates the probabilistic state of the environment for the individual decision maker, and nature is assumed to be indifferent to the motives, goals, and possible future behaviors of the decision maker.

In sharp contrast, in models of social choice, decision making involves different conditions of uncertainty or risk, conditions that are not independent of a decision maker's own goals, strategies, and future actions. A first condition of risk in social decision making is that in assigning expected values to particular choices, an actor must generally assign likelihoods to various choices the other player may make. This obtains, of course, because actor's achievement of valued outcomes is determined both by own and other's choices. Hence, other's goals, strategies, and resulting actions can affect actor's outcomes as well as his or her own. In most instances, this assignment of likelihood involves uncertainty, since actor knows neither other's dominant value nor other's perception of actor's own values.

There is another kind of risk that an actor must consider when a particular choice is aimed not at short term gain, but at modifying other's behavior so as to increase the value of an actor's future outcomes. Here, the risk associated with the actor's choices relates to the likelihood that the overt or covert strategy or instrumental behavior being undertaken will be successful. Because of the complexity of studying social values in exchange settings, most work on decision making between interdependent actors has assumed that the actors are pursuing a single goal or value, namely, the classical economic motive of maximizing their own material outcomes. Such an assumption, however, leads to inappropriate explanations of human decision making in instances where actors are concerned with others' as well as own outcomes—a concern that may be cooperative, altruistic, aggressive, or competitive in orientation.

Defining Social Values

Social values, given the preceding discussion, can be defined as preferences for particular distributions of outcomes to self and other, preferences that may be motivational (goal oriented) or strategic in intent. Griesinger and Livingston (1973) describe a two-person preference model of social values in which the magnitude of actor's outcomes (their utilities) is defined by the horizontal axis, and the magnitude of the outcomes received by other by the vertical axis. These researchers further assume that payoffs increase monotonically along each axis. Any point in the plane formed by these two axes would thereby represent a particular combination of payoffs to actor and other. An actor's dominant value can be represented as a vector that defines actor's preferences between two or more combinations of outcomes to self and other. That is, given such a vector, one assumes that an actor, in making choices between combinations of own and other's outcomes, will prefer those that have the greatest projection on the line defining this most preferred vector. Such a definition of social values bears a close resemblance to Lewin's (1951) topological representation of actor's utilities. A review of his work suggests further that the simple structure proposed here may be appropriate only for rather simple decisions regarding distributions of own and other's outcomes.

If one assumes that an actor's values are consistent over time within or between some subset of situations, and if one further assumes that these values reflect a linear combination of payoffs to self and other, then one can depict social values as utility functions that form linear vectors in the two-dimensional payoff space described above. Figure 3.1 depicts eight of an infinite number of possible linear combinations of own and other's

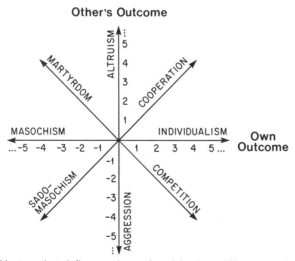

Figure 3.1. Vectors that define a subset of social values. (Given a particular value orientation, an actor should select that combination of available own and other's outcomes that has the greatest projection on the correspondent vector.)

outcomes. The eight are often cited among the major personal and inter-personal orientations that actors take towards own, other's or own and other's outcomes. It can be seen that these linear vectors are formed by assigning different weights to own and other's outcomes. For example, *cooperation* is defined by the weights of + 1 to own and to other's outcomes, *individualism* by + 1 to own and 0 to other's, *competition* by + 1 to own and − 1 to other's outcomes, and so forth.

As in the case of the economic model of commodity preference discussed earlier, one can also define indifference curves within an own–other outcome space. Sets of indifference curves for four of the eight values depicted in Figure 3.1 are given in Figure 3.2. One assumes, of course, that an actor would prefer outcomes on that indifference curve that has the highest projection on the vector defining the actor's preferred value. However, by definition, an actor would be indifferent between two points falling on a particular indifference curve. For example, a person with a competitive value orientation would prefer the combination of outcomes of 8 to self and 2 to other to that of 5 to self and 5 to other. In effect, the first point would fall on an indifference curve that would have a greater projection on the preferred vector of competition. For a cooperatively oriented actor, however, given the indifference structure depicted in Figure 3.2, these two outcomes would fall on the same indifference curve since both produce a

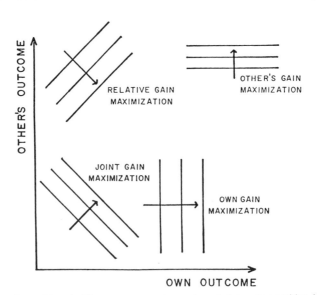

Figure 3.2. Sets of four indifference curves for vectors defining competition (relative gain maximization), altruism (other's gain maximization), cooperation (joint gain maximization) and individualism (own gain maximization).

joint outcome of 10. Hence, the cooperative actor should be indifferent between the two.

It is obvious that an actor who is cooperatively oriented might not show such indifference, and that a model other than an additive one may be required to depict the indifference structure of some actors. The economists who work with actors' preferences for various combinations of two commodities, for example, tend to relax a strictly additive combination rule by invoking the notion of diminishing rates of marginal substitution. This principle asserts that the more a consumer has of a given commodity, the more he or she will be willing to give up additional units of that commodity for fewer units of another. Such an assumption generates indifference curves that are not linear but convex to the origin and that have a negative slope. Such a proportionally cooperative actor might prefer a 52–48 distribution of outcomes to self and other rather than 98 for self and 2 for other, or 2 for self and 98 for other, though the joint outcome is identical in all three instances.

There are numerous ways in which one can define the preference structures underlying social values such that indifference curves need not be linear in form. MacCrimmon and Messick (1976) examine a number of these. And in later sections we will review the empirical work of Radzicki (1976), who finds a form of nonlinearity in own and other outcome preferences that points toward the need to consider the prosocial orientation of equity as another human social value.

Value Measurement

In the present section we will describe several ways that have been employed to measure social values, particularly as they function as social motives and as distinct from interpersonal strategies. An assessment of value measurement procedures will be important to our subsequent discussion of equity. In order to assess equity as a social value, it is necessary to be able to define and distinguish other related values as well. And, of course, measurement is essential to such a definitional process.

In order to interpret the choice behaviors of an actor as reflecting a particular value, it is necessary to demonstrate not only that the behaviors are consistent with a certain decision rule but also that they are discriminable from related but different rules. Of course, one cannot ever be certain that one has successfully discriminated between all relevant alternative explanations of an actor's choice. But one can feel considerably more confident concerning the explanation that one imposes on an actor's preferences if one has a more or less coherent theory of social value, one that includes a measurement procedure that permits both the identification of and the discrimination between various theoretically relevant choice rules.

MATRIX GAMES

Early attempts to assess social values generally involved observing actors make choices in particular two-person, two-choice matrix games, that is, in games where on any given trial, the actor's outcomes were determined both by his or her own as well as another's choices. The utility of this procedure for measuring social values proved with time to be problematic for several reasons. The capacity to discriminate between more than two values, for example, proved difficult. Thus, if one's theory assumed that any one of four social goals—aggression, cooperation, individualism and competition—might account for a particular sequence of actor choices, then the repeated play of a particular two-choice game could not provide sufficient behavioral information to discriminate between these various possible explanations.

Furthermore, differences in the interdependence structure of two-person, two-choice games—for example, between the often used prisoner's dilemma game (PDG), maximizing difference games (MDG), and chicken game (CG)—can have more or less subtle implications for the measurement of both the goal and the strategic aspects of performance. The logical and social psychological implications of the structural properties of matrix games have only recently been clearly described by the insightful theoretical efforts of Kelley and Thibaut (1978). The complexities they describe create even further difficulties in using two-choice matrix games as a method for assessing social values.

Finally, there is a problem with utilizing matrix games both to infer people's values and their social preferences. As Grzelak (1976) and Grzelak, Iwinski, and Radzicki (1977) observe, if one employs matrix games to infer values, then game behavior can be explained but not predicted. Often in decision making tasks, we are concerned not only with explanation but with making predictions based on a knowledge of actors' utility functions. To do this, it is necessary to measure either utilities (social values) or decisions outside of the game paradigm. A similar point is made by Wyer (1969) in commenting on Messick and McClintock's (1968) use of decomposed games as a method for assessing both values and subsequent choice behaviors. We turn next to consider the decomposed game paradigm as a value assessment method.

DECOMPOSED GAMES

A number of researchers have recognized that the theoretically relevant determinants of choice behavior in even simple two-person, two-choice matrix games are far too complex to support the use of such games as a way to attempt to discriminate between various value orientations. As a result they developed a variety of new methods for measuring values. Thus, for example, Messick and McClintock (1968) theoretically identified three value orientations that might underlie actors' choices in game settings: cooperation, or joint gain maximization (*j*); individualism, or own gain maximization (*o*); and competition, or relative gain maximization (*r*). They then looked at all possible combinations of two-choice, two-person games that could logically be formed, given these three values. Of the six possible classes of two-choice games that can be so formed, three place values in opposition to one another: *o* and *r* in opposition to *j*, for example, the PDG; *o* and *j* in opposition to *r*, for example, the MDG; and *j* in opposition to *r* with *o* controlled, that is, the same own (*o*) outcome attends each choice. The other three classes of games are ones in which one particular choice alternative is dominant in regard to two or three of the three values, and any other is nondominant. For example, in one game class one choice is dominant in regard to all three values. This would obtain if one were confronted with a choice that afforded self 8 points and other 4 as versus one that afforded self 3 points and other 2. The choice of 8 for self and 4 for other dominates in terms of joint, own, and relative gain.

Messick and McClintock noted that the repeated presentation of these six classes of games to a chooser, particularly those classes where values were in opposition, should permit an observer to infer the chooser's predispositions toward *o*, *j*, and *r* choice rules and hence provide the beginnings of a procedure for differentiating cooperative, individualistic, and competitive goals. They further observed that a procedure was needed for presenting choices so as to reduce the possible confounding of social goals and interpersonal strategies, a confounding that is a serious problem when matrix games are employed to assess values. Hence, they developed a method for presenting choices to subjects that afforded the choosing actor at the moment of choice complete fate control over both own and other's outcomes, a method that employed what they termed *decomposed games*. In effect, this procedure reduces the joint interdependence between actors since the chooser can completely determine, at least at the moment of choice, both his or her and other's outcomes. For this reason, the chooser has less opportunity to make choices for the strategic reason of modifying other's behavior.

Formally, Messick and McClintock defined a two-choice decomposed game as one in which a player is given a choice between two alternatives, *x* and *y*, each of which specifies the payoffs to the player and the simulated other. Each alternative consists of two commodities, for example, two numbers (*a*, *b*) where *a* is the payoff to the chooser and *b* that to the other if the choice is made. A typical two-choice decomposed game is depicted in Figure 3.3. It is a variant of the MDG developed earlier by McClintock and McNeel (1967), to assess competitive as contrasted to cooperative and individualistic preferences. The x choice maximizes chooser's own (a) and joint $(a + b)$ gain, and the y choice maximizes chooser's gain relative to other $(a - b)$.

Messick and McClintock presented subjects with 80 instances of the six game classes described earlier, and scored their choices in terms of the three values: own gain (o), joint gain (j), and relative gain (r). They then examined the degree to which an external factor—the feedback presented the chooser concerning the status of his or her own, joint, or relative outcomes—would affect the dominance of o, j, and r choices. They observed that both the motivational structure of the decomposed games (membership in one of the six game classes), and the nature of the feedback provided choosers significantly affected the dominance of the various choice rules. The researchers then went on to develop a two-choice stochastic model of social value in which subjects were assumed to be in one of four possible value states: o, j, r, or i (indifference, a state that leads to random choosing). The model, by assuming a probability distribution over these four sets of states, successfully permitted the prediction of subjects' subsequent behavior on the basis of their prior behavior and the estimation of the strengths of various value orientations.

In subsequent work (McClintock, Messick, Kuhlman, & Campos, 1973), the procedure was extended to three-choice decomposed games, and one additional value was added to the analysis: aggression, or the minimization of other's outcomes (m). Choices in three-choice games obviously permit one to discriminate more clearly among various preference rules. For example, in a three-choice but not in a two-choice decomposed game, one can simultaneously isolate individualism from both cooperation and competition. In analyzing the results of the studies, it was observed that for the task employed, aggression (m) was not a frequently used decision rule, but o, j, and r *were* frequently employed rules. The use or dominance of these

	Player's choice	
	x	y
Player's outcome, a	9	7
Other's outcome, b	8	2

Figure 3.3. Two-choice decomposed game with maximizing difference game structure. Choice x maximizes player's own and joint gain; choice y maximizes player's relative gain.

rules varied as a function of game case (whether other was systematically afforded more or fewer points than chooser), and in certain games by sex of chooser.

Subjects' choices in decomposed games have subsequently been employed in a variety of ways such as, for example, to investigate the development of values in children (McClintock & Moskowitz, 1976; McClintock, Moskowitz, & McClintock, 1977); cross-cultural variations in childrens' values (Toda, Shinotsuka, McClintock, & Stech, 1978); and variations in value orientation of ingroup members to ingroup and outgroup members (Brewer & Silver, 1978). Further, Kuhlman and his students (Kuhlman & Marshello, 1975; Mills, 1978) have employed decomposed game measures of social value in a number of studies concerned with individual differences in value. For example, they have found that the value orientation of an actor significantly affects the actor's choice behavior when confronting others playing different strategies in the PDG. Further, they have observed that actors with different values encode affect such as happiness, sadness, and anger with differing accuracy.

Finally, in recent research, Maki, Thorngate, and McClintock (1979) have found that observers are differentially successful in detecting choosers' preferences for the choice rules dictated by the eight vectors described in Figure 3.1. The order of detection from most successful to least successful was as follows: individualism, competition, aggression, cooperation, altruism, masochism, martyrdom, and sadomasochism. The fact that observers can detect with reasonable accuracy both the altruistic and the aggressive choice rules suggests that these orientations should be incorporated into any theory of social value. Common sense, as well as prior theoretical and empirical work, would suggest that the expression of these values, as well as the others already discussed, is in part situationally dependent. And one can make an empirical case that, where own gain maximization is dominated by values that concern other's outcomes—whether these values emphasize maximizing or minimizing other's gains—behavior becomes more situationally dependent. Later in the present chapter we will argue that various rules of fairness regarding distributions of outcomes between self and other should also be included in any general theory of social value, and that fairness values may also be more situationally defined than those of individualism, cooperation, and competition.

JUDGMENTAL MEASURES OF VALUE

A second example of a procedure for assessing an actor's orientation toward own and other's outcomes comes from the early and important work of Robert Wyer (1969, 1971). Instead of employing a behavioral measure of social value, Wyer suggested using a judgmental procedure for defining actors' orientations toward own and other's outcomes. He proposed such a method for two reasons. First, he believed the procedure for validating the decomposed game method of value measurement, as followed by Messick and McClintock, might be circular insofar as the games were employed to both estimate and evaluate the parameters of their model. And second, by using judgmental procedures, Wyer observed that one could achieve a more quantitative assessment of the utility of particular combinations of own and other's outcomes—that is, of social value.

Wyer, as in the earlier work by Griesinger and Livingston (1973), defined value in linear terms:

$$U_{est} = w_1 \delta R_s + w_2 (1 - \delta) R_s + w_3 R_o \qquad (1)$$

where U_{est} refers to the estimated utility of particular combinations of outcomes, R_s represents the number of points received by the subject in a particular choice alternative, δ is defined as a step function that is equal to 1 if $R_s < 0$ and to 0 if $R_s > 0$, and w_1, w_2, w_3 are weights attached to R_s and R_o, where R_o is the number of points received by other. Different weights are assigned to R_s depending upon whether it is positive or negative, under the assumption that the utility of each point gained by the subject might differ from each point lost by the subject.

Given this definition of value, Wyer proceeded to construct choice situations that had the same structure as decomposed games except that, rather than being requested to choose between two own-other outcome combinations, subjects were asked to evaluate combinations of own and other's outcomes on a 21-point scale ranging from $+10$ (very desirable) to -10 (very undesirable). To determine whether subjects would vary their ratings of outcomes under various external contingencies, Wyer varied the monetary values associated with outcomes (high, low, or none), and the attractiveness of other (high, low, not manipulated).

From a measurement standpoint, Wyer's major finding was that the rated desirability of own and other's outcomes did indeed approximate a linear function as defined by Eq. (1). Further, by dividing and correlating two subsets of own and other outcome evaluations, he was able to show that the linear function was consistent across both subsets. He also observed that across subjects, the average correlation between predicted and obtained values of U for the two subsets was .876 and .864. Wyer (1969) went on to evaluate his measurement procedure in several other ways that we will not review here except to note that they further strengthen his assertion that the estimates of the desirability of outcomes in a payoff matrix can be predicted fairly well as a linear function of R_s and R_o, at least within the range of values considered in this study. Finally, Wyer observed that the weight attached to R_s and R_o varied as a function of the values of the payoffs but was not influenced by the attractiveness of other.

Wyer's linear model, of course, admits an infinite variety of preferred combinations of own and other's outcomes, and makes no a priori assumptions about the existence of particular social values. Messick and McClintock's definition of a particular set of values, namely, cooperation, competition, individualism, and aggression, is logically consistent with the linear definitions of value assumed both by Griesinger and Livingston and by Wyer. The particular importance of Wyer's work is his finding concerning the consistency and reliability of his carefully conceptually defined measurement procedures for estimating and assessing an actor's orientations towards various combinations of own and other's outcomes, as well as the evidence he presents within the study that subjects' preference rules approximate the linear model defined in Eq. (1). The work on measurement to be considered next, however, would indicate that a simple linear model is sufficient for describing the social choice rules of only some subjects.

ASSESSING VALUE BY CONJOINT MEASUREMENT

In more recent work, Radzicki (1976) has extended Wyer's measurement techniques by employing conjoint procedures (Luce & Tukey, 1964). However, before reviewing Radzicki's work, we should note that an earlier, somewhat parallel effort to value assessment was undertaken by Sawyer (1966). Sawyer also defined cooperation as $(P + O$, where P = person's outcome, and O = other's outcome), competition as $(P - O)$ and individualism as (P). He asserted that the preceding represented pure forms of the above three orientations, and that a more general, useful linear statement of interpersonal orientations is given by:

$$\text{Orientation} = P + aO \qquad (2)$$

where a (which Sawyer defined as altruism) could range in value from $+1.0$ to -1.0. He then measured a either directly by asking subjects to assign values ranging from $+1.0$ to -1.0 to other's outcomes, or indirectly by having them rank preferences for various combinations of outcomes for self and other. Sawyer employed a rather complicated weighting technique to obtain a single estimate of a. He did not test, however, whether subject's preferences were linear or followed some other composition rule. For one thing, of course, conjoint measurement procedures such as those subsequently employed by Radzicki were just beginning to appear in the literature at the time.

Sawyer's data analysis did indicate that systematic differences in the value of a occurred within and between subjects given differing characteristics of P and O. Thus (a) college student subjects differentiated between friend, stranger, and foe in terms of the value they assigned a; (b) YMCA members of the preceding population were generally more positively oriented towards others' outcomes than non-YMCA members; (c) business majors preferred to maximize their own outcomes more than did other majors; and (d) social science students differentiated more strongly between friends and foes in assigning a value to a.

Radzicki's conjoint method of measurement provides a common scale by which to assess both the dependent variable (e.g., the utility attached by subjects to various pairs composed of own and other's outcomes) and the independent variable (e.g., the utilities of two different kinds of values). To achieve this, one must admit a certain kind of composition rule by which the component factors (independent variables) will be integrated producing a certain joint effect (dependent variables). The rule can be of any variety, for example, additive or multiplicative. By examining each subject's choice behavior one can gain insight into the specific composition rules (values) employed by actors.

We will not attempt to detail the methodology of conjoint measurement here. We would note, however, that Wyer's efforts evaluated a single composition rule as given in Eq. (1) by having subjects make independent evaluative judgments of each of a number of own–other outcome combinations. In the present work, Radzicki asked subjects to evaluate simultaneously 25 outcomes to self and other by ordering outcomes in terms of whether they were most or least preferred. Subjects were informed prior to the ordering that the experimenter would select randomly two of the own–other outcomes and afford them money (zlotys) associated with the one they ranked higher.

Radzicki's study produced a number of important findings. First, the choices of 22 of the 53 subjects he used were consistent with a simple linear model such as that proposed by Wyer. For four additional subjects, the model best fitting their choice was a nonlinear additive model in which the utility attributed to partner's gains (as well as own gains) is a nonlinear function of payoff magnitude, but does not depend upon own payoff. The function defining this state, Radizicki observed, can be expressed by the following equation:

$$u(x,y) = ax + by + cx^2 + dy^2 \qquad (3)$$

For the remaining half of the subjects, no additive model provided a good fit of their choice data. However, there were a variety of polynomial functions that provided reasonably good fits across the rank orderings of the individuals tested. Radzicki, following Tversky's (1967) assertion that the selection of appropriate functions in such instances must simultaneously take into consideration both substantive and measurement theory, observed that in a number of instances subjects' choices reflected a concern with decreasing potential "inequity," or more accurately in this instance, equality. Hence, subjects showed favor for outcomes with smaller discrepancies between own and other's outcomes.

This concern is reflected in the polynomial that provided the best fit for 14 subjects:

$$u(x,y) = ax + by + cx^2 + dy^2 + \exp|x - y|^q \qquad (4)$$

where $q < 1$. Here the factor of inequality is nonlinear. Finally, in about 8% of the cases the respondents' ratings were just too inconsistent or chaotic to be ordered.

The preceding study has several important implications. First, it suggests that in the types of tasks employed here, some subjects show concern for fairness. Second, it appears that with or without fairness as a consideration, some subjects' choice rules are nonlinear. And although the phenomenological basis for the latter decision rule is not yet clear, MacCrimmon and Messick (1976), in developing their framework for the evaluation of social values, do suggest a number of nonlinear rules that may dictate subjects' preferences for various combinations of own and other's outcomes, rules that may help provide phenomenological meaning for nonlinear choices.

In concluding, it should be emphasized again that the measurement of social values involves both making and testing the implications of assumptions concerning measurement and substance. The work in the tradition of Messick and McClintock (1968) has emphasized the substantive nature of social values, whereas the efforts of Wyer (1969, 1971) and Radzicki (1976) have focused more on identifying an adequate combinatorial mode of measurement. The two emphases are obviously complementary to one another and to the long-term goal of understanding the etiology of social values and their impact upon human action.

Fairness Rules

The model of social values outlined in the first section of this chapter has defined social values as distinct sets of motivational or strategic preferences among distributions of outcomes to self and other. These values are assumed to play an important role in determining an actor's behavior in settings of outcome interdependence. Until recently, the above model has not explicitly considered the relationship between social values and various rules of fairness—such as equality and equity—that have received considerable attention in recent theoretical and empirical analyses of interdependent behavior. In the present section, we will be directly concerned with this relationship. Following a brief general characterization of current social psychological approaches to fairness, we will examine whether rules of fairness can be formally defined in terms of a two dimensional own–other outcomes space. Next, the functional relationship between rules of fairness and other social values will be discussed. Finally, attention will be given to the research implications of our analysis.

The Social Psychological Approach to Equity and Other Rules of Fairness

In a generic sense, the concept of fairness refers to any of a variety of decision rules that people may employ to evaluate the correctness, that is, the justice implied by various distributions of valued resources between actors or groups. Ever since the time of Aristotle, philosophers, sociologists, and more recently, social psychologists have attempted to define, distinguish, and relate the various criteria and rules that can serve as a basis for fair or just distributions of resources. Ability, effort, need, accomplishments or productivity, social utility, scarcity of services provided and many other dimensions, including even sheer humanity, have been considered as instances of such criteria (Deutsch, 1975; Lerner, 1977; Rescher, 1966; Walster, Walster, & Berscheid, 1978).

In addition to defining various fairness rules, social philosophers have attempted, from a prescriptive point of view, to rank order these rules in terms of which are the more fundamental (Rawls, 1971; Sen, 1970). Sociologists have focused more on the functional value of the various fairness rules for collective problem solving and survival (Davis & Moore, 1945; Quinton, 1975/1976; Walster & Walster, 1975). Social psychologists, although not ignoring the value of other approaches, have concentrated their attention on the psychological origin of people's concern with fairness and justice and on its behavioral manifestations. More specifically, they have set forth various models that specify how actors subjectively define the fairness of particular exchange relationships, under which conditions various rules of fairness are elicited, and which behavioral and/or cognitive means actors use to bring fairness or justice to a relationship.

In view of the discussion that follows, it is appropriate to list, without going into detail, some of the more distinguishing characteristics of the various social psychological models of fairness. Some models, for instance, deal with only a single fairness rule. Adams (1965) and Walster et al. (1978) define fairness as equity, a distributional rule that states that actors' outcomes should be proportional to their contributions or inputs to a relationship. Without denying the existence of other fairness rules, they argue that they can all be subsumed under the proportionality formulation. Other approaches (Deutsch, 1975; Lerner, 1977; Leventhal, 1976; Mikula, 1980; Sampson, 1975) make a formal distinction between a number of fairness rules. For example, they distinguish an equity rule (to each according to his inputs), an equality rule (equal outcomes for all), and a need rule (to each according to his individual needs). Whereas Walster *et al.* (1978) argue that these rules differ only in that they refer to different classes of inputs that are considered salient in particular contexts, the defendants of the multirule approach feel that Walster's approach formally and abstractly unifies what are phenomenologically distinct definitions of fairness, and thereby severely reduces the predictive quality of theories of justice in general (Mikula, 1980).

A distinction can also be made between models that examine fairness behaviors reactively and those that emphasize their proactive character (Van Avermaet, McClintock, & Moskowitz, 1978). Adams (1965) and Walster *et al.* (1978), for example, view fairness (equity) primarily as a motivational disposition that is activated after an actor perceives that a state of unfairness (inequity) obtains. Fair behaviors are thus conceived in a reactive manner, as resultants of attempts to escape the aversive internal states of dissonance produced by the perception of unfairness. In contrast to such drive reduction approaches, other models, particularly those that maintain a distinction between various rules of fairness, have a more proactive, purposive conception of fairness. They view distribution behaviors as governed by one or another fairness rule and as purposively directed toward achieving some positively valued state. As such, their conception of behavior is quite similar to the decision theoretical approach proposed in McClintock's model of social values. Hence, the two kinds of models make differing motivational assumptions regarding the role of fairness in human behavior. Reactive models view behavior as motivated by unfairness, whereas proactive models conceive of behavior as motivated by a positive concern with fairness.

It should also be observed that much of the social psychological research in this area creates at least the impression that fairness represents *the* dominant motivational force in human social interaction. In many instances both fairness models and research fail to specify explicitly the relationship between a fairness orientation and other social motivational orientations, such as those described in the first part of this chapter. Finally, most of the theoretical and empirical efforts in this area have been largely restricted to examining the role of fairness in allocation settings and have not given sufficient attention to its role in situations of exchange or reciprocation (McClintock & Keil, forthcoming).

The importance of some of these considerations will become clear, as we now turn to a discussion of fairness within the context of a general model of social values. For reasons of brevity, our discussion will focus on a subset of the possible fairness rules, namely, those of equity and equality. Among the rules of fairness, they appear to be the most prevalent, and at the same time they have received the most attention in the empirical literature.

Rules of Fairness as Social Values

Earlier we defined various social values as distinct sets of preferences among distributions of outcomes to self and others. If one also conceives of fairness in proactive decision theoretical terms, the interesting question arises as to whether various rules that define fair distributions of outcomes can be formalized and discriminated from other social values. For the value model we are proposing, rules of fairness only formally qualify as social values if, as other social values, they can be uniquely represented as preferences defined by a set of indifference curves in a two dimensional own–other outcome space. And it can be shown, in fact, that equity and equality, as two of the more specific rules of fairness, satisfy this criterion.

EQUITY

Following Adams's (1965) proportional definition of equity, individuals intent on maximizing the equity of their and other's outcomes want the ratio of their to others' outcomes to be proportional to the ratio of their respective inputs. Hence, such individuals should be indifferent among all own–other outcome points falling along a line that satisfies this criterion. This line is, by definition, a line passing through the origin and with a slope equal to the I_o/I_p ratio, where I_o are inputs made by others and I_p those made by self. Moreover, these individuals should prefer points on that line to points falling along lines with smaller *or* larger slopes. This implies first that, because fairness is defined in ratio terms, an equity preference structure is not linear, and second that there is no unique equity vector since the highest indifference curve varies with different input ratios. It is, however, possible to map an equity preference structure into this space for any given ratio.[1] The ability to represent equity in the space in this rather limited manner is useful because it reveals the measurement criteria that have to

[1] Two additional restrictions should be mentioned. Adams's definition of equity becomes problematic when one leaves the region of positive inputs and outcomes, and therefore only in the positive quadrant of the payoff space can it be represented in a logically meaningful manner. Second, the geometrical representation suggested here specifies only the location and slope of the highest (equity) indifference curve. Nothing is said about the location of other indifference curves except that they are lower and that they cannot meet or cross the equity indifference curve.

be met if one wants to verify empirically the existence of equity as a value distinct from other values.

Consider, for example, a case where the own–other input ratio is 1/2, that is, where an individual perceives other's inputs to be twice his or her own. As shown in Figure 3.4, the highest indifference curve is then a ridge line with a slope of +2. An individual who is equity oriented should prefer points on that slope or line to all other points in the outcome space. Such an individual should also prefer points on indifference curves closer to the ridge than those further removed (see direction of arrows).

Comparing this preference structure with, for example, a relative gain structure suggests that in this case, an equity utility surface coincides with and dictates the same choices as a relative-gain utility surface for that region of the payoff space where own and other outcomes fall on or to the left of the ridge line. Only in the complementary region falling to the right of the ridge do the two values imply indifferent and opposite preferences. Similar analyses on other own–other input ratios would show that in each instance the corresponding equity preference structure can be mapped onto the payoff space, but in each case the choices dictated by equity will partially overlap others that are consistent with other social values.

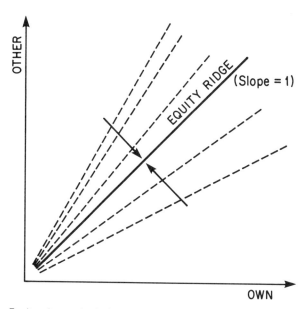

Figure 3.4. Equity given other's inputs are twice own inputs. (The most equitable distribution falls on the equity ridge. Dashed lines represent indifference curves defined as in Figure 3.2.)

EQUALITY

An equality rule dictates that an actor should prefer an identical distribution of outcomes between self and other regardless of inputs. This rule can also be represented by a set of indifference curves in an own–other outcome space where the highest curve or ridge line assumes a slope of +1. Persons making choices consistent with an equality rule should prefer own–other outcome points that most closely approximate the ridge line on either side, and hence, as in the instance of equity, the preference structure for equality cannot be described as linear. The equality rule differs in terms of its preference structure from equity in two fundamental ways. First, there is a unique equality ridge line that does not obtain for equity since the latter necessarily varies by definition as a function of changes in the ratio of own to other's inputs. Second, although in the one instance where own and other inputs are equal, both equity and equality can be represented as having a highest indifference curve or ridge line with a slope of +1, the shape of neighboring indifference curves varies for the two rules. In the case of equality, all other indifference curves run parallel to the ridge line. As depicted in Figure 3.4, because equity rules are defined in terms of ratios, the indifference curves are not parallel to one another regardless of the slope of the dominant ridge.

CONCLUSION

In concluding, equity and equality as rules of fair distribution imply a set of preferences distinct from those dictated by other values. The same is true also with respect to other distribution rules that can be or have been defined as fair or just. At a formal level, it appears therefore appropriate to treat rules of fairness the same as other potential values that individuals may attempt to maximize as they interact with others in allocation or exchange settings. But at the same time, and here we repeat a point made in the first part of this chapter, in empirically assessing whether one or another fairness orientation underlies an actor's behavior, one must be careful to observe behavior over a number of regions in the outcome space and not just in those subregions where, for example, preferences for equitable payoffs coincide, that is, covary with one or more other motivational orientations.

The Functions of Fairness Rules and Their Relationship to Other Social Values

The preceding analysis is primarily a logical one, and as such, it does not address the question of the psychological equivalence between social values such as cooperation or competition and various rules of fairness. As discussed elsewhere (Van Avermaet *et al.*, 1978), rules of fairness, like other social values expressed within interdependent relationships, can be viewed as the goals of an actor, or as the stretegies one actor employs to influence the future behaviors of others. But in addition, rules of fairness seem also to be employed normatively to modulate the expression of self-interest and reduce the potential for interpersonal conflict. The normative use of fairness rules seems particularly likely to obtain, given choices in the presence of external observers or when the choices of actors are to be made public. In such instances the particular behaviors followed may not be consistent with either the preferred goals of a particular actor or the strategies the actor might employ to influence an interdependent other in less public settings. The specific rule-governed behaviors expressed when values are under strong normative control fall in two major categories. *First,* there is the direct substitution of rules of fair distribution such as equality or equity for other preferred outcomes. *Second,* there are numerous rules of fair procedure that serve to constrain the way in which the other major social values may be expressed.

FAIRNESS AS A GOAL

Individuals may behave fairly because of the intrinsic reward value of the corresponding distributions of outcomes to self and others. In this conception fairness becomes an intrapersonal motive, functionally comparable to the motives of individualism, competition, etc.

This conception of fairness is quite similar to those set forth in some of the more influential social psychological theories of justice. Lerner's (1977) justice motive theory "assumes a preeminent guiding principle or motive in the commitment to deserving which serves to organize most goal-seeking behavior [p. 23]." Walster's equity theory postulates that, as a consequence of a variety of socialization experiences, individuals develop a strong orientation toward fairness that manifests itself primarily in psychological discomfort or distress when rules of fairness have been violated (Walster, Berscheid, & Walster, 1973). Leventhal (1976), although placing more emphasis on the instrumental functions of fairness, states that one of the reasons for fair behavior stems from an individual's desire for fairness and justice as ends in themselves.

Viewing fairness as a goal does not necessarily imply that situational factors do not affect an individual's distributions behavior. As we have argued elsewhere (McClintock & Keil, forthcoming), although some people might show a strong cross-situational preference for fair distributions, it is obvious that situations also can strongly affect the relative dominance of various social values. In addition, given a fairness orientation, situational factors, such as the structure of the interdependence relationship, can influence the choice among various fairness rules. Equality, for example, might predominate as a goal in long-term relationships, whereas equity could be a stronger orientation in one-time interactions.

RULES OF FAIRNESS AS ACCOMMODATIVE STRATEGIES

Besides functioning as a social goal, the various rules of fairness can also be employed as interpersonal strategies designed to induce others with whom one is interdependent to emit behaviors congruent with one's own most preferred outcomes. Thus, an actor may behave equally or equitably so as to influence another party in an exchange relationship to reciprocate or to continue the relationship. Such behaviors are strategic insofar as the actor is dependent on other for achieving some valued outcome.[2] Viewed from this perspective, fairness is, of course, psychologically equivalent to the various other social values discussed in the first part of this chapter. Just as cooperative choices can be made for the purpose of ingratiation, equitable behavior by an actor who has made only small contributions to a relationship can be interpreted as a tactic to induce more generosity by the other on future occasions, particularly when the other has control over resources that the actor values highly.

RULES OF FAIRNESS AS SOCIAL NORMS

Walster and others have proposed that rules for a fair distribution of outcomes emerge in settings of outcome interdependence when the values of the actors are in conflict or when some form of outcome coordination is required to distribute the limited available resources. These rules may be normative either in the sense that they emerge within a given relationship over time or in the sense that they are prescribed by society at large. They specify which particular modes of fair outcome distribution behavior are expected, appropriate, and even obligatory. Because fair distributions are not always congruent with those most preferred by the parties to an interdependence relationship, the participants in the relationship themselves or external third parties may employ material and social rewards and punishments as a means of ensuring rule-compliant behavior. As a result, people may come to behave fairly because of the various benefits associated with norm compliance, including those related to the favorable presentation of self.

---

[2] In this latter case, behavior can be viewed as strategic only if the actor perceives himself or herself in an interdependence relationship with this third party rather than with the person with whom he or she is sharing outcomes or resources. The distinction between strategy and norms also becomes blurred when the term *strategy* is used in the very general sense of a means to achieve a goal, rather than in the more restricted sense of an interpersonal influence device (see for example Leventhal, 1976).

If rules of fairness indeed function as social norms, rule-correspondent behavior can be expected whenever an individual decision maker perceives that his or her choices are being scrutinized by someone who has the power to invoke the rewards and costs associated with norm compliance and violation. Whether the decision maker's rule-correspondent behavior will take on the specific form of equity or equality would then depend on the nature of his or her relationship with the other person. For example, in an employment–productivity relationship equity might be expected, whereas in relationships characterized by status congruence, common fate, or peer-group membership, equality would be more normative (Reis & Gruzen, 1976).

FAIRNESS AS A CONSTRAINT ON THE EXPRESSION OF OTHER VALUES

Finally, rules of fairness can be used as procedural constraints for achieving those social values we have already defined. Earlier we argued that rules of fairness become salient in settings in which some form of outcome coordination is required. It appears that, given such conditions, the application of rules of fair procedure reduces the conflict and the costs involved in repeated negotiations (Pruitt, 1972; Mikula, 1980), thereby producing more satisfactory outcomes for all parties and increasing the likelihood of relational longevity. Instances of this kind of procedural constraint can be found with respect to various values.

For example, there are usually upper limits in regard to an actor's maximizing other's outcomes, that is, altruism. One does not normally provide other with all the resources one might have available. To establish what is fair in regard to altruism, various norms tend to be established. Thus, churches may set more or less strict rules regarding their members' tithing. Such limits not only establish normative expectations regarding the minimal proportion of one's income to contribute but also simultaneously establish upper limits on proportionate giving so that the implied requests may not be viewed as an unduly large amount.

Fairness, as a constraint, can take several forms in regard to cooperation. Given that one defines goodness of outcomes in terms of the maximization of joint gain, there are often constraints in terms of the willingness of actors to afford themselves or others a disproportionate amount of the outcome resources. For example, two actors who are strongly cooperative in value orientation may prefer a non-optimal "cooperative" resource distribution of 45–45, to either one of 100–0 or 0–100. MacCrimmon and Messick (1976) make note of this when they extend their definition of cooperation beyond a simple linear model and describe possible preferences for proportionate cooperation.

Finally, sports provide a number of examples of the types of constraints that equity or fairness can place upon both competitive procedures. Thus, once a team has built up an insurmountable lead over an opponent, there are normative constraints that operate against "pouring it on." Teams ignoring such constraints, are often judged to be quite unfair by coaches, sportswriters, and fans.

Measurement Implications

In this final section, we would like to note briefly the more important measurement implications of the above analysis. In view of the distinction that has been made between the various functions of fairness rules, it becomes imperative to follow measurement procedures that enable one to discriminate between the various rules, and to determine *when* and *how* interdependent actors behave in ways so as to produce outcomes that are consistent with one or more definitions of fairness. In this context it should be observed that most prior research has assessed the role of fairness rules mainly in allocation settings, where a subject unilaterally makes outcome distributions between himself and another person (or between two others) while being observed by the experimenter and the other actor. While these measurement situations definitely permit one to gain some insight into the role of fairness as a social norm or as a goal in short-term relationships, they fall short of considering the functions of fairness in genuine exchange relationships that extend over long periods of time.

McClintock and Keil (in press) have recently attempted to order interdependence situations along a continuum that ranges from the simplest to the most complex interdependence setting, with allocation behavior at one end and continuing reciprocation or exchange at the other. They then examine how being located at varying points on this continuum differentially affects the expression of fairness rules. An even more complete analysis would require one to assess the values of the actors involved, other characteristics of the situation in which resources are being distributed, and the utility of the resources distributed (see also Sampson, 1975; Mikula, 1980; Schwinger, 1980).

Conclusion

The model of social values set forth in this chapter reflects the fundamental social fact that in many settings, the behavior of individual actors affects not only their own but others' outcomes as well. Such interdependence has major implications for understanding human social behavior. It implies first that the value an actor attaches to a given outcome is determined by its resource implication for both self and other. Further, it assumes that individuals will select those behaviors that are more likely to yield the preferred distributions of resources to both self and other. Hence, values should necessarily be defined in social terms.

The fact of outcome interdependence further implies that a distinction should be made between values as goals and values as strategies. In order to achieve a preferred outcome, actors may have to adopt behaviors that appear on the surface to be inconsistent with their preferred outcomes. To the extent, however, that one depends partially on others' behaviors to achieve one's goals, such behaviors may be instrumental in the long term in maximizing valued outcomes.

Against this general background several social values were distinguished, and various attempts at defining and assessing these values described. Because measurement is essential to the process of defining values, considerable attention was afforded the several ways that can and have been employed to measure them. In this context, we stressed in particular the theoretical and pragmatic significance of being able to discriminate the various values from one another and of assessing values as goals as distinct from values as strategies.

This emphasis was carried over into the second part of the chapter in which we discussed the formal and psychological relationship between rules of fairness and social values. At a formal level, it was demonstrated that rules of fairness also qualify as social values, but at the same time we argued that they can and should also be viewed as social norms and as normative constraints on the expression of other values.

Looking ahead, our analysis suggests that research into the determinants of behavior in situations of outcome interdependence will have to move away from the rather simple game and allocation settings and in the direction of more complex exchange relationships. As McClintock and Keil (forthcoming) recently stated: "The greatest advances in understanding rules of fairness in relation to human behavior will occur when we begin to understand how they help to define and to determine the structure and the ongoing processes of human interdependence and exchange."

Acknowledgments

Preparation of this chapter was partially supported by NSF Grant No. 77-03862 and by a Faculty Research Grant, University of California, Santa Barbara. The first author would like to thank the London School of Economics for providing an appropriate intellectual environment for the effort involved in preparing this chapter. We are both indebted to Dr. David Messick and Linda Keil for their cogent criticisms.

References

Abelson, R. Script processing in attitude formation and decision making. In J. S. Carroll & J. Payne (Eds.), *Cognition and social behavior*. Hillsdale, N.J.: Lawrence Erlbaum, 1976.

Adams, J. S. Inequity in social exchange. In L. Berkowitz (Ed.), *Advances in Experimental Social Psychology* (Vol. 2). New York: Academic Press, 1965.

Brewer, M., & Silver, M. Ingroup bias as a function of task characteristics. *European Journal of Social Psychology*, 1978, *8*, 393–400.

Davis, K., & Moore, W. E. Some principles of stratification. *American Sociological Review*, 1945, *10*, 242–249.

Deutsch, M. Equity, equality and need: What determines which value will be used as the basis of distributing justice? *Journal of Social Issues*, 1975, *31*, 137–149.

Eckhoff, T. *Justice: Its determinants in social interaction*. Rotterdam: Rotterdam University Press, 1974.

Griesinger, D., & Livingston, J. Towards a model of interpersonal motivation in experimental games. *Behavioral Science*, 1973, *18*, 173–188.

Grzelak, J. L. Game theory and its applicability to the description of prosocial behavior. *Polish Psychological Bulletin*, 1976, *7*, 197–203.

Grzelak, J. L., Iwinski, T. B., & Radzicki, J. J. "Motivational" components of utility. In H. Jungermann & G. de Zeeuw (Eds.), *Decision making and change in human affairs*. Dordrecht, Holland: D. Reidel, 1977.

Heath, J. *Rational choice and social exchange*. Cambridge: Cambridge University Press, 1976.

Kelley, H., & Thibaut, J. *Interpersonal relations: A theory of interdependence*. New York: John Wiley, 1978.

Kuhlman, D., & Marshello, A. Individual differences in game motivation as moderators of preprogrammed strategy effects in Prisoner's Dilemma. *Journal of Personality and Social Psychology*, 1975, *32*, 922–931.

Lerner, M. J. The justice motive. Some hypotheses as to its origins and forms. *Journal of Personality*, 1977, *45*, 1–52.

Leventhal, G. S. The distribution of rewards and resources in groups and organizations. In L. Berkowitz & E. Walster (Eds.), *Advances in Experimental Social Psychology* (Vol. 9). New York: Academic Press, 1976.

Lewin, K. *Field theory in social science: Selected theoretical papers*. New York: Harper, 1971.

Luce, R. D., & Tukey, J. Simultaneous conjoint measurement: A new type of functional measurement. *Journal of Mathematical Psychology*, 1964, *1*, 1–27.

MacCrimmon, K., & Messick, D. Framework of social motives. *Behavioral Science*, 1976, *21*, 86–100.

Maki, J., Thorngate, W., & McClintock, C. Prediction and perception of social motives. *Journal of Personality and Social Psychology*, 1979, *37*, 203–220.

McClelland, G. Who accepts the Pareto axiom. The role of utility and equity in arbitration decisions. *Behavioral Science*, 1978, *23*, 446–456.

McClintock, C. G., & Keil, L. Equity and social exchange. In G. Greenberg & L. Cohen (Eds.), *Equity and justice in social behavior*. New York: Academic Press, forthcoming.

McClintock, C., & McNeel, S. Prior dyadic experience and monetary reward as determinants of cooperative and competitive game behavior. *Journal of Personality and Social Psychology*, 1967, *5*, 282–294.

McClintock, C., Messick, D., Kuhlman, M., & Campos, F. Motivational bases of choice in three-choice decomposed games. *Journal of Experimental Social Psychology*, 1973, *9*, 572–590.

McClintock, C., & Moskowitz, J. Children's preferences for individualistic, cooperative and competitive outcomes. *Journal of Personality and Social Psychology*, 1976, *34*, 543–555.

McClintock, C., Moskowitz, J., & McClintock, E. Variations in preferences for individualistic, competitive and cooperative outcomes as a function of age, game class and task in nursery school children. *Developmental Psychology*, 1977, *48*, 1080–1085.

Messick, D., & McClintock, C. Motivational bases of choice in experimental games. *Journal of Experimental Social Psychology*, 1968, *4*, 1–25.

Mikula, G. On the role of justice in allocation decisions. In G. Mikula (Ed.), *Justice and social interaction*. New York: Springer-Verlag, 1980.

Mills, J. *Social motivations and the encoding and decoding of nonverbal affect*. Honors thesis, University of Delaware, 1978.

Pruitt, D. G. Methods for resolving differences of interest: a theoretical analysis. *Journal of Social Issues*, 1972, *28*, 133–154.

Quinton, A. Elitism: A British view. *The American scholar*, Winter 1975/76, 719–732.

Radzicki, J. Technique of conjoint measurement of subjective value of own and others' gains. *Polish Psychological Bulletin*, 1976, *7*, 179–186.

Rawls, J. *A theory of justice*. Cambridge, Mass.: Harvard University Press, 1971.

Schwinger, T. Just allocations of goods: Decision among three principles. In G. Mikula (Ed.), *Justice and social interaction*. New York: Springer-Verlag, 1980.

Reis, H. T., & Gruzen, J. On mediating equity, equality and self-interest: The role of self-presentation in social exchange. *Journal of Experimental Social Psychology*, 1976, *12*, 487–503.

Rescher, N. *Distributive justice*. New York: Bobbs-Merrill, 1966.

Sampson, E. E. On justice as equality. *Journal of Social Issues*, 1975, *31*, 45–64.

Sawyer, J. The altruism scale: A measure of cooperative, individualistic and competitive interpersonal orientation. *American Journal of Sociology*, 1966, *71*, 407–416.

Sen, A. *Collective choice and social welfare*. San Francisco: Holden Day, 1970.

Toda, M., Shinotsuka, H., McClintock, C., & Stech, F. Development of competitive behavior as a function of culture, age, and social comparison. *Journal of Personality and Social Psychology*, 1978, *36*, 825–839.

Tversky, A. A general theory of polynomial conjoint measurement. *Journal of Mathematical Psychology*, 1967, *4*, 1–20.

Van Avermaet, E. F., McClintock, C. G., & Moskowitz, J. Alternative approaches to equity: Dissonance reduction, prosocial motivation and strategic accommodation. *European Journal of Social Psychology*, 1978, *8*, 419–437.

Von Neumann, J., & Morgenstern, O. *Theory of games and economic behavior*. Princeton: Princeton University Press, 1944.

Walster, E., Berscheid, E., & Walster, G. W. New directions in equity research. *Journal of Personality and Social Psychology*, 1973, *25*, 151–136.

Walster, E., & Walster, G. W. Equity and social justice. *Journal of Social Issues*, 1975, *31*, 21–43.

Walster, E., Walster, G. W., & Berscheid, E. *Equity: Theory and research*. Boston: Allyn and Bacon, 1978.

Wyer, R. Prediction of behavior in two-person games. *Journal of Personality and Social Psychology*, 1969, *13*, 222–228.

Wyer, R. The effects of outcome matrix and partner's behavior in two person games. *Journal of Experimental Social Psychology*, 1971, *7*, 190–210.

Chapter 4

Cognitive Processes Underlying Cooperation: The Theory of Social Representation

JEAN CLAUDE ABRIC

Research conducted on the processes of interindividual cooperation and competition has generated a large number of varied and often interesting studies in social psychology. However, taking a closer look at this work, one is soon faced with the rather embarrassing question of what can be retained from these studies. That is, what have we learned about the fundamental mechanisms leading to cooperative or competitive interaction? The general impression derived from reading the research accounts is that although numerous studies have investigated a multitude of variables by means of a very elaborate methodology, the findings are often contradictory or relevant only to the specific laboratory setting.

Examining research in this area suggests that there may be a decisive flaw that explains the limited value of past research projects. Most studies have ignored or set aside what we consider to be a fundamental factor in all psychological processes: the cognitive dimension. Despite Zajonc's (1968) opinion, expressed some years ago, about the pervasiveness of cognitive phenomena in all human interaction, most of the research work seems to be based on a neo-behavioristic approach. That is, learning and reinforcement are often taken as essential processes. The objective components of situations are taken as determining factors; interaction is always studied

73

COOPERATION AND HELPING BEHAVIOR
Theories and Research

through its explicit manifestations and processes. The cognitive dimension, the symbolic register, is infrequently mentioned as being a relevant feature of interaction.

A number of fairly recent studies, particularly those conducted by Kelley and Stahelski (1970) and Kelley and Thibaut (1978), show that these cognitive factors can play an essential role in interaction. In fact, these studies indicate that factors such as the perception of intentions or attitudes toward the other or the perception of the situation intervene in the determination of behavior. The theory of social representation elaborated below seems to offer an interesting and broad-based analysis for studying cognitive factors.

The Theory of Social Representation

The theory of social representation, elaborated and developed in social psychology by Moscovici (1961), was introduced around the turn of the century by Emil Durkheim (1898). The theory has been applied in both field studies (Chombart de Lauwe, 1971; Herzlich, 1969; Jodelet, 1979; Kaes, 1968; Milgram, 1979), and experimental laboratory studies (Abric, 1971; Codol, 1968; Doise, 1972; Flament, 1979). Furthermore, the theory has led to a new trend in research on conflict and the processes of cooperation (Abric, 1976; Apfelbaum, 1967; Faucheux & Moscovici, 1968; Flament, 1967).

Conceptual Framework

The general postulate of the theory of social representation states that the behavior of an individual or of a group in any given situation will be governed, to a large extent, by the representations held by that individual or group of the situation and of each of its components. This representation constitutes reality for the subject. The term *representation* refers to the actual process of construing social reality and the result of this construction. It is thus defined as

> the product as well as the actual process of that mental activity whereby an individual or a group reconstrues the reality which confronts the particular individual or group and invests it with a specific meaning. This meaning results directly from the attitudes and opinions, whether conscious or unconscious, developed by the individual or the group [Abric, 1976, p. 106].

When an individual is faced with any given situation or participates in this same situation, the basic postulate of the theory tells us that he or she will develop a representation not only of the situation as a whole, but also of its different parts. This set of representations about the situation (which we will call the *representation of the situation*) is what makes up the actual reality for the subject (the subject is the person from whose point of view things are to be considered). The corollary to this proposition is that there is no such thing as an objective reality for the subject, since he or she appropriates, reorganizes, and interprets the components of that reality by means of the cognitive construction of a subjective reality. Thus, a representation of reality results which *is reality itself* to the subject. That is why, as we have already stated, an individual's behavior is determined largely by his or her system of representations and, accordingly, any attempt to acquire knowledge about behavior must necessarily be carried out through investigation and analysis of the subject's representations.

It would be impossible, within the limited scope of this chapter, to review the theory of social representation in detail. For more information about this topic see Moscovici (1961) and Abric (1976). However, some essential features of this theory will be briefly described.

WHAT IS CONTAINED IN A REPRESENTATION?

A representation is composed mainly of two types of elements. On the one hand are available elements of information about objects. An object is that part of social reality that is elaborated or formed by the subject into a representation; for example, a situation, a tree or another subject.

On the other hand, the subject has opinions, attitudes, stereotypes, or beliefs that are related to the object and to the immediate situation. These attitudes or opinions are such fundamental components of the representations that Moscovici (1961) has called them their *keystones*. In fact, they bring a subjective, normative dimension to the representation; that is, they induce their meaning by giving weight to and transforming the data made available to the subject.

HOW IS A REPRESENTATION ORGANIZED?

A representation is an organized subdivision of the subject's cognitive world. In other words, the subject's information, attitudes, opinions, and beliefs are organized as a coherent whole in which every part takes on a meaning through its relationship with all of the other parts. It is also probable that these components have some kind of internal hierarchy (Abric, 1979) whereby each representation is organized around a *central core*. This central core is none other than the fundamental element of the representation, since it plays an essential role in determining the representation's meaning.

HOW DOES THE REPRESENTATION WORK?

Although the representation is the subject's interpretation of the world around him, it is by no means a simple or static image of reality. Quite to the contrary, the representation will play a dynamic role in the interaction between the subject and the object, and far from being a mere reflection of this interaction, the representation prepares the future of the relationship and determines what it is to become.

This dynamic and inductive effect results from the fact that the representation determines and produces a system of categorization for reality. It consists of "the building of a 'doctrine' that simplifies the task of disclosing, planning, or anticipating actions or conjunctures [Moscovici, 1969, p. 11]." The representation is fundamentally an interpretive filtering device inserted, as it were, between the subject and the situation. That is to say, the information or the events confronting the subject will be interpreted in accordance with the nature of the already existing representation and in such a manner so as to avoid any doubt about the latter. The meaning read into the information, the place assigned to it, and the way it is used will be the result of a personal subjective interpretation, being itself determined by expectations, or anticipations, produced by the representation.

These mechanisms turn the representation into an oriented system for decoding reality, which explains why the representation is at the roots of these reactions developed by the subject within the situation.

Application to the Study of Cooperation

In social psychology most studies on interindividual cooperation and competition use the same approach: The experimental method and the given situation rely on a game. We shall therefore be concerned mainly with the value of applying the theory of social representation to the experimental study of cooperation in the game situation.

REPRESENTATION AND COOPERATION IN GAME-TYPE STUDIES

In the experimental game situation, there appear to be three different types of intervention: the subject himself or herself; the partner; and the game being proposed, or the task to be accomplished. As a matter of fact, it is possible to classify most of the research carried out in this area under these three headings. However, when analyzing the studies, one notices that each of these dimensions is taken on its own, which means that one manipulates the objective components of the situation and places importance essentially on these. Thus the researcher will be concerned with the investigation of existing behavioral variations as determined by, for example, the type of matrix used, the absence or presence of a threat, the psychological characteristics of the actors, or the partner's actual behavior and strategy. However, in most cases, whether at the level of the question asked or of the analysis of the findings, the meaning these variables hold for the subject is not taken into account. It seems to be taken for granted that the experimental situation has only one meaning for all of the subjects and that this meaning is actually the one emphasized by the researcher, who assumes it is shared by everyone and identical for all others. We believe that this is a fundamental theoretical and methodological error that hinders all further comprehension and analysis of the actual reasons behind behavior. It is our conviction that subjects do not react to the situation as it really is, but that they interpret it and lend a meaning to it, producing final interpretations that are specific to each subject. As long as these interpretations, or representations, remain unknown, it will be impossible either to understand or to explain the foundations of behavior or the nature of the processes involved.

This critical analysis seems to have been anticipated by Vinacke (1969), when he wrote that "the perception and aims of players should be considered more explicitly, even when these factors are not directly manipulated [p. 310]." Pincus and Bixenstine (1977) were even more explicit: "How we behave in mixed motive situations depends on our subjective interpretation of the situation rather than strictly the situation itself [p. 529]." (See also Grzelak (1976) and Young (1977) for a similar analysis.)

Our overall hypothesis is that the appearance of cooperative or competitive behavior in a situation will be determined largely by the representations held by the protagonists in that situation. This general hypothesis is built up around three more specific hypotheses:

1. Cooperation is determined by the *subject's self-image*, which is a representation that actually determines the kinds of implications one draws about a situation and the level of aspiration that the subject shows.

2. Cooperation is determined by the *representation that the subject holds of the partner* versus what the partner actually is. This representation, in fact, is used to monitor one's behavior by determining the kind of relationship it is possible or desirable to have with the partner, thereby inducing finality into the interaction. ("Finality" in this context refers to the individual's goals and objectives for a situation as perceived by that individual.)

3. Cooperation is determined by the *representation of the task* held by the subject. This representation actually fixes the goals that the subject relates to the task and, accordingly, makes the subject develop such behavior as corresponds to the perceived finality.

These hypotheses have been stated in very general terms. We will describe later on how we have tried to make them more precise and how we have validated them in our research. We will now consider the way the introduction of the notion of representation brings about a complete reconsideration of certain questions regarding the experimental study of cooperation.

QUESTIONS RAISED BY STUDIES OF COOPERATION IN THE GAME SITUATION

The introduction of the notion of representation as a fundamental element in interaction processes raises at least two types of problems about the experimental procedures that have generally been used until now in game situations.

The first type of problem concerns the meaning of the subject's choices. The prisoner's dilemma game (PDG) has been the source of a great deal of research. Let us look at the way in which investigators have used this game, that is to say, let us study the dependent variables used to characterize cooperation or competition. It is common knowledge that in the PDG, each player has a choice between two alternatives, for instance, in Figure 4.1, he may choose C or D. Almost all investigators make use of the number of C choices as an indicator of the subjects' cooperation and the number of D choices as an indicator of their competitive tendencies. It seems to us that this way of measuring is partially inadequate, since it does not take into account the subject's anticipation of the partner's choice. Obviously, this expectation is an essential factor when it comes to the subject's own decision.

This points out the necessity of integrating the representation of the other's choice within the dependent variables, since this representation confers two radically different meanings on one and the same choice made by the subject. It is incorrect to state that the number of D choices are indicators of competition, since this is only the case when the player plays D, believing that the other plays C. Otherwise, supposing that the subject believes that the other has also played D, there is a defensive choice. Once this has been established, how can results be validated through an indicator that blends two motivations, two radically different behaviors?

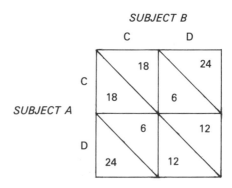

Figure 4.1. Prisoner's dilemma matrix.

Taking into consideration the representation of the other's choice, it seems necessary to classify the behaviors observed in the prisoner's dilemma game as follows:

Cooperative behavior	Subject plays C, believing that partner also plays C.
Opening behavior	Subject plays C, believing that the other has played D. This may either be an opening to cooperation or a trap leading to exploitation (causing partner to play C so that subject may play D afterwards).
Defensive behavior	Subject plays D, believing that the other also plays D.
Exploiting behavior	Subject plays D, believing that the other plays C.

The second type of problem concerns the meaning of the earnings for the subject. We do not think that the numbers, or earnings, stipulated in the game matrices can usefully inform the investigator about the kinds of implications a subject draws in any given situation. In our opinion, earnings have no meaning per se. The point total or the amount of money won or lost takes on value for the subject only insofar as he or she *gives* it a meaning. The latter is directly derived from the subject's representation of the context and, more specifically, from the representation pertaining to the partner. For instance, it seems evident to us that only the capacities of the opponent and the image held of him or her will confer value to a victory or a defeat.

The two questions we have just raised illustrate the difficulties encountered and the precautions which must be taken when studying any interaction. They reveal how the representation which subjects elaborate of the situation which confronts them must be checked by the researcher, even when the part played by the representation per se is not directly studied. Were the subjects' representations to be simply inferred from the investigator's own representations, chance might have it that the latter does not include those of the subjects.

A Critical Analysis of Some Experimental Studies of Cooperation

We do not intend to present a complete examination of the studies on cooperation. But, by means of a few examples, we shall try to show the criticisms which can be made of analyses which do not take into account the part played by representation processes.

We have chosen examples from some well known studies which seem to us to represent the process of analysis used in this area of study. They all raise questions which are fundamental concerning the role of the three elements which constitute the interaction situation: self, the partner, and the task to be accomplished.

The Subject's Role in Cooperation

Deutsch (1960) carried out a study of the impact of subjects' initial behavioral tendencies on their ultimate cooperative or competitive behavior. It appears from the findings of this study that a subject's initial "cooperative" tendency leads to cooperative behavior in those situations in which the subject believes he can trust his partner. A "competitive" inclination results in uncooperative behavior and an "individualistic" tendency produces competitive behaviors of varying degrees, depending on the payoff structure of the situation.

Let us consider the procedure used by Deutsch. Initial inclinations were induced in subjects by means of the following three instructions:

1. Cooperative orientations: "Try to get the highest score possible for yourself and make your partner win as much as possible. Your partner has the same goals."
2. Competitive orientation: "Try to get the highest score possible for yourself and try to make more than your partner. He has the same goals."
3. Individualistic orientation: "Try to get the highest score possible for yourself without paying any attention to your partner's earnings. Your partner has the same goals."

Considering these instructions and Deutsch's general procedures, it seems to us that Deutsch did not study the initial inclination of his subjects. He was not measuring the orientation of individuals but, rather, the effect of a set of instructions. His interpretation of his results on the basis of "initial" orientation makes no sense, in our opinion, since it is the representation of the task and its goals that he has manipulated.

In fact, the task proposed to the "cooperatively" oriented subjects is essentially a task of coordination; it does not set up a conflictual situation. Consequently, the absence of competitive behavior is due not to the subjects' characteristics but to the fact that such behavior would be in direct opposition to the stated aims of the interaction. The induced task representation is focused on cooperation, and subjects react accordingly.

On the other hand, in the competitive orientation, the instructions induce a radically different task representation, focused on differential earnings.

Once again, the subjects conform to their representation of the task. We have formulated the hypothesis that under these conditions, even those subjects who had genuine cooperative tendencies to start with would have adopted the same competitive behavior as genuinely competitive subjects.

Actually, the "individualistically" oriented subjects are the only ones who have a real choice, since the task representation induced by their instructions does not focus explicitly on either cooperation or competition. In this study, it is with these subjects only that inclinations, which are their own, may well result in different strategies.

We believe that the subjects' initial orientation plays an important role, as has been confirmed incidentally in other studies (Apfelbaum, 1969; McNeel, 1973). Results demonstrate that subjects do not approach the interaction situation in a neutral and objective manner, but rather on the basis of a certain number of a priori assumptions, derived from a representation of the situation that is determined either by psychological variables (initial orientation) or by the context of the experiment (particularly by the instructions).

The Partner's Role in Cooperation

The literature contains a great number of studies of the part played by the partner in establishing cooperation. These studies either seek to show the importance of the kind of partner the subject is faced with and of the kind of relationship established between them, or the studies investigate the impact of the partner's actual behavior on the subject's reactions. We have chosen an example of the latter type of study.

The actual behavior of the partner is an important factor in establishing a cooperative relationship. Most of the studies done show that it is a partner's conditionally cooperative behavior that is most favorable to setting up cooperation (Apfelbaum, 1971; Gallo, 1966; Pareck & Dixit, 1977). Furthermore, it has been found that systematically cooperative behavior on the part of the other generally leads the subject to exploit him or her (Sermat, 1964; Solomon, 1960). The actual behavior of the other plays an important role because it gives the subject the information he or she needs in order to understand the partner's strategy and aims. The other's actual behavior is thus one of the components of the subject's representation of the partner, although it is not the only one.

In order to analyze the importance of the other's behavior as a building block in the subject's representation of that other, we must recognize that the part this behavior plays varies radically as a function of the partner's representations. Since it is the representation that induces meaning, we conclude that the meaning of a given behavior can vary when the partner's representation varies and that there is no unequivocal link between the partner's behavior and the subject's reaction. A study conducted by Mack (1976), concerning the role of the status and behavior of the partner, appears to confirm our point of view. Mack found that an identical behavior on the part of the partner may result in a cooperative relationship when the partner is of superior status but may produce a competitive relationship when both partner and subject are of the same status. We can interpret these results by noting that differences in status bring about different representations of the partner, which in turn make for different interpretations of the partner's behavior.

The Impact of the Kind of Task Used

In our studies we have been impressed by the importance both of the kinds of earnings that appear in the interaction matrices and of the way the task is introduced. We believe that the latter is a crucial point, since the introduction of the task determines a representation and defines and reinforces the goals of the interaction.

EFFECTS OF FEEDBACK AND OF TYPE OF EARNINGS PROPOSED

Rapoport and Chammah (1965), along with Bixenstine and Blundell (1966), have shown that cooperative choices depend on the numbers written in the matrices. We believe that these clear-cut and undeniable findings may be explained easily by our statement of the issue: Not only will the subject's choice depend on the attractiveness of whatever numbers (gains) are written into the matrix, inasmuch as these numbers refer to a representation of the situation at large (and more specifically of the task), this representation will be an equally determining factor in the subject's behavior. The numbers carry a meaning for the subject, and it is the existence of the numbers that, in turn, creates the competitive or cooperative nature of the task. Along these lines, we (Abric et al., 1967) have shown how the presence of positive or negative numbers in a prisoner's dilemma game matrix makes for two different meanings: We have, on the one hand, a situation in which there are earnings to be had, on the other, a situation in which one tries to avoid losses.

HOW TASK INTRODUCTION AFFECTS INTERACTION

The work of Pruitt seems to us essential in showing that what is fundamental is by no means the logical structure of the situation, but rather the subject's interpretation or representation. We know that Pruitt (1967) made use of a decomposed version of the prisoner's dilemma game since he surmised that this novel presentation, because it was closer to the reality usually confronting the subjects, would entail an increase in cooperation.

When he found that different results ensued from the use of different kinds of decomposed matrices, Pruitt (1970) formulated a second explanatory hypothesis: The structure of the game induces a given motivation. Finally, in a third stage of his analyses (Pruitt & Kimmel, 1977), he came to the conclusion that "this kind of display emphasizes one's dependence on the other party's willingness to cooperate and thus facilitates development of the mutual cooperation goal [p. 378]."

Presentation of decomposed matrices induces a different representation than does the presentation of a complete matrix; accordingly, the situations are no longer defined along the same dimensions or by the same aims. As we have shown elsewhere (Abric, 1976), certain decomposed matrices lead subjects to represent a task in terms of coordination or the collusion of interests, which would make the degree of cooperation increase substantially. This view is shared, although stated in different terms, by others (Gallo, 1966; Pincus & Bixenstine, 1977). For instance, Pincus and Bixenstine (1977), as mentioned earlier, note that behavior in mixed motive situations depends on the "subjective interpretation of the situation." This interpretation is determined, according to these authors, by the information revealed and stressed during the introduction of the task.

We believe that this task representation is, in fact, derived not only from the actual introduction of the task, but also from the entire context, that is, the semantic, spatial, social, and ideological environment.

Research Perspectives

The analysis so far of a few research projects supports our thinking that any study of social interaction, including that of cooperation, should systematically incorporate the social representation dimension. In a way, this approach is quite close to the theories of symbolic interaction and their applications to the analysis of cooperative relationships, especially when they take into account what is called the "definition of the situation" (Blumer, 1969; Scheff, 1967).

We have carried out a series of experimental studies to demonstrate precisely the part that social representation plays in a situation of conflictual interaction. We have also investigated the relationship between representation and behavior. These studies are described in the next section of this chapter.

Experimental Studies of the Importance of Social Representation in Cooperative Processes

Our studies of the role of representations can be classified in two groups: One deals with the representation of the partner, the other with task representation. Because of the methodological difficulties involved, we have not yet carried out any studies of self-representation.

Cooperation and Representation of the Partner

By *representation of the partner*, we mean the set of hypotheses that the subject formulates about the partner—the set of attributes the subject assigns to his or her partner and the subjective importance given to these attributes in respect of interaction. It is important to remember that as far as we are concerned, this representation determines not only the subject's anticipation of the partner's behavior but the subject's interpretation of the partner's actual behavior and his or her reactions to it.

EXPERIMENT I: INTERACTION AND REPRESENTATION OF THE PARTNER

In order to study the part played in cooperation by representation of the partner, we conducted an experiment in which the subjects were placed in a prisoner's dilemma game setting (Abric, 1967). Subjects were given "individualistic" instructions, and the partner's responses to their moves were run according to a "tit for tat" strategy. The partner facing the subject was either a "student" or a "machine." Using a questionnaire, we were able to collect the subjective representations induced by each of these presentations of the partner. The subjects then played a series of 50 trials. At the end of this first period, subjects were told that their partners would now be "machines" (for those who believed they had played against a fellow student) or "students" (for those who believed they had played against a machine). Once again the representation about the future partner was checked by means of a questionnaire. The subjects then proceeded to play a new series of 50 trials. The partner's strategy remained identical (tit for tat) across both experimental conditions and during the entire experiment. Two control conditions, in which no change of partner was announced at half-time, completed the experimental design.

In each of the experimental conditions, the subject was actually confronted with an identical partner during the whole interaction. Differences between conditions were based simply on the representation of the partner as developed by the subjects.

Two fundamental hypotheses were formulated:

Hypothesis 1: Whereas the representation of a student partner favors the establishment of cooperative interaction, that of a machine partner, to the contrary, leads to defensive behavior.

Hypothesis 2: The change in representation of the partner induced at half-time causes an immediate transformation of the behavior that was shown by the subjects during the first phase: As the introduction of a representation of the partner as a machine entails an immediate lowering of the degree of cooperation, the presentation of the partner as a student produces an immediate increase in cooperation.

Without going into all the details of our findings (see Abric, 1976, for a full account), we can note that both hypotheses were confirmed in the study (see Figure 4.2). The representation of the partner as a student produced significantly more cooperative behavior than did the representation of the partner as a machine. Moreover, even in the absence of any actual change of behavior on the part of the partner, the induced transformation of the representation of the partner produced a marked change in the behavior of those subjects who were exposed to these conditions. The behavior of the subjects in the control groups developed during the first period and was stable throughout, whereas the initial behavior of subjects in conditions in which representations changed between the two phases of the experiment was completely modified. These results may be explained by differences in the representation of the partner. As a matter of fact, we have found that the main components of the representation of a student

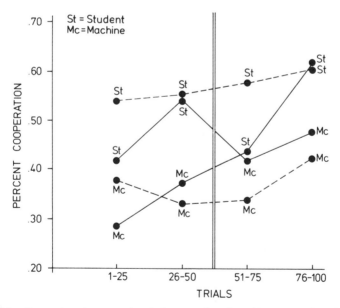

Figure 4.2. Proportion of cooperative choices as a function of representation of a partner. Trials 1–50 (to the left of the double vertical) were before change of representation; Trials 51–100 were after change of representation.

partner are (a) "subjective," (b) "has no pre-established strategy," and (c) "can be influenced." The machine partner, on the other hand, is seen as (a) "objective" and as (b) "adhering to a pre-established strategy," and as being (c) "not open to influence."

The nature of these two representations permits us to understand and explain the obtained differences in behavior. The representation of a responsive partner over whom the subject can exert some influence makes it possible to search for a basis of cooperation. The representation of a rigid partner makes such cooperation impossible and results in defensive, blocking behavior on the part of the subject.

One last finding seems worthwhile mentioning. Although the actual behaviors of the partners were identical the representations of the partners, when checked *after* the interaction, remained different for each of the two experimental conditions. In particular, the dimension "open to influence or not" was not affected by the actual tit for tat behavior adopted by the partner. This finding confirms that the representation acts as an interpretive filter. Identical behavior is interpreted differently, depending on the representation held about the partner. The tit for tat strategy means "open to influence" within the context of the student representation and "rigidity" within that of the machine representation. The existence of representations somehow sets the stage for a situation in which the game is over before the interaction has even begun.

EXPERIMENT II: REPRESENTATION, ACTUAL BEHAVIOR OF THE PARTNER, AND COOPERATION

The next study we will describe concerns the representation of the other as induced by his or her social status (Abric, 1976). Like the preceding experiment, this one makes use of the PDG and has been carried out with high school students.

The first variable we studied was the representation of partners of two different social ranks. In one condition, the students were told that their partner, whom they never actually saw, was a teacher at their high school. The "teacher" supposedly did not know them and had no more experience than they did themselves with the subject matter covered by the research project. In the other condition, the bogus partner was introduced as a "student" in the subject's own grade who (also) did not know anything about the experimental subject matter. In each condition subjects were given "individualistic" instructions ("try to get the highest score possible without paying any attention to your partner's score"). Before interaction, information about the representations built up by the subjects for each type of partner was collected by the experimenter.

The second experimental variable was the partner's actual behavior. As in the preceding experiment, this partner was fictitious. Each status condition was now matched with two kinds of actual behavior: an unconditionally cooperative behavior (95% cooperative choices) or a "tit for tat" behavior. The four resulting experimental conditions were as follows:

1. Teacher partner, cooperative strategy
2. Teacher partner, tit for tat strategy
3. Student partner, cooperative strategy
4. Student partner, tit for tat strategy

Three major hypotheses were tested:

Hypothesis 1: The partner's status forms a specific representation of the partner.

Hypothesis 2: The nature of these representations of the partner will influence subjects' behaviors in the interaction.

Hypothesis 3: Reactions of subjects are not determined by the partner's actual behavior but by the relationship between this behavior and the representation of the partner. To be more precise, consistency between the representation of the partner and his or her actual behavior facilitates the emergence of stable behavioral standards during interaction. In particular, consistency between a cooperative representation of the partner and his or her systematically cooperative behavior will favor the development of cooperation. On the other hand, inconsistency between the representation of the partner and his or her actual behavior will bring about either aggressive (exploitative) or defensive reactions

Status and Representation of Partner   Representations collected from this experimental population varied as a function of the status of the partner. Subjects thought of the teacher as closed to any influence and focused on an egalitarian goal rather than on the pursuit of differential earnings. Subjects thought of the student, on the other hand, as being open to influence and as focusing on competitive goals, that is, as pursuing differential earnings.

Representation of Partner and Subject Behavior   It was found that, after a preliminary period of indecision, the representation held about the partner systematically influenced the subjects' behavior. The level of cooperation was significantly greater with a teacher partner. Moreover, one of the conditions seemed to be more conducive to cooperation than all of the others: the interaction with a teacher who played an unconditionally cooperative strategy. The proportion of cooperative choices on the part of subjects in this case reached 90% near the end of the experiment. This condition's results may appear to be exceptional, especially in view of the studies of the effect of partners' unconditionally cooperative behavior mentioned earlier. However, it is precisely the one condition in which there is complete consistency between the representation of the partner ("cooperative," for a teacher partner) and the actual behavior of the latter. This allows for the establishment of a *norm* for the situation, defined in terms of cooperation. Subjects will conform to this norm as long as the partner's behavior indicates that this goal is maintained.

Where the representation of the partner is that of a student (and thus focused on competition), there will be disagreement between that representation and the unconditionally cooperative behavior of a partner. This inconsistency will prevent the emergence of a stable behavioral norm, and in our experiment, observed behaviors in the student–cooperative condition were actually much less cooperative than behaviors in the teacher–cooperative condition.

In the other two conditions, the partner's actual behavior (tit for tat) is not as obvious to the subjects and the differences in their reactions that could be attributed to their representation of the partner, although real, are less marked. For example, a positive representation of the teacher partner would lead to defensive rather than competitive behavior in response to the partner's draws.

These results thus confirm our hypotheses and demonstrate clearly that the connection between the components of the representation of the partner and his or her actual behavior determines to what extent the latter will affect the subject's reactions. The representation of the partner is really the central determining factor of the subject's reactions to the other's behavior. It is not the actual behavior of the other that leads to cooperation or competition but the entire setting—the whole relational context within which the behavior appears.

Cooperation and Representation of the Task

We define *representation of the task* as the "theory or system of hypotheses that individuals work out regarding the nature of the task, its finality (i.e. its aims), the means to be employed to carry out the task and the behavior conducive to efficiency [Abric, 1971, p. 313]." Since task representation induces a certain way of reading and decoding information, it facilitates or inhibits cognitive control of the situation. It intervenes in the subject's motivation by determining, in part, the finality of the situation and highlights the interpretation made of the partner's behavior.

EXPERIMENT III: INTERACTION AND REPRESENTATION OF
THE TASK

This study (Abric & Vacherot, 1976), which was conducted after the two
we have already described, takes into consideration the representation of
the task as well as that of the partner. We used a prisoner's dilemma game
with a population of student subjects.

As in Experiment I, two different representations of the partner were
used, either "student" or "machine." In order to study the task representation
variable, we conducted a rather complex analysis of the representations that
the subjects held of the PDG. The subjects were given a neutral presentation
of a matrix and of the rules of the prisoner's dilemma game (with "individualistic" instructions). They were then asked to fill out a form about the
image that they held at this point of the task proposed to them. The answers
to this questionnaire were analyzed with a relatively new mathematical
method that is useful in the analysis of representation, the method of
similarity analysis (Flament, 1962; Flament, 1979). This technique consists
of locating, within a group of components (in our study, these were the
answers to a questionnaire), the structural relations of proximity and resemblance that exist between the elements.

Distinct types of representations emerged from the application of this
method. One group of subjects saw the task as a *problem-solving* process;
for another group the task was a *game*. Thus, we had four experimental
conditions:

1. Student partner, problem task representation
2. Machine partner, problem task representation
3. Student partner, game task representation
4. Machine partner, game task representation

Subjects received identical (individualistic) instructions in each condition.
Three major hypotheses were tested:

Hypothesis 1: A single task can result in two different representations.

Hypothesis 2: Subjects' behavior is determined by their representation of
the task and not by the nature of the task. More specifically, in the case
of the prisoner's dilemma game, the "problem-solving" representaton is
conducive to cooperation, whereas the "game" representation reduces the
amount of cooperation.

Hypothesis 3: The different elements composing the representation of the
situation are interdependent. Both the task representation and the representation of the partner act simultaneously and in a complementary manner
to define the situation for the subject.

Representations produced by Prisoner's Dilemma Game   In our experiment, the representation served first as a dependent variable and then as an independent variable. The similarity analysis carried out on the subjects' answers to the questionnaire confirmed our first hypothesis. The prisoner's dilemma game evokes two different representations, or two distinct interpretations, which separate the subjects placed in the identical experimental situation, objectively speaking. One group of subjects (about 25%) sees the PDG essentially as a problem-solving task. Another group sees the task as a game. Not only is this finding important; it is also somewhat disturbing, since past studies with the PDG have not controlled or checked for this variable of task representation. It is therefore likely that subjects who were not necessarily comparable have been mistakenly considered to be so, even though they thought of themselves as being in quite different situations: Some subjects played, while others solved problems.

The representation of the PDG in terms of a game is characterized mainly by association with situations of play (distraction, amusement, gambling) as well as with unpredictable (due to luck or chance) and competitive situations. The representation in terms of problem-solving, on the other hand (see Figure 4.3), is composed mainly of associations with situations that require significant intellectual effort (mathematical computations, in-

A.   Nature of the "game" representation of the task

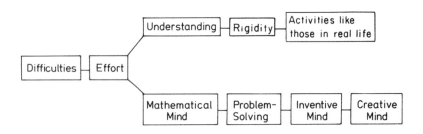

B.   Nature of the "problem-solving" representation of the task

Figure 4.3.   Representations of the task obtained by the similarity analysis.

venting, resolving difficulties). It should be noted that in this representation there is no allusion to any competitive aspect of the situation.

Having identified these two representations, it becomes possible to understand and predict the subjects' behaviors. The "problem-solving" representation (coordination, no competitive connotation) necessarily results in more cooperative behavior. Once again, we contend that the subject's behavior is predetermined, prior to the interaction, by the representation of the task.

Task Representation and Behavior   If we consider the task representation per se as a separate unit, we can state that it operates mainly to influence the quantity of defensive behavior observed in the experiment. The representation in terms of a game, with its competitive connotations, actually yields a much higher rate of defensive behavior than the problem-solving representation.

On analyzing cooperative, exploitative, and competitive behaviors (i.e., not defensive behavior), it is not possible to separate the effects of the task representation from the representation of the partner. It appears that the task representation operates when the subject interacts with a partner thought to be like himself (representation of partner as student).

When the partner is represented as a student, the representation of the task as problem-solving leads to one-sided behavior by the subject: Cooperation is increased at the expense of the three other possible behaviors. Thus, the representation that combines problem-solving and a student partner is the most favorable condition, in this experiment, for the establishment of a cooperative relationship. This can be explained by the fact that this condition is the only one where the positive effects on cooperation are cumulative across both the task representation and the representation of the partner. On the contrary, when the subject believes that he is interacting with a machine, the effects induced by the representation of the partner wipe out those brought on by the task representation. In other words, the relational and cognitive problems brought about by a nonhuman partner have precedence over all other aspects of the situation.

DISCUSSION

Although we have described only a few studies of representations of the task and of the partner, our discussions should sensitize readers to the fundamentally polysemous, or ambiguous, nature of all social situations. The reasons why individuals attribute certain a priori meanings to the tasks they are asked to accomplish remain to be discovered. However, we can confidently state that the components of this representation will be the basis of guidelines that will influence the subject's future actions. For instance, we are convinced that the differences resulting from the use of different decomposed matrices must be attributed to the fact that each matrix corresponds to a distinct task representation.

Generally speaking, the framework we have presented confirms the existence of a connection between behavior and the representation of the situation and allows one to see how the internal working mechanism of the representational system operates. Also emphasized is the fact that task and partner, task representation and representation of the partner, must be considered as belonging to a single entity.

Summary

We have presented a theoretical orientation and have described related experimental studies that together, it seems to us, represent a relatively original and fundamental approach to studying social interaction. Within this theory, subjects themselves are of great importance, since it is they who produce their own environment instead of merely being an element of that environment. This approach allows us to take into account, directly or not, conscious or unconscious social factors that affect an individual's behavior. The representations that an individual produces are not only the image of his or her own involvement and link with all of the elements of the situation; they also carry the stamp of the history of the person's social group and of its dominant ideology. Thus social representations make it possible to define active subjects who are situated within an individual and collective history and impregnated with the norms and stereotypes of their group or of the class to which they belong.

It is within this context that we disagree with Pruitt when he defines his goal expectation theory and adds that "our theory does not deal with such forces (attitudes, feelings and norms), because they have little influence on behavior in strategic environments such as the gaming laboratory [Pruitt & Kimmel, 1977, p. 376]." Quite to the contrary, we feel that these forces, as our studies seem to demonstrate, play a central role in every situation, be it strategic or not, even within the artificial setting of a laboratory.

We would in fact argue that representations are actually a means of strategic adaptation to reality inasmuch as they invest the reality with a meaning, so that it is consistent with the individual's whole cognitive and ideological universe. The processes brought into action by the representation—that is, interpretation, categorization, anticipation—are all strategic tools for maintaining the subject's internal equilibrium in the face of a changing and varied environment. In this sense, an individual's system of representation seems to be the essential factor in the maintenance and defense of his identity.

References

Abric, J. C. Experimental study of group creativity: Task representation, group structure and performance. *European Journal of Social Psychology*, 1971, *1*, 311–326.

Abric, J. C. *Jeux, conflits et représentations sociales.* Thèse doctorat d'Etat, Université de Provence, 1976.

Abric, J. C. *Représentations sociales et interaction conflictuelle: Etudes expérimentales.* Paper presented to Conference on Social Representations, Laboratoire européen de psychologie sociale, Paris, January 1979.

Abric, J. C., Faucheux, C., Moscovisi, S., & Plon, M. Rôle de l'image du partenaire sur la coopération en situation de jeu. *Psychologie française*, 1967, *12*, 267–275.

Abric, J. C., & Vacherot, G. Méthodologie et étude expérimentale des représentations sociales: Tâche, partenaire et comportements en situation de jeu. *Bulletin de psychologie*, 1976, *29*, 735–746.

Apfelbaum, E. Représentations du partenaire et interaction à propos d'un dilemme du prisonnier. *Psychologie française*, 1967, *12*, 287–295.

Apfelbaum, E. *Interdépendance, renforcement social et réactivité.* Thèse doctorat d'Etat, Faculté des Lettres, Paris, 1969.

Apfelbaum, E., & Moscovici, S. Some cognitive dimensions of conflict. Unpublished manuscript, *Laboratoire de Psychologie Sociale*, Paris, 1971.

Bixenstine, V. E., & Blundell, M. Control of choice exerted by structural factors in two-persons non-zero-sum games. *Journal of Conflict Resolution*, 1966, *10*, 478–487.

Blumer, H. *Symbolic interactionism: Perspective and method*, Englewood Cliffs, N.J.: Prentice-Hall, 1969.

Chombart de Lauwe, M. J. *Un monde autre: l'enfance.* Paris: Payot, 1971.

Codol, J. P. Représentation de la tâche et comportements dans une situation sociale. *Psychologie française*, 1968, *13*, 241–264.

Deutsch, M. Trust, trustworthiness and the F Scale. *Journal of Abnormal and Social Psychology*, 1960, *61*, 138–140.

Doise, W. An experimental investigation into the formation of intergroup representation. *European Journal of Social Psychology*, 1972, *2*, 202–204.

Durkheim, E. Représentations individuelles et représentations collectives. *Revue de métaphysique et de morale*, 1898.

Faucheux, C., & Moscovici, S. Self-esteem and exploitative behavior in a game against chance and nature. *Journal of Personality and Social Psychology*, 1968, *8*, 83–88.

Flament, C. L'analyse de similitude. *Cahier du centre de recherches opérationnelles*, 1962, *4*, 63–97.

Flament, C. Représentations dans une situation conflictuelle. *Psychologie française*, 1967, *12*, 297–304.

Flament, C. *L'analyse de similitude: Une technique pour les recherches sur les représentations sociales.* Paper presented to Conference on Social Representations. Laboratoire européen de psychologie sociale, Paris, January 1979.

Gallo, P. S. The effects of score feedback and strategy of the other on cooperative behavior in a maximizing differences game. *Psychonomic Science*, 1966, *5*, 401–402.

Grzelak, J. Game theory and its applicability to the description of prosocial behavior. *Polish Psychological Bulletin*, 1976, 7, 197–205.

Herzlich, C. *Santé et maladie: Analyse d'une représentation sociale*. Paris: Mouton, 1969.

Jodelet, D. Le corps représenté et ses transformations. Paper presented to Conference on Social Representations. Laboratoire européen de psychologie sociale, Paris, January 1979.

Kaes, R. *Images de la culture chez les ouvriers français*. Paris: Cujas, 1968.

Kelley, H. H., & Stahelski, A. H. Social interaction basis of cooperator's and competitor's beliefs about others. *Journal of Personality and Social Psychology*, 1970, 16, 66–91.

Kelley, H. H., & Thibaut, J. *Interpersonal relations: A theory of interdependence*. New York: John Wiley, 1978.

Mack, D. Status and behavior in the reiterated prisoner's dilemma game. *Psychological Record*, 1976, 26, 529–532.

McNeel, S. P. Training cooperation in the prisoner's dilemma. *Journal of Experimental and Social Psychology*, 1973, 9, 335–348.

Milgram, S. Cities as social representations. Paper presented to Conference on Social Representations. Laboratoire européen de psychologie sociale, Paris, January 1979.

Moscovici, S. *La psychanalyse, son image et son public* (2nd ed.). Paris: Presses universitaires de France, 1976.

Moscovici, S. Préface à C. Herzlich: *Santé et maladie: analyse d'une représentation sociale*. Paris: Mouton, 1969.

Oskamp, S., & Perlman, D. Effects of friendship and disliking on cooperation in a mixed-motive game. *Journal of Conflict Resolution*, 1966, 10, 221–226.

Pareck, V., & Dixit, V. Effect of partner's response and communication on competitive and cooperative game behavior. *Psychologia*, 1977, 20, 38–48.

Pincus, J., & Bixenstine, V. E. Cooperation in the decomposed prisoner's dilemma game. A question of revealing or concealing information. *Journal of Conflict Resolution*, 1977, 21, 519–530.

Pruitt, D. G. Reward structure and cooperation: The decomposed prisoner's dilemma game. *Journal of Personality and Social Psychology*, 1967, 7, 21–27.

Pruitt, D. G. Motivational processes in the decomposed prisoner's dilemma game. *Journal of Personality and Social Psychology*, 1970, 14, 227–238.

Pruitt, D. G., & Kimmel, M. J. Twenty years of experimental gaming: Critique, synthesis and suggestions for the future. *Annual Review of Psychology*, 1977, 28, 363–392.

Rapoport, A., & Chammah, A. M. Sex differences in factors contributing to the level of cooperation in the prisoner's dilemma game. *Journal of Personality and Social Psychology*, 1965, 2, 831–838.

Scheff, T. J. A theory of social coordination applicable to mixed-motive games. *Sociometry*, 1967, 30, 215–234.

Sermat, V. Cooperative behavior in a mixed-motive game. *Journal of Social Psychology*, 1964, 62, 217–239.

Solomon, L. The influence of some types of power relationships and game strategies upon the development of interpersonal trust. *Journal of Abnormal and Social Psychology*, 1960, 61, 223–230.

Vinacke, W. E. Variables in experimental games: Toward a field theory. *Psychological Bulletin*, 1969, 71, 293–318.

Young, J. W. Behavioral and perceptual differences between structurally equivalent two person games. A rich versus poor context comparison. *Journal of Conflict Resolution*, 1977, 21, 299–322.

Zajonc, R. Cognitive theories in social psychology. In G. Lindzey and E. Aronson (Eds.), *Handbook of social psychology* (2nd ed., Vol. 1). Reading, Mass.: Addison-Wesley, 1968.

Chapter 5

Preferences and

Cognitive Processes

in Interdependence

Situations: A Theoretical

Analysis of Cooperation

JANUSZ L. GRZELAK

In everyday life there are many social situations in which an action taken by one party (i.e., a person or a group) influences another's outcomes or well-being. Situations differ with respect to the amount and type of that influence. At one extreme of a continuum we may posit *dependence* situations; at the other extreme, *interdependence* situations. In dependence situations the first party influences the second, but the second does not influence the first. If social situations are analyzed on the basis of external, observable outcomes, helping behavior or charity-giving would be good examples of dependence situations. (A helper can influence a person helped, but the latter does not influence the helper's outcomes—at least not in a visible way.) In social interdependence situations all parties' actions affect their own outcomes as well as the outcomes of others. Examples of interdependence include the sharing of household chores between roommates, contributing to a collaborative research project, and conserving energy or other social resources.

The analysis of people's behavior in interdependence situations usually focuses on two basic problems: (*a*) When do people cooperate or sacrifice their own profits to benefit others; and (*b*) what rules do people apply in their decision making, and are these rules rational or irrational? In at-

COOPERATION AND HELPING BEHAVIOR
Theories and Research

tempting to answer these questions, psychologists have relied heavily on concepts derived from the theory of decision making, especially game theory. The game theory approach assumes that individuals are rational in the sense that they try to maximize the subjective utility or value of outcomes. The most common psychological interpretation of this assumption is that every individual tries to maximize his or her own gains.

Critics have become increasingly skeptical of the value of game theory or, at least, of its psychological interpretation. People frequently do not follow game theory prescriptions about the best solutions even in the simplest situations, as in games with dominating strategies (e.g., prisoner's dilemma or some no-conflict games). Three reasons may be suggested for the failure of the game theory approach to predict behavior in interdependence situations:

First, it is an oversimplification of human motivation to assume that people maximize only their own gains in interdependence situations. There is a tendency to assume that if a game has a dominating strategy, rational behavior will consist in selecting that strategy. It is difficult to believe that people erroneously choose a solution that is worse than other available ones. However, rather than suspect people of irrationality when they select a dominated strategy, it may be worthwhile to assume that they seek out values other than to maximize their own absolute gains. This issue will be discussed in greater detail later in the chapter.

Second, departures from optimal solutions, especially in relatively complex situations, may occur because subjects apply maximization rules that have not been incorporated into decision making theory. A plausible interpretation for a large portion of choices in n-person games is that individuals use some very simplified ways of maximizing utility, such as assuming that their partners will choose certain strategies and then choosing the best responses to those strategies (Grzelak, Iwinski, & Radzicki, 1977). (For other discussions of this issue see de Zeeuw & Wagenaar, 1974; Grzelak, 1976, 1978; Kozielecki, 1975; Tyszka & Grzelak, 1976.)

Third, people's social knowledge and their perceptions of the actual degree of interdependence may influence their behavior. Decision theory itself has not considered how a variety of transformational processes, perceptions of partners' characteristics, perceptions of the task, etc., influence people's behavior.

In sum, people's reactions to conflict situations may be understood in terms of differences in their (a) structures of values, (b) preferred maximization rules, and (c) subjective interpretations of the entire decision-making situation.

Recently psychologists have been developing new and more sophisticated approaches to interdependence. These theories are frequently based on either a reinterpretation of the utility concept (e.g., the social motivation approach) or an emphasis on the cognitive mechanisms underlying behavior in interdependence situations. We will argue that both motivational and cognitive factors are necessary to account for behavior in interdependence situations.

The following major ideas will be discussed in this chapter:

1. Human preferences (social motivation) determining the subjective value of outcomes in any given interdependence situation are fairly complex and multidimensional. The structure of preferences is related to two basic aspects of interdependence: (a) the distribution of outcomes among the parties involved, and (b) the distribution of control or power among the parties.

2. A strong relationship exists between an individual's preferences and his or her information processing.

3. Interpersonal differences in preferences and information processes produce different systems of social knowledge and different subjective interpretations of any given social situation.

4. These differences in preferences, social knowledge, and subjective interpretations account for the observed variety in people's reactions to social interdependence. These differences may also have important implications for the analysis of human rationality, of social influence, etc.

In the next section some basic beliefs underlying our approach are presented. After that, we discuss the structure of social motivation (or structure of preferences), the relationship between preferences and the perception of interdependence, and finally, the relationship between preferences and behavior.

Basic Assumptions

Although it is difficult to describe all the assumptions that underlie our approach, some general beliefs about human nature and the social world should be stated explicitly. Attempts to specify such basic beliefs seem worthwhile, particularly at a relatively early stage of theory development.

1. *For any two outcomes an individual is either indifferent (if the outcomes are not important) or prefers one over the other.*[1] An individual tries to gain

---

[1] The term *outcome* is used here in a very broad sense. It includes external outcomes (e.g., money, prestige, fatigue, etc.) as well as internal ones (e.g., satisfaction from complying with someone's norms, or standards).

some outcomes and to avoid others. The subjective value, or subjective utility, of any outcome for a person can be inferred from these preferences if they are sufficiently consistent.

2. *Individuals are basically rational; they tend to maximize the subjective value associated with the consequences of their actions.* Persons try to select actions that bring about the most preferred outcomes, that is, those associated with the highest subjective value.[2] We assume that "selfless" motivation does not exist and that people invariably try to maximize their own interests. People of course may differ in the way they construe their self-interest. People's actual behavior may occasionally depart from what appears to be the best way of maximizing their interests. In general, though, all behavior attempts to gain the most valuable outcomes for individuals.

3. *Individuals' attempts to maximize their interests are mediated by a subjective, cognitive interpretation of the social situation.* Individuals interpret and transform pieces of information on the basis of the unique system of meanings that they develop throughout their lives. This system includes individuals' knowledge of others, of social settings, and of social norms.

Relatively automatic and impulsive behavior is possible. However, we believe that behavior (with the exception of unconditioned responses) is or at least at some point in the past was mediated by information processing. This processing includes one's recognition of the structure of interdependence, inferences about partner's characteristics, thoughts about the best way to maximize one's interests, and so forth. This analysis implies that even in the case of seemingly impulsive and automatic behavior, an adequate explanation requires knowledge of the behavior's cognitive antecedents.

The perfect rationality of all players that is posited by game theory implies that players' rules of interest maximization depend only on the structure of interdependence. Everyday experience does not support this view. Our behavior may vary as a function of how we perceive the partner as well as of what we believe is acceptable behavior in the given situation. Thus we use different strategies for solving interdependence problems based on the structure of interdependence (as perceived by the individual) as well as on the interpretation of the partner's and the social situation's characteristics.

4. *The behavior of individuals depends on both their intellectual ability and their repertory of skills.* Given the complexity of many social situations, information processing is necessary to comprehend the situation and to

---

[2] We will use the broader term, *subjective value* of outcomes, rather than *subjective utility* of outcomes since the measures of preferences employed in our studies often fail to satisfy all the requirements imposed by mathematical utility theory (von Neuman & Morgenstern, 1953).

select the best action. Thus, among other factors, individuals' intellectual levels contribute to their success in maximizing goals (see Mischel, 1973).

5. *The maximization of one's interests often requires coaction with others.* Individuals frequently are not self-sufficient in satisfying their needs. Some preferred outcomes can be obtained only by the joint action of two or more parties (e.g., conceiving a child requires joint action by a male and a female). Individual differences in preferred outcomes and in resources make exchanges with others valuable as a means of obtaining desirable outcomes. For instance, a babysitter provides services that are considered valuable by parents who, in turn, provide money to the babysitter.

6. *The maximization of outcomes by one individual often affects the maximization of outcomes by others (in terms of probability and amount).* Examples include the mutual dependence of individuals on energy and other material resources.

Statements 5 and 6 indicate that social interdependence is an important and inevitable property of social life. Individuals' outcomes depend not only on their own actions but on the actions taken by other members of their group, community, or society. In some cases individuals have the same or corresponding preferences for outcomes. In other cases, individuals have different or at least not entirely corresponding preferences. When individuals disagree about their most preferred outcomes, we have a situation with high conflict of interests.

Individuals are motivated to maximize their own interests. Hence, high conflict situations may induce competitive and exploitive behaviors that could destroy existing social structures or exhaust social resources. As a result, groups impose restrictions (by means of both informal norms and legislation) on the amount of goods individuals can obtain and/or on the way these goods can be obtained. These rules serve to reduce socially undesirable outcomes like violence, aggression, and the destruction of social structures and, at the individual level, to reduce uncertainty about how much and under what conditions persons can gain what they want. Social norms about input–output distributions among members in any social structure seem to derive from a concern about conflict in situations of social interdependence.

Structure of Preferences

It is assumed that individuals seek to obtain the most valuable outcomes. However, individuals may use different criteria to evaluate the consequences of their actions. First, the quality of preferred outcome varies among individuals (e.g., someone may prefer making money to enjoying family happiness, or vice versa). Second, people evaluate not only specific outcomes but whole actions or strategies, especially in the light of the social approval and moral value they assign to such actions. Their preferences vary according to their concern for and knowledge about what is "good" and what is "bad" to do in a particular social setting. Third, the subjective value resulting from any combination of choices in an interdependence situation depends on how these outcomes are shared between the individual and others. Fourth, preferences vary depending on whether gains are brought about by an individual's own action or by the actions of others. We will focus on the third and fourth of these criteria since they embody the most prominent features of an interdependence situation.

Outcome Preferences

We have noted that the diversity of behavior in interdependence situations is partly due to differences in individuals' preferences for outcomes. People differ in how they define their self-interest (i.e., in what they consider suitable criteria for subjective evaluations of available outcomes). People's preferences about outcome distributions for themselves and others seem to reflect individualistic tendencies (to maximize one's own gains), concern for partner's gains (to maximize or minimize the partner's gains), and concern for relative differences between one's own and the partner's outcomes (to maximize that difference). Thus, individuals' subjective value, or utility, of outcomes consists of many components. (The notion that utility is a function of more than the one variable of the individual's own gain has been developed theoretically and empirically confirmed by many researchers, including: Grzelak et al., 1977; MacCrimmon & Messick, 1976; McClintock & McNeel, 1967; McClintock & Van Avermaet, Chapter 3, this volume; Messick & Thorngate, 1967; Pruitt, 1970; and Radzicki, 1976.)

Control Preferences

The idea of control as a value was inspired by a number of theories. Ultimately, it seemed justified by our inability to predict people's behavior from their outcome preferences and expectations about partners (Kranas, 1977). This failure could be explained in many ways. For one thing, outcome preferences do not provide sufficient information about an individual's interests, that is, about what he or she tries to maximize. Interdependence situations not only differ in the magnitude and distribution of outcomes as a consequence of the choices made by all the parties, they also differ in how much and to what extent each party can control his or her own and other parties' outcomes (Kelley & Thibaut, 1978). In every interdependence situation each party has a certain level of control over its own outcomes and the other party's outcomes, as determined by the payoff structure. The amount or level of that control can be defined, as proposed by Kelley and Thibaut (1978), by the magnitude of the difference in own and others' outcomes that the party can produce by changing from one strategy to another. Control in the simplest, two-person situation can thus be described, from an individual's point of view, in terms of individuals' control of their own outcomes; partners' control of their own outcomes; individual's control of the partner's outcomes; and partner's control of the individual's outcomes.[3]

Theoretically these dimensions are independent, though in real life situations one party's high control over one domain of outcomes often implies low control by the other party over the same domain. My high control over my own outcomes frequently means that others have low control over my outcomes.

Kelley and Thibaut's (1978) theory of interdependence provides an elegant and comprehensive analysis of control. The present chapter offers a simpler analysis based on the four dimensions just listed. We postulate that it matters to people who controls what outcomes in any given situation. In other words, people care about the characteristics of any given situation in terms of each of the four dimensions. Individuals may like or dislike the opportunity to control their own outcomes (positive or negative self-control preferences), like or dislike controlling partners' outcomes (power preferences), like or dislike partners' ability to control their own outcomes (preferences for partners' self-control), and, finally, like or dislike partners' ability to affect their own outcomes (preferences for partners' power).

We further postulate that people are sensitive not only to the amount of control they and their partners have over outcomes but to relative differences in control exercised by themselves and their partners. For instance, some people may try to gain more control over their own and/or partner's outcomes than the partner has himself, whereas other people value highly equitable distributions of control above all else. Thus within each domain of outcomes (own or partner's) we can speak of the value of equity in control (or simply of "partnership").

Individuals can satisfy their preferences by moving from one situation to another, as in the following examples or, in a given situation, by choosing

---

[3] For the sake of simplicity we have not considered a control based on *coordination* of moves taken by the parties (i.e., *behavioral control*, in Kelley's and Thibaut's theory). We do not believe that this type of control plays a crucial role in individuals' preferences.

actions that maximize their specific needs for control. If party A has strong preferences *only* for his or her own self-control or independence, the two examples (1 and 2) presented in Table 5–1 should have about the same high positive value for A. That is, in both examples, A has the same amount of control over his own outcomes (compare the differences in outcomes associated with strategies a_1 and a_2). If party A, in addition to his preferences for self-control, also prefers to have control over his partner, then "Example 2" should be evaluated more favorably. If A prefers that all parties should be able to control themselves, then "Example 1" better satisfies his desires since it provides both parties with an equally high possibility for self-control.

An example of exercizing control within a situation is shown in Table 5–2. If A places high value on his own independence and/or control over partner's outcomes, then strategies a_1 and a_2 in the situation presented in Table 5–2 are more valuable to him than a_3 and a_4 since in switching from a_1 to a_2 or from a_2 to a_1 he produces bigger differences in partner's outcomes and at the same time partner's choices have very little influence on his own outcomes. Knowledge about A's preferences over control should make our predictions of his choices more accurate. If A's control preferences are very strong, and stronger than, say, his individualistic preferences for outcomes (to gain as much as he can), he should choose a_1 or a_2 even though a_3 and a_4 are likely to bring him higher outcomes (since b_1 is a dominating strategy for B).

It should be noted at this point that subjective value of control (unlike subjective value of outcomes) is not based on outcomes themselves but on *differences* in outcomes as produced by either own or others' choices. In the case of one's own choices (that is, control over one's own and/or partner's

Table 5.1
Two Examples of Varying Control over Outcomes

	Party B					Party B	
	b_1	b_2				b_1	b_2
Party A a_1	10, 1	11, 10			Party A a_1	10, 10	11, 9
a_2	3, 2	1, 9			a_2	3, 1,	1, 2

Example 1: Low interdependence; high bilateral self-control (each party controls its own outcomes and has little control over other party's outcomes).	**Example 2:** High self-control and power (A controls own outcomes and B's outcomes; B's choices do not affect either party's outcomes).

Table 5.2
Exercising Control within a Situation

	B	
	b_1	b_2
a_1	15, 12	16, 10
a_2	16, 23	14, 22
a_3	20, 17	10, 13
a_4	24, 18	11, 15

outcomes) it is not possible to determine which single action maximizes control, that is, either self-control or control over other. We can only compare any two strategies. In our example, when A changes choices from a_1 to a_2 in Table 5–2 he or she can exercise more control over partner than by choosing between a_3 and a_4 or even between a_1 and a_2. Thus our predictions, if based only on A's preferences over his or her own control, are limited to a set of strategies rather than to a single strategy. In the case of A's preferences over partner's control, we can speak of the degree to which any *single* strategy by A maximizes B's control interests. For instance, strategy a_3 maximizes B's possibility to control his own outcomes $(17 - 13 = 4)$, strategy a_4 maximizes B's possibility to control A's outcomes, and strategy a_1 minimizes B's possibility to control A's outcomes.

Of the types of control discussed so far, the need to control one's own outcomes has the longest theoretical tradition, beginning with Adler (1929). White (1959) provides a major statement of the motivational aspects of self-control in his concept of effectance motivation. De Charms' (1968) theory of personal causation states that behaviors stemming from own choices are more valuable and more strongly motivated than those stemming from external pressures. Brehm's (1966) theory of reactance seems to be based on the assumption that individuals need to control their own outcomes. Theory and research on privacy (see Derlega & Chaikin, 1977) can be interpreted in terms of an individual's desire to maintain control over the interpersonal flow of information, and findings about human territorial behavior and crowding (e.g., Altman, 1975) can be interpreted in terms of control over the physical and social environment.

Control over others' outcomes as a value seems to underlie research on the Machiavellian personality (Christie & Geis, 1970). If we possess control over other people, we obviously force them (by the use of threats, promises, rewards, and/or punishments) to act in a way that suits our interests.

The notion of control seems to function in psychology at *two* levels of generality. At a general level, control means the fundamental ability of individuals to satisfy their needs effectively. This meaning is probably most closely related to that proposed by White (1959), and we can quite safely assume that all people want to control themselves and the environment in this sense (except perhaps in cases of severe mental pathology). However, general control may be gained and maintained through such means as asserting one's own needs and wishes, submitting one's fate to another person (a spouse or a boss), or gaining power over other people. In these cases the meaning of control refers to more specific ways of attaining individual goals. People may handle control in a general sense quite effectively even if they are and want to be very dependent on others (as is often the case in neurotic patients). Similarly, all the other specific preferences for control discussed above may be viewed as derivatives of a general need for control.

Thus, the general idea of control as a value has a long tradition in psychology. However, most theories have focused either on the general concept or on one specific type of control (i.e., control over one's own outcomes), assuming that the proposed motivation exists in most people. We postulate that the need for control is multidimensional and that there are individual differences in patterns of people's values concerning control. These differences in preferences about control will affect people's behavior in various social situations. For instance, people with high preferences for self-control will tend to resist attempts by others to influence their attitudes or behavior. The reactance phenomenon (Brehm, 1972) may be limited to those people who have high preferences for control over own outcomes and should not be observed in people for whom self-control does not seem to be valuable. The effectiveness of directive or nondirective psychotherapy may also depend on patient's control preferences.

Measurement of Preferences

MEASURES OF OUTCOME PREFERENCES

In our studies, individuals' outcome preferences have been measured with two similar methods. The first method is based on a type of conjoint measurement developed by Radzicki (1976). The technique is based on a set of "offers," each of which contains two payoffs: one payoff for the subject and the other for the anonymous partner. A complete set of offers may include the various possible combinations of five levels of payoffs (e.g., $1, $2, $3, $4, $5) for a subject and and his or her partner. Subjects are asked to rank the offers in terms of their preference, from the most to the least attractive. Subjects are told that their rank order will determine their own as well as their partner's payoffs but that in another (albeit nonexistent) group the partners' rank orders will determine payoffs.[4]

The best approximation of each subject's utility as a function of his or her own payoffs (x) and the partner's payoffs (y) is calculated from the subject's payoff ranking. Sometimes polynomials of the second degree are used. But we find that the simplest but quite satisfactory piecewise linear class of functions can be used,[5] that is,

$$u(xy) = ax + by + c(x - y).$$

The first term in this equation can be interpreted as the utility of one's own gains, the second term as the utility of the partner's gains, and the third as the utility of the absolute difference between one's own and the partner's outcomes.[6] The best fitting function of this type, that is, parameters a, b, and c, would be calculated for each subject to match her or his rank order. (The criterion of best fit is based on either the least square method or the correlation between the subject's ranking and the rank of values derived from the utility function.) The results can be interpreted in psychological terms that are similar to a proposal by McClintock (1977). That is, purely "individualistic" persons are those whose best fitting functions show b and c parameters as close to 0. "Altruistic" persons are those with $b > 0$ and $b > a$. Persons with $c < 0$ and $c > a$ and $c > b$ are basically concerned with equity.

A second method was used to measure outcome preferences in our most recent research (we will refer to this research as the "Warsaw study").[7] This technique also relies on rank ordering a set of offers, but a different method is used to reveal the main criterion for a person's ranking. The criteria are identified by correlation coefficients between a subject's rank order and "ideal" one-dimension patterns of preferences. The formal analysis (Wieczorkowska, 1979) showed that any consistent preferential order can be described by a three dimensional space with the diemnsions being individualism, altruism, and equity (see Table 5–3).

---

[4] The payoffs to subjects are real, not imaginary.

[5] The piece-linear function usually fits 80–90% of the subjects' rank orders. The polynomials of the second degree give, of course, good approximation in all cases of consistent rank orders; however, psychological interpretation of the terms is less straightforward than in the case of the simpler function.

[6] For detailed discussion of the procedure and the theoretical basis of the technique, see J. Radzicki (1976), and Grzelak (1977).

[7] The Warsaw study (which is not yet published) consists of six experiments conducted in one large project. Outcome and control preferences were measured in all 656 subjects, and the experiments differed in respect to type of dependent variables. The study was designed and conducted in collaboration with the author's M.A. students and with the assistance of Z. Czwartosz and G. Wieczorkowska.

Table 5.3
Outcome Preferences

| | Pattern | | | | | |
| | Individualistic | | Altruistic | | Equity | |
Rank	Me	Partner	Me	Partner	Me	Partner
1	40	40	40	40	40	40
2	40	30	30	40	30	30
3	40	20	20	40	20	20
4	40	10	10	40	10	10
5	30	40	40	30	40	30
6	30	30	30	30	30	40
⋮	⋮	⋮	⋮	⋮	⋮	⋮
16	10	10	10	10	10	40

The three formally independent dimensions have proven to be empirically independent too. The highest correlation coefficient between any two of the criteria in the Warsaw study was .16.

MEASURES OF CONTROL PREFERENCES

A technique employed in our recent studies reconciles theoretical requirements (described in section on "System of Preferences: Some General Comments") and the need for a technique that is easy to use and easily understood by subjects. The method is similar to that used in measuring outcome preferences. Subjects believe that, in dyads, they will perform 100 short tasks and that they will be paired randomly with an anonymous partner of the same age and social status. Both members of the pair have to solve *all* 100 tasks to receive a monetary reward. The magnitude of the reward depends on the level of the dyad's performance and is to be divided equally (so that each member will get the same share). Although both members have to solve 100 tasks, the dyad's level of performance is to be evaluated on the basis of a selection of tasks from the subject's set of tasks and another from the partner's set. The subjects are asked to evaluate the attractiveness of different ratios of such selections, for example, 20% of subject's tasks vis-à-vis 80% of partner's tasks. All possible combinations (summing to 100% or less) of subject's and partner's percentages make up a set of 15 offers, each describing what proportion (or percent) of subject's and partner's tasks will account for the final dyad performance. Subjects are informed that in cases where two percentages do not sum to 100 (e.g., 35% subject's tasks and 20% partner's tasks) the answers to the remaining portion of the tasks (45%) will be decided randomly (based on a random drawing from the pool of correct and incorrect answers). The evaluation of the attractiveness of the offers is based on subjects' rank ordering of all the offers from most to least desirable. The subjects believe that they will not be able to identify their partners. Subjects' preferences are identified by the similarity (correlation coefficient) of their rank orders to the selected one-dimensional "ideal" patterns of preferences (see Table 5–4).

Thus each subject's structure of control preferences is described by four correlation coefficients that reflect how the subject values self-control, partner's self-control, fate control, and equity of control (or partnership). The final analysis in our study revealed that these dimensions were relatively independent. The highest correlation coefficient between any two control preference dimensions in the Warsaw study was .39; others were all below .24. Very low correlations were also found between all possible dimensions of control and outcome preferences (coefficients were below .18), showing that the two components of preference structure are independent.

System of Preferences: Some General Comments

RELATIONSHIP BETWEEN THE TWO SYSTEMS OF PREFERENCES

So far we have discussed the two systems of preferences separately. In presenting our empirical findings, we will limit ourselves to the simple effects of one or the other dimension of preference. It is important to note,

Table 5.4
Patterns of Preferences for Control

	Pattern							
	Self-control		Partner's control		Fate control		Partnership	
Rank	My tasks	Part-ner's Tasks	My tasks	Part-ner's tasks	My tasks	Part-ner's tasks	My tasks	Part-ner's tasks
1	80	20	20	80	20	20	50	50
2	65	35	35	65	35	20	65	35
3	65	20	20	65	20	35	35	65
4	50	50	50	50	35	35	50	35
5	50	35	35	50	50	20	35	50
6	50	20	20	50	20	50	⋮	⋮
⋮	⋮	⋮	⋮	⋮	⋮	⋮	80	20
15	20	20	20	20	20	80	20	80

Note: Numbers show the percentage of subject's and his or her partner's tasks that account for dyad's performance.

however, that an individual's preferences should be described in terms of both components of preferences and their relative strength.

Interesting theoretical hypotheses about differences in behavior and cognitive processes can be related to specific configurations of control and outcome preferences. For instance, we can expect the behavior of "altruistic" individuals to be different, depending on their control values. Individuals with high respect for others' self-control should be sensitive and responsive to others' needs (respecting others' right to define what is good for them), whereas "altruistic" individuals with high need for power should be more aggressive in enforcing whatever they consider to be good for others. For instance, overprotective parents may attempt to control a child's outcomes, disregarding his or her own needs. We may also expect competitive persons who respect others' need for self-control to solve interpersonal conflicts in a more peaceful way (obeying socially acceptable rules, which usually affirm equal control rights for both parties) than competitive and power-oriented individuals.

The Warsaw study showed that a substantial number of people can be found at the extremes of any preference dimension (indicated by a correlation coefficient between ideal preference order and a given point on the dimension of .40 or more). For instance, we found over 20% of subjects selecting even improbable preferences, such as preferences for not having control over own outcomes. We also found that for many subjects outcome preferences were stronger than central preferences and that for other people the opposite was true. Thus it seems realistic to analyze preferences in terms of various configurations of their dimensions and strength.

THEORETICAL AND METHODOLOGICAL STATUS OF PREFERENCES

We do not consider preferences to be stable, traitlike characteristics of personality. They vary from situation to situation depending on partner's characteristics, group norms, etc. It was found in the Warsaw study that preferences revealed by subjects are strongly influenced by their images of their partners. Outcome and control preferences were measured twice by the methods described above. In the first session the subject's partner was described only as a fellow student. In the second session (a week later) the subject's partner was specifically described by his position on each of several continua such as prestige; wealth; ability (higher or lower than that possessed by the subject) to solve intellectual tasks; and possession of skills similar to those required by the experimental tasks. A number of significant differences in preferences were observed in intrapersonal comparisons (changes from the first to the second session) as well as in intergroup comparisons (across different partners' characteristics in the second session).

Outcome and control preferences were most affected by the wealth of the partner, the partner's prestige, and information about level of subjects' abilities as compared to their partners' abilities.

The results demonstrate the interactional nature of preferences. The lack of stability across various kinds of situations does not imply that the preferences are not consistent at all (Endler & Magnusson, 1976; Magnusson & Endler, 1977). What is stable and characteristic for a person is his or her individual pattern of preference variability across situations. For instance, if person A displays less competitiveness when facing a more prestigious partner than when facing a partner of similar status, this difference should occur systematically whenever person A is exposed to partners of various levels of social prestige. Thus, a person's preferences will be defined by both preference (or, rather, preference configuration) factors and situational factors. Knowledge about both kinds of factors is still limited, and further research should assess what factors account for most of the variance in people's preferences. Like other variables, preferences in any given situation or across situations should be characterized by a probability distribution over different preference values or at least by a range within which individuals' preferences vary. Any single measurement may lead, for a number of reasons, to a preference assessment that is far from the best representation of the individual's actual preferences.

It is highly desirable (but it will be extremely difficult) to develop new methods of measurement that would permit us to collect a large sample of any single individual's preferences in various situations. This project would probably require the use of repeated measures, which are inconvenient and time-consuming for a researcher as well as for his or her subjects. The absence of such methods, together with financial restraints, explains why we use relatively simple techniques in our present research. The use of an anonymous, "average" partner in measuring preferences is based on the assumption that preferences revealed by subjects in such a setting represent an "average" of subjects' preferences across at least different situations. This technique, however, is not appropriate if we assume the probabilistic and interactional nature of preferences.

Preferences, Cognitive Processes, and Behavior

Preferences and Information Processing

INFORMATION SEEKING

Any effective, deliberate course of action requires knowledge about both outcomes and the means to achieve them. Not every bit of knowledge we possess has an immediate, instrumental value. However, it seems reasonable to assume that individuals search primarily for information that will be useful in obtaining desirable outcomes. Thus information seeking is selective in nature: An individual searches for information that is consistent and instrumental to his or her structure of preferences. A general hypothesis is that in interdependence situations, people with highly individualistic outcome preferences and/or with high self-control preferences will show lower interest in others and their outcomes than people with any other type of preference. An individualistic person should be interested in a partner's outcomes only to the degree to which that knowledge is necessary for maximization of the person's own gains. For example, once the person discovers that one of his or her strategies is dominating, the person does not need more information about the interdependence structure, especially information related to a partner. On the other hand, someone who is either competitive, altruistic, or equity oriented needs to know at least what a partner's outcomes are in order to maximize, respectively, his or her own gains, losses, or equity. Sometimes information may be needed about the subjective value of outcomes for partners. For example, an equitable solution for a person may be any equal distribution of external outcomes or a solution that creates the same level of satisfaction for the person and the partner. In the latter case the person would want information about the external outcome distribution and about the other person's preferences. In either case we expect stronger interest in the partner's outcomes and in the partner himself or herself. Similarly, someone motivated to respect partner's self-control, to control other's outcomes, or to have control equal to a partner, has to collect more extensive information about the interdependence structure in order to fulfill his or her own needs.

These predictions have been partially verified in two of our studies (Grzelak, 1978; Warsaw study). In both studies subjects were placed in a two-person, non-zero-sum, gamelike situation that was not well defined. They were told only that they could earn some money and that how much they earned depended on both what strategy (X or O) they chose themselves and what strategy their partners chose. The experimenters provided no information either about the specific outcomes for possible combinations of choices or about the partners' identity except that they were high school students. Before making their own choice, subjects could ask any question and as many questions as they wanted in order to understand the situation. The numbers and types of questions asked made up the dependent variable. The independent variables were outcome preferences in the first study (Grzelak, 1980) and both types of preferences in the Warsaw study.

A summary of the main findings is presented in Table 5–5. The first

Table 5.5
Preferences and Information Seeking

Type of preferences	Type of information searched for	Level of exploratory activity
Individualistic: *high* versus low	Strategic: High interest in own outcomes[a,b] Low interest in partner's outcomes[b] Nonstrategic: High interest in partner's personality and background[b]	High[a,b]
Altruistic or *aggressive* versus neutral	Strategic: High interest in partner's outcomes[a,b] Nonstrategic: High interest in partner's personal characteristics[a,b]	—
Equity versus Inequity	Strategic: High interest in own and partner's outcomes[a,b] Nonstrategic: Low interest in partner himself[b]	High[a,b]
Own control: *high* versus low	Strategic: Low interest in partner's strategic position[b]	—
Partner's control: *high* versus low	Strategic: Low interest in own and partner's outcomes[b] Nonstrategic: Low interest in partner's characteristics not related to the situation[b]	Low[b]
Fate control: *high* versus low	Strategic: Low interest in partner's outcomes, relations among outcomes and partner's strategic position[b]	—
Partnership: *high* versus low	Strategic: High interest in relationship between own and partner's outcomes, and in partner's strategic position[b]	—

[a] Results from Grzelak (1980).
[b] Results from Warsaw study.
[c] This is the only case in which one of the two extremes is compared with the middle of the continuum.

column in Table 5–5 identifies dimensions for which dichotomous comparisons were made. The second column specifies the type of question that was asked more or less frequently by subjects located at one end of the continuum (indicated by italicized terms in the first column) versus subjects who were at the other end. The questions are grouped into two broad categories: strategic and nonstrategic. The strategic questions are those related to the payoff-matrix (that is, they seek to define the decision problem); and all other questions are nonstrategic, having to do mainly with partner's characteristics and the rules of the game. Significant differences were found on every preference dimension, confirming the relationship between preferences and the selective nature of information seeking. However, the direction of the specific differences was not quite what we predicted. For instance, although the individualistically oriented subjects as compared with nonindividualistic subjects asked more questions about their own and fewer about the partner's strategic position, unexpectedly, they asked more questions about the partner himself or herself. Also, contrary to predictions, high preferences for partner's control resulted in low interest in both the strategic properties of the situation and in the partner himself. Subjects with a tendency to either maximize or minimize partner's gains showed, as expected, strong interest in partner's as well as in their own outcomes. The equity-oriented subjects showed strong interest in the strategic aspects of the situation and little interest in their partner's situation. This may reflect a general tendency for equity oriented persons to be concerned with external outcomes rather than in their subjective value to both parties. Strong interest in strategic properties of the situation, including partner's position, was also shown by subjects with high preferences for equal control distribution (a partnership orientation). Some of the preferential dimensions also were correlated with level of exploratory activity as measured by total number of questions asked. Subjects with individualistic, equity, and low partner's control preferences asked more questions than subjects located on, respectively, the other ends of these continua.

The results, though not definitive, suggest that a strong linkage exists between preferential factors and informational inputs. The elements used by individuals to construct their view of a situation vary on the basis of their outcome and control preferences. In other words, individuals are sensitive to different aspects of the external world based on their preferences. A further question for research is: Once received, do the pieces of information remain unchanged in a person's memory storage or are they transformed after memory processing so that they depart from the original ones? The studies described next provide some preliminary answers to this question.

MEMORY TRANSFORMATION

In two experiments (Grzelak, 1978; Warsaw study) a PDG payoff matrix was presented to subjects. The properties of the game were explained in detail during a 7–10-min period of instruction. Next the experimenter hid the matrix and asked subjects to fill out a short questionnaire, to divert their attention from the game. Then subjects were asked to recall all the payoffs that had been seen before. Number and type of errors in recalling the payoff matrix were the dependent variables.

One major effect of preferences for equity was found in the Grzelak (1978) study. Subjects with high equity preferences recalled payoffs so that differences between their own and partner's outcomes were smaller than in the original matrix. Inaccuracy in recalling payoffs was in many cases large enough to change completely the strategic quality of the game. Subjects with high preferences as compared with those with low preferences for equity showed a strong tendency to equalize payoffs (especially payoffs that were originally most different).

A simple explanation of this "equalizing effect" assumes that high equity preferences reveal subjects' motivation to gain and maintain equity with respect to outcome distribution. Perception of inequitable outcomes could then produce negative emotional tension. This tension could be reduced by finding and justifying inequity, by attempting to restore equity or, as in our experiment, by transforming, in memory, the original perception of inequity (i.e., denying its existence).

A number of significant effects appeared in the Warsaw study among the measured outcome and control preferences. However, some results were unexpected and difficult to interpret. For instance, the "equalizing effect" for equity oriented subjects observed in the first study was found for one pair of outcomes: that associated with subject's competitive and partner's cooperative strategy. The same equity subjects, however, tended to increase differences between outcomes that were originally similar (for mutual competition or cooperation). Thus the defensive equalization of outcomes postulated after the first study is not the only response of equity oriented people, and there are probably other factors that influence types of memory transformations.

Some transformations were either consistent with preferences or at least easy to understand:

Subjects with individualistic, as compared with nonindividualistic, orientation did not change outcomes substantially in either direction. However, subjects tended to recall the payoff matrix such that partner's control over their outcomes appeared to be stronger (i.e., larger changes were produced by partner's choices) than in the original matrix. Does threat that results from partner's control provide a good justification for making a defensive choice that also suits the subject's individual interest?

Altruists increased partners' outcomes associated with their own cooperative strategy, whereas equity oriented people tended to increase both own and partners' outcomes in the same case.

Subjects with high preferences for self-control recalled payoffs that gave them higher control over own outcomes than the original matrix did. They also recalled that the partner had higher control over his or her own outcomes. Their recollections of their own payoffs was at the same time more accurate than recollections of subjects with low preferences for self-control.

Subjects with preferences for partner's control increased partner's payoffs, and subjects with preferences for partnership increased differences between own and partner's outcomes, to the partner's advantage.

SUBJECTIVE REPRESENTATION OF THE INTERDEPENDENCE SITUATION

Preferences affect the type of information that an individual searches for and, probably, the way information is transformed in memory. Individuals may see the same situation differently based on how they process information. Kelley and Thibaut (1978) present a similar idea in their analysis of interdependence. They postulated that any interdependence situation (as represented by a given matrix) is transformed through various mental operations into an effective matrix to which we finally respond. Abric (1976; see also Chapter 4, this volume) expresses a similar view.

Not only are there interpersonal differences in subjective representations, but one's system of preferences accounts for these differences to a great extent. If preferences affect information seeking and memory processing, people with different preference patterns should also build up different systems of general beliefs about others (implicit personality theories) and the social world (implicit theories of the social world). We have some evidence from the Warsaw study to support this hypothesis dealing with one type of beliefs about others, that is, expectations about others' preferences over outcome and control distributions.

Preferences and Expectations about Others

According to game theory, players' knowledge about interdependence is limited to their information about the game matrix. Thus, the player's anticipation of his or her partner's future move is based only on what can be inferred from the game matrix to be a rational choice for the partner. The game situation is also termed decision making under uncertainty because of this assumption.

This situation seems to contradict our everyday experiences with social interdependence, in which we try to anticipate our partner's moves based on our social stereotypes and/or the information that we already possess about the person with whom we are dealing. At the present time, we do not have a clear picture of the relationship between a player's decisions and his or her expectations about a partner's behavior. Kelley and Stahelski (1970), on the basis of their research, hypothesized that expectations about others depend on motivational factors. Cooperatively as compared with competitively inclined people tend to perceive the social world as more differentiated. A cooperatively oriented individual expects others to be cooperative as well as competitive, whereas a competitive person perceives others to be like himself (that is, competitive too). Codol (1975) questioned this relationship by asserting that the dominant tendency in anticipating others' behavior is to expect other people to behave "as I do" ("but a little worse than me"). Tyszka and Grzelak (1976) observed the same tendency in some game situations, and in other situations they reported slightly higher differentiation of expectations about partner's moves in cooperative than in competitive players.

In an experiment conducted as part of the Warsaw study, subjects played five two-person games differing in strength of conflict and in type and amount of control (from high subject's to high partner's control over outcomes). The subjects were asked about their expectations concerning people's, as well as their actual anonymous partner's, preferences or intentions before all the games and then in each game separately. In questions about people in general, subjects were asked to put down the percentages of people they believed made up different categories of outcome preferences (competitive, individualistic, equity-oriented, cooperative, and altruistic) and control preferences (preferring each party's independent control; own control over all outcomes, or own power; partner's control over all outcomes, or partner's power; and "reverse" control, in which each party controls the other party's outcomes). We tested for differences in expectations for every preference dimension. No systematic differences in expectations were found across game situations. In most cases the comparisons between subjects' expectations about others in five games revealed differences in the same direction although only some of them reached a conventional level of statistical significance. Taking into account only those differences that were significant in at least two game situations, the results can be summarized as follows:

1. Subjects with individualistic preferences expected others not to value partner's power.
2. Equity-oriented subjects perceived others more often as being equity oriented and less often as power oriented.

3. Subjects with high preferences for own control perceived others less often as competitive, altruistic, and preferring partner's control, and more often as cooperative.
4. Subjects who respected partner's control expected others less often to be altruistic.
5. Subjects who minimized fate control expected others less often to be competitive and altruistic. They also expected others to value power and/or the independence (self-control) of each party.
6. Subjects with a partnership orientation perceived others as being competitive more often, and as individualistic and preferring partner's control less often.

The results did not consistently support the hypotheses about expectations of others discussed earlier. We observed a tendency in subjects to perceive others as similar to themselves only in cases of preferences for equity and, to some extent, for own control. The results did not support Kelley and Stahelski's hypothesis either. However, the number of significant results obtained in the present study and their consistency across various interdependence situations indicates that a strong relationship exists between preferences and expectations about other people's motivation.

Preferences and Level of Performance

People's actual behavior in a given social situation depends on what they want to gain (i.e., their preferences) and their subjective representation of the situation. An important aspect of the subjective representation is recognition about how well the situation enables one to satisfy preferences, that is, about the outcome and control structure of the situation. Thus the type, intensity, and quality of responses performed by people should depend on both the structure of their preferences and the perceived interdependence structure. We have already shown that there is a relationship between preferences and perception. A separate part of the Warsaw study was designed to test this relationship as well as behavior in different interdependence situations.

Subjects thought that they were paired with an anonymous partner with whom they were supposed to perform a number of simple calculations in 12 3-minute periods. They were told that the amount of money that each dyad would earn for the task depended on the number of correct calculations completed by the dyad. There were nine 3 × 3 experimental conditions varying in the amount of control the subject had over the dyad's performance and in the subject's share in the dyad's earnings. The "control" conditions differed in terms of the number of subject's work-periods the subject believed were used to calculate the dyad's performance: 4 in low control, 6 in equal control, and 8 in high control condition. The remaining work-periods used were supposedly the partner's. In the three pay conditions, the subject earned 35%, 50% or 65% of the dyad payoff. The number of calculations in all 12 periods (level of performance) and number of errors (quality of performance) were the dependent variables.

The type of interdependence itself did not produce any differences in subjects' performance. All the significant differences were associated either with the type of subjects' preferences or with the interaction between preferences and situation. Subjects with low preferences for equity, fate-control, and partnership, and high preferences for own control had a higher overall level of performance than subjects representing the other sides of these dimensions. However, high level of preferences for partnership and a non-fate-control orientation were associated with a low level of quality in performance (high number of errors).

The major results were that performance and its quality depend on both the nature of the interdependence and specific outcome and control preferences. Table 5–6 shows what types of preferences are associated with level and quality of performance in each interdependence situation. The observed differential effects of type of preferences and type of interdependence may have important implications. For instance, the validity of Adams' (1965) theory of equity may be limited in interdependence situations to people with high preferences for equity and possibly partnership. Adams assumed that people are motivated to gain and maintain equity. Our results show that there were interpersonal differences in level of motivation for equity that are large enough to produce considerable differences in behavior. Besides the theoretical value of the results, they may also have important practical implications (e.g., in industry) if confirmed in further research.

Summary and Concluding Remarks

This chapter's theoretical approach incorporated both motivational and cognitive components to study interdependence. For many years a psychological interpretation of game theory heavily influenced our investigation of interdependence. We learned from a number of experiments about the importance of the external outcome structure and of the strategic features of interdependence. However, we also learned that these strategic aspects of the situation (if interpreted on the basis of a simple one-dimension concept of utility) accounted for only part of the variance in people's choice behavior. In an attempt to construct more powerful theories, psychologists focused their attention either on developing more complex theories of utility of outcomes (values that people tend to maximize) or on cognitive processes

Table 5.6
Preferences, Interdependence and Level of Performance

"Control" conditions	Payoff conditions							
	Low		Equal		High		Overall	
	P	Q	P	Q	P	Q	P	Q
Low	Eq: low	Eq: —	Par: low	Par: —			Eq: low	Eq: —
			Nf: high	Nf: —			Nf: high	Nf: —
Equal	P_{con}: —	P_{con}: low	Ind: high	Ind: —	Alt: high	Alt: —	Ind: high	Ind: —
			O_{con}: high	O_{con}: low			Alt: —	Alt: low
			Nf: high	Nf: low			Eq: low	Eq: low
							O_{con}: high	O_{con}: low
							Nf: high	Nf: low
							Par: low	Par: —
High	P: —	Q: —	P_{con}: —	P_{con}: high	P: high	Q: —	Alt: —	Alt: high
Overall	Eq: low	Eq: —	O_{con}: high	O_{con}: —	Ind: high	Ind: —	Eq: low	Eq: —
	O_{con}: high	O_{con}: —	P_{con}: —	P_{con}: high	Nf: —	Nf: low	O_{con}: high	O_{con}: low
	P_{con}: low	P_{con}: —	Nf: high	Nf: low			Nf: high	Nf: low
			Par: low	Par: —			Par: low	Par: —

P = level of performance
Q = quality of performance
Ind = high individualistic preferences
Alt = altruistic preferences
Eq = equity preferences

O_{con} = own control preferences
P_{con} = partner's control preferences
Nf = nonfate control preferences
Par = partnership preferences

underlying decision making under interdependence. McClintock and Van Avermaet's chapter in this book (Chapter 3) represents the first approach; Abric's chapter (Chapter 4) represents the second approach. In agreement with both approaches, we assume that there is a continuous interplay between people's values and their cognitive processes.

Three theoretical ideas advanced in this chapter should be reemphasized:

First, the various components of an interdependence structure influence the subjective value of the consequences of actions taken by individuals. The most important features of the interdependence structure are defined by the outcome and control distributions that exist among the involved parties. People have preferences over both who can gain (and how much can be gained) in any given situation and who can determine the actual outcomes (and to what degree). Thus a theory of social values should incorporate people's preferences over control.

Second, any deliberate behavior in interdependence situations is mediated by people's knowledge or interpretation of the situation. This knowledge is based on information that the individual collects in a given situation, inferences he or she makes from this information, and information that the individual already possesses about the social world.

Third, there is a strong linkage between people's preferences and information seeking, subjective representations of the situation, and general beliefs about others and the social world.

In general, the empirical results presented in this chapter strongly support these theoretical ideas. We found that interpersonal differences in preferences for both outcome and control distribution produce differences in individuals' cognitive functioning and behavior. The present results do not always create a clear and consistent picture of the relationships among the specific preferences, cognitive processes, implicit social knowledge, and behavior. However, they show that these variables are strongly interrelated. The nature of these interrelationships must be investigated in future research.

We have demonstrated the various effects of differences in preferences. In most cases the findings did not permit straightforward causal interpretations. We have emphasized the preferential aspects of choice behavior under interdependence. However, the chapter does not provide any answer to the basic question about what comes first: preferences or cognitive processes (cf. Zajonc, 1980). As a matter of fact we believe that at the general level of analysis presented in this chapter, the relationship between preferences and cognitive processes is not one-directional. We have shown that people's information seeking greatly depends on the system of preferences they already possess. On the other hand, the individual's environment may influence the development of his or her view of the social world so as either to strengthen or call into question (and possibly modify) the individual's value system.

Findings reported in the chapter were mainly limited to simple cognitive and behavioral correlates of single preference dimensions. They did not show the interactions among preference dimensions in their full complexity. However, it seems that progress in exploring interdependence will require clarification of basic concepts and improvement in our measurement techniques. More precise definitions of preferential space and methods to measure a variety of possible configurations of preferences are needed. Eventually, we should be able to define individual's preferences by their location in a multidimensional space of preferences.

The findings showing that people's behavior correlates with the subjective representation of social interdependence and subjective evaluation of outcomes may substantially change the way we try to answer questions about people's rationality and cooperation. In order to evaluate people's rationality we have to know not only what are the subjective values of outcomes but also how they perceive these outcomes and what they expect from their partners. The assumptions made in game theory that partners are alike and perfectly rational are incorrect. We have shown that decision makers may have different views of partners, depending on their preferences. If so, what seems irrational to an external observer may in fact be rational if we relate the individual's behavior to what he or she knows about the situation. In addition, an individual's subjective representation and preferences may change over time within the same interaction as new information about the partner or structure of the situation becomes available. Thus, if we relate rationality to the logical analysis of subjective reasons for behavior rather than to external standards of rationality (e.g., as proposed by normative theories of decision making) we have to investigate carefully people's preferences, their subjective representations, and their dynamics.

The same issue may be raised about cooperation. It may, for example, happen that we interpret someone's behavior as being competitive even though he or she is cooperative, at least in terms of conscious intentions. This person might simply misperceive the structure of interdependence and hurt others when in fact he or she wants to help. Is he then a cooperative or an aggressive person? The answer always depends on our theoretical perspective. The person is aggressive in terms of what he or she really did to other people. The person is cooperative if we think only in terms of his subjective representation and intentions. He may be either cooperative or aggressive in terms of his structure of preferences measured independently from the analyzed situation.

In this chapter we discussed preferences and some aspects of cognitive processes underlying behavior in interdependence situations. It should be mentioned that our approach can also be extended to the analysis of other types of behavior, including helping behavior. As we pointed out in the first chapter of this book, differences between cooperation and helping behavior are not substantial in most cases. Helping behavior is also influenced by one's system of preferences and the subjective representation of the other person as well as by the entire social situation. However, a detailed discussion of the issue lies beyond the scope of this chapter.

Acknowledgments

I would like to thank Z. Czwartosz (University of Warsaw), V. J. Derlega (Old Dominion University, Norfolk, Virginia), G. Wieczorkowska (University of Warsaw), my group of master's students at the University of Warsaw, and W. Colson (Norfolk State University), for their very stimulating discussions. Special acknowledgment is due to V. J. Derlega for his help in editing the chapter. The final draft of the chapter was written during my visit at Old Dominion University in the spring of 1980. I wish to thank my colleagues in the Psychology Department at Old Dominion University, and particularly Raymond Kirby, for arranging my visit and providing access to office and computer facilities.

References

Adams, J. S. Inequity in social exchange. In L. Berkowitz (Ed.), *Advances in social psychology* (Vol. 2). New York: Academic Press, 1965.

Adler, A. *The science of living.* Greenberg, 1929.

Altman, I. *The environment and social behavior.* Monterey, Calif.: Brooks/Cole, 1975.

Brehm, J. W. *Responses to loss of freedom: A theory of psychological reactance.* Morristown, N.J.: General Learning Press, 1972.

Christie, R., & Geis, F. (Eds.), *Studies in Machiavellianism.* New York: Academic Press, 1970.

Codol, J. P. Contre l' hypothèse du triangle. *Cahiers de Psychologie,* 1976, *19,* 381–394.

de Charms, R. *Personal causation: The internal affective determinants of behavior.* New York: Academic Press, 1968.

Derlega, V. J., & Chaikin, A. L. Privacy and self-disclosure in social relationships. *Journal of Social Issues,* 1977, *33,* 102–115.

de Zeeuw, G., & Wagenaar, W. A. Czy prawdopodobienstwa subiektywne sa prawdopodobienstwami? (What is subjective probability?), *Prakseologia,* 1974, *3–4,* 227–261.

Endler, N. S., & Magnusson, D. Toward an interactional psychology of personality. *Psychological Bulletin,* 1976, *83,* 956–974.

Grzelak, J. L. Game theory and its applicability to the description of prosocial behavior. *Polish Psychological Bulletin,* 1976, *7,* 197–203.

Grzelak, J. L. *Konflikt interesow. (Conflict of interests.)* Warsaw: Państwowe Wydawnictwo Naukowe, 1978.

Grzelak, J. L. Social interdependence: Do we know what we want to know? Unpublished manuscript, University of Warsaw, 1980.

Grzelak, J. L., Iwinski, T. B., & Radzicki, J. J. Motivational components of utility. In H. Jungermann & G. de Zeeuw (Eds.), *Decision making and change in human affairs.* Dordrecht, Netherlands: D. Reidel Publishing Company, 1977.

Kelley, H. H., & Stahelski, A. J. The inference of intentions from moves in prisoner's dilemma game. *Journal of Experimental Social Psychology*, 1970, *6*, 401–419.

Kelley, H. M., & Thibaut, J. W. *Interpersonal relations: A theory of interdependence*. New York: Wiley, 1978.

Kozielecki, J. *Psychologiczna teoria decyzji. (Psychological theory of decision making.)* Warsaw: PWN, 1975.

Kranas, G. *Utility, subjective probability and liking in interdependence situations*. Unpublished doctoral dissertation, University of Warsaw, 1977.

MacCrimmon, K., & Messick, D. Framework of social motives. *Behavioral Science*, 1976, *21*, 86–100.

Magnusson, D., & Endler, N. S. Interactional psychology: Present status and future prospects. In D. Magnusson & N. S. Endler (Eds.), *Personality at the cross-roads*. New York: Wiley, 1977.

McClintock, C. Social motivations in settings of outcome interdependence. In D. Druckerman (Ed.), *Negotiations: Social psychological perspectives*. Beverly Hills, Calif.: Sage, 1977.

McClintock, C., & McNeel, S. Prior dyadic experience and monetary rewards as determinants of cooperative and competitive game behavior. *Journal of Personality and Social Psychology*, 1967, *5*, 282–294.

Messick, D., & Thorngate, W. B. Relative gain maximization in experimental games. *Journal of Experimental Social Psychology*, 1967, *3*, 85–101.

Mischel, W. Toward a cognitive social learning reconceptualization of personality. *Psychological Review*, 1973, *80*, 252–283.

Pruitt, D. G. Motivational processes in the decomposed prisoner's dilemma game. *Journal of Personality and Social Psychology*, 1970, *14*, 227–238.

Radzicki, J. A. Technique of conjoint measurement of subjective value of own and other's gains. *Polish Psychological Bulletin*, 1976, *7*, 143–152.

Tyszka, T., & Grzelak, J. L. Criteria and mechanisms of choice behavior in *n*-person games. *Journal of Conflict Resolution*, 1976, *20*, 357–376.

von Neumann, J., & Morgenstern, *Theory of games and economic behavior* (3rd ed.). New York: Wiley, 1953.

White, R. W. Motivation reconsidered: The concept of competence. *Psychological Review*, 1959, *66*, 297–323.

Wieczorkowska, G. *Formal analysis of preferences*. Unpublished manuscript prepared in collaboration with G. Majcher. University of Warsaw, 1979.

Zajonc, R. B. Feeling and thinking: Preferences need no inferences. *American Psychologist*, 1980, *35*, 151–175.

Chapter 6

The Effects of

Intergroup Competition

and Cooperation on

Intragroup and

Intergroup Relationships

JACOB M. RABBIE[1]

In comparison with the enormous amount of research on the small group (McGrath & Altman, 1966), the experimental research on intergroup relations is relatively sparse. In a recent review of the literature on intergroup relations (Brewer, 1979), fewer than 70 references are mentioned, and about 50 of these are experimental studies that were conducted in the last decade. One of the reasons for experimental social psychologists' neglect of this area may be that it is very difficult to create intergroup relations in the laboratory (Gerard & Miller, 1967). Because of the complexities of the interaction processes in small groups, there has been an inclination to consider social groups relatively closed social systems (Katz & Kahn, 1978). Incorporating transactions with the environment, and especially with other groups, would complicate the research paradigm considerably. Intergroup research is also more costly in terms of both time and money, for groups instead of individuals have to be used as the unit of statistical analysis. Perhaps the most

[1] This chapter is based on earlier reviews (Rabbie, 1974a, 1974b, 1979a, 1979b). Most of the studies reported in this paper were supported by the Netherlands Organization for the Advancement of Pure Research (ZWO), grant 57-7.

important reason for the slow development of this area of research has been the absence of an integrated theory. Intergroup relations can be studied at various levels of analysis: at the intraindividual, interpersonal, intergroup, organizational, and societal levels (Deutsch, 1973; Doise, 1978; Rabbie, 1979a; Rabbie, Visser, & van Oostrum, 1978). Intergroup research introduces the problems of what level of analysis should be used to study phenomena and how the various levels relate to each other (Kelman, 1965).

Although the literature offers a number of hypotheses about intergroup relations, these hypotheses do not form an integrated theory. They are usually stated at one particular level of analysis, they are sometimes contradictory, and their supporting evidence varies widely. This unfortunate state of affairs is clearly documented in a review by Rosenblatt (1964), which offers an inventory of propositions dealing with the origins and consequences of ethnocentrism, nationalism, and other forms of intergroup behavior in which the own group is deemed superior to other groups. A more recent review of the literature on conflict and cohesion (Stein, 1976) conveys the same impression of friction and lack of integration.

Social psychology has been criticized for being too individualistic in its approach to social behavior (Billig, 1976; Steiner, 1974; Tajfel, 1972). The experimental study of intergroup relations cannot be exempted from this criticism. Large-scale social conflicts such as war and racial disturbances are often interpreted in terms of individual frustrations and personal aggressive reactions (Berkowitz, 1962, 1972). Ethnocentrism, racial prejudice and intergroup hostility are similarly viewed as symptomatic expressions of a deeply rooted authoritarian personality (Adorno, Frenkel-Brunswik, Levinson, & Sanford, 1950). In these approaches the irrational, expressive origins of intergroup relations are emphasized, and little attention is given to the instrumental conflicts in which one group competes with another group to achieve valued goals (Coser, 1956; Levine & Campbell, 1972). Likewise, the phenomenon of national socialist Germany that spawned a generation of authoritarian citizens is ignored by an idiographic search for discriminating personality variables among individuals with high F-scale scores.

The individualistic orientation in theory and research is prevalent among other approaches within experimental social psychology as well. Most current research on social conflict is based on the game behavior of isolated individuals, and the findings are then extrapolated to conflicts among groups (Nemeth, 1972; Rabbie, 1974a). Even those researchers who have been sharply critical of the individualistic approach to intergroup relations (Billig, 1973; Billig & Tajfel, 1973; Tajfel, 1978; Tajfel, Billig, Bundy, & Flament, 1971) have focused their empirical work on intraindividual processes.

Kurt Lewin (1948) and Muzafer Sherif (e.g., Sherif & Sherif, 1969) were among the first social psychologists to try to rectify the balance between the individualistic and social approaches to intergroup behavior. Sherif has argued that intergroup relations should be studied at their own level of analysis, and to that end he has devised an appropriate research strategy. In his classic boys' camp experiment, groups were brought into competition with one another and during the intergroup conflict a number of changes within and between the groups were observed (Sherif, Harvey, White, Mood, & Sherif, 1961). In this way Sherif was able to show that the ingroup attraction and outgroup hostility in these experiments could be attributed mainly to the actual intergroup conflict rather than to deep-seated individual frustrations or other intrapersonal dynamics. One of the few attempts to replicate this study was that of Diab (1970), a Lebanese social psychologist at the American University of Beirut. Diab's experiment had some frightening consequences for the subjects as well as for the researcher, who had to be hospitalized for exhaustion after the experiment was abruptly terminated. He had been too successful in arousing intergroup hostility. The conflict got completely out of hand; some boys knifed each other and the police had to evacuate the camp to prevent further violence (L. N. Diab, personal communication, 1965).

This incident not only illustrates the occupational hazards for subjects and research workers in this area but also highlights the strength of the intergroup conflict that can be attained in a field situation, an intensity that can rarely be found in the confines of the conventional laboratory. Blake and Mouton (1961) and Bass and Duntemann (1963) are among the few researchers in the United States who have extended Sherif's work. Probably because of their background as organizational consultants they became impressed with the wide-ranging effects of intergroup conflict in industrial organizations and used training exercises with managers of industrial firms in order to give them experientially based insights into the origins and effects of intergroup conflict. In these exercises groups of managers were put into competition with each other, and during the intergroup conflict a number of predictable phenomena occurred within and between the groups involved. The findings of Blake and Mouton (1961) can be briefly summarized as follows: Within the groups the members close ranks; there is an increase in group cohesiveness and solidarity; the own group and its product are considered to be superior to the other group and its product; each group becomes more hierarchically organized; there is a greater willingness to accept centralized leadership; deviating opinions are barely tolerated; the group demands more loyalty and conformity from its members; there is more emphasis on the task than on the social–emotional relationships among members. Between the groups negative stereotypes tend to develop; communication between the groups decreases, preventing the correction of negative stereotypes; during intergroup negotiations, members pay more attention to points of disagreement than they do to agreement; distrust and hostility toward the other group rises, sometimes erupting into open aggression; tactics and strategy for winning are emphasized at the expense of concern about the merits of the problem to be negotiated.

These experiments have been very important in the social psychology of social conflict. They demonstrate that hostile attitudes and prejudices against other groups do not develop only as a consequence of deeply rooted frustration, aggression, or an authoritarian personality structure, but may occur as a consequence of realistic conflicts between groups. It should be noted that Sherif's view of realistic conflicts does not always involve an opposition of "material and objective interests" as is sometimes suggested (Brown, 1978, p. 106; Turner, 1978, p. 235). Sherif (1966) makes it clear that groups may compete about both material and nonmaterial interests; "the issues at stake" he reminds us "may relate to values and goals shared by group members, a real or imagined threat to the safety of the group, an economic interest, a political advantage, a military consideration, prestige, or a number of others [Sherif, 1966, p. 15]."

From a methodological point of view, the experiments of Sherif (1966) and Blake and Mouton (1961) leave much to be desired. In these before-and-after studies, highly cohesive groups were brought into competition with each other and observations were made of the processes that developed within and between these groups. In the final stages of Sherif's study (Sherif et al., 1961), compatible or "superordinate goals" were introduced to examine the effects of intergroup cooperation. Anticipated or actual intergroup competition or cooperation were not varied independently of one another. It is very difficult to assess whether the dramatic effects they obtained can be attributed to one or another of the following factors:

1. The classification of individuals into distinct groups
2. The experience of sharing a common interdependence of fate with other members in the group
3. Anticipated or actual intragroup interaction
4. The compatibility or incompatibility of the goals of the group, that is, anticipation of competing or cooperating with each other
5. The mutually frustrating intergroup interaction during the actual intergroup competition
6. The anticipated or actual experience of having won over or lost to the other group

Each of these factors alone or in combination could have accounted for Sherif's results. In the absence of appropriate controls, this design can be characterized as a preexperimental design (Campbell & Stanley, 1966), one that leaves too much room for alternative interpretations.

Taking Sherif's work as the point of departure, we have tried in the course of our own research over the past 15 years to make a systematic examination of the contribution of each of these factors in order to arrive at a better understanding of group processes in intergroup competition and cooperation.

In our first series of studies we attempted to specify the minimal conditions under which an evaluative bias would occur, that is, a tendency to evaluate the ingroup more positively than the outgroup. Our main problem was to discover whether the random classification of individuals into distinct groups—without any social interaction between them—would be sufficient to induce a sense of belongingness or "we-feeling" in the groups, leading to an evaluative bias in favor of the own group, or whether it would be necessary to induce an additional common group fate (Lewin, 1948) to produce this bias. The results of this research will be summarized in the next section of this chapter.

The findings of Sherif (1966) and Blake and Mouton (1961) can be attributed to intragroup and intergroup processes. In an effort to exclude the consequences of actual intergroup interaction, a second series of studies was conducted in which groups anticipated having to compete or to cooperate with each other. By asking subjects to rate their own and the other group on various attributes before and after they had the opportunity to work together, it was possible to determine the effects of expected versus actual intragroup interaction on the bias in favor of the own group.

In a third series of experiments actual intergroup interaction was introduced, enabling us to examine the effects of mutual frustration during the intragroup competition and the effects of winning and losing from another group. A comparison between the second and third series of experiments should give some indication of whether the anticipation of intergroup competition or cooperation is sufficient to elicit the effects found by Sherif (1966) and Blake and Mouton (1961) or whether actual intergroup interaction is a necessary condition. The results of this comparison will be discussed in the second major section of this chapter.

In combination with intergroup competition and cooperation manipulations, a variety of other variables were empirically analyzed in this research program: for example, the presence or absence of intragroup conflict (Rabbie & Huygen, 1974; Rabbie & Visser, 1976); the bargaining strength of the parties (Rabbie, Benoist, Oosterban, & Visser, 1974; Rabbie & Visser, 1972); the opportunity to monitor each other's discussions during the intergroup conflict (Visser, 1974); the time perspective of the groups (van Oostrum, 1977); the motivational orientation and counterstrategy of the groups (Rabbie, Visser, & van Oostrum, 1975); the size of the groups involved (Rabbie, Visser, & van Oostrum, 1978); the organizational context in which the intergroup conflict occurs (Rabbie & van Oostrum, 1977; Rabbie, Visser, & Vernooij, 1976; van der Linden & Rabbie, 1976); the capability to deliver noxious stimulation to the other party (Rabbie, 1980); the influence of the constituency (Rabbie & de Brey, 1971; Rabbie & van Oostrum, 1977; Visser, 1975); and the tenure of power of the leader in the group (Bekkers, 1977; Rabbie & Bekkers, 1976; Rabbie & Bekkers, 1978). Since it is impossible to discuss these experiments in any detail, a selection had to be made.[2] In the third section of this chapter the question is raised whether the absence or active involvement of constituencies in intergroup negotiations facilitates or hinders the resolution of intergroup conflict. The fourth section presents research that suggests leaders who feel uncertain of their tenure of power are more likely to engage in intergroup competition than those who feel certain of their leadership positions. Finally, in the discussion section the body of results generated by our research program will be briefly summarized and evaluated.

Intergroup Bias in Minimal Groups

Sherif has asserted that intergroup bias (the tendency to have a more positive attitude about the ingroup than about the outgroup) occurs under a very complex set of circumstances. In his view the groups involved should have all the attributes commonly ascribed to well developed social groups, for example, awareness of group membership; social interaction among group members; role and status relationships; and shared values and norms that regulate the attitudes and behavior of the members, including those directed toward the in and outgroup (Sherif & Sherif, 1969). There is little doubt that under all these conditions the intergroup bias will occur. However, the question is whether all these conditions are necessary to produce the bias. The presence or absence of social interaction in the group appears to be of special importance, since it is through social interaction that these various attributes may develop.

In a number of studies (Rabbie, 1979a) we have dealt with the issue of whether an intergroup bias would occur in "minimal groups," or social categories in which the members have no opportunity to interact with each other. Specifically, we wondered whether the experience of being classified as a distinct group by a prestigious authority would be sufficient to induce a sense of group belongingness or "we-feeling" leading to an intergroup

---

[2] A more extensive review of these studies can be found in Rabbie, 1979a.

bias or whether the bias would require the introduction of an additional "interdependence of fate" (Lewin, 1948) or a "common predicament" (Sherif, 1966). In these experiments, an interdependence of fate was created by rewarding or depriving individuals, not because of their individual merits, previous performance, esthetic preferences or any other preexisting ingroup identification, but solely on the basis of their membership in an arbitrary social category. Typically, these minimal groups had a competitive relationship with each other: their fates were "contriently interdependent" (Deutsch, 1973), since a gain by one group always implied a loss by the other. The common fate of one group implied a differential fate for the other group.

All studies were modeled after the first experiment in this series (Rabbie & Horwitz, 1969). Subjects in these experiments were randomly divided into two distinct groups: a "blue" and a "green" group. The two groups were asked, respectively, to write with blue or green pens on blue or green paper and were always addressed by the experimenter as the "green" or "blue" group. A differential common fate was introduced by rewarding or depriving the members of these "minimal" groups on the basis of chance, the arbitrary decision of the experimenter, or the alleged decision of one of the groups. In a control condition, subjects were categorized into two distinct groups but their other experiences remained identical, since they were not rewarded or deprived by virtue of their membership. Under the guise of studying first impressions, the experimenter requested subjects to rate the groups and their members on a variety of attributes scaled along a favorable–unfavorable dimension.

The main finding was that a chance win or loss was sufficient to produce intergroup bias. In the control condition no significant intergroup bias was obtained, which led to the conclusion that "group classification *per se* appears to be insufficient to produce discriminatory evaluations [Rabbie & Horwitz, 1969, p. 272]."

In retrospect this conclusion was premature because with additional subjects in the control condition, evidence of intergroup bias was found on items referring to feelings of group belongingness (Rabbie, 1979a). (Comparable findings were obtained in similar control conditions in later studies.) This new evidence was rather damaging to our ad hoc explanation of the original findings of no intergroup bias in the control condition. In view of these and other results it has been suggested that Heider's (1958) balance theory provides the most parsimonious explanation for the finding that members become attached to the social unit of which they perceive themselves to be a part (Rabbie, 1979a; Rabbie & Visser, 1976; Rabbie & Wilkens, 1971). According to this theory, perception of cognitive unity and sentiments about a unit tend toward a balanced state. Perceptions of cognitive unity with the ingroup members rather than with outgroup members generates more positive sentiments about the ingroup and its members than about the outgroup and its members. The experiments that followed were designed to specify the unit-forming factors that may contribute to intergroup bias. For example, members of minimal groups were rewarded with or deprived of a large or a small reward, threatened by a strong or a weak electric shock, rewarded or deprived independently of each other or at each other's expense, and informed they would or would not interact with their own or the other group. Finally, subjects were rewarded or deprived on an individual rather than on a group basis. The results of these experiments justified the conclusion "that the random division of individuals in two distinct groups by a prestigious authority providing them with arbitrary names and labels seems sufficient to produce perceptions of belongingness to a 'we' rather than to a 'they' group, triggering responses that lead to more positive evaluation of ingroup members than of outgroup members [Rabbie, 1979a, p. 28]."

Intergroup Competition and Cooperation

In the previous experiments (Rabbie, 1979a), intergroup bias could be demonstrated in groups that lacked the usual attributes required by Sherif and Sherif (1969); for example, intragroup interaction was minimized in these experiments. Sherif further suggested that mutually incompatible goals between groups is a "sufficient condition for the rise of hostile attitudes and deeds toward another group [Sherif, 1968, p. 49]." This assertion raises the question whether the incompatibility of the goals of the group, that is, the anticipation of competing with another group, is sufficient to reproduce all the findings of Sherif (1966) and Blake and Mouton (1961).

A second series of experiments was designed to study the effects of group goal incompatibility per se. In the first study of this series (Rabbie & Wilkens, 1971), groups expected to be either rewarded or not rewarded independently of each other or as a result of direct competition with each other. In the remaining studies, the groups prepared themselves for negotiations with another group that never materialized. All of these experiments excluded any possible effects of intergroup interaction or of the actual experience of winning and losing. Because the mere expectation to compete or to cooperate might not be sufficient to produce a strong enough contrast between the competitive and cooperative groups (Rabbie, 1974a; Rabbie, 1974b), actual intergroup competition and cooperation was introduced. In these studies the groups were able to help or hinder each other in the achievement of their goals; thus, they could win or lose from each other.

Two types of studies were conducted, one of which was closely modeled after the previous experiments. Groups prepared themselves for intergroup negotiations and were instructed to compete or to cooperate with another group through actual negotiations of appointed representatives. In other experiments the *prisoner's dilemma game* (PDG) and other mixed-motive games were used to study the effects of actual intergroup interaction. Contrary to the current individualistic tradition in the social psychology of conflict, the game was played by groups instead of individuals.[3] Each group made a collective decision about each choice. Cooperative or competitive orientations were induced either by instruction or by confronting each group with a tough, "competitive" or a soft, "cooperative" strategy.

In the following sections we will first discuss the effects of expected versus actual *intra*group interaction on intergroup bias. Then we will make a comparison between the effects of expected and actual *inter*group interaction.

Expected versus Actual Intragroup Interaction

Anticipated or actual social interaction is an important unit-forming factor (Heider, 1958). In the following experiment it was predicted "that in addition to other unit-forming factors such as physical proximity, common labels, etc. . . . , the anticipation of future interaction in the group would enhance the perception of a cognitive unity with oneself and the group and hence would lead to an increase in ingroup belongingness and consequently to ingroup–outgroup differentiation [Rabbie & Wilkens, 1971, p. 217]." A comparison of subjects who did or did not expect to work with group members on a construction task corroborated this hypothesis. In each of the following experiments (Rabbie, Benoist, Oosterbaan, & Visser, 1974; Rabbie & de Brey, 1971; Rabbie & Huygen, 1974; Rabbie & Visser, 1976), subjects who expected to work together were asked to rate their own and the other group members *after* they were categorized as distinct groups but *before* they actually worked with each other. The results were very clear: Subjects classified into two distinct groups and expecting to work with each other showed a significant bias in favor of the own group. As can be expected, cooperative processes during the actual intragroup interaction invariably increased the intergroup bias (Deutsch, 1973; Homans, 1950). The increased bias, moreover, can be attributed to an enhancement of the ingroup evaluation rather than to a devaluation of the outgroup. Other studies have obtained similar results (Dion, 1973; Reyen & Kahn, 1975; Stephenson, Skinner, & Brotherton, 1976; Worchel, Lind, & Kaufman, 1975).

---

[3] A systematic comparison between the game behavior of individuals and groups indicates that groups and individuals handle conflicts in different ways (Rabbie, Visser, & van Oostrum, 1978).

Actual interaction within the group thus appears to operate as a stronger unit-forming factor than expected interaction.

Expected versus Actual Intergroup Interaction

INTERGROUP COMPETITION AND INGROUP COHESION

One of the main themes of Sherif (1966) and Blake and Mouton (1961) is that intergroup competition produces an increase in ingroup cohesion or solidarity. Various explanations have been proposed to account for this effect (Bramel, 1969). Perhaps the most important one is that intergroup competition provides the group with a simple operational objective: the superordinate goal of winning from the other group, which overrides possible interpersonal animosities in the group (Boulding, 1962). There is much less support for this popular hypothesis in "realistic conflict theory" (LeVine & Campbell, 1972) than one would expect.

Indeed, our own studies show that groups that expect to compete do not exhibit a greater ingroup cohesion than groups that do not expect to compete (Rabbie & Wilkens, 1971) or than groups that expect to cooperate (Rabbie et al., 1974a,b; Rabbie & Visser, 1976). In one instance (Rabbie & de Brey, 1971), a slight tendency in the opposite direction was found; cooperative groups felt more positive about themselves than competitive groups. The expectation of intergroup competition per se does not appear to produce greater solidarity than the expectation of intergroup cooperation.

Coser (1956) has suggested that if a group expects to lose, intergroup competition may lead to disruption rather than cohesion. This effect was witnessed during the period when the Vietnam war dragged on without a decisive military victory in sight for the United States of America. An increase in divisiveness and disunity occurred first among that nation's youth but then spread through many sectors of American life.

To test Coser's hypothesis, a labor–management simulation was conducted (Rabbie et al., 1974a,b) in which groups had either strong or weak bargaining positions. It was found that groups with strong bargaining positions were more cohesive when they were instructed to prepare for competition than for cooperation, but that groups with weak bargaining positions were less cohesive when they were instructed to compete than to cooperate.

In the competitive context of labor union negotiations, unions with a stronger bargaining position were able to get more out of the management group in which they are instructed to compete rather than to cooperate with each other. Instructions to cooperate prevented them from taking full advantage of their stronger bargaining position vis-à-vis the other party. If the union teams had a weak bargaining position they were likely to gain more for themselves when they were expected to cooperate rather than to compete with each other. Competition would lead to a certain loss, whereas the instructions to cooperate prevented the management group from taking full advantage of their greater bargaining power. Thus, it is not the expectation of either competition or cooperation as such but the likely advantage to the group of either form of intergroup interaction that determines ingroup cohesion.

The foregoing conclusion is supported by studies in which actual intergroup competition and cooperation is introduced. Competitive intergroup competition produces sometimes more (Rabbie & van Oostrum, 1977), sometimes less (Rabbie et al., 1975; Visser, 1974) or sometimes about the same degree of cohesiveness (Visser, 1975) as intergroup cooperation. The crucial factor in producing more cohesiveness in all these studies seems to be whether the group members view themselves as achieving the goals they have set for themselves, whether in a cooperative or a competitive relationship with another group (Cartwright, 1968).

INGROUP COHESION AND OUTGROUP HOSTILITY

It is a common notion that ingroup cohesion is accompanied by outgroup hostility. According to Sumner (1906), "The relation of comradeship and peace in the we-group and that of hostility and war toward other groups are correlative to each other [p. 12]." However, in all our studies positive rather than negative correlations are found between the ingroup and outgroup ratings, although these correlations are not always statistically significant (Rabbie & de Brey, 1971; Rabbie & Wilkens, 1971; Rabbie et al., 1974a,b). Generally these correlations are slightly higher among cooperative than among competitive groups. Other researchers have obtained similar findings (Wilson, 1971; Wilson & Miller, 1961). These results are obtained not only in the laboratory. In a recent survey among ethnic groups in East Africa, no consistent relations could be found between self-regard indices of ethnocentrism and the perceived social distance toward the outgroups (Brewer & Campbell, 1976). At least for laboratory groups it appears that when little or no information is available about the other group, the experiences in the ingroup seem to be used as a frame of reference to evaluate the outgroup.

As noted earlier, Sherif has asserted that group goal incompatibility is sufficient to generate outgroup hostility. In this view, groups that expect to compete, that is, whose goals are incompatible with each other, should show more negative attitudes toward the outgroup than groups that expect to cooperate. There is little support for this hypothesis. Although the results are in the predicted direction, no significant differences could be obtained between the outgroup ratings of groups that expected to compete or not to compete (Rabbie & Wilkens, 1969) or groups that expected to compete or to cooperate (Rabbie & de Brey, 1971). Only in a labor–management simulation study in which the conflict was unusually intense did competitive groups express more hostile feelings toward the other group and expect more hostility from the outgroup toward themselves than cooperative groups did. It is possible that these findings reflect the actual state of affairs that obtained in the Netherlands between labor and management at the time the experiment was conducted. Our student subjects strongly identified with the union roles they had to play, thus enacted them with a vigor uncharacteristic for experimental subjects.

Where the parties have the opportunity to help or hinder each other in an active way to their goals, intergroup competition invariably produces more negative attitudes than intergroup cooperation (Rabbie & van Oostrum, 1977; Rabbie et al., 1975; van Oostrum, 1977; Visser, 1974; Visser, 1975). These results call into question the notion that group goal incompatibility per se is sufficient to generate negative attitudes toward other groups unless the intergroup conflict is quite intense. There is strong support for the hypothesis that actual interference with goal-directed activities among competitive groups creates more outgroup hostility than intergroup cooperation in which the groups help each other to attain their goals.

OVEREVALUATION OF GROUP PRODUCT

It has often been found that competitive groups have a more favorable attitude toward the products of their own group than toward those of other groups (Ferguson & Kelley, 1964). Our studies reveal a more differentiated picture. When groups have little or no information about their own and the other group, there is a slight tendency to overestimate the expected performance of the other group relative to one's own. It is only when they have completed the group product and are asked to evaluate both group products that the characteristic overevaluation of the own group product occurs (Rabbie & de Brey, 1971).

We also did not find an overevaluation of the completed product of the own group where groups were awaiting the judgment of independent observers who had to decide about the quality of the group product (Rabbie & Wilkens, 1971). A possible explanation is that competitive groups seem to protect themselves against the possibility that they will perform more poorly than the other group or will be judged by independent observers as not having done as well as the other group. By rating the other group slightly higher at the beginning of the intergroup contest they protect themselves against a possible failure. It is no shame to lose a better adversary, and victory tastes sweeter when it is won over a stronger opponent. After the product has been completed, all members are then responsible for it—

they share in its success or in the blame for its inadequacy. At this time they really "own" the product, and the liking of the group should lead to a liking for its product (Ferguson & Kelley, 1964; Heider, 1958).

Actual intergroup competition introduces the possibility that one group may win or lose from another group. Obviously winning groups have a more positive attitude about their group product than losing groups, although there is considerable reluctance on the part of the losing group to accept the reality that their own product is in fact inferior to that of the other group (Visser, 1975).

CENTRALIZATION OF LEADERSHIP

Groups have been found likely to accept strong and centralized leadership in the face of intergroup competition (Mulder & Stemerding, 1963), as was seen in Rome when a dictator was appointed in reaction to an imminent war. Simmel (1964) believes that in times of war a dictatorship is the best way to mobilize the energy of the group. Coser (1956) is doubtful of this proposition and suggests that strong leadership is needed when the ingroup cohesion is weak and when the execution of the intergroup competition requires a great deal of coordination and role differentiation. In our studies the degree of centralization that characterized a leadership hierarchy was operationalized by a modified version of Tannenbaum's "control graph" (1968). The greater the difference between the influence attributed to the low and the high influence person, the more hierarchical the leadership structure. In general, expected intergroup competition does not produce a more hierarchical leadership than does a cooperative orientation (Rabbie & de Brey, 1971; Rabbie & Visser, 1976). It was only when we used a construction task that required a great deal of coordination on the part of the most influential person that a more hierarchical leadership structure appeared in groups that operated competitively with each other rather than independently of each other—that is, where one group's success or failure was not contingent on that of the other group (Rabbie & Wilkens, 1971).

One explanation for these disappointing results might be that the mere expectation to compete or to cooperate does not generate sufficient pressure among competitive groups to accept more centralized leadership. Another possibility is that our control graph measure is not sensitive enough to detect differences in the influence distribution among groups that are expected to compete or to cooperate with each other.

Both notions receive some support. As indicated by the control graph measure of the degree to which influence was hierarchical, actual intergroup competition did not lead to a greater centralization of leadership than actual intergroup cooperation in three studies (van Oostrum, 1977; Rabbie et al., 1975; Visser, 1975). However, in two of these studies members of competitive groups reported a greater "willingness to accept more centralized leadership" than members of cooperative groups. Although there might be a greater willingness to accept more centralized leadership among competitive than among cooperative groups, such willingness would not necessarily lead to differential attributions of influence in these laboratory groups.

TASK AND CONFORMITY PRESSURES

According to Blake and Mouton (1961), competitive groups focus on the task at the expense of the social–emotional relationships within the group. Presumably social and emotional issues are suppressed because they detract from the primary task facing the group: to defeat the common enemy. Since intergroup competition requires a unified effort by all the members, there is strong pressure toward conformity and little tolerance of deviating opinions.

The support for this hypothesis is rather weak. In two studies (Rabbie & de Brey, 1971; Rabbie & Visser, 1976) no greater task and conformity pressures were reported in groups that expected to compete than in those that expected to cooperate with one another. However, in one study (Rabbie & Visser, 1976) it was found that competitive groups had a more negative attitude toward a deviating subgroup than did cooperative groups. This finding may reflect a lower tolerance among competitive groups for deviant opinions in the group. In the same study, competitive groups showed a greater reluctance to inform the opposing party about the internal dissension in the group than did cooperative groups. Apparently, there is a stronger pressure among competitive groups to form a "united front" against an opponent than there is among cooperative groups. Some support for the hypothesis was found in a labor–management simulation study in which the competition was unusually intense. Subjects in the competition condition reported greater pressures to conform and were somewhat less motivated "to create a relaxed atmosphere" in the group than subjects in the cooperation condition (Rabbie et al., 1974).

Members engaged in actual intergroup competition did not report greater task and conformity pressures than members who cooperated with other groups (Rabbie & van Oostrum, 1977; Rabbie et al., 1975; van Oostrum, 1977). In the first of several studies, both cooperative and competitive groups characterized the atmosphere in the group as more "relaxed" than members of individualistic groups. Presumably, members of cooperative and competitive groups could simply follow the instructions given them. They did not have to take the actions of the other party into account. Therefore, they might have been less tense than the individualistic groups, who had to decide each time what the most appropriate strategy would be in order to gain as much as possible for themselves.

Although there are some indications that competitive groups may have experienced greater task and conformity pressures than cooperative groups, the evidence is minimal. Part of our problem might have been that the subjects found it very difficult to admit that these kinds of pressures were being exerted on them. The scores on the items that were designed to measure these pressures were very low indeed. On the other hand, it should be noted that the cooperative groups were often just as motivated to do a good job and to perform the task as were the competitive groups.

WINNING AND LOSING

It was suggested earlier that intergroup competition may lead to internal disruption instead of cohesion when the members expect to lose rather than to win from another group (Coser, 1956). When their stronger bargaining position led competitive groups to expect to win, they showed greater in-group cohesion than when their weak bargaining position created an expectation of probable loss (Rabbie et al., 1974).

Actual experiences of winning and losing produced similar results. In an organization simulation study (Rabbie & van Oostrum, 1977) one department achieved better results than another. Consistent with the findings of Blake and Mouton (1961) and Bass and Duntemann (1963), winners showed a greater cohesiveness and task satisfaction than did losers. Moreover, the winners described the other group as less cohesive and less competitively motivated than was true in the losers' description of the winners. Generally there was a greater intergroup bias among the winning than losing groups, but this greater bias among the winners can be attributed more to an enhancement of the ingroup evaluation than to a downgrading of the losers.

It has been argued that cohesiveness and attraction among individuals will be greater for winners than for losers the more the win or loss can be attributed to internal rather than to external sources (Lott & Lott, 1965; Weiner, 1972). There is some support for this hypothesis. In an organizational simulation study, we varied systematically the management regimes of the "firms." In a "democratic" condition, the departments could exert a great deal of influence on the managerial decisions by the coordinator that affected the outcomes of the departments. In an "autocratic" condition, the coordinator had the final say in determining departments' outcomes. As compared with autocratic departments, the democratic departments could attribute their wins and losses more easily to themselves than to the coordinator. Consistent with the hypothesis of Lott and Lott (1965), the winners were more positive about their group performance and showed a greater cohesiveness than the losers in democratic than in autocratic groups.

In a follow-up study (Rabbie & van Oostrum, 1977), winning and losing were systematically manipulated by varying the structure of the task that gave one department more of a chance to win than the other. As expected, the winners showed a greater cohesiveness and task satisfaction than the losers did. They also showed a greater acceptance of and appreciation for their leader–representative than did the members of the losing groups. Apparently his actions had led to success rather than to failure. This difference between the winning and losing groups was greater in the consultation than in the no consultation condition. In the consultation condition the representatives had to consult with their departments on what organizational decisions were to be made. In the no consultation condition the representatives could make these decisions on their own. Presumably in the consultation conditions the success or failure of the winning and losing groups could be attributed more to themselves than to their representatives. In the no consultation condition the representatives could be held responsible for their respective fates. Thus, the more winning and losing can be attributed to internal rather than to external sources, the greater will be the difference in cohesion and task satisfaction between winning and losing groups.

Winning does not always involve a gain in material or tangible outcomes but may also reflect an attainment of more intangible goals like status, prestige and superiority. Most of the time these two kinds of outcomes are intercorrelated. Material outcomes often serve as a measuring stick for intangible outcomes. Sometimes the opposite may occur, as in a PDG study by Rabbie et al. (1975). Groups of three persons were instructed to play competitively, cooperatively, or individualistically (Deutsch, 1960; McClintock, 1972) against a programmed opponent who followed either a "soft," cooperative or a "tough," competitive strategy. Subjects evaluated their own and the other group midway and at the end of the trials. In all experimental conditions the own group was rated more favorably than the other group, but cooperative groups rated themselves higher than competitive groups and individualistic self-ratings fell in between. This result is remarkable since the groups that were instructed to cooperate almost always lost money as compared with the competitive and individualistic groups, especially when they were paired with a competitive opponent. This finding was not totally surprising. An earlier pilot study we had conducted revealed that groups that had played cooperatively, in accordance with the experimental instructions, felt morally superior to their competitive opponents, who appeared not to comply with these experimental instructions. The cooperative groups in these experiments lost materially but were "moral winners": They had played by the rules, whereas the other party had not. In line with this interpretation, cooperative groups felt more strongly than competitive and individualistic groups that in this game "moral issues were at stake," and they considered the task "more as a serious business than as a game." Moreover, the cooperative groups felt less "guilty" about their behavior than competitive and individualistic groups.

These results suggest once more that it is not intergroup competition or cooperation per se that determines ingroup cohesion but the satisfaction of having achieved one's goals, whatever these goals might be.

The Influence of Constituencies

In the exercises developed by Blake and Mouton (1961), the intergroup negotiations were conducted through representatives under public negotiation conditions, that is, the members of the groups were seated behind their representatives and were able to communicate with them via written messages. Midway in the negotiations the representatives met with their constituencies and consulted with them as to the kinds of steps to be taken in the future negotiations. The constituency, or audience, whose tangible and intangible outcomes depended on the negotiation behavior of their representatives (Rubin & Brown, 1975) exerted considerable influence on the course of the intergroup negotiations. Throughout the negotiations the representatives could be held accountable for their behavior. Through their messages and consultations, the constituencies steered the representatives close to the groups' preferred position. In a review of the literature it has been concluded that "salient dependent audiences are likely to generate pressures of considerable strength toward loyalty, commitment, and advocacy of their preferred positions [Rubin and Brown, 1975, p. 54]." The question is whether the intensity of the intergroup conflict in the exercises conducted by Blake and Mouton (1961) is not partly due to the *public* character of the intergroup negotiations. What would happen if the representatives negotiated in the absence of their constituency?

It has often been assumed that the presence of an audience invariably heightens pressures on groups and individuals to compete with one another and to defeat the other party, especially when they support one party rather than another. There is some evidence that soccer teams in the Netherlands do considerably better when they play at their "home base," before their own public constituency, than when they are the guests of another team. However, in these games the teams have a competitive orientation toward each other that is heightened by the presence of their supporters. If negotiation groups have a cooperative orientation toward each other, it is to be expected that the presence of a salient dependent audience will increase the pressure on the representative to act more cooperatively with the other party.

Evidence for this hypothesis comes from groups that expected to cooperate with each other. Their attitudes toward their own and the other group were more positive where they anticipated public rather than private negotiations. However, when the groups expected to compete they had more negative attitudes toward both their own and the other group if they anticipated public rather than private negotiations (Rabbie & de Brey, 1971). Apparently, the anticipation of public rather than private negotiations strengthens the prevailing normative orientations in the group. This facilitative factor leads to more cooperation, positive attitudes, and mutual agreement among groups that are instructed to cooperate, but to the reverse among groups that are instructed to compete.

If group members are actually able to influence the course of intergroup negotiations, we can expect that competitive groups will experience more difficulties in reaching an agreement with the other party than when the negotiations are left to the representatives alone. The normative pressures to compete stimulate the group members to defeat the other party rather than to reach an agreement. Where the representatives are acting on their own, they are freed from the increase in normative pressures and are able to find some interpersonal accommodation (Morley & Stephenson, 1977). For cooperative groups the opposite should occur: They should find it easier to reach an agreement with the other group when they can influence the course of the negotiations, in open communication with the other group, than when they are prevented from doing so, possibly because the representatives acting on their own cannot check on the changes in their group's position and consult with them as to the optimal cooperative solution. This hypothesis is consistent with a theory of Walton and Dutton (1969), which assumes that intergroup cooperation is facilitated by an open and free exchange of information between the parties, whereas intergroup competition is heightened in rigid and formal interaction situations characterized by a careful rationing of information between the parties.

This hypothesis receives strong support. In an intergroup negotiation study (Visser, 1975) representatives and their groups were instructed to compete or to cooperate with each other in the presence or absence of their constituencies. When they were present, the constituencies could actively influence the intergroup negotiations. When they were absent, they could follow the negotiations through closed circuit television but they could not exert any influence on the negotiations.

As expected, cooperative groups found it easier to reach an agreement with the other group and also had more positive attitudes toward own and other group when they could influence the intergroup negotiations than when they could not. Competitive groups found it more difficult to reach agreement with the other group and had more negative attitudes about themselves and others in the influence condition than in the no influence condition.

Similar findings were obtained in an organization simulation study (Rabbie & van Oostrum, 1977). In this experiment three-man groups, or "departments," had to work together toward a common organizational goal, which took six trials to complete. The departments had either a competitive or a cooperative relation with each other. In half of the cooperation and competition conditions, representatives of the departments consulted regularly with their groups. In the no consultation condition, the representatives acted on the initial proposals of their groups but did not have to consult with their groups during the intergroup negotiations.

Consistent with our predictions, cooperative groups showed a greater cohesiveness and task satisfaction than competitive groups in the consultation condition, but they showed less cohesiveness and task satisfaction in the no consultation condition. Generally, competitive groups reported a greater hostility toward the outgroup than did cooperative groups, but this difference is more pronounced in the consultation than in the no consultation condition. Apparently, the involvement of all members in the intergroup competition intensified the conflict and generated more disagreements and mutual hostility among them than when the negotiations were left to the representatives, who found it easier to accommodate to each other's desires. When groups were expected to cooperate with each other the opposite trend occurred.

Taken together, these studies suggest that the anticipated or actual presence of a dependent audience enhances the prevailing normative orientations in the group leading to more intense desires to win from the other party among competitive groups or to greater efforts among cooperative groups to reach the best joint solution.

Threatened Leadership and Intergroup Competition

In the studies we have discussed, we examined the effect of intergroup competition and cooperation on the centralization of leadership in the group. In these studies leadership was the dependent variable. In the latter research we have tried to specify some of the conditions that may motivate leaders to engage in intergroup competition rather than in intergroup cooperation.

There is a great deal of anecdotal evidence to suggest that in times of crisis people will rally around their leaders. President Carter's spectacular rise in the opinion polls during the Iran and Afghanistan crises (of 1980) is a case in point. It is a common notion that uncertainty about their tenure of power may motivate leaders to start a war in an effort to save their position and unify the nation behind them. However, the subjective probability of a successful outcome of such intergroup conflict must be rather high; otherwise leaders will shy away from it (Rosencrance, 1963). These hypotheses have been tested in a number of studies.

In one series of experiments (Rabbie & Bekkers, 1976, 1978) leaders had a choice to opt for intergroup competition or for intergroup cooperation under the threat of being deposed or not by their followers. Consistent with our expectations, leaders were more likely to opt for intergroup competition rather than for intergroup cooperation, especially when their groups were internally divided and when they had a stronger bargaining position than their opponents. Where their tenure of power was very precarious, they choose to compete rather than to cooperate, regardless of their chances of bringing the intergroup conflict to a successful conclusion. To broaden the generalizability and external validity of these laboratory findings, a field study was conducted among members of 29 labor unions in the Netherlands (Bekkers, 1977). The chairmen, members of the executive committee and a sample of the rank and file of these unions were questioned about the present policies of the unions, their satisfaction or dissatisfaction with the leadership of the union, etc. In interviews with each chairman, it was determined whether he felt threatened in his leadership position by the other members of the executive committee. Content analyses of the annual speeches of the chairmen to their constituencies over the last 2 years and the articles which were written in the journals of the unions over the same period yielded a measure of outgroup hostility toward employers' organizations, the government, political parties, and other unions. As expected, the more the chairmen felt threatened in their leadership positions, the more hostility they expressed in their annual speeches and journal articles. Moreover, significant correlations were found between the dissatisfaction of the committee members with the leadership of their chairmen and the degree to which these leaders made hostile remarks toward outgroups in their speeches and articles. These findings suggest that under some conditions threatened leaders are more likely to engage in intergroup conflict and to be more hostile toward other groups than leaders who feel more certain of their tenure of power.

Discussion

A sense of group identity or a differentiation into a "we" or "they" is a product of intragroup interaction according to Sherif and Sherif (1969). In his view, "the 'we' thus delineated comes, in time, to embody a host of qualities and values to be upheld, defended and cherished [Sherif, 1966, p. 69]." However, the minimal group studies show that social interaction is not necessary to produce a positive attachment to one's own group or social category. The random classification of a collection of individuals into two distinct social categories, imposed by an external authority, seems sufficient to produce a more positive evaluation of the ingroup than of the outgroup. This would seem surprising since, on the face of it, the names and labels attached to these social categories had no "intrinsic psychological significance" to the subjects (Gerard & Hoyt, 1974; Tajfel et al., 1971). It should be noted, however, that almost any intergroup categorization in a laboratory setting will probably generate attributions, on the part of the subjects, that the experimenter must have had some purpose in categorizing them in this way leading to expectations of potential consequences on the part of individuals or groups thus categorized (Zimbardo, 1975).

The relative ease with which the experimental world of the subjects can be divided into a "we" and "they" seems important in view of the well-documented finding that strangers are likely to be more helpful and co-operative with people they consider one of "us" than one of "them" (Hornstein, 1978). In fact, it has been observed that members of minimal groups who are able to act in terms of "we–they" distinctions are likely to favor anonymous individuals who are identified as ingroup members rather than outgroup members (Tajfel, 1978; Tajfel et al., 1971).

In the minimal groups studied in our laboratory, the members were the passive recipients of a common fate. They could not affect the outcome of others, either directly or indirectly. It seems appropriate in these situations to employ explanatory concepts that refer exclusively to inferred intra-individual processes such as attempts to achieve balance between cognitions and sentiments (Heider, 1958), a search for a positive social identity (Tajfel, 1978; Turner, 1978), a need for social differentiation (Lemaine, 1974), or the accentuation of cognitive differences between social categories (Doise, 1976). However, as soon as social interaction is introduced among members of a social category, group processes occur that lead to the development of role and status relationships and to the emergence of common goals, values, and norms that cannot be reduced to the operation of intraindividual processes alone. These patterns of intragroup relationships cannot be explained exclusively in terms of intraindividual motives and perceptions but should be complemented by analyses of group processes that occur as a consequence of the structural interdependence of the members of the group with respect to their goals (Deutsch, 1973), or their outcomes (Kelley, 1979). These intragroup processes are affected by the structure of the intergroup relations and the wider social context in which the interacting groups have to operate (Tajfel, 1972; Billig, 1976). A multilevel theory of intergroup relations is required to take all these levels of analysis into account.

Our efforts to replicate the findings of Sherif (1966) and Blake and Mouton (1961) under more controlled laboratory conditions have been only partially successful. As was to be expected, actual intergroup interaction produced more significant differences in the predicted direction between competitive and cooperative groups than expected intergroup interaction. Appealing as the results of the early, classic studies might be, they seem to occur only under very specific circumstances. What could be the reason for some of the differences between Sherif's and Blake and Mouton's results and ours? The natural groups employed in their studies had long histories and anticipated futures together. In contrast, the cohesiveness in our ad hoc laboratory groups was very low to begin with. There was little emotional identification of the members with the ingroup; thus what happened to members within their groups probably had little impact on their self-image and self-esteem. The situation was quite different in the training groups used by Blake and Mouton (1961). There is also a difference in intensity of conflict: For example, in the studies by Blake and Mouton (1961) the representatives and their groups were instructed to agree among each other on which of the groups had developed the best position. This all or none, zero-sum situation contrasts sharply with the mixed motive situations used in our experiments. Even where groups were instructed to compete with each other, to get as much as possible of their own position included in the joint proposal of the groups, they were expected to come to some kind of an agreement with the other party. If they failed, and the negotiations ended in deadlock, neither group would be rewarded. The polarity between competitive and cooperative groups was not that strong. Both groups had a need to preserve the group's identity and were motivated to measure their own strength against the strength of the other group.

Hostile actions from one group to the other were not condoned nor were they engineered as in Sherif's experiment. For example, on one occasion the experimenter in Sherif's study (Sherif et al., 1961) had intentionally left spoiled food on the table, making it appear that the other group was to blame for it. In our laboratory experiments the relationship between the groups was highly regulated, and the experimenter played a strictly impartial role. In this sense, the intergroup relations in our experiments can be considered more as a game or a debate than a "fight" (Rapoport, 1960).

The anticipated presence and actual involvement of a dependent audience in intergroup negotiations seem to enhance the prevailing normative orientations in the group, leading to more cooperation, agreement, and positive attitudes among groups that were instructed to cooperate, but to the reverse among groups that were instructed to compete with each other. These results can be considered an instance of "group polarization," that is, a "group-produced enhancement of a prevailing individual tendency [Lamm & Meyers, 1978, p. 146]." However, in these studies as in previous ones (Rabbie & Visser, 1972; Rabbie, Visser, & Bagger, 1974), the group-induced enhancement refers to a strengthening of normative orientations induced by experimental instructions rather than to an enhancement of existing individual tendencies. In any case, it is quite likely that the processes that have been invoked to explain group polarization, for example, responsibility dynamics, informational influence, and social comparison (Lamm & Meyers, 1978), may also account for the present findings, although it is difficult to specify which of these processes are the most important in producing the obtained effects.

Finally, our research seems to show that leaders who are uncertain of their tenure of power are more likely to opt for intergroup competition than for intergroup cooperation than leaders who feel certain of their leadership position. The other party in our experiments, unlike groups and nations in the real world, could not respond in kind; to have done so might have led to an escalation of the intergroup conflict. To end on a more optimistic note, it should also be said that leaders who were certain of their tenure of power persisted in making cooperative proposals toward the other party even though a stronger bargaining position permitted them to defeat the other group. Freed from the preoccupation with power, they found it easier to engage in a helpful and cooperative relationship with the other party.

Acknowledgments

The author is indebted to the many co-workers and students who participated in this research. He wishes to thank Dr. Norman Berkowitz for his constructive criticism of an earlier draft of the paper and Dr. Philip Zimbardo for his editorial advice. The author is particularly grateful to Dr. Murray Horwitz, who helped him in so many ways.

References

Adorno, T. W., Frenkel-Brunswick, E., Levinson, D., & Sanford, N. *The authoritarian personality.* New York: Harper & Row, 1950.

Bass, B. M., & Duntemann, G. Biases in the evaluation of one's own group, its allies and opponents. *Journal of Conflict Resolution*, 1963, 7, 16–20.

Bekkers, F. Threatened leadership and intergroup conflicts. *Journal of Peace Research*, 1977, 14, 223–237.

Berkowitz, L. *Aggression: A social psychological analysis.* New York: McGraw-Hill, 1962.

Berkowitz, L. Frustrations, comparisons and other sources of emotional arousal as contributions to social unrest. *Journal of Social Issues*, 1972, *28*, 77–91.

Billig, M. Normative communication in a minimal intergroup situation. *European Journal of Social Psychology*, 1973, *3*, 27–52.

Billig, M. *Social psychology and intergroup relations*. London: Academic Press, 1976.

Billig, M., & Tajfel, H. Social categorization and similarity in intergroup behavior. *European Journal of Social Psychology*, 1973, *3*, 27–52.

Blake, R. R., & Mouton, J. S. Reactions to intergroup competition under win-lose conditions. *Management Science*, 1961, *7*, 420–435.

Boulding, K. E. *Conflict and defence*. New York: Harper & Brothers, 1962.

Bramel, D. H. Interpersonal attraction, hostility and perception. In J. Mills (Ed.), *Experimental social psychology*. New York: Macmillan, 1969.

Brewer, M. B. In-group bias in the minimal intergroup situation: A cognitive motivational analysis. *Psychological Bulletin*, 1979, *86*, 307–324.

Brewer, M. B., & Campbell, D. T. *Ethnocentrism and intergroup attitudes: East African evidence*. New York: Halstead Press, 1976.

Brown, R. Divided we fall: An analysis of relations between sections of a factory work force. In H. Tajfel (Ed.), *Differentiation between social groups: Studies in the social psychology of intergroup relations*. London: Academic Press, 1978.

Campbell, D. T., & Stanley, J. C. *Experimental and quasi-experimental designs for research*. Chicago: Rand McNally, 1966.

Cartwright, D. The nature of group cohesiveness. In D. Cartwright & A. Zander (Eds.), *Group dynamics*. New York: Harper & Row, 1968.

Coser, L. *The function of social conflict*. New York: Free Press, 1956.

Deutsch, M. The effect of motivational orientation upon trust and suspicion. *Human Relations*, 1960, *13*, 123–139.

Deutsch, M. *The resolution of conflict: Constructive and destructive processes*. New Haven: Yale University Press, 1973.

Diab, L. N. Personal communication, 1965.

Diab, L. N. A study of intragroup and intergroup relations among experimentally produced small groups. *Genetic Psychology Monographs*, 1970, *82*, 49–82.

Dion, K. L. Cohesiveness as a determinant of ingroup-outgroup bias. *Journal of Personality and Social Psychology*, 1973, *28*, 163–171.

Doise, W. *L'articulation psychosociologique et les relations entre groupes*. Brussels: DeBoeck, 1976.

Doise, W. Images, représentations, idéologies et expérimentations psychosociologues. *Social Science Information*, 1978, *17*, 41–69.

Ferguson, C. K., & Kelley, H. H. Significant factors in the overevaluation of one's own group's product. *Journal of Abnormal and Social Psychology*, 1964, *69*, 223–228.

Gerard, H. B., & Hoyt, M. F. Distinctiveness of social categorization and attitude toward ingroup members. *Journal of Personality and Social Psychology*, 1974, *29*, 836–842.

Gerard, H. B., & Miller, N. Group dynamics. *Annual Review of Psychology*, 1967, *18*, 287–332.

Heider, F. *The psychology of interpersonal relations*. New York: John Wiley & Sons, 1958.

Homans, G. C. *The human group*. New York: Harcourt, Brace & World, 1950.

Hornstein, H. A. Promotive tension and prosocial behavior: A Lewinian analysis. In L. Wispe (Ed.), *Altruism, sympathy and helping: Psychological and sociological principles*. New York: Academic Press, 1978.

Katz, D., & Kahn, R. L. *The social psychology of organizations* (2nd ed.). New York: John Wiley, 1978.

Kelley, H. H. *Personal relationships: Their structures and processes.* Hillsdale, New Jersey: Lawrence Erlbaum, 1979.

Kelman, H. C. Social-psychological approaches to the study of international relations: The question of relevance. In H. C. Kelman (Ed.), *International behavior: A social-psychological analysis.* New York: Holt, Rinehart & Winston, 1965.

Lamm, H., & Meyers, D. G. Group-induced polarization of attitudes and behavior. In L. Berkowitz (Ed.), *Advances in experimental social psychology,* (Vol. 11). New York: Academic Press, 1978.

Lemaine, G. Social differentiation and social originality. *European Journal of Social Psychology,* 1974, *4,* 17–52.

LeVine, R. A., & Campbell, D. T. *Ethnocentrism: Theories of conflict, ethnic attitudes and group behavior.* New York: Wiley, 1972.

Lewin, K. *Resolving social conflict.* New York: Harper & Row, 1948.

Lott, A. J., & Lott, B. E. Group cohesiveness and interpersonal attraction: A review of relationships with antecedent and consequent variables. *Psychological Bulletin,* 1965, *64,* 259–309.

McClintock, C. G. Game behavior and social motivation in interpersonal settings. In G. McClintock (Ed.), *Experimental social psychology.* New York: Holt, Rinehart & Winston, 1972.

McGrath, J. E., & Altman, I. *Small group research: A synthesis and critique of the field.* New York: Holt, Rinehart & Winston, 1966.

Morley, I. E., & Stephenson, G. M. *The social psychology of bargaining.* London: George Allen & Unwin, 1977.

Mulder, M., & Stemerding, A. Threat, attraction to group, and need for strong leadership. *Human Relations,* 1963, *16,* 317–334.

Nemeth, C. A critical analysis of research utilizing the P.D.G. paradigm for the study of bargaining. In L. Berkowitz (Ed.), *Advanced in Experimental Social Psychology* (Vol. 2). New York: Academic Press, 1972.

Rabbie, J. M. Effecten van een competitieve en coöperatieve intergroepsoriëntatie op verhoudingen binnen en tussen groepen. *Nederlands Tijdschrift voor de Psychologie,* 1974, *29,* 239–257. (a)

Rabbie, J. M. Effects of expected intergroup competition and cooperation. Paper presented to symposium, *On the development and maintenance of intergroup bias.* Annual convention of the American Psychological Association, New Orleans, 1974. (b)

Rabbie, J. M. *Categorization and common fate in intergroup relations.* Unpublished manuscript, Institute of Social Psychology, University of Utrecht, 1979. (a)

Rabbie, J. M. Competitie en cooperatie tussen groupen. In J. M. F. Jaspars & R. van der Vlist (Eds.), *Sociale Psychologies in Nederland.* Deventer: Van Loghum Slaterus, 1979. (b)

Rabbie, J. M. *Conflict and aggression among individuals and groups.* Paper presented at the Twenty-second International Congress of Psychology, Leipzig, 1980.

Rabbie, J. M., & Bekkers, F. Bedreigd leiderschap en intergroepscompetitie. *Nederlands Tijdschrift voor de Psychologie,* 1976, *31,* 269–283.

Rabbie, J. M., & Bekkers, F. Threatened leadership and intergroup competition. *European Journal of Social Psychology,* 1978, *8,* 9–20.

Rabbie, J. M., Benoist, F., Oosterbaan, H., & Visser, L. Differential power and effects of expected competitive and cooperative intergroup interaction on intragroup and outgroup attitudes. *Journal of Personality and Social Psychology,* 1974, *30,* 46–56.

Rabbie, J. M., & de Brey, J. H. C. The anticipation of cooperation and competition under private and public conditions. *International Journal of Group Tensions,* 1971, *1,* 230–251.

Rabbie, J. M., & Horwitz, M. The arousal of ingroup-outgroup bias by a chance win or loss. *Journal of Personality and Social Psychology*, 1969, *69*, 223–228.

Rabbie, J. M., & Huygen, K. Internal disagreements and their effects on attitudes toward in- and outgroup. *International Journal of Group Tensions*, 1974, *4*, 222–246.

Rabbie, J. M., & van Oostrum, J. *The effects of influence structures upon intra and intergroup relations*. Paper presented to the International Conference on Socialization and Social Influence, Warsaw, Poland, September, 1977.

Rabbie, J. M., & Visser, L. Bargaining strength and group polarization in intergroup negotiations. *European Journal of Social Psychology*, 1972, *4*, 401–416.

Rabbie, J. M., & Visser, L. Gevolgen van interne en externe conflicten op verhoudingen tussen groepen. *Nederlands Tijdschrift voor de Psychologie*, 1976, *31*, 233–251.

Rabbie, J. M., Visser, L., & Bagger, K. *Bargaining strength, pre-assessment of own and other's aspirations and group induced shifts in intergroup negotiations*. Unpublished manuscript, Institute of Social Psychology, University of Utrecht, 1974.

Rabbie, J. M., Visser, L., & van Oostrum, J. *Motivational orientation and strategy of other groups in a Prisoner's Dilemma Game*. Unpublished manuscript, Institute of Social Psychology, University of Utrecht, 1975.

Rabbie, J. M., Visser, L., & van Oostrum, J. *Conflict behavior of individuals, dyads and triads in mixed motive games*. Paper presented at Conference on Group Decision Making, Reisensburg, West Germany, August 1978.

Rabbie, J. M., Visser, L., & Vernooij, G. Onzekerheid van omgeving, differentiatie en invloedsverdeling in universitaire instituten. *Nederlands Tijdschrift voor de Psychologie*, 1976, *31*, 285–303.

Rabbie, J. M., & Wilkens, G. Intergroup competition and its effects on intra-group and intergroup relations. *European Journal of Social Psychology*, 1971, *1*, 215–234.

Rapoport, A. *Fights, games and debates*. Ann Arbor: University of Michigan, 1960.

Reyen, A. H., & Kahn, A. Effects of intergroup orientation on group attitudes and proxemic behavior. *Journal of Personality and Social Behavior*, 1975, *31*, 302–310.

Rosenblatt, P. C. Origins and effects of group ethnocentrism and nationalism. *Journal of Conflict Resolution*, 1964, *8*, 131–146.

Rosencrance, R. N. *Action and reaction in world politics*. Boston: Little Brown, 1963.

Rubin, J. Z., & Brown, B. R. *The social psychology of bargaining and negotiation*. New York: Academic Press, 1975.

Sherif, M. *In common predicament*. Boston: Houghton Mifflin, 1966.

Sherif, M. If the social scientist is to be more than a mere technician. *Journal of Social Issues*, 1968, *24*, 41–61.

Sherif, M., Harvey, O. J., White, J., Hood, W. R., & Sherif, C. W. *Intergroup conflict and cooperation: The Robberts Cave Experiment*. Norman, Oklahoma: University Book Exchange, 1961.

Sherif, M., & Sherif, C. W. *Social psychology*. New York: Harper & Row, 1969.

Simmel, G. *Conflict and the web of group affiliation*. New York: Free Press of Glencoe, 1964.

Stein, A. A. Conflict and cohesion: Review of the literature. *Journal of Conflict Resolution*, 1976, *20*, 143–172.

Steiner, I. D. Whatever happened to the group in social psychology? *Journal of Experimental Social Psychology*, 1974, *10*, 94–108.

Stephenson, G. M., Skinner, M., & Brotherton, C. J. Group participation and intergroup relations: An experimental study of negotiation groups. *European Journal of Social Psychology*, 1976, *6*, 51–70.

Sumner, W. G. *Folkways*. Boston: Ginn, 1906.

Tajfel, H. Experiments in a vacuum. In J. Israel & H. Tajfel (Eds.), *The contexts of social psychology, a critical assessment*. London: Academic Press, 1972.

Tajfel, H. The psychological structure of intergroup relations. In J. Tajfel (Ed.), *Differentiation between groups, studies in the social psychology of intergroup relations.* London: Academic Press, 1978.

Tajfel, H., Billig, K., Bundy, R., & Flament, C. Social categorization and intergroup behavior. *European Journal of Social Psychology*, 1971, *1*, 149–175.

Tannenbaum, A. S. *Control in organizations.* New York: McGraw-Hill, 1968.

Turner, J. Social comparison, similarity and ingroup favouritism. In H. Tajfel (Ed.), *Differentiation between social groups, studies in the social psychology of intergroup relations.* London: Academic Press, 1978.

Van der Linden, W. J., & Rabbie, J. M. Doeldifferentiatie en-integratie in gesimuleerde organisaties. *Nederlands Tijdschrift voor de Psychologie*, 1976, *31*, 305–320.

van Oostrum, J. *Group size and future perspective in an intergroup game.* Unpublished manuscript, University of Utrecht, 1977.

Visser, L. *The effects of open and closed channels of communication on intergroup behavior in the Prisoner's Dilemma Game.* Unpublished manuscript, Institute of Social Psychology, University of Utrecht, 1974.

Visser, L. *De invloed van de achterban op coöperatieve intergroepsonderhandelingen.* Unpublished manuscript, Institute of Social Psychology, University of Utrecht, 1975.

Walton, R. E., & Dutton, J. W. The management of interdepartmental conflict: A model and review. *Administrative Science Quarterly*, 1969, *14*, 73–84.

Weiner, B. *Theories of motivation: From mechanisms to cognition.* Chicago: Markham, 1972.

Wilson, W. Reciprocation and other techniques for inducing cooperation in the Prisoner's Dilemma Game. *Journal of Conflict Resolution*, 1971, *15*, 167–195.

Wilson, W., & Miller, N. Shifts in evaluation of participants following intergroup competition. *Journal of Abnormal Social Psychology*, 1961, *63*, 428–431.

Worchel, S., Lind, E. A., & Kaufman, K. H. Evaluations of group products as a function of expectations of group longevity, outcome of competition, and publicity of evaluations. *Journal of Personality and Social Psychology*, 1975, *31*, 1089–1097.

Zimbardo, P. G. Transforming experimental research into advocacy for social change. In M. Deutsch & H. Hornstein (Eds.), *Applying social psychology.* Hillsdale, N. J.: Lawrence Erlbaum Associates, 1975.

Chapter 7

The Development

of Integrative

Agreements

DEAN G. PRUITT
PETER J. D. CARNEVALE

This chapter concerns the processes and conditions leading to the adoption of integrative agreements in situations where there is a divergence of interest between two parties. An agreement is said to be integrative to the extent that it reconciles the parties' interests and thus provides high benefit to both of them. The term *integrative* has its origins in the concepts of *integration* (Follett, 1940) and *integrative bargaining* (Walton & McKersie, 1965), which refer to the processes by which high joint benefit is developed in social conflict. The concept of integrative agreement is akin to Deutsch's (1973) notion of a "constructive" consequence of conflict, which he describes as one in which "the participants all are satisfied with their outcomes and feel that they have gained as a result of the conflict [p. 17]."

The first section of this chapter will define terms and discuss the importance of achieving high joint benefit. In the second section, four types of integrative agreement will be examined. The third section will deal with a process that is often essential for the development of integrative agreements: the unlinking of elements in bundles of demands, goals, aspirations, or values. A research method for studying the development of integrative agreements will be described in the fourth section. The fifth and sixth sections will present findings on the conditions and processes that foster such agreements.

COOPERATION AND HELPING BEHAVIOR
Theories and Research

Problem Definition and Importance

Divergent Interests

The situations of concern here are those in which two parties are trying to make a joint decision between two or more alternatives. Interests are divergent in the sense that the two parties have differing evaluations of these alternatives, such that an alternative that nicely satisfies one party's needs seems quite unsuitable to the other. Joint decision making in such a situation is sometimes called *bargaining*.

The alternatives under consideration can be of three types, which we call Cases 1, 2, and 3. These are illustrated by the three reward structures shown in Figure 7.1. Case 1 alternatives concern how *one* of the two parties will behave. In the example in Figure 7.1, this party (the son) has three alternative courses of action: to spend 1 week, 2 weeks, or 3 weeks at home during his college vacation. His evaluations of these alternatives are shown by the numbers in the bottom left corner of each cell. His mother's evaluations of the same alternatives are shown in the upper right corner of each cell. The divergence of interest can be seen in the fact that the son gets his largest reward from staying 1 week and the mother gets her largest reward if he stays 3 weeks.[1]

Case 2 alternatives concern how each of the *two* parties will behave in situations where their independent actions have a combined effect on reality. The example is taken from Kelley and Thibaut (1978). Both husband and wife face a choice between having a cocktail or going bicycling at 5:30 in the evening. They can cycle or drink together (NW and SE cells) or each can do his or her own thing (SW and NE cells). Divergence of interest is reflected in the fact that the wife most prefers cycling together but the husband most prefers having cocktails together.[2]

---

[1] An important question for Case 1 is how one party (e.g., the mother) can gain enough power over the other (e.g., the son) to bargain with him about his own behavior. This question is beyond the scope of this chapter, which starts with the assumption that people are already engaged in joint decision making.

[2] The matrix shown for Case 2 resembles those employed by game theorists (e.g., Rapoport, 1966). However, our assumption about the rules for decision making in situations modeled by such matrices differs from that made by most game theorists. We assume that the parties are engaged in *joint* decision making about which cell to occupy. Game theorists ordinarily assume that the parties make *independent* decisions, the row player choosing between his or her options without knowledge of the column player's choices and vice versa.

In the context of joint decision making, a matrix presentation such as the example shown for Case 2 implies that the two parties see the actions represented by the rows and columns of the matrix as somehow *interrelated* and hence worthy of being linked in thought and discussion. How they reach such a conclusion will not be discussed in this chapter.

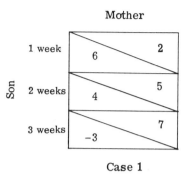

Case 1

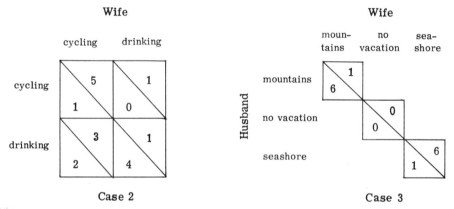

Case 2   Case 3

Figure 7.1. Three types of alternatives that can be the subject of two-party decision making. The alternatives are the cells in the matrices shown. Case 1 involves the behavior of a single party (the son, in this example), Case 2 the separate behaviors of two parties (husband and wife), Case 3 the joint behavior of two parties (husband and wife). The benefit in the lower left corner of a cell goes to the person named on the left of the matrix, and the benefit on the upper right to the person named above the matrix. The Case 2 example is adapted from one given by Kelley and Thibaut (1978).

Case 3 alternatives concern what *joint action* should be taken by the two parties. The example is one of a husband and wife trying to decide where to spend their vacation. Again interests diverge. The husband prefers to go to the mountains and the wife to the seashore (though both prefer taking a vacation over no vacation). In Case 3 situations, independent action (e.g., going on separate vacations) is not under consideration, either because it is impossible (they have only one car and one slim budget), it is seen as undesirable (togetherness is a value in this marriage), or it has never been thought of (the couple has never read *Open Marriage* [O'Neill & O'Neill, 1972]).

In presenting the examples of Cases 1, 2, and 3, we have made the simplifying assumption that both parties are aware of the same alternatives. Cases 1 and 2 also assume that the parties are trying to make a joint decision and are unwilling to take independent action without talking things over. These assumptions are accurate in many bargaining settings but by no means in all.[3]

Joint Benefit

Between any two alternatives one can be said to be more "integrative" than the other if it provides greater joint benefit to the two parties. Unfortunately there is no general agreement among scholars about the proper definition of *joint benefit*, or **"social utility"** as it is sometimes called (Sen, 1970).

Three definitions of joint benefit are worth mentioning. The first assumes that one alternative is of greater joint benefit than another if it is better than the other for one party and equal or better for the other party. For instance, in the Case 3 example shown in Figure 7.1, either type of vacation is of greater joint benefit than no vacation. This "equal-or-better" definition has considerable face validity but poses a fatal flaw for empirical research. In many cases, it does not allow us to say which of two alternatives provides the greater joint benefit. For instance, in the Case 1 example, none of the three alternatives is preferred over the others by both parties. This means that it is not possible to assign unambiguously a joint benefit value to every alternative. This poses difficulty for statistical analysis.

The second definition equates joint benefit with the sum of the two parties' individual benefits. For instance, in the Case 1 example, a 2-week stay has the largest sum of benefits (9). We have employed this "joint-sum" definition in our empirical research because it has face validity and permits assignment of numerical values to all alternatives. However, it has the drawback in some people's thinking of not sufficiently reflecting both parties' outcomes. The joint sum can be high when one party does very well and the other somewhat poorly. Thus in the Case 2 example, cycling together has the highest joint sum (6) but is unlikely to appeal to the husband because he gets so little out of it (1).

Sen (1970) has proposed a third definition that resolves the latter problem. This equates joint benefit with the outcome achieved by the less rewarded individual. On the basis of this criterion, the best alternative in the Case 2 example would be the wife cycling and the husband drinking, which

---

[3] For a partial analysis of the conditions under which people will try to make a joint decision, see Pruitt and Gleason (1978).

provides a benefit of 2 to the less benefited party (in this cell the husband), in contrast to 1, 0, and 1 in the other three cells. This "lesser-outcome" criterion improves on the joint-sum criterion in that high joint benefit requires that *both* parties do well. However it is inferior to the joint-sum criterion in another way. It gives the same score to two alternatives that provide equal benefits to the less advantaged individual even if the more advantaged individual does better on one alternative than on the other. Thus suppose you and I must choose between cherry and apple pie and I am lukewarm about both while you love cherry pie and only like apple pie very much. These two alternatives would be equal by the lesser-outcome criterion because I am less interested in pie than you and like both kinds of pie equally. Yet common sense suggests that cherry pie provides greater joint benefit than apple pie because it provides you more benefit without providing me any less benefit.

In summary, the joint-sum and lesser-outcome definitions of joint benefit are superior to the equal-or-better definition in providing a numerical value for every alternative. However, it is hard to choose between the first two definitions, because each has both an advantage and a disadvantage in comparison to the other. Hence we have employed both of these definitions in most of our research.

The Development of New Alternatives

One of two kinds of process may be at work when an integrative agreement is reached: (*a*) *choice* of an integrative alternative among those currently available and (*b*) *development* of a new alternative that is more integrative than those currently available. Scholars who employ matrix analyses of the kind shown in Figure 7.1 often overlook the latter process. But it is reasonable to view joint decision-making as a phenomenon that endures for a period of time and in which changes can occur in the alternatives under consideration. Old alternatives may be dropped from the agenda and new alternatives that were not previously known may come under examination. Hence sets of alternatives like those shown in Figure 7.1 should not be seen as fixed but as representing the situation at some particular point in time.

Suppose in the Case 1 example of Figure 7.1 that the son's objection to staying home for 3 weeks is that he wants to travel and spend time with his girlfriend who lives 500 miles away. A new, more integrative alternative might be for his family to take a vacation trip to an area close to the girlfriend's home, so that he can spend time with both of the women in his life, an alternative that could be worth say 6 and 6 to the two parties. In the Case 2 example, one party might discover a beautiful and inexpensive cocktail lounge reached by a 3-mile bicycle ride—an alternative that is worth say 3 and 4 to the husband and wife. In the Case 3 example, the parties might find a fresh water lake in the foothills with the best features of the mountains and the seashore, providing a value of say 5 to each of them. In all three cases, the new alternative would provide higher joint benefit than any of the prior alternatives by either the joint-sum or the lesser-outcome definition of joint benefit.

The notion that parties can develop new, more integrative alternatives implies that divergent interests can be reconciled in the course of a controversy. A controversy that starts out with sharp disagreement can end up with consensus and good feelings because an option has been discovered that provides the two parties a good deal of what they set out to get (e.g., an outcome worth 5 instead of the hoped-for 6 for each member of the married couple in the Case 3 example). This conclusion may seem strange to those who view divergence as an inherent property of a set of interests. We believe that interests (i.e., goals and values) never clash inherently but only by virtue of the alternatives under consideration by the parties.

Why Study the Adoption of Integrative Agreements?

There are at least five reasons why it is important to understand the processes leading to the adoption of integrative agreements:

1. High joint benefit has intrinsic validity, in the sense of providing the greatest good to the greatest number of people.

2. When aspirations are high on both sides, it may be impossible to reach agreement unless an alternative providing high benefit to both parties is found and adopted. Hence these processes are relevant to understanding how a controversy will end.

3. The higher the joint benefit attained, the less likely agreements are to be repudiated after they have been reached (Follett, 1940). Hence processes leading to such agreements contribute to the stability of normative systems.

4. When two parties provide high joint benefit to one another, their mutual attraction is likely to be enhanced (Lott & Lott, 1965). This means that they will enjoy their relationship more and their relationship is more likely to persist. Furthermore, attraction will probably produce trust, contributing to the capacity to find integrative agreements in the future.

5. The capacity to develop integrative agreements in organizations is likely to contribute to organizational effectiveness. The units of an organization (individuals, work groups, departments) ordinarily strive for differing goals that reflect the divergent responsibilities assigned to them. If

these separate goals are legitimate, the organization as a whole will prosper provided that its units are able to find creative ways to reconcile these goals. In this interpretation, the processes leading to integrative agreements are a source of "total power," as that term is used by Tannenbaum (1968). In other words, when integrative processes are in operation, all units are more capable of achieving their goals in their dealings with one another.

Types of Integrative Agreement

Four types of integrative agreement will be distinguished in this section: those that cut one party's costs; those that compensate one party for costs incurred; those that bridge the two parties' positions; and those that involve logrolling, that is, an exchange of concessions on different issues. These four types of agreement can be thought of as models for the development of new alternatives that provide higher joint benefit than those currently under consideration.

Before turning to these types of agreements, it is necessary to deal with a misconception that may have been fostered by what was said in the first section of this paper. This is that people always evaluate an alternative on a single utility scale. It is sometimes useful to treat people as if they behaved this way, because it allows us to make entries in payoff matrices, such as those shown in Figure 7.1. Furthermore it is clear that people are capable of making such judgments (Thus Kelley [1979] gets subjects to fill in Case 2 matrices concerning their interactions with significant figures in their lives.) However, when evaluating an alternative in the normal course of events, people are more likely to make a *set of judgments*, one for each of the needs affected by the alternative. For example, in evaluating the alternative of staying home for 3 weeks of vacation, the son in the Case 1 example might give this alternative high points because it allows him to save money and get to know his parents better and low points because it blocks his goal of seeing other parts of the country and being with his out-of-town girlfriend. (The latter two judgments can be considered anticipated "costs" associated with this alternative.) Such judgments may eventually be summarized into a single overall assessment of the alternative. But, for a period of time, they will be separate elements in the individual's thinking, which will often contribute to the development of more integrative alternatives.

Cost Cutting

When interests are divergent, successful goal achievement by one party (party A) is likely to impose costs on the other (party B). One way of developing an integrative agreement is for party A to get what he or she wants while cutting party B's costs. The result is diminished divergence of interest, not because A has diluted his or her goals but because B suffers less.

Many forms of cost cutting can be found; however, in this chapter we shall examine only two particularly interesting varieties: those designed to relieve party B's concern about the future implications of an agreement and those designed to protect party B's public image, or self-image, from harm.

CONCERN ABOUT FUTURE IMPLICATIONS

At times, party B's costs derive not so much from acceding to party A's wishes as from the perceived implications of such a concession for the future. B fears that A will see his or her concession as a signal of willingness to continue acquiescing.

A major solution to concern about such implications is *decoupling* the present from the future. Either A's demands or B's acquiescence must be portrayed as a one-shot event, providing no precedents for the future. According to Jervis (1970), decoupling takes one of three forms:

1. Explicit denial of precedents associated with an action. One example would be a man who tells his new wife that her parents can come over this weekend but "don't get the idea I want to see them every Sunday" (O'Neill & O'Neill, 1972).
2. Attempting to show that the current action is a product of special circumstances. A girl who asks her father to take over her job of mowing the lawn "just this once because we're having a special tournament at school" would be using this technique.
3. Taking additional actions that contradict the undesired impression. A person who accepts a kiss and then draws away is employing such a strategy. The point of this and the other strategies is to signal that the action has no implications beyond itself.

IMAGE PROTECTION

Sometimes A's efforts to achieve his or her goals produce costs for B by imperiling B's public image, or self-image. Three image sensitivities can be identified: B may be concerned about diminished status vis-à-vis A; rejection by A; or a reduced sense of freedom, that is, of being hemmed in by A's demands. The latter feeling has been called "reactance" (Brehm, 1966).

Many tactics are available to party A for dealing with these three sensitivities and thus getting B to comply with or acquiesce to A's wishes. Among them are the following seven classes:

1. Using disclaimers to deny the relevance of A's behavior to B's sensitivities
2. Diminishing the size or significance of what the source is doing or asking
3. In stating a demand, using indirect methods such as signaling, hinting, or employing humor or roundabout channels of communication; these techniques enhance the sense of freedom and status by not seeming to apply direct pressure

The other four tactics are aimed at structuring B's attributions about the origin of A's behavior or of B's compliance. The goal is to avoid attributions such as "A is motivated by a sense of superiority or a negative attitude," or "B lacks freedom of action because he/she is acting out of pressure from A."

4. Blaming external forces for A's actions: If A's actions can be seen as responding to external imperatives, his or her behavior is less likely to be interpreted as an effort to display enhanced status or as a rejection of B.
5. Shifting responsibility for A's actions to motives acceptable to B: A favorite argument of this kind is that these actions are in B's best interest.
6. Encouraging a belief that B has participated in the decision making: If B believes that he or she is responsible for the costs being experienced, B will not attribute them to A's pressure or unfavorable attitude.
7. Employing sanctioned forums: Some societies have settings within which high status individuals can be criticized without implying that the source of the criticism feels equal or superior, e.g., the galley of a traditional sailing ship where all were equal under the authority of the cook (Goffman, 1959).

All seven of these tactics have been described from the viewpoint of A as user. Yet it should be noted that party B will sometimes cut his or her *own* costs, so as to be able to accept and live with unavoidable decisions that benefit A. A third party may also help B cut costs by designing a formula on one of these seven models.

Compensation

Compensation is a second way of generating more integrative alternatives. When party A takes unwelcome actions or makes costly demands, party B is sometimes indemnified for his or her losses. Compensation usually comes from A, because of a desire to buy acquiescence from B. But it can also originate with B or with a third party.

TYPES OF COMPENSATION

Three kinds of compensation can be distinguished: specific, homologous, and substitute. In specific compensation, other ways are found to satisfy those of B's needs that have been frustrated by A's initiatives.[4] An example of specific compensation would be the American guarantee not to invade Cuba, which helped to end the Cuban Missile Crisis. This action partly compensated Russia for withdrawing its missiles, since the missile installations were at least partly designed with the goal of deterring American aggression against Cuba. In homologous compensation, B receives a benefit in the same realm of reality and of roughly equal appearance as the benefit lost, but the needs being served are not those that have been frustrated. An example of homologous compensation can also be seen in the Cuban Missile Crisis. In exchange for Russian withdrawal of the missiles from Cuba, the United States is reported to have pledged covertly to withdraw its missiles from Turkey. This pledge was homologous compensation because, while not satisfying the goals that led the Russians to put missiles into Cuba, it provided a benefit that looked similar to the withdrawal of those missiles. Substitute compensation is in a coin unrelated to the costs experienced by B. Different needs are served, and a different realm of reality is involved. An example would be a cash settlement for the loss of a limb.

A benefit is not always equivalent in value to the loss sustained. Partial compensation is not uncommon, especially when A is more powerful than B and has little intrinsic interest in B's welfare. Nevertheless, pressures to *equalize* compensation (or to make it proportional to the inputs of the two parties) often exist (Walster, Walster, & Berscheid, 1978). An unequal agreement may seem unfair to the less advantaged party and may cause him or her to lose face with third parties. Hence he or she may not be willing to enter into such an agreement or may violate it as soon as the opportunity arises.

In specific compensation, it is relatively easy for the recipient (party B) to determine whether the compensation is equivalent to the loss sustained, because he or she can tell whether the need that was frustrated is now satisfied. However specific compensation is not always practical, because of environmental rigidities or lack of information about the exact nature of B's costs. This explains why we sometimes find homologous compensation, which does not serve the needs that have been frustrated but looks outwardly similar to the sacrifices B has made in acceding to A's demands.

---

[4] Specific compensation is like cost cutting in dealing with the precise needs frustrated by A's goal attainment. Hence these two forms of integrative agreement are sometimes hard to distinguish.

Such compensation has the appearance of equivalence, allowing party B to save face and party A to believe that he or she has acted justly.

The problem of equivalency is most acute in the case of substitute compensation, because the target's sacrifice and the compensation provided by the source are on such different dimensions.

TRUST

The problem of trust is acute in any compensatory scheme if one party must go first and the other second. In this context, "trust" refers to the first party's belief that the second party is willing and able to honor his or her commitment to compensate.

When trust is low, substitutes for trust are sometimes available. For instance, if one party is less reliable than the other, he or she can be required to go first. If the party going first fails to comply with the agreement, the party going second is still free to move in another direction. When the less trustworthy party *must* go second, physical or legal restraints can sometimes be imposed on this party; for example, in supermarkets the customers may be forced to exit past a cash register after taking or receiving their merchandise.

When none of these solutions is available, piecemeal reciprocity can sometimes be employed. This involves breaking each party's contribution into small parts and delivering them alternately over a period of time. The risk here is minimal to both parties because each, in a sense, goes both first and second over most of the period of exchange. Exchanges of concessions in formal negotiations frequently take a similar form, with each party giving up only a little and waiting for compensation from the other before making a further concession.

In the absence of trust or a suitable substitute device, compensatory schemes tend not to develop. Hence, it is harder to reconcile divergent interests. Interpersonal relationships are likely to be less harmonious and need satisfaction to be diminished.

OVERTNESS OF COMPENSATION

Sometimes one or both parties fear community awareness of a compensatory scheme. The scheme may be illegal, such as a bribe; improper, such as the awarding of advancement for sex; or potentially embarrassing, such as paying somebody for providing praise. If the exchange is nevertheless desired by both parties, this dilemma can be solved in three basic ways: making a secret agreement, secretly transferring one or both benefits, or delaying enactment of the second part of the exchange so that the two parties' actions are so separated in time that outsiders do not see the connection.

In the two types of integrative agreement discussed so far, cost cutting and compensation, party A does not retreat from his or her preferred action or demand, but party B's pot is sweetened in one way or another. By contrast, the remaining two types, bridging and logrolling, require *both* parties to change their positions in an effort to reconcile their interests with one another.

Bridging

Bridging occurs when a new option is developed that achieves both parties' major goals. Follett (1940) gives a homely example in a story of two women reading in the same library room. One wanted to open the window for ventilation, the other wanted to keep it closed to avoid a draft. The ultimate solution was to open a window in the next room, which was sufficiently close to bring in fresh air yet sufficiently far to avoid a draft.

In constructing a bridging formula, it is often useful to analyze the basis for the apparent divergence of interest. Sometimes the problem lies in a seeming environmental constraint, such as a resource shortage. In other cases, it resides in a culturally mediated constraint, such as the assumption that husband and wife should spend their leisure time together. A bridging formula can be developed by either party working separately, the two parties working together, or a third party acting as a mediator. Different types of bridging formulas are useful for different sorts of constraints, the following being examples:

1. Sometimes an apparent divergence of interest is due to time constraints, that is, the seeming impossibility of taking both parties' preferred actions at the same time. A person or object cannot simultaneously be in two places or in two mutually exclusive states (such as listening and not listening to the radio). Nor can two people use a limited resource at the same time. Two related types of formulas are available for resolving time constraints:

Alternation, in which one party goes first and the other second. Alternation is useful to the extent that the party going second does not experience prohibitive costs as a result of the delay. Hence, alternation may not be an effective solution if the constraint is due to the scarcity of a resource that is quickly used up.

Contingent sequence, in which one party's proposal is enacted so long as it is successful; but if it is unsuccessful, the other's is enacted.

Alternation would appear to be the more appropriate approach when the two parties have opposing preferences; contingent sequence makes more sense when they have differing values about how to achieve a common goal.

2. Sometimes the difficulty is due to a resource shortage. In these cases, it may be possible to *broaden the pie*, that is, to increase the fund of resources.

3. Assumptions about the necessity of joint action sometimes underlie an apparent divergence of interest. For example, negotiators may assume that substantive agreement must be reached on all issues where action is taken. This assumption can produce failure to reach agreement if feelings are deep and interests quite opposed on one or more issues. An alternative approach is to reach agreement on tractable issues and *agree to disagree* on intractable ones.

Logrolling

When bargaining concerns a set of issues, it may be possible to arrange an exchange of concessions: One party concedes on issues *a*, *b*, and *c* and the other on issues *d*, *e*, and *f*. This exchange will be successful in reconciling interests to the extent that the parties have differing priorities across the set of issues, that is, to the extent that *a*, *b* and *c* are more important to the second party than to the first while *d*, *e*, and *f* are more important to the first party than to the second. This is the process of logrolling. Logrolling is closely related to compensation, the main difference being that in logrolling each party rewards the other for making a concession, whereas in compensation only one party does so.

Logrolling formulas can be developed in two ways. Sometimes logrolling is insightful, in the sense that the party devising the logrolling scheme has an understanding of both parties' priorities. At other times, logrolling simply emerges from concession making. One or both parties drop goal after goal until a mutually satisfactory deal is found. If the parties have differing priorities and each party drops his or her low priority goals, the result is likely to be a reasonably integrative solution. This will be discussed later under the heading, "Heuristic Trial and Error."

Unlinking

We turn now to a process that is often essential to the development of new, more integrative options—the process of unlinking.

When integrative agreements are being devised, it is usually necessary for one or both parties to make *selective concessions*. They must give up certain goals or demands, diminish certain aspirations, or compromise certain values while they adhere firmly to others. Such concessions are most clearly seen in the case of logrolling, where each party's demands must be assigned priorities so as to decide which ones can be relaxed in exchange for concessions by the other party. Selective concessions can also be seen in cost cutting and compensation, since party A must often make sacrifices in order to cut costs for or compensate party B. Bridging does not always require concession making. For example, a marital controversy about whether to go out to dinner or see a movie can sometimes be settled by doing both. But it is usually necessary in bridging for one or both parties to give up certain minor goals or compromise certain less essential values.

Demands, goals, aspirations, and values often come in *bundles*, in the sense of being psychologically linked to other demands, goals, aspirations, and values. Hence in order to make a selective concession, there must occur a process of unlinking, in which a set of related cognitions is disaggregated and certain items are dropped or altered. The bonds between the elements of a bundle are often strong, making it hard to unlink them.

Types of Linkage

There are various forms of linkage, each posing a different obstacle to concession making. Among these we can distinguish substantive linkage, strategic linkage, linkage on behalf of group maintenance and linkage that reflects unresolved past grievances.

Two demands or goals are *substantively* linked when one of them seems to imply the other logically. For example, consider the following problem of a married couple: The husband proposes to buy a car and drive it to Florida for a vacation, and the wife dissents on the grounds that a new car will be too expensive. The purchase of a new car seems a prime candidate for unlinking from this proposal since it is the element that bothers the wife. Yet it cannot simply be dropped since it is instrumental to the shared goal of visiting Florida. Instead, a new element must be invented to take its place, such as renting a car. If imagination is deficient, such an invention may not materialize. Substantive linkage can also be due to the fact that two elements of a proposal are part of the same traditional concept. Some linkages are so strong that a party may not even see the possibility of disaggregation. Such an obstacle is likely to be particularly acute if *both* parties share the same concept, so that neither is able to imagine a way of unlinking its separate parts. Here a third party may be useful.

Other forms of linkage are *strategic* in nature, in the sense of being designed to gain advantage in the negotiation. For example, a "rider" that cannot be sold per se to the other party may be attached to a proposal that the other seems prepared to accept. Since they are not logically tied together, strategic links might appear to be easier to sever than substantive links.

However bargainers frequently become so committed to strategic links that they run the risk of losing face by breaking them.

Where the source of a demand or action is a group (or organization) and different elements are contributed by different group members, linkage is often due to the *desire for group maintenance*. If an element is unlinked and dropped, the group member who sponsors that element may become alienated and create conflict within the group or political problems for the negotiator.

Some elements are hard to drop from a larger package because they reflect unresolved past grievances against the other party. Such grievances are often only tangentially related to the current issues, making them particularly hard to overcome because they are not out in the open. To reach agreement on the manifest issue, one must either resolve the unexpressed controversy or unlink it from the manifest issue. In either case, insight into the dynamics of the controversy is needed.

Unlinking and Bridging

Successful bridging often depends on successful unlinking. For example, alternation is only possible where the party who goes second is willing to drop his or her demand for immediate gratification. Sometimes unlinking precedes bridging, a new option being discovered only after certain goals have been dropped. At other times the order is reversed, with goals being dropped only after an attractive bridging proposal comes into view.

A Method for Studying the Development of Integrative Agreements

The rest of this chapter will be based mainly on the results of a series of laboratory experiments on the development of integrative agreements. These studies employed a common methodology, involving a simulated bargaining task adapted from one used by Kelley (1966). This task simulates the interaction between buyer and seller in a wholesale home appliance market. Pairs of subjects, taking the roles of buyer and seller, must agree on prices for three appliances: television sets, vacuum cleaners, and typewriters.[5]

Each bargainer is given a schedule showing the dollar profits achieved at each price for each appliance. These schedules are shown in Figure 7.2.

[5] In earlier studies in this series, agreement had to be reached on prices for iron, sulfur, and coal.

	Television Sets		Vacuum Cleaners		Typewriters	
Player	Price	Profit	Price	Profit	Price	Profit
	A	$4000	A	$2400	A	$1600
	B	$3500	B	$2100	B	$1400
	C	$3000	C	$1800	C	$1200
	D	$2500	D	$1500	D	$1000
Buyer	E	$2000	E	$1200	E	$ 800
	F	$1500	F	$ 900	F	$ 600
	G	$1000	G	$ 600	G	$ 400
	H	$ 500	H	$ 300	H	$ 200
	I	$ 000	I	$ 000	I	$ 000
	A	$ 000	A	$ 000	A	$ 000
	B	$ 200	B	$ 300	B	$ 500
	C	$ 400	C	$ 600	C	$1000
	D	$ 600	D	$ 900	D	$1500
Seller	E	$ 800	E	$1200	E	$2000
	F	$1000	F	$1500	F	$2500
	G	$1200	G	$1800	G	$3000
	H	$1400	H	$2100	H	$3500
	I	$1600	I	$2400	I	$4000

Figure 7.2. Buyer and seller profit schedules.

The prices are represented by letters so as not to be confused with the profits; A is the lowest price and I the highest price on each appliance. The profit associated with each price is shown to the right of that price. As is frequently the case in multi-issue situations, the issues are of differing priority to the two parties: Television sets provide greatest benefit to the buyer, and typewriters provide greatest benefit to the seller. Hence the largest joint benefits are achieved by means of logrolling, with the buyer granting concessions on the price of typewriters in exchange for seller concessions on the price of television sets. (An example of such an agreement would be A–E–I.) Compromise agreements in which the two parties make equal concessions on all three appliances are also possible but do not yield as high joint benefits or as large individual profit as when logrolling takes place. (An example of such an agreement would be E–E–E.)

Because of the differing priorities among the issues, our research task can be said to have "logrolling potential." This is a subcategory of "integrative potential," a term that refers to the opportunity for cost cutting, compensation, bridging, *or* logrolling.

In most of our studies, the negotiators meet face-to-face. Each negotiator receives a separate profit schedule giving information about only his or her own outcomes. They can say anything they want to each other, including talking about their profit schedules, but they may not show their profit schedules.

Our measures of joint benefit are the sum of the profits achieved by the two parties and the profit achieved by the less successful party. (Results for these two measures are ordinarily quite similar.) In addition, we have often constructed an index of insight into the other negotiator's priority structure on the basis of postquestionnaire items concerning which of the issues was most and which least important to the other party. This index is always moderately correlated with joint benefit (average $r = .49$), suggesting that many though by no means all integrative solutions are accompanied by insight into the other party's priority structure.

Orientation and Aspiration

This section will deal with the impact of orientation and level of aspiration on joint benefit. In the following section, we shall describe (a) a number of bargainer tactics that are associated with, and hence possibly causally antecedent to, the development of high joint benefit and (b) some conditions affecting the use of these tactics. Both discussions will rely heavily on the results of studies using the method just described, though other results and theoretical speculations will also be presented.

The Cooperative Orientation

Deutsch (1973) distinguishes three orientations: "*Cooperative*—the person has a positive interest in the welfare of the others as well as his own welfare; *individualistic*—the person has an interest in doing as well as he can for himself and is unconcerned about the welfare of the others; and *competitive*—the person has an interest in doing better than the others as well as in doing as well as he can for himself [p. 182]."

Deutsch's cooperative orientation is tantamount to a desire to find an integrative agreement. Hence it is not surprising that bilateral instructions inducing this orientation ordinarily lead to high joint benefit (Schulz & Pruitt, 1978). There is, however, one exception to this prediction. When bargainers cannot converse but can only send messages containing their proposals and these proposals carry little or no information about the values that give rise to them, the cooperative orientation can actually undermine joint profit by interfering with an orderly sequence of concessions (Kelley & Schenitzki, 1972). (The importance of an orderly sequence of concessions will be discussed below in the section on heuristic trial and error.)

The Flexible Rigidity Hypothesis

Bargainers who start with an individualistic orientation must translate it into one of two approaches, which can also be called "orientations": the problem-solving orientation and the win/lose orientation. A party with a problem-solving orientation treats the situation as a solvable problem in which he or she is seeking an alternative that is acceptable to both self and other. A party with a win/lose orientation perceives the situation as one in which it is not possible for both parties to succeed and hence seeks to persuade or force the other party to adopt his or her favored option.

Despite a superficial similarity, our problem-solving orientation differs from Deutsch's cooperative orientation in that the emphasis is on finding an alternative the other party can accept rather than one that is in the other's interest. Likewise our win/lose orientation differs from Deutsch's competitive orientation in that the emphasis is on extracting concessions from the other rather than achieving a greater benefit than the other.

As might be expected, integrative agreements ordinarily arise out of a situation in which one, and preferably both, parties adopt a problem-solving orientation. However such an orientation is not sufficient for the development of an integrative agreement. It is also necessary for both parties to have high, relatively inflexible aspirations, that is, to be relatively stubborn. (An "aspiration" is a goal that lies on a continuum of valued outcomes.) The reason for this is that, if aspirations are low or fall rapidly, neither party will be motivated to look beyond easily available compromise alternatives.

Another way of putting this point is that high joint benefit derives from an approach that can be termed *flexible rigidity* (Pruitt & Lewis, 1977). Flexibility of means and flexibility of ends are distinguished in this approach. Flexibility of means refers to the extent to which a party is willing to try out various solutions in search of one that satisfies his or her goals and aspirations, that is, to engage in problem solving. Flexibility of ends refers to the extent to which a party is willing to make concessions on basic goals and aspirations. A party who is rigid about ends can be said to be stubborn, in the meaning of the term used earlier. Flexible rigidity is found when a party is flexible with respect to means but relatively stubborn with respect to ends. He or she starts with high goals and gives them up only gradually if at all yet remains open-minded and explorative about how to achieve them.

Evidence supporting the flexible rigidity hypothesis can be seen in a study by Pruitt and Lewis (1975) and a set of data generated by S. A. Lewis and B. Edwards (personal communication, 1976). Both sets of investigators used the research method described earlier. Orientation (flexibility of means) was manipulated by instructions, with half the subjects receiving a problem-solving orientation and half an individualistic orientation. Stubbornness (flexibility of ends) was manipulated by instructions about limit (maximal fall-back level). Half the subjects were told that they had to make at least $2300 (high) and the other half that they had to make at least $2000 (low). These numbers are equivalent to $4600 and $4000 in the task shown in Figure 7.2. Two findings were achieved in these studies: (a) Higher joint benefits were achieved under a combination of stubbornness and a problem-solving orientation (flexible rigidity) than in any other condition. (b) Fewer agreements were reached under a combination of stubbornness and an individualistic orientation (rigid rigidity) than in any other condition. The second study employed both men and women as subjects.

The Importance of Social Conflict

By endorsing stubbornness (rigid ends), we are saying that social conflict is often necessary for the emergence of high joint benefit. Each party must make demands on the other while resisting the other's demands, which is the essence of conflict.

This reliance on conflict is paradoxical, because conflict has the capacity to undermine the problem-solving orientation. This is likely to occur when a party makes demands that seem illegitimate or too large or employs tactics that seem overly harsh. The other's response is usually to become defensive and to adopt a win/lose outlook that diminishes the likelihood of achieving high joint benefit.

The solution to this paradox lies in the type of conflict waged. Productive conflicts (those leading to integrative outcomes) are in the category of "vigorous discussions" or "mild arguments," where both parties state their preferences and stick to their goals while remaining flexible about their means of goal attainment. Aspirations need to be high, yet demands cannot seem "unreasonable" to the other party. This suggests the importance of being sensitive to the other party's standards of reasonableness, explaining the motives behind one's demands so as not to seem arbitrary, and employing tact. It is also desirable to build a "conflict cushion" of positive feelings between the parties, prior to the onset of conflict, so that they do not become defensive at the first hint of an unacceptable demand or tactic from the other. Many social norms contribute to the development of these elements of productive conflict because integrative agreements are much in the interest of society.

THE ROLE OF HARSH DISPUTES

Harsh disputes, involving win/lose orientations and associated pressure tactics, are sometimes found *before* the advent of a problem-solving process, the conflict taking the form of a two-stage sequence. Despite the fact that they are not constructive themselves, disputes that are initially harsh can contribute to the problem-solving process in three ways:

1. They can motivate the parties to engage in problem solving as an alternative to making a fight to the finish. Having looked over the abyss at the possibility of knock-down-drag-out warfare, the parties often draw back and become quite reasonable. (An important unresolved theoretical question concerns the circumstances under which the parties draw back from, as opposed to going over, such an abyss.)

2. They can motivate the parties to sharpen their understanding of their own interests so that they can develop priorities and reasonably explain their stubborn stands in the ensuing problem-solving stage.

3. They can provide a forum in which the parties can communicate clearly and dramatically with one another about the limits beyond which they are unwilling to concede. When such limits become clear, the parties are likely to drop those demands which the other side finds especially unpalatable, thereby diminishing the perceived divergence of interest and making it easier to adopt a problem solving orientation. Information about such limits also provides guidance about the realms within which to search for an agreement.

In addition to the two-stage sequence, another common pattern is one that moves back and forth between win/lose and problem-solving phases. As each new issue arises or old issue resurfaces, there is a period of harsh dispute followed by a period of problem solving.

CONFLICT AVOIDANCE

Failure to be stubborn about one's goals often results from a desire to avoid conflict (Pruitt & Lewis, 1977). Hence the desire to avoid conflict can undermine the development of integrative agreements.

The desire to avoid conflict is found when each party is attracted to the other party but is distrustful of the other's feelings. This situation, which has been termed "false cohesiveness" (Longley & Pruitt, 1980), is especially common at the beginning of a relationship when people are feeling each other out. This suggests that agreements reached in early stages of group development will often be less integrative than those reached in later stages *or in relations between people who do not know each other.*

The latter part of this hypothesis is counter-intuitive, since we can expect people who are developing a relationship with each other to be more likely than strangers to take a problem-solving orientation, which should encourage the development of integrative agreements. Yet solid evidence can be cited in favor of this proposition. Using the research task developed in our laboratory, Fry, Firestone and Williams (1979) found that dating couples achieved lower joint outcomes than male–female stranger dyads. Evidence that this was due to conflict avoidance can be seen in the fact that the former couples typically terminated negotiation as soon as an alternative that satisfied both parties' limits had been mentioned, whereas the latter continued negotiating beyond this point. Other evidence suggests that members of the dating couples had more of a problem-solving orientation than members of the stranger dyads. But their lack of stubbornness appears to have offset this favorable orientation so that the net effect was reduced integrativeness.

In a related study (Mullick & Lewis, 1977), it was found that the diminished outcomes in dating couples were more characteristic of the women than of the men, suggesting that the women were especially conflict avoidant. Furthermore, women who favored the traditional sex-role in which males are dominant did particularly poorly in comparison to those with more modern, egalitarian attitudes. However, we must be careful not to generalize these results to sex differences as a whole. They were found in a study of mixed-sex dating dyads. In studies of same-sex stranger dyads (Kimmel *et al.*, 1980; Lewis & Edwards, personal communication, 1976) no sex differences were found in outcomes.

The willingness of two parties to engage in constructive conflict, and hence to develop integrative agreements, is probably enhanced if they are *equal in power*. When they are unequal, the more powerful party is likely to avoid joint problem solving because of a belief that he or she can dominate the other, and the less powerful party is likely to follow suit out of fear of reprisal or because of a sense of hopelessness about achieving an equitable agreement. This prediction is supported by the experimental research of Thibaut and Faucheux (1965) and by Bach's clinical observations (Bach & Wyden, 1968).

Tactics Leading toward and Away from Integrative Agreements

In studies employing the task shown in Figure 7.2, we have content analyzed the subjects' verbalizations, in an effort to identify the tactics they are using. Examples of the categories used are "stating a new proposal" and "making a threat." The score for each category is the proportion of verbalizations coded in this way.

Most of our statistical analyses of these measures employ *dyad scores*, the sum of the buyer and seller scores for each dyad. These scores are justified on three grounds: (*a*) We wish to correlate these scores against joint outcome, which is a dyad score; (b) since the two negotiators talk with one another, their data can hardly be regarded as statistically independent; (c) the two members of a dyad ordinarily use much the same tactics (Kimmel et al., 1980), so that they are often indeed acting as a unit.

The tactics coded in this fashion are of four general types: information exchange, incorporation, heuristic trial and error, and pressure tactics. The first three types are usually found to be positively correlated with joint benefit and can be viewed as manifestations of the problem-solving orientation. Pressure tactics are usually negatively correlated with joint benefit and can be thought of as deriving from the win/lose orientation. The fact that the two bargainers are ordinarily quite similar in their level of usage of a tactic suggests that they imitate one another's approach.

Information Exchange

Integrative agreements are sometimes achieved because one party has developed insight into the other's motivational structure (goals, aspirations, values, constraints, priorities) and seeks a way to unite the two viewpoints. Such insight can be developed in a number of ways, of which information exchange is the most prominent. In information exchange, one party provides the other with some sort of information about the first party's motivational structure. This information can be either explicit (direct talk about motives) or implicit (indirect reference to motives).

EXPLICIT INFORMATION EXCHANGE

Our subjects often discuss the numbers in their profit schedules. We view this as analogous to talking about the nature of the motives underlying one's proposals. Explicit information exchange has been positively though often weakly correlated with both insight and joint benefit in most of our studies (Kimmel et al., 1980; Pruitt et al., 1978; Pruitt & Lewis, 1975; Schulz & Pruitt, 1978), suggesting that it produces integrative agreements by a process of insight into the needs underlying the other party's demands.

We have found three conditions under which explicit information exchange is especially predictive of high joint profit. One (Pruitt & Lewis, 1975) involves pairs of negotiators who are both high in cognitive complexity as measured by the Streufert and Driver (1967) technique. These people provide no more information than their less complex compatriots but appear to be more capable of using the information effectively.

The second condition involves a cooperative orientation, in Deutch's (1973) sense of the term. Under this orientation, the parties seek to maximize both their own and the other's outcomes. This orientation produces more explicit information exchange than an individualistic orientation, and, under this orientation, explicit information is particularly likely to lead to high joint profit (Schulz & Pruitt, 1978).

There is also evidence (Pruitt *et al.*, 1978) that explicit information exchange is more useful under low than under high accountability to a constituent. (*High accountability* means that the constituent has considerable power over the bargainer. *Low accountability* means either that the constituent has little power or that there is no constituent.) We suspect that this result is due to the reduced social distance and hence greater trust between bargainers under low accountability. Trust presumably both enhances the amount of information exchanged and makes it more likely to be believed.

It should be noted that while explicit communication about values can lead to integrative agreements under some conditions, it can actually be counterproductive under others. For example, when the bargainers disagree about basic values, explicit statements about values may evoke a reaction of shock and outrage, reducing the motivation to coordinate interests (Druckman & Zechmeister, 1973). Such statements can also reveal hostility where it exists, similarly poisoning the atmosphere. In such cases, other forms of communication may be preferable, such as communication through an intermediary.

Having a problem-solving orientation—as opposed to an individualistic orientation—has been found to encourage explicit information exchange (Pruitt & Lewis, 1975). However, information exchange is not inevitable under this orientation because it involves *risks*. The main risk is that the other party will use the information obtained about one's goals and values to develop threats that hit where it hurts. Hence, to get information exchange, the problem-solving orientation must be coupled with *trust*. In this context, the term "trust" is used somewhat differently from the way we employed it before. Here it means a belief that the other party also has a problem-solving orientation (Kimmel *et al.*, 1980). In the study where this was found, trust produced an especially high level of explicit information exchange when aspirations were high as opposed to low. This was presumably because the bargainers sensed little need for problem solving when their aspirations were low, since an obvious compromise agreement (e.g., E–E–E) could be easily achieved. Hence trust was less relevant in this condition.

IMPLICIT INFORMATION EXCHANGE

Where explicit talk about one's motives seems unwise or unproductive, implicit approaches may be used. One such approach is to make statements about the dimension(s) on which the other party's position can be improved. For example, in a negotiation concerning several issues, labor might ask management to improve its offer on hospital benefits, failing to mention other issues such as overtime pay. We call this *directional information*, because the communicator is indicating the direction in which he or she wants the other to move on a particular matter.

In the Kimmel *et al.* (1980) study, directional information was especially prominent when the bargainers had high aspirations and low trust, presumably because directional information is a low risk form of problem solving. The reader may wonder why we regard this kind of behavior as a form of information exchange, since it could conceivably contribute *directly* to high joint profit by encouraging the listener to suggest a proposal favorable to the speaker. Our conclusion is based primarily on a partial correlation that was calculated between directional information and joint profit, with insight into the other's priorities held constant. This correlation was negligible and nonsignificant, suggesting that insight mediates the relationship between the other two variables.

Another form of implicit information exchange that has been coded in two of our studies (Kimmel *et al.*, 1980; Pruitt *et al.*, 1978) involves statements of preference between two offers made by the other party. Such statements can apparently be decoded into information about the communicator's priorities which can then be used to develop a bridging solution. As with directional information, such statements are predictive of both insight into the other party's priorities and joint outcome.

However, in contrast to directional information (and also explicit information), bargainers who employ statements of preference between two offers do not regard themselves as having been "cooperative." Hence this tactic should probably not be regarded as a manifestation of the problem-solving orientation. Rather it appears that one party blunders into statements of preference for individualistic reasons and the other decodes information about the first party's priorities from these statements.

Incorporation

In the absence of information about the other party's motivational structure, it may still be possible to take his or her viewpoint into account by formulating a proposal that serves one's own interests even though it includes elements of the other party's latest proposal. One need not understand the rationale behind the other's proposal to incorporate parts of it into one's own. This tactic has the capacity to produce an integrative agreement if the elements incorporated are important to the other party and not too costly to the self.

Evidence of the value of incorporation can be seen in two studies that employed our methodology (Fry, Firestone, & Williams, 1979; Williams & Lewis, 1976). An incorporation index was also used in several of our studies, with results that were always positive but never statistically significant. Hence the evidence that incorporation produces integrative agreements is positive but weak.

Heuristic Trial and Error

Heuristic trial and error is our name for a set of intercorrelated tactics that contribute to the development of high joint profit. Taken collectively, these tactics can be thought of as a single strategy, which gets its name as follows: "Trial and error" means that it involves throwing out a variety of proposals without insight into how they will affect the other bargainer; "heuristic" means that it employs several devices (heuristics) for enhancing the likelihood of finding a proposal with high joint benefit.

Heuristic trial and error entails both elements of the flexible rigidity formulation: flexibility with respect to means (in the sense of willingness to explore many possible approaches to agreement) and rigidity (stubbornness) with respect to ends. Ambitious goals are initially adopted, and alternatives aimed at satisfying these goals are sought. Each alternative that is located in this way is submitted to the other party. If the other rejects it, a new alternative is sought. Only when it appears that no new alternatives can be found to satisfy the initial set of goals is one or more of these goals dropped, and a modified search begun. Such modification, when it occurs, takes the form of unlinking and dropping the goals that are lowest in priority, so that as little as possible is sacrificed. This process continues until an alternative is found that satisfies the other party.

In our research, we have coded three tactics that represent different aspects of heuristic trial and error:

1. Frequently changing one's offer, operationalized by the proportion of statements involving a new and different proposal
2. Presenting all proposals possible at one profit level before moving to another, a form of orderly concession making first described by Kelley and Schenitzki (1972)
3. Making larger concessions on low priority than on high priority issues

The first of these three tactics can be viewed as simple trial and error. Tactics 2 and 3 can be viewed as "heuristics," methods for generating new alternatives that are valuable to oneself.

The codes employed to measure these three tactics are usually moderately intercorrelated, suggesting that these tactics are manifestations of a unified strategy. In addition, people who use this strategy tend to ask for the other party's reactions to each of their proposals, presumably a manifestation of the underlying problem-solving orientation.

Heuristic trial and error was found to be positively related to joint profit in most of our studies (Kimmel *et al.*, 1980; Lewis & Fry, 1977; Pruitt *et al.*, 1978; Pruitt & Lewis, 1975; Schulz & Pruitt, 1978). Again, the strength of this relationship was moderated by accountability to constituents, with heuristic trial and error being more effective the *greater* the accountability (Pruitt *et al.*, 1978). This latter finding may be due to the fact that high accountability fosters a competitive atmosphere with a concomitant lack of trust. This presumably reduces the amount of information exchange, leaving heuristic trial and error as the only means for achieving high joint profit. Heuristic trial and error is always uncorrelated with insight, indicating that it encourages the development of high joint profit without an understanding of the other party's needs or priorities. Like information exchange, the use of heuristic trial and error results from having a problem-solving orientation (Pruitt & Lewis, 1975).

Pressure Tactics

Four of our codes are viewed as measures of the use of *pressure tactics*.[6] These codes are: (*a*) *persuasive arguments* aimed at changing the other's attitudes on the issue; (*b*) *putdowns*, aimed at trying to impress the other with one's higher power or status; (*c*) *positional commitments*, designed to persuade the other that one cannot or will not move from one's current proposal and hence that the other must concede if he or she wishes to avoid a deadlock; (*d*) *threats*, which have the purpose of persuading the other that failure to concede will be punished. These four measures are usually highly intercorrelated across dyads, suggesting that they represent a single strategy. The aim of this strategy is apparently to elicit concessions from the other party.

Unequal use of pressure tactics leads to an agreement favoring the heavier user (Williams & Lewis, 1976). But such victories are likely to be pyrrhic in situations with integrative potential, because the use of pressure tactics ordinarily hurts both parties' interests, interfering with the attainment of high joint benefit (Carnevale, Pruitt, & Britton, 1979; Kimmel *et al.*, 1980; Lewis & Fry, 1977; Pruitt & Lewis, 1975; Schulz & Pruitt, 1978). How can this latter finding be explained? The problem with pressure tactics may be in part that they block problem-solving behavior. Bargainers employing them are so busy pursuing their own interests that they do not see the possibility that both parties can win. The problem may also be in part a failure of imagination, since one of the main pressure tactics involves stand-

---

[6] In previous publications (e.g., Pruitt & Lewis, 1977), we have called these tactics *distributive behavior*, following the terminology of Walton and McKersie (1965), but the term *pressure tactics* seems to communicate better.

ing firmly on a single proposal and trying to persuade the other to move in that direction.

Pressure tactics are a manifestation of the win/lose orientation and hence are largely incompatible with the problem-solving orientation (Pruitt & Lewis, 1975). In the context of a win/lose orientation, placing a barrier between two bargainers so that they can talk to but not see each other reduces the use of pressure tactics and increases joint profit (Lewis & Fry, 1977). When aspirations are high, the use of pressure tactics is also encouraged by the absence of trust (Kimmel et al., 1980). A possible explanation for this result is that low trust precludes information exchange, forcing the bargainer to turn to other methods for pursuing agreement. Since concession making is ruled out by the bargainer's high aspirations, the use of pressure tactics may seem like the only remaining strategic option.

Other antecedents of the use of pressure tactics include perceived relative power over the other party (Carnevale, Sherer, & Pruitt, 1979; Michener et al., 1975), slow concessions from the other party when there is a prominent alternative (Gruder, 1971; Michener et al., 1975), closeness of one's demands to one's limit (Kelley, Beckman, & Fischer, 1967), and hence the height of one's limit (Carnevale, Sherer, & Pruitt, 1979; Fischer, 1969). By "limit" is meant a bargainer's ultimate fall-back position. The closer bargainers' demands are to their limits, the less capable they are of making concessions. Hence they must rely more on pressure tactics if they want to reach agreement.

The use of pressure tactics is also related to bargainer accountability. (A bargainer is accountable when representing constituents that have power over him or her.) Pruitt et al. (1978) have found that high accountability produces pressure tactics and diminished joint profit in comparison to low accountability.

Following the lead of Lewis and Fry (1977), Carnevale, Pruitt, and Seilheimer (1981) have shown that this accountability effect occurs only in face-to-face interaction. When bargainers could see and hear each other, high accountability produced a heavy use of pressure tactics and low joint benefit. However, this effect disappeared when they could not see each other.

This finding and the one mentioned earlier by Lewis and Fry can be summarized as indicating that, in a win/lose context (i.e., where both parties have a win/lose orientation), visual access tends to promote the use of pressure tactics and the attainment of low joint benefit. In the Lewis and Fry study, a win/lose context was produced by individualistic (as opposed to problem solving) instructions. In the Carnevale study, this context was produced by bilateral high (as opposed to low) accountability. There are at least two possible explanations for this effect. One is that a large component of win/lose behavior is nonverbal; for example, staring, in an effort to dominate the other party. In a win/lose context, a party who can see the other will be tempted to try to stare the other down and will interpret the other's staring in the same way. Such events will heighten the competitive tone of the interaction, promoting the use of verbal pressure tactics. In the absence of a win/lose context, the eyes will not be used or interpreted in this way. Evidence favoring this interpretation can be seen in the Lewis and Fry finding of a correlation between the incidence of staring and the use of verbal pressure tactics. The second explanation suggests that in a win/lose context, the visual image of the adversary acts as a cue that elicits hostile and domineering verbal behavior.

In another study of the bargainer as representative (Carnevale, Pruitt, & Britton, 1979), constituent surveillance was found to diminish joint profit. Process measures suggested that constituent surveillance compelled bargainers to appear strong, which encouraged the use of pressure tactics and consequently interfered with the development of integrative agreements.

Conclusions

Integrative agreements have practical as well as intrinsic value. The capacity to develop such agreements makes it less likely that bargainers will break off negotiation and more likely that an agreement once reached will be maintained. Integrative agreements contribute to mutual attraction and to the effectiveness of the group or organization reaching them.

Taking an overview of our theory, we have essentially described joint decision making as a two-stage process. In the first stage, the parties indicate their preferences. If a divergence of interest exists, these preferences will not be identical and the parties will have to go on to the second stage where an effort is made to resolve their controversy.

Two main orientations can be taken to the second stage, each implying a particular range of strategies. One is a win/lose orientation, in which the parties are motivated to try to persuade each other to concede. This orientation produces pressure tactics such as threats, positional commitments, efforts to establish an image of strength, and persuasive arguments of all kinds. The other is a problem-solving orientation, in which the parties are motivated to try to locate a mutually acceptable option. The problem-solving orientation encourages heuristic trial and error and discourages the use of pressure tactics. Where trust and high aspirations exist, the problem-solving orientation also encourages exchange of information about values and priorities aimed at locating an option to which both can agree. The problem-solving orientation in conjunction with bilaterally high aspirations produces high joint benefit. The win/lose orientation encourages low joint benefit. This theory helps explain a number of empirical findings about the conditions affecting joint benefit. One is that high joint benefit is especially hard to reach in the early stages of group formation when people are reluctant to risk conflict by maintaining high aspirations. A second is that bargainers who can talk without seeing each other achieve higher joint benefit than those who can also see each other because they make less use of pressure tactics. This implies a testable hypothesis, that, in a win/lose context, telephone contact is more productive than face-to-face contact. A third finding is that bargainers who are more accountable to the people they represent achieve lower joint benefit because they make more use of pressure tactics. The same effect is found when the constituents watch the negotiation instead of only learning about it later. The latter two findings suggest that, in situations with integrative potential, representatives who are given considerable decision latitude and are not closely monitored are likely to achieve higher benefits for their constituents than those who are strictly supervised.

These findings have been established in a laboratory task with logrolling potential. It makes theoretical sense that they should extend to settings where the integrative potential lies with cost cutting, compensation or bridging. But generality research needs to be done on this question.

Acknowledgments

Preparation of this manuscript was supported by two awards to the first author: National Science Foundation Grant BNS7610963A03, and a fellowship from the John Simon Guggenheim Memorial Foundation. The authors wish to thank the following people for their useful comments on earlier drafts: Pamela S. Engram, Jeanne Longley, Brenda Major, Robert W. Rice, D. Leasel Smith, and Helena Syna.

References

Bach, G. R., & Wyden, P. *The intimate enemy*. New York: Avon Books, 1968.

Brehm, J. W. *A theory of psychological reactance*. New York: Academic Press, 1966.

Carnevale, P. J. D., Pruitt, D. G., & Britton, S. D. Looking tough: The negotiator under constituent surveillance. *Personality and Social Psychology Bulletin*, 1979, 5, 118–121.

Carnevale, P. J. D., Pruitt, D. G., & Seilheimer, S. Looking and competing: Accountability and visual access in integrative bargaining. *Journal of Personality and Social Psychology*, 1981, 40, 111–120.

Carnevale, P. J. D., Sherer, P., & Pruitt, D. G. *Some determinants of concession rate and distributive tactics in negotiation*. Presented at the annual meeting of the American Psychological Association, New York, 1979.

Deutsch, M. *The resolution of conflict*. New Haven, Conn.: Yale University Press, 1973.

Druckman, D., & Zechmeister, K. Conflict of interest and value dissensus: Propositions in the sociology of conflict. *Human Relations*, 1973, *26*, 449–466.

Fischer, C. S. The effects of threats in an incomplete information game. *Sociometry*, 1969, *32*, 301–314.

Follett, M. P. Constructive conflict. In H. C. Metcalf & L. Urwick (Eds.), *Dynamic administration: The collected papers of Mary Parker Follett*. New York: Harper & Brothers, 1940.

Fry, W. R., Firestone, I. J., & Williams, D. *Bargaining process in mixed-singles dyads: Loving and losing*. Presented at the annual meeting of the Eastern Psychological Association, Philadelphia, 1979.

Goffman, E. *The presentation of self in everyday life*. Garden City, N.Y.: Doubleday, 1959.

Gruder, C. L. Relationship with opponent and partner in mixed-motive bargaining. *Journal of Conflict Resolution*, 1971, *15*, 403–416.

Jervis, R. *The logic of images in international relations*. Princeton, N.J.: Princeton University Press, 1970.

Kelley, H. H. A classroom study of the dilemmas in interpersonal negotiations. In K. Archibald (Ed.), *Strategic interaction and conflict*. Berkeley, Calif.: Institute of International Studies, University of California, 1966.

Kelley, H. H. *Personal relationships: Their structure and processes*. Hillsdale, N.J.: Lawrence Erlbaum, 1979.

Kelley, H. H., & Schenitzki, D. P. Bargaining. In C. G. McClintock (Ed.), *Experimental social psychology*. New York: Holt, Rinehart & Winston, 1972.

Kelley, H. H., & Thibaut, J. W. *Interpersonal relations: A theory of interdependence*. New York: John Wiley & Sons, 1978.

Kelley, H. H., Beckman, L. L., & Fischer, C. S. Negotiating the division of reward under incomplete information. *Journal of Experimental Social Psychology*, 1967, *3*, 361–398.

Kimmel, M. J., Pruitt, D. G., Magenau, J. M., Konar-Goldband, E., & Carnevale, P. J. D. Effects of trust, aspiration and gender on negotiation tactics. *Journal of Personality and Social Psychology*, 1980, *38*, 9–23.

Lewis, S. A., & Fry, W. R. Effects of visual access and orientation on the discovery of integrative bargaining alternatives. *Organizational Behavior and Human Performance*, 1977, *20*, 75–92.

Longley, J., & Pruitt, D. G. A critique of Janis' theory of groupthink. In L. Wheeler (Ed.), *Review of personality and social psychology*. Beverly Hills, Calif.: Sage, 1980.

Lott, A., & Lott, B. Group cohesiveness as interpersonal attraction: A review of relationships between antecedent and consequent variables. *Psychological Bulletin*, 1965, *64*, 259–309.

Michener, H. A., Vaske, J. J., Schleifer, S. L., Plazewski, J. G., & Chapman, L. J. Factors affecting concession rate and threat usage in bilateral conflict. *Sociometry*, 1975, *38*, 62–80.

Mullick, B., & Lewis, S. A. *Sex-roles, loving and liking: A look at dating couples' bargaining behavior*. Presented at the annual meeting of the American Psychological Association, San Francisco, 1977.

O'Neill, N., & O'Neill, G. *Open marriage*. New York: Avon, 1972.

Pruitt, D. G., & Gleason, J. M. Threat capacity and the choice between independence and interdependence. *Personality and Social Psychology Bulletin*, 1978, *4*, 252–255.

Pruitt, D. G., & Lewis, S. A. Development of integrative solutions in bilateral negotiation. *Journal of Personality and Social Psychology*, 1975, *31*, 621–633.

Pruitt, D. G., & Lewis, S. A. The psychology of integrative bargaining. In D. Druckman (Ed.), *Negotiations: A social psychological perspective*. Beverly Hills, Calif.: Sage-Halsted, 1977.

Pruitt, D. G., Kimmel, M. J., Britton, S., Carnevale, P. J. D., Magenau, J. M., Peragallo, J., & Engram, P. The effect of accountability and surveillance on integrative bargaining. In H. Sauermann (Ed.), *Bargaining behavior*. Tübingen: Mohr, 1978.

Rapoport, A. *Two-person game theory: The essential ideas*. Ann Arbor, Mich.: University of Michigan Press, 1966.

Schulz, J. W., & Pruitt, D. G. The effects of mutual concern on joint welfare. *Journal of Experimental Social Psychology*, 1978, *14*, 480–491.

Sen, A. K. *Collective choice and individual values*. New York: Holden-Day, 1970.

Streufert, S., & Driver, M. Impression formation as a measure of the complexity of conceptual structure. *Education and Psychological Measurement*, 1967, *27*, 1025–1039.

Tannenbaum, A. S. *Control in organizations*. New York: McGraw-Hill, 1968.

Thibaut, J., & Faucheux, C. The development of contractual norms in a bargaining situation under two types of stress. *Journal of Experimental Social Psychology*, 1965, *1*, 89–102.

Walster, E., Walster, G. W., & Berscheid, E. *Equity: Theory and research*. Boston: Allyn and Bacon, 1978.

Walton, R. E., & McKersie, R. B. *A behavioral theory of labor negotiations: An analysis of a social interaction system*. New York: McGraw-Hill, 1965.

Williams, D. L., & Lewis, S. A. *The effects of sex-role attitudes on integrative bargaining*. Presented at the annual meeting of the American Psychological Association, Washington, 1976.

Chapter 8

Social Trap Analogs:

The Tragedy

of the Commons

in the Laboratory

DARWYN E. LINDER

The natural resources of the planet Earth are being depleted at an alarming rate. Species are becoming extinct; our air and water are increasingly befouled; timber and minerals are increasingly scarce; and energy shortages have begun to plague the highly developed, technologically oriented nations of the world. As we watch our resources disappear, some gradually and others with astonishing quickness, the need for effective solutions grows. We must find ways to live together, using the resources of the "spaceship Earth" but not exhausting them.

Many of the resources in the natural environment can be considered "commons" in the sense that Hardin (1968) has used the term. His "tragedy of the commons" is the prototype for a number of structurally similar situations in which a group of individuals uses resources drawn from a common pool. As Hardin describes it, the commons originally referred to pasturage that was available to any and all of the livestock owners in a given locality. Each owner could put to pasture a herd of animals and reap the entire benefit from the products of the herd: meat, milk, wool, and offspring. Each person was motivated by economic factors to increase the size of his or her herd. Thus, the number of animals grazing on the commons would be increased whenever it was possible to do so. As long as war,

COOPERATION AND HELPING BEHAVIOR
Theories and Research

famine, disease, and natural disasters kept the population of humans and animals relatively small the system worked quite well. But as humans gained mastery over the environment and controlled the impact of these naturally limiting factors, the size of the herd grew until it exceeded the carrying capacity of the commons, the rate at which grass could be regenerated from one season to the next. Even after the carrying capacity of the commons had been exceeded it was to the advantage of each individual owner to continue to increase the herd. The reduction in the productivity of the commons caused by adding another animal was suffered by all users, but the profit from owning another animal accrued directly to the individual. Thus the users of the commons, pursuing individual gain, destroyed the very resource that had sustained them.

Social traps are "situations in society that contain traps formally like a fish trap, where men or organizations or whole societies get themselves started in some direction or some set of relationships that later prove to be unpleasant or lethal and that they see no easy way to back out of or to avoid [Platt, 1973, p. 641]." The tragedy of the commons is a prototype of a social trap, but there are many such examples in both the recent and distant past. Social traps can be defined quite easily in the language of Skinnerian behaviorism (Platt, 1973). A social trap occurs when individuals respond by seeking and gaining immediate gratification but the collective impact of many such responses by many people leads to a long-term negative consequence for all. Brechner (1977) has restated the definition of social traps as "situations in which (1) responses by an organism generate at least two consequences of oppositive valence, (2) the positive consequence is immediate while the negative consequence is delayed, and (3) the responses of other organisms in the environment affect the length of the delay [Brechner, 1977, p. 555]." The language of behaviorism provides for a convenient definition of social traps, but the analysis of social traps need not be confined to the behaviorist perspective. In later sections of this paper we will examine behavior in social traps and ways of avoiding social traps that are based on an analysis of behavioral as well as cognitive, motivational, and social factors.

A social trap is a distinct form of interdependence, overlapping in part but in several ways different from prisoners' dilemmas and other conflict-of-interest situations. Kelley and Thibaut (1978) have provided an elegant analysis of the various forms of interdependence that can be captured in the interaction matrix. They have shown that the variety of games that have been used in research on interdependence and conflict of interest—the prisoner's dilemma, chicken, and others—can be derived from the general principles of interdependence matrices that they have developed. The two-person matrix games analyzed by Kelley and Thibaut can be expanded to

n-person games in which each player may either cooperate or defect. Such games provide one model of a commons dilemma if every player gains by defecting no matter how many others defect, but the payoff to each person for unanimous cooperation is greater than the payoff to each person when all defect (Dawes, 1980). In these games the defecting response may be to continue to behave in such a way as to exploit or pollute a common-pool resource. Thus, some situations that are social traps, as we have defined the concept, can also be modeled by these games. For example, Kelley and Grzelak (1972) argue that failing to install automobile pollution control devices is a defecting response that provides a gain for each individual, but if all defect, air quality is much worse than if all cooperate. In most instances of matrix interdependence the outcomes for all participating parties are determined by the intersection of their individual actions, and the consequences are applied immediately. Within the matrix the degree of interdependence is fixed, and the impact of each person's behavior on each other person's outcomes is immediately known. In a social trap individuals are nearly independent, for short-term outcomes. It is only in the long run or after a long period of time in the situation that interdependence becomes apparent. And it is only when the commons has been very nearly destroyed that the behavior of one individual has an immediate impact on the outcomes of others. There is the possibility of continual change in the degree of interdependence embodied in a particular social trap situation and the valence of the various response options may shift continuously over time. Of course it is true that low rates of responding or some form of restraint could be considered a cooperative move in a social trap situation and that high rates of responding or excessive consumption could be considered a competitive move. However, such an attempt to map the dynamic situation of a social trap into the relatively more static configuration of a prisoners' dilemma matrix would obscure the very features of the social trap that are important to understand for the development of solutions or ways to avoid the eventual tragedy.

The traditional definition of a social trap does not include the notion of a commons, or *common pool resource*, the term we shall use in the remainder of this chapter. And in many situations that can be characterized as social traps the concept of the common pool resource simply does not apply. For example, wage–price inflation is brought about by the demand for higher wages, leading producers of goods and services to charge higher prices which in turn lead to another round of demands for higher wages. Another example is the rise of street crime in urban neighborhoods. If individuals believe there is some danger of being victimized they may withdraw from the streets of the neighborhood behind locked doors and drawn shades. As the streets become more and more deserted, the probability of an attack increases until the streets are truly dangerous, and the probability of other crimes (e.g., burglary) is also increased.

Thus the social trap concept encompasses a broader range of problems than just the common pool resource type. However, since most of the problems that we confront as we attempt to live together in the twentieth century are problems of managing a common pool resource, most of our examples will be taken from that class of situations. In the remainder of this chapter we will attempt a conceptual analysis of the development of social traps, and we will try to apply several psychological perspectives to behavior in social trap situations. Those perspectives will be used to develop ways of avoiding or escaping from social traps. Social trap analogs—laboratory situations in which the structure of a social trap is embodied in a game-like situation—will be introduced as a useful tool for evaluating the potential effectiveness of solutions. Finally, we will attempt to construct some general principles for the escape from or avoidance of social traps.

The Development of Social Traps

A situation is not a social trap until the collective responses of the participants summate to produce an eventual negative outcome. This can be shown most clearly by using the example of a renewable common pool resource. There is a period of time during which the individual users of the common pool resource are objectively independent of one another. As long as the resource is under-used and is fully replenished after each cycle of use—whether that cycle is one of the seasons, of mating and reproduction, or of some slow, nearly continuous process such as the percolation of new water into existing aquafers—the actions of one individual user have no impact on the availability of the resource to other users. But when the carrying capacity of a common pool resource has been exceeded it is no longer fully replenished after each cycle, and the more of the resource that is demanded and used by each individual the less will remain for the consumption of all other users. The degree of interdependence usually grows slowly, starting just after the carrying capacity has been exceeded, and in many instances interdependence will not be obvious for quite some time. In Hardin's tragedy of the commons, for example, it may have been difficult to discern that the grass was no longer as lush as it had been in previous springs. In other situations, the shift from independence to interdependence can be abrupt and obvious. When the carrying capacity of an electrical generating utility in a given area has been exceeded, a brown-out or black-out occurs with startling suddenness. When gasoline supplies are no longer adequate for the consumption of automobile users, lines appear at gasoline stations and we are dramatically informed of our new state of interdependence. As overuse continues interdependence grows, and the ability of the commons to replenish itself diminishes. Eventually interdependence is complete, and the resource is exhausted by the killing of the last passenger pigeon or the consumption of the last blade of grass.

In many such situations however, the utility of continued individual use of the resource remains quite high. As Crowe (1969), who has also explored the tragedy of the commons, has shown, the utility of adding additional animals to one's own herd remained very high even after the carrying capacity of the commons had been far exceeded. A gallon of gas is as useful in a period of gasoline shortage as in a period of plenty even though the increased cost experienced lately has somewhat diminished that utility. However, the number of cars traveling on the streets and highways indicates that the utility has not been greatly diminished. In many instances the cost of exploiting the commons increases continually after carrying capacity has been reached and the shortage continues to grow. It is no doubt more expensive to find and kill the last whale than it was to find and kill whales prior to the great reduction in their numbers that we have seen in the last few decades. But the cost factor is perhaps the only force that reduces the utility of the consummatory response, the utility of exploiting the commons. In some instances the motivation to obtain the short-term benefit, whether that is a large herd of cattle, a full tank of gasoline, or a temperature of 72 degrees, is unaffected by the shortage of the resource. In other instances the motivation to obtain the short-term benefit may be increased by the recognition of a shortage.

A social trap, then, may develop suddenly or gradually, but in either case the utility of exploitation, consumption of the resource, maintains individual responding even as the resource grows more and more scarce or more and more difficult to obtain. Furthermore, the behavioral patterns and the cognitive schemata developed during the period of independence may prove disastrous during the period of interdependence.

Psychological Perspectives

Behavior in a social trap situation can be viewed from a variety of psychological perspectives. Platt (1973) used the language of Skinnerian behaviorism to develop both a definition and some analyses of the ways behavior in social trap situations is maintained and might be changed. Subsequent research on behavior in social traps has continued to use the behaviorist approach (Brechner, 1975; 1977), but other researchers have adopted cognitive and social perspectives, taking account of the way in which an individual thinks about and understands a social trap or a commons dilemma (Stern, 1976; Edney & Harper, 1978a). Others have examined the impact of social forces on behavior in social traps and commons dilemmas (Dawes, McTavish, & Shacklee, 1977; Shippee, 1978).

The behavioral perspective leads to a quite simple statement of the contingencies that are in effect in a social trap situation. Put simply, the consummatory response is maintained by continuous reinforcement. Each time an individual exploits or uses the commons he or she is rewarded with a positive outcome, a personal gain of some kind. The long-term negative outcome, the tragedy, can be viewed as punishment; however, there is a long delay between the consummatory response and the eventual punishment, the total depletion of the resource. Brechner (1977) has proposed that a social trap can be considered as a system of superimposed schedules of reinforcement. The contingency that maintains consummatory behavior could be either continuous reinforcement, as in exploiting pastureland, or some variable ratio schedule, as in harvesting whales. The long-term negative consequence can be viewed as a variable interval schedule of punishment in which the length of the interval is a function of the number of other organisms using the resource. We will see later that the behavioral perspective leads to a certain class of interventions in social trap situations that are designed to reduce the frequency or intensity of the consummatory response.

From a cognitive perspective, the actor in a social trap situation may be viewed as behaving in accord with one or more cognitive schemata selected on the basis of the individual's understanding of the situation. When a person understands the situation to be one of independence, whether that is objectively true, as in the case of the commons before carrying capacity has been exceeded, or is instead the individual's failure to perceive the true state of interdependence that exists, a rational schema may be simply to maximize one's own gain by exploiting the common pool resource as fully as possible. If the individuals involved in a social trap situation all adopt a "maximizing own gains" schema, the outcome is the tragedy of the commons. If persons involved in a social trap recognize the interdependence that exists, several other schemas may be adopted. Kelly and Thibaut (1978) have provided a useful list of the schemata that might be adopted in transforming an interdependence matrix from the objective state of interdependence, the given matrix in their terms, to the effective matrix that actually guides the behavior of participants. Once an individual recognizes the state of interdependence he or she may select a schema in which an attempt is made to maximize the other person's outcomes, or a schema in which an attempt is made to maximize outcomes of the entire group. A third schema that might be adopted would minimize the difference in outcomes across the group of participants. This third schema might also be viewed as an equity schema (Adams, 1965). Still another schema that might be adopted by individual participants would maximize the relative difference between own outcomes and the outcomes of others. Under such a schema, one would adopt a competitive set. Combining these various schemas to arrive at strategy for action may be considered from the perspective of multicomponent utility theory (Grzelak, Irwinski, & Radzicki, 1977). The utility of a particular solution is determined by considering factors in addition to the absolute value of one's own outcomes. Of course participants may choose simply to continue with the schema appropriate for the state of independence—to maximize own gains irrespective of the gains or losses incurred by other participants. A cognitive approach may also examine the way in which individuals process information about the interdependent situation in which they find themselves. Participants may or may not believe that a shortage exists—that the carrying capacity of the common pool resource has been exceeded. The impact of information about the dynamics of social trap situations, the effectiveness of information concerning optimizing strategies and the ways in which participants perceive and evaluate others can also be examined from a cognitive perspective. A class of interventions can be developed based on this kind of analysis of the cognitions and cognitive processes of participants in social traps.

Social factors such as the ability to communicate among participants, the existence of norms and standards of behavior, and the existence of leadership and decision-making structures may all affect the way people behave in social trap situations. When all of these factors are absent individuals may simply continue to consume the resource according to a maximizing-own-gain schema, and the tragedy of the commons will ensue. In general, then, any social–structural variable that can direct some force against individual consumption of the resource should be effective in reducing the intensity or frequency of the consummatory response. Thus, a class of solutions to social traps can be developed by considering the ways in which social structures could be established that would affect the behavior of individuals in social traps.

Breaking Out of Social Traps

Each of the perspectives on behavior in social traps that we have outlined can be used to generate a class of solutions, or ways of reducing the frequency or intensity of the consummatory response, thereby avoiding the depletion of the resource. There is one difficulty with which all potential solutions must deal; the utility of the consummatory response remains very high even though the resource may be very nearly depleted. As argued earlier, a gallon of gas, a whale, or another animal added to one's herd is certainly as desirable in a time of shortage as in a time of plenty. In some instances shortages may make the economic benefit of harvesting even greater. Thus, the motivation to obtain the resource will remain quite high, regardless of the level of the resource. As a result, all potential solutions to social traps must attempt to diminish the frequency or intensity of the consummatory response even though the motivation driving that response will remain strong.

Platt (1973) developed a number of proposed solutions to social traps, many of which had been tried in some historical context. Most of Platt's solutions were developed from the behavioral perspective on social traps. From that perspective, one way to reduce the intensity of the consummatory response is to make more salient the eventual long-term negative outcome; that is, to bring the punishment contingency to bear on the consummatory response. However, since the tragedy—the total depletion of the resource— is exactly the outcome that is to be avoided, the contingency must be made salient in a symbolic manner. This may be accomplished with the use of feedback about the current level of the resource or about the time remaining until the resource is depleted. Unfortunately, in most situations feedback alone does not seem to deter consumption. When a species becomes endangered, when gasoline supplies are low, or when air pollution begins to rise, feedback alone does not seem to deter responding. Instead, some form of regulatory authority must be used to limit poaching, to place limits on the amount of gasoline that may be sold, and to eliminate or shut down some sources of air pollutants. However, some forms of feedback have been effective in reducing the frequency or intensity of responding. For example, Seligman and Darley (1977) demonstrated that when households were given feedback about electrical usage they were able to achieve an 11% average decrease in the total power used. Some of the social trap analog experiments that will be described later have employed feedback and have shown it to be moderately effective in reducing the frequency or intensity of consumption. The eventual depletion of our resources can also be made salient with slogans that predict, sometimes dramatically, what will occur. "We shall freeze in the dark," "Give a hoot, don't pollute," and "Every litter bit hurts" are all examples of attempts to make more salient the consequences of continued overconsumption of our resources.

Platt (1973) has also suggested that a social trap may be avoided by increasing the cost of the consummatory response: We can reduce the utility of consumption by adding an artificial cost not normally incurred. The 55-mile-an-hour speed limit is a familiar example of this tactic. The cost of traveling at high rates of speed is increased by the possibility of arrest and a fine. As long as surveillance and enforcement are possible, traffic fines, laws against killing endangered species, and air pollution requirements for automobiles may be effective. But in many instances the regulatory authority to provide surveillance and enforcement is lacking, and under such circumstances it is difficult to add costs to the consummatory behavior. Some forms of taxation may be used to add artificial costs and thereby reduce consumption. During the 1979 gasoline shortage, in some localities a minimum purchase requirement of $10 was quite effective in reducing "tank hoarding" and minimizing gas station waiting lines. However, high gasoline taxes in Western Europe do not seem to have reduced overall consumption. Thus, it may be that taxation focused on discretionary purchases will reduce consumption but that taxes on all purchases of a given resource will have less impact.

From the behaviorist perspective, the probability of any given behavior may be reduced by reinforcing competing, alternative, or incompatible behaviors. Thus, social traps may be avoided if some behavior other than the consummatory response becomes more attractive. Incentives for car pooling, reduced rates for electric use at times other than the peak-load period, and reduced rates for long-distance telephone calls in the evenings and on weekends are all examples of ways in which competing behaviors can be made more attractive. One difficulty with this approach, however, is that usually the contingencies for reinforcement of competing behaviors must be set up for large numbers of people. Arranging such contingencies may be very costly, in both monetary and political terms. Mass transportation can reduce fuel consumption and air pollution. However, it is usually very costly to the community and deficits must be paid for by increasing tax burdens or the fare for riding must be raised to a point at which the alternative becomes unattractive.

The kinds of solutions that we have discussed thus far, taken from a behavioral perspective, almost always require the creation of some superordinate agency to regulate access and consumption of some resource. Historically, the establishment of regulatory agencies has a preferred response to social trap situations, whether those designing such agencies consciously apply the behavioristic perspective or not. Thus the Federal Communications Commission, the Federal Aeronautics Administration, and state fish and game agencies have been created to regulate access to and consumption of some of our public resources. As we have already noted, when there is sufficient funding available so that surveillance and enforcement can be maintained, regulatory agencies can provide a way to avoid a social trap.

Platt (1973) has also pointed out that if the nature of the long-term consequences can be changed the social trap may very well disappear.

Changing the nature of the long term consequence almost always involves some form of technological advance. The energy shortage can be ameliorated if technology can find a way to burn cheap and plentiful coal without creating unacceptable levels of air pollution. But technological solutions do not always exist, and even when they do unintended negative consequences may occur, as in the problems associated with using nuclear power to generate electricity.

From a cognitive perspective, the problem of finding solutions to social traps becomes one of specifying the kinds of information that will enable the person to develop and adopt some schema other than maximizing one's own gain. One important aspect of the cognitive field will be the participants' understanding of whether the situation is one of independence or interdependence. Maximizing own gain is a quite rational response to a situation of independence, the situation that exists prior to exceeding the carrying capacity of some common pool resource. Preservation of the resource, adopting a schema of maximizing own *long-term* gain or of maximizing the group's long-term gain can be adopted only after the participant realizes the nature of the interdependence that exists when carrying capacity has been exceeded. It is possible that the realization of interdependence, in the absence of any sense of trust that others will adopt a prosocial schema, may lead an individual to continue with the goal of maximizing own gain or to shift to a schema of maximizing relative gain, adopting a stance of competition for the resource that is growing increasingly scarce. There is evidence in the research to be reported shortly that the realization of interdependence can lead to more rapid depletion of the resource.

Encouraging participants to adopt a new schema to guide their actions may draw on the entire armamentarium of theory and data in the areas of social influence and social perception. Persuasive communication, compliance techniques, and attributions about the motivations and characteristics of other participants will all have an impact on determining the actions of any individual participant in a social trap situation. Taking a cognitive perspective on social traps suggests an almost endless array of possible interventions.

If the participants in a social trap situation cannot communicate with one another, have no leadership, are not affected by group norms or standards, and have no effective decision-making structure, each person will respond independently to the contingencies that create the social trap. Any social structure that can be created and that will bring to bear some force to reduce the intensity or frequency of the consummatory response will then be at least a partial solution to the social trap. It is often the case that social structures exist for a group of people who find themselves in a social trap, but those structures are not employed to direct forces that will reduce the frequency or intensity of consumption. Where no social structure exists a general class of solutions is to create some structure that will allow for the development of norms and standards of behavior, leadership, or decision-making structures so that self-regulation or regulation by the group may occur. Where some structure does exist, as in neighborhood organizations, churches, or simple proximity, the task is to focus the impact of that social structure on reducing the level of consumption of the resource. The development of norms and the application of group sanctions can have a remarkable impact on consumption patterns. Anecdotal evidence from the recent California water shortage indicates that standards of personal cleanliness were significantly altered during that shortage under normative pressures that developed in many communities. The class of solutions that may be developed from taking a social–structural perspective on social trap situations could draw on a quite large array of theories and research in the areas of leadership, group dynamics, group decision making, and conformity in response to normative pressures.

Evaluating Solutions: Social Trap Analogs

As the preceding discussion illustrates, the list of possible solutions to social trap situations is almost endless. From this array the most promising can be selected and developed in some detail for application to the variety of social traps that confront us. However, assessing the effectiveness of interventions in social trap situations will be quite difficult. First, the researcher must gain access to the situation and somehow acquire the power to implement some intervention. That power may require the cooperation or active assistance of a government agency, a corporation or some large societal institution. Should a researcher be fortunate enough to acquire sufficient power somehow, the intervention could be implemented only on a one-shot, case study basis (Campbell & Stanley, 1963). The evaluation of the effectiveness of any intervention would be totally confounded with the specifics of the situation in which it was employed. Knowledge of the relative effectiveness and limitations of interventions and of the kinds of situations in which specific interventions are most effective would accrue very slowly. We must attain a more detailed understanding of the kinds of interventions that will be effective in reducing the intensity and frequency of the consummatory response. To do so by conducting research in naturally occurring social traps would lead to only a very slow accumulation of relatively imprecise knowledge. Because of these difficulties a number of researchers have begun to explore social trap analogs, situations that capture the structure of a social trap but that can be created in laboratory settings. These analogs have been used to explore the effectiveness of a number of possible solutions to social traps.

In this section of the chapter, although we report the results of research using a variety of social trap analogs, we shall not maintain a rigid classification of results into behavioral, cognitive, and social categories. Our purpose here is to illustrate the usefulness of social trap analogs rather than to begin to compile a catalog of results classified according to the perspective from which they are viewed.

The first social trap analog was constructed by Brechner (1975, 1977) in an attempt to bring the tragedy of the commons into the laboratory. Brechner's analog used a pool of points as the commonly shared resource from which groups of subjects could harvest points for individual benefit. The analog was operated by electromechanical programming equipment which will not be described in detail. Instead, we shall focus on the functional aspects of the analog. The pool of points was displayed as a column of lights. The light that was illuminated indicated the number of points remaining in the pool at any given time. Participants could harvest points by pressing a response button mounted on a gray metal box. The box also contained a counter, which indicated to each participant the number of points he or she had accumulated. The pool was continually replenished with points by a series of timers. If the pool level was in the top quartile, a point was replaced every 6 seconds for each subject participating. In the second quartile, the replenishment rate was one point per subject every 12 seconds. In the third quartile one point per subject was replaced each 18 seconds and in the bottom quartile, one point per subject each 24 seconds. If the pool level reached zero, the session terminated and subjects could harvest no more points. Points were valuable to participants because they could be exchanged for extra experimental credit. Participants were introductory psychology students subjected to a research participation requirement of 3 hours. They were informed that if they earned 150 or more points they would receive credit for the entire 3-hour requirement. Smaller point totals could be exchanged for lesser amounts of experimental credit. The subjects were informed that enough points would be available during the session, through replenishment of the pool, so that all participants could earn the maximum credit. This statement was objectively true. However, subjects would have had to respond with a near optimizing strategy in order for all participants to obtain 150 points. Brechner's analog, then, created a commons type social trap. If subjects responded at a faster rate than points were being replaced in the pool, the pool would be continually depleted until the resource was entirely exhausted. Lower rates of responding would preserve the pool as a resource and still allow subjects to obtain a substantial benefit. The analog meets the definitional requirements of a social trap and provides a convenient laboratory setting in which to evaluate solutions and test hypotheses about the determinants of behavior in social trap situations.

Brechner also created an individual version of his analog in which a single participant responded for points from the pool. The replenishment times were adjusted so that the number of points replaced per person per unit of time were identical to those in effect during the group version of the analog.

Three different measures of management effectiveness were obtained from Brechner's analog and, as we shall see, the same three measures may be obtained from most other social trap analogs. The first was simply the amount of time that the resource was maintained above zero. The second measure was the number of points harvested by each participant. The third measure was the number of points replaced in the pool during the time in which participants attempted to manage the resource. This last measure, "points replaced" has been the main dependent variable in many experiments. It reflects somewhat more clearly the effectiveness of resource management, and it is not artifactually affected by manipulations of initial pool size or other basically parametric independent variables.

The participants in the individual version of Brechner's analog were able to manage the resource quite effectively. When given an initial pool size of 24 points and a 15-minute time period, individual participants allowed an average of 71 points to be replaced in the pool. Groups of three subjects who had the same initial pool size and time limit and who were instructed not to communicate with one another, allowed an average of only about 40 points per session or 13 points per person to be replaced in the pool. Furthermore, they depleted the pool in a mean time of 90 seconds, whereas individual subjects maintained the pool for an average of about 12 minutes. The comparison of the effectiveness of groups and individuals as managers of the resource in a social trap analog is of interest for two reasons. First, it indicates that the situation can be effectively managed by individuals, whereas groups of subjects depleted the resource, recreating the tragedy of the commons in the laboratory. Thus, the analog does allow the occurrence of the behavior of interest, the total depletion of a common pool resource. A second point of interest, however, is that group members were well aware of their interdependence, aware that others were drawing points from the same pool. Knowledge of interdependence did not lead to effective management, at least in this instance. We shall return to this point later in the chapter.

The main experiment reported by Brechner was a 2 × 2 factorial design in which the ability to communicate among group members was either present or absent and the initial size of the pool was either 24 points or 48 points. The study was designed to test the hypothesis that a small initial pool would make more salient the necessity for some management strategy and that with communication available the small pool could be managed most effectively. Brechner ran six groups of three persons in each of the four conditions of the experiment. He found no support for the hypothesis that the salience of the long-term negative outcome, as manipulated via a small initial pool size, would interact with communication to lead to more effective management. Instead, he found a main effect for the availability of communication—communicating groups managed the pool more effectively—and a main effect for initial pool size—groups with a larger initial pool size performed more effectively than groups given a small pool.[1] A recent review by Dawes (1980) cites a number of studies of commons dilemmas in which communication has had salutary effects. The groups of subjects with a small pool who were not allowed to communicate were the least effective managers. As already mentioned, they allowed relatively few points to be replaced in the pool and depleted it rapidly, usually within 90 seconds. Brechner interpreted his findings from a behavioral perspective in terms of the impact of superimposed schedules of reinforcement. However, it is clear that the communication manipulation affects social and cognitive factors and that the manipulation of pool size could be considered from a cognitive perspective.

Another social trap analog was constructed by Cass (1975; Cass & Edney, 1978). Cass was interested in the effects of feedback about the amount of resource remaining in a common pool resource and in the effect of subdividing the resource so that individuals exercised something like private ownership. To allow manipulation of these variables he designed an analog in which the resource was displayed in 12 separate pools, each designated by a letter of the alphabet. A computer program was written to display the pools on CRT terminals, and participants could harvest from the pools by depressing the key on the terminal corresponding to the letter name of the pool from which they wished to take a point. The pools were replenished periodically by doubling the number of points that remained in each pool, with an upper limit of four points available in each pool. If a pool was ever depleted to zero it was never again replenished during the experimental session. Once again the analog created the structure of a social trap. If subjects responded too rapidly, the pools would be depleted and the resource totally consumed. If subjects responded at a rate that matched or nearly matched the replenishment schedule, each subject would continue to benefit individually from harvesting the points.

In the feedback conditions the number of points available in each of the

---

[1] The results reported in this section of the chapter are based on statistical analyses in which the various null hypotheses were rejected with the probability of Type I error no greater than .05.

12 pools was continuously displayed on the terminal. In the no-feedback conditions the subjects were told that there were 4 points initially in each pool, but no information regarding the number of points in the pools was ever displayed on the terminal. When the resource was commonly owned, all subjects could harvest points from any one of the 12 pools. When the resource was subdivided for private ownership, each subject was assigned three pools and could not harvest points from any of the pools belonging to other participants. Points were made valuable in Cass's analog by determining the grade the subject received for the field assignment that was fulfilled by participating in the study.

Subjects participated in groups of four. The dependent measure that Cass employed to indicate the effectiveness with which the resource was managed was the number of points remaining in each pool just prior to replenishment. The optimum strategy in his analog was to harvest 2 points from each pool, wait until the pool was replenished to 4 and then harvest 2 points once again. This optimum strategy would allow all four participants to acquire the number of points needed to earn an "A" in the field assignment. Cass found that when the resource was commonly owned, subjects depleted the pools quite rapidly. In most of the experimental sessions in which subjects harvested from a commonly owned resource without feedback, the pools were all depleted prior to the third replenishment. With feedback, the life of the commonly owned pools was extended somewhat, but all groups still depleted the pools prior to the fifth replenishment. When the resource was subdivided for private ownership, subjects with feedback harvested at nearly the optimum rate, leaving 2 points in each pool just prior to replenishment. With private ownership and no feedback, subjects actually behaved somewhat conservatively, harvesting fewer than the optimum number of points from each pool. These results, in combination with the results from the individual version of Brechner's analog, lead us to conclude that knowledge of interdependence may hasten the depletion of a resource rather then prevent it. When subjects in Brechner's study knew that they were interdependent they harvested much more quickly and managed the resource much less effectively than the individual subjects. In Cass's study when subjects were aware of their interdependency they, too, depleted the pool more rapidly than did subjects who were in fact independent of one another. Of course it is imperative to determine the conditions under which resource depletion is impeded by knowledge of interdependence. Cass's analog was also successful, in the same sense as Brechner's, in that the behavior of interest—the depletion of the resource, or the tragedy of the commons—had been demonstrated in the laboratory setting. Furthermore, independent variables that could be manipulated in that laboratory setting did have an impact on behavior in the social trap situation.

The laboratory analogs created by Cass and Brechner required sophisticated equipment that was difficult if not impossible to move to new locations. Furthermore, once programmed, the analogs were relatively inflexible with regard to changing parameters such as the replenishment rate, the size of the initial pool, or the number of responses required to harvest a point. The advantage of the Cass and Brechner analogs was that, once programmed, the experimental sessions could be run with relatively little effort on the part of the experimenter. Replenishment and record keeping was handled by the equipment, and the task of the experimenter was simply one of greeting and instructing the subjects. However, it became clear that more portable and more flexible analogs would be desirable, and several of these were constructed by other researchers.

Edney (1979) developed a social trap analog that he has called "the nuts game." In the nuts game, groups of three or more subjects are seated around a table that holds a bowl that is about 30 mm in diameter. Hexagonal hardware nuts are placed in the bowl and represent the resource to be harvested. Subjects harvest the resource simply by reaching into the bowl and taking as many nuts as they wish. The bowl can be replenished according to a schedule devised by the experimenter. If the resource is ever completely consumed the session ends and the tragedy of the commons has again occurred.

The nuts game as described by Edney (1979) has been used primarily for demonstration purposes and some pilot work. However, a modification of the nuts game was developed by Shippee (1978) to explore hypotheses about the effects of leadership and variations in decision-making rules on behavior in a social trap situation. In Shippee's analog a bowl and hardware nuts are again used, but the bowl is attached to a small scale so that replenishment can occur according to the weight of the nuts remaining in the bowl. Subjects are also limited to harvesting one nut at a time so that the total and sudden depletion of the resource is not so likely to occur. It should be noted that both of these analogs require a great deal of attention from the experimenter during the experimental session. The experimenter must maintain the replenishment schedule and in addition keep any records of responding that are desired. For example, if the experimenter wishes to obtain a cumulative record of responses from the group he or she must simultaneously monitor the responses by each subject, record them, and maintain the replenishment schedule. Both analogs, however, have the advantage of being simple to construct and highly portable.

Shippee (1978) wished to explore the ways in which limitations on the accessibility of a resource are implemented and the effectiveness with which they allow a group to maintain a resource. A moratorium on responding is a common solution to a social trap. The endangered species act, the quotas placed on harvesting of whales by the International Whaling Commission, and many other examples illustrate the popularity of this solution. Shippee wished to explore the effects of various forms of leadership and of variations in the decision-making rules governing the application of a moratorium. He created three levels of leadership: no leader, appointed leader, or elected leader. In each experimental session one of three kinds of decision-making rules was established: a unilateral-decision condition, in which a single person could place a moratorium on responding; a majority-decision condition, in which two members of the group of three had to agree to the moratorium; and a unanimous-decision condition in which all three members of the group had to concur. In the no-leader–unilateral-decision condition any member of the group could call for a moratorium on responding that would then be observed by all subjects until the individual who called the moratorium cancelled it. In the no-leader–majority-decision condition, any subject could initiate a request for a moratorium, and if one other member of the group agreed the moratorium was put into effect. In the no-leader–unanimous-decision condition any subject again could initiate the request, and all three members had to concur before the moratorium went into effect. The moratorium was cancelled in both instances by a similar vote. When there was an appointed or elected leader, only the leader in the unilateral-decision conditions could institute the moratorium. Only the leader could initiate the request for a moratorium in the majority- and unanimous-decision conditions. During the moratorium, the pool was replenished according to the replenishment schedule. The moratorium, then, could be used to allow the pool to refill to a level at which the replenishment rate was higher after it had been depleted by a period of rapid responding.

Shippee's experiment generated a wealth of data concerning the times at which a moratorium was proposed, the success of individuals in leaderless groups at instituting a moratorium and the success of leaders in getting a request for a moratorium accepted. In addition, he collected the now traditional three dependent variables—points replaced, points harvested, and time until the pool was depleted. The only experimental group that differed reliably and consistently from a control group in which no moratorium option was available was the elected-leader–unanimous-decision condition. Groups in that condition allowed more points to be replaced, harvested more points, and maintained the pool for a longer period of time than did any other experimental group. It was the only condition in which performance was significantly better than in the no-moratorium control group. Shippee interpreted his results from a cognitive and motivational perspective. He argued that subjects in the elected-leader–unanimous-decision condition experienced the greatest sense of participation in the determination of when to use the moratorium and therefore were more willing to institute a moratorium when requested by the leader. He further argued that the leader may have sensed this group support and called for a moratorium at an earlier time, before the pool was seriously depleted. The net result of these factors was that the pool was maintained generally at a higher level with a correspondingly higher replenishment rate in the elected-leader–unanimous-decision groups. These results may have important implications for public policy, but the mediating processes must be explored in replications and extensions of Shippee's work.

Still another analog, just as portable and simpler to operate for the experimenter, has been developed by Harper (1978) and employed in a variety of studies by Edney and Harper (1978a, 1978b). In this analog the pool of points appears simply as a number written on a transparency for an overhead projector. Subjects are seated in front of the experimenter and indicate the number of points they wish to harvest on each trial by holding up a card with the number 0, 1, 2, or 3 displayed. On each trial the experimenter awards each subject the number of points requested, reduces the pool by a corresponding number of points, and maintains the replenishment schedule. The pool is replenished by doubling on a random schedule that averages every other trial, but the pool cannot exceed the size limit set by the experimenter. If on any trial the number of points in the pool is exceeded by the number of points requested, the pool is considered to have been depleted and the experimental session ends. Once again, the analog captures the structure of the social trap situation. However, in this instance responding is on a trial-by-trial basis rather than being continuous, as in the analogs previously described.

Harper (1978) used this analog to explore hypotheses about the effectiveness of communication and the impact of a cooperative versus a competitive set. Groups were either allowed to communicate or were instructed not to communicate during the experimental session. Communicating groups managed the resource significantly more effectively than did noncommunicating groups. Harper's manipulation of a competitive versus cooperative set essentially changed the structure of the social trap into a communal system. In the competitive orientation subjects were instructed that each person would benefit from the number of points he or she harvested individually. In the cooperative set subjects were instructed that the group as a whole would benefit from the number of points harvested. Not surprisingly, groups with a cooperative set managed the resource much more effectively.

The overhead projector analog has been used by Edney and Harper (1978a, 1978b) to examine the impact of a variety of variables. In one study (Edney

& Harper, 1978a) they examined the effect of information about useful strategies in a social trap situation. They found, as Cass had earlier, that explicit instructions concerning the optimizing strategy did not prevent depletion of the resource. Subjects given full instructions on how to optimize management of the resource still depleted it in every session. However, subjects given the optimizing strategy and allowed the opportunity to communicate managed the resource more effectively, maintaining it through the experimental period in about 60% of the sessions.

In another study using the overhead projector analog, Harper and Gold (1978) examined the impact of various kinds of feedback on responding in the social trap situation. Subjects were given feedback about two different aspects of resource management. First, they were given feedback on the amount of the resource remaining in the pool after each trial. This feedback was either factual—the number of points remaining—or subjective—statements indicating that the pool was "abundant" (the resource was at or near capacity), "stable" (the resource was sustaining itself), or "endangered" (the pool was getting dangerously low). Subjects were also given feedback about the amount of the resource harvested on each trial. They were given either objective feedback (a statement of the total number of points taken on the last trial by all subjects) or subjective feedback (a description of the number of points selected on the last trial as "proper use" or "overuse"). Harper and Gold found that objective feedback about the level of the resource led to better management than either no feedback or subjective feedback. However, subjective feedback about trial-by-trial behavior led to more effective management than did objective feedback. Thus, subjects managed the resource most effectively when they had objective information about the number of points remaining in the pool and subjective feedback that was stated in terms of overuse or proper use concerning their trial-by-trial behavior.

Many of the results reported in this section may have implications for public policy. However, it is important to begin to develop a more comprehensive theory about the impact of various interventions in various kinds of social traps. Some of the effects that we have reported may be peculiar to the particular analog that was employed, for there are important structural differences between the analogs. The most obvious of these differences is the continuous versus trial-by-trial character of harvesting. Questions about the limits of applicability of various interventions or solutions to social traps and about the impact of parametric and structural differences in social trap situations can only be answered in a comprehensive program of research that employs social trap analogs that can be systematically varied, both parametrically and structurally.

Programmatic research of this sort has been initiated by Linder and Braver (1979) using a PDP-11 computer system in which the analog is displayed through CRT terminals and subjects respond using the terminal keyboards. Software has been developed to drive both a continuous version of the social trap analog and a trial-by-trial version.

The programs themselves allow variation in the parameters of the social trap, pool size, number of points per trial or number of responses required to harvest a point, and replenishment rates. The number of subjects can also be varied to explore the effects of group size, although limitations of equipment will constrain the group size variations to a relatively small range. Variations in social structure and in cognitive and motivational aspects of the game can be manipulated using the techniques of experimental social psychology, cognitive psychology, and the psychology of individual differences. It is much too early to anticipate the details or even the major outlines of a theory of social trap behavior that may emerge from this program of research. We can only hope that other researchers will be encouraged to develop alternative analogs and to participate in the exploration of what appears to be an extremely promising research paradigm.

Living with Others

Many of the resource management problems that confront us in the physical environment can be viewed as social traps. They can also be viewed from the perspective of other disciplines—economics and biology, for example. But economic and biological analyses of resource management problems do not often suggest the development of interventions or solutions. One important aspect of the social trap analysis of resource management problems is that one is led quite naturally to speculate on how the behavior of individuals might be changed so that the resource would not be depleted. Even when one has come to the problem first from the perspective of the behaviorist, one can still adopt a cognitive or social–structural perspective and develop potential solutions to social traps that draw on a wide range of theories and empirical results in psychology. The research conducted within the social trap analog paradigm that has been reported in this chapter has, indeed, drawn on a variety of perspectives. The researchers have not sought to confirm or support a specific theoretical position but have attempted to assess the effectiveness of potential solutions to social traps. Some regularities have begun to emerge from the body of data collected thus far. First, it seems that communication almost always leads to more effective management in a social trap situation. Thus, the establishment of effective communication channels among the participants in a social trap should be one of the first interventions instituted. Second, information alone seems not to improve performance in a social trap. In several of the experiments we have reported, subjects have been informed explicitly of the optimizing strategy and have failed to employ it. The dynamic quality of the interdependence established in a social trap situation seems to prevent the easy application of information about an optimizing strategy. However, information combined with the ability to communicate has been shown to lead to more effective management. Third, simple knowledge of interdependence seems, if anything, to exacerbate the exploitation of a resource in a social trap. Subjects deal quite well with individual resource management problems, but management becomes much less effective when groups of three or four are confronted with a management problem comparable in terms of the parameters of replenishment rate, pool size, and the ability to harvest points from the resource. Careful research is needed to explore the cognitive and motivational effects of knowledge of interdependence. But at this point it seems clear, both from observations in naturally occurring social traps and from the research conducted thus far, that knowledge of interdependence most often leads to increased exploitation of the resource rather than to the development of restraint and cooperative strategies. Finally, it appears that a sense of meaningful participation in determination of how the resource is to be managed allows a group to develop ways of restraining exploitation, with the result that group members are able to obtain more personal benefit than in other settings where such restraint is not developed.

These results have been obtained in analog experiments, and it is natural and reasonable to question the degree to which they may be generalized to naturally occurring social traps. Certainly, research in field settings must be conducted. However, there does seem good reason to expect that results will generalize from the laboratory setting of social trap analogs to the natural settings in which the social traps that confront us occur. The structure of social trap analogs carefully models the structure of naturally occurring social traps. Furthermore, in the analogs constructed thus far, behavior very similar to that in natural social traps—the total depletion of the resource—has occurred reliably and sometimes dramatically. If the interventions selected for study—the independent variables manipulated in social trap analogs—are chosen with attention to their relevance in natural settings (Cialdini, 1980), it may be possible to establish their relative effectiveness quite reliably by using the laboratory analogs. We may then move into applications choosing the interventions to be employed, guided by our knowledge of their relative effectiveness in laboratory settings. Such knowledge may help us to manage our commons more effectively and to live together on spaceship Earth, using our resources wisely.

References

Adams, J. S. Inequity in social exchange. In L. Berkowitz (Ed.), *Advances in experimental social psychology* (Vol. 2). New York: Academic Press, Inc., 1965.

Brechner, K. C. *An experimental analysis of social traps: A laboratory analog.* Unpublished doctoral dissertation, Arizona State University, 1975.

Brechner, K. C. An experimental analysis of social traps. *Journal of Experimental Social Psychology*, 1977, *13*, 552–564.

Campbell, D. T., & Stanley, J. C. *Experimental and quasi-experimental designs for research.* Chicago: Rand McNally, 1963.

Cass, R. C. *Subdividing communal resources: A social trap analysis of management outcomes.* Unpublished doctoral dissertation, Arizona State University, 1975.

Cass, R. C., & Edney, J. J. The commons dilemma: A simulation testing the effects of resource visability and territorial division. *Human Ecology*, 1978, *6*, 387–395.

Cialdini, R. B. Full cycle social psychology. In L. Bickman (Ed.), *Applied social psychology annual* (Vol. 1). Beverly Hills, Calif.: Sage, 1980.

Crowe, B. The tragedy of the commons revisited. *Science*, 1969, *166*, 1103–1107.

Dawes, R. M. Formal models of dilemmas in social decision making. In M. Kaplan & S. Schwartz (Eds.), *Human judgment and decision processions: Formal and mathematical approaches.* New York: Academic Press, 1975.

Dawes, R. M. Social dilemmas. In M. R. Rosenzweig & L. W. Porter (Eds.), *Annual review of psychology* (Vol. 31). Palo Alto, Calif.: Annual Reviews Inc., 1980, 169–193.

Dawes, R. M., MacTavish, J., & Shaklee, H. Behavior, communications, and assumptions about other people's behavior in a commons dilemma situation. *Journal of Personality and Social Psychology*, 1977, *35*, 1–11.

Edney, J. J. The nuts game: A concise commons dilemma analog. *Environmental Psychology and Nonverbal Behavior*, 1979, *3*, 252–254.

Edney, J. J., & Harper, C. S. The effects of information in a resource management problem: A social trap analog. *Human Ecology*, 1978, *6*, 387–396. (a)

Edney, J. J., & Harper, C. S. Heroism in a resource crisis: A simulation study. *Environmental Management*, 1978, *2*, 523–527. (b)

Grzelak, J. L., Irwinski, T. B., & Radzicki, J. J. "Motivational" component of utility. In H. Jungermann & G. deZeeuw (Eds.), *Decision making and change in human affairs.* Dordrecht, Holland: D. Reidel Publishing Company, 1977.

Hardin, G. The tragedy of the commons. *Science*, 1968, *162*, 1243–1248.

Harper, C. S. *The role of communication and cooperative or individualistic orientation in a simulated resource management dilemma.* Unpublished master's thesis, Arizona State University, 1978.

Harper, C. S., & Gold, B. *The role of feedback in the management of a group resource.* Unpublished manuscript, Arizona State University, 1978.

Kelley, H. H., & Grzelak, J. Conflict between individual and common interest. *Journal of Personality and Social Psychology*, 1972, *21*, 190–197.

Kelley, H. H., & Thibaut, J. W. *Interpersonal relations: A theory of interdependence.* New York: John Wiley & Sons, 1978.

Linder, D. E., & Braver, S. L. *Psychological aspects of sharing common-pool resources: Research plan.* Unpublished manuscript, Arizona State University, 1979.

Platt, J. Social traps. *American Psychologist,* 1973, *28,* 641–651.

Seligman, C., & Darley, J. M. Feedback as a means of decreasing residential energy consumption. *Journal of Applied Psychology,* 1977, *62,* 363–368.

Shippee, G. E. *Leadership, group participation and avoiding the tragedy of the commons.* Unpublished doctoral dissertation, Arizona State University, 1978.

Stern, P. C. Effects of incentive and education on resource conservation decisions in a simulated commons dilemma. *Journal of Personality and Social Psychology,* 1976, *34,* 1285–1292.

Chapter 9
Altruism and
the Problem
of Collective Action

GERALD MARWELL

Background and General Approach

Social psychological attempts to understand the process of cooperation and mutual aid have long been substantially influenced by what has been variously termed decision theory, game theory, and economic theory. Such theory has generally taken a simplified, hedonistic, and calculating view of the motives of social actors, and has examined the impact of various situational contingencies on the emergence of cooperation. Perhaps the most common example of such research is the enormous body of studies utilizing the prisoner's dilemma. But a large number of other studies have also grown essentially from an "exchange" or otherwise economic model.

More recently, social psychologists have joined scholars from the other social sciences in considering a large-group paradox of cooperation that, in several ways, is similar to the prisoner's dilemma. In the language of at least one of the economists who formally postulated it, the paradox is called *the problem of collective action* (Olson, 1968). In recent social psychological discussion it is sometimes referred to as one of a series of *social dilemmas* (Dawes, 1980) or *social traps* (Platt, 1973; Linder, Chapter 8, this volume). At base, the problem of collective action has to do with conflict

COOPERATION AND HELPING BEHAVIOR
Theories and Research

between the interest of some group of which an individual is a member and the individual's own interest. Because it is often possible for individuals to profit from actions taken by a group, even when they themselves did not contribute to, or participate in, those actions, individuals' self-interested calculations lead them to not contribute or participate. This is called *free riding*, and the paradox of collective action is that even though the group as a whole would profit from the collective activity, each individual group member calculates that he should not personally join the effort—so the activity does not get done.

The logic of the problem of collective action is both compelling and illuminating. The problem with this logic, however, is that empirical evidence for its ability to predict actual behavior is either scant or nonexistent. The fact seems to be that under the conditions described by the theory as leading to free riding, people often cooperate instead. Naturally, this brings up the question of why they behave in this illogical fashion.

It is not the purpose of this paper to prove that the reason why is X or Y. I shall not attempt cunningly to undermine or out-logic the logic of the collective action paradox. Instead, I shall merely take as given the fact that under the specified conditions people do cooperate. I shall then postulate a fundamental assumption as to why—an assumption that has to do with altruism. Arguing the reasonableness of this assumption will occupy the next segment of the paper. The central concern of this chapter, however, is a discussion of three ways in which altruism affects collective action: through altruism's effects on the *noticeability* of individual contributions; through the reduction of the costs of *side payments*; and through the *expansion* of the group.

The Problem of Collective Action: A Brief Review

The problem of collective action centers on what has come to be called the *free rider hypothesis*, developed by a number of scholars, particularly economists. The version presented here leans heavily on the well-articulated analysis of Olson (1968). Many readers may be more familiar with the discussion of the *commons dilemma* by Hardin (1968).

In the analysis of Olson and other economists, the concept of *group* is itself radically different from the concept common to social psychologists and most behavioral scientists, and this difference has led to much confusion. For Olson, a group consists of a collection of individuals who have some interest in the provision of some good. That is to say, a group therefore has little (although not necessarily nothing) to do with interaction, or identity, or commitment, or any of the other factors commonly used by social psychologists to define the construct. Olson's group is closer to the concept of *interest group* in political science, and the theory of collective action was developed in part as a reaction to interest group theories of social movements and related behavior.

The free rider problem concerns the provision of public goods by groups. Public goods may be defined as "any good such that, if any person $X_1, \ldots, X_i, \ldots, X_n$ consumes it, it cannot feasibly be withheld from others in that group [Olson, 1968, p. 14]." For example, the use of more expensive unleaded gas may produce the public good of less air pollution. If half of all cars convert to unleaded gas the air will be markedly cleaner. However, regardless of who converts and pays for the more expensive gas, the cleaner air accrues to all of the people in the area. Clean air is a public good because it is nonexcludable.[1]

The free rider problem may be understood by considering the economic logic facing each car owner in the example above. If a given owner converts to unleaded gas, pollution may decrease, but if other car owners keep using leaded gas the effect on pollution will be small. In fact, the effect will be almost zero, although the cost may be over $100 per year to the owner who converts. How much smarter it is to let the other drivers use unleaded gas and free ride on the cleaner air they cause, without paying for the more expensive gas yourself. You have little impact on air quality yourself, anyway, so why not keep your money? Unfortunately, all of the other car owners think the same way, so no reduction in pollution is likely. Therefore, no public good of cleaner air will be provided to anyone. Even though all would have been better off with some change to unleaded gas, no such change will occur because of the free rider problem.

Other examples of such problems are legion, ranging from assembling volunteer armies, to building bridges, to forming unions, to arranging a church picnic. The free rider hypothesis states that except under certain specifiable conditions the provision of such public goods will either not occur at all (what Brubaker, 1975, calls the "strong" version), or will be "suboptimal" (the "weak" version). The group will provide either no public goods at all, or less than it would provide if it were a single individual making an economic decision on how to act under the same conditions.

The Voluntary Provision of Public Goods in Societies and Experiments

Of course, we see public goods provided all around us, regardless of the free rider proposition. Armies abound, bridges are built, unions are formed,

---

[1] Some economists use a more restrictive definition of public goods, involving "jointness of supply" as a second characteristic. We will use the less restrictive definition that is common to almost all empirical—especially experimental—work on the topic. We shall also use the terms public good and collective good interchangeably, and the term "collective action" to mean activity that is oriented toward producing public (collective) goods.

people use unleaded gas, church groups have picnics, etc. Many of these facts do not constitute empirical refutations of the analysis by Olson and others. Some of these public goods are provided by government, through coercive powers such as those of taxation and the draft. Military defense, for example, is no longer a matter of each of us choosing to pick up his rifle to join in the great crusade. Laws require the manufacture of cars that use only unleaded gas. Similarly, we often get cooperation through *side payments*. The bridge is built because it is worth the cost to the person who has to get goods to the other side of the creek, and he or she *pays* the contractor to cooperate in its building. Unions offer health insurance or social clubs as inducements to join. The theory does not dispute the power of coercion or side payments to produce public goods. Only where no coercion is available, or where nobody is so interested in the good that he or she is willing to pay the cost of getting cooperation, will free riding obtain.

Still, examples of voluntary cooperation without side payments appear readily to any mildly observant eye. Students join together to take over buildings (or used to). The United Fund finds many anonymous donors. Even when they can afford the gas, people choose to use less. Cynical though we may be, we recognize the sometimes foolish, sometimes selfless patterns of cooperation in the face of need, disaster, or simply the pursuit of what seems to be useful, that characterizes incidents of behavior on the part of others—perhaps even ourselves from time to time. We do not always ride free.

My own experimental work (Marwell & Ames 1979, 1980, in press; Alfano & Marwell, 1980) makes me particularly sensitive to the fact that even in highly abstract and controlled situations people do not behave in accordance with the theory. In over 13 experiments we have found that subjects persist in investing substantial proportions of their resources in public goods despite conditions specifically designed to maximize the impact of free riding and thus minimize investment. The prevalence of such economically "illogical" behavior was replicated over and over. Nor do other experimenters find their subjects behaving much differently (e.g., Bohm, 1972; Brubaker, 1979; Schneider & Pommerehne, 1979).

All of which is not to say that people do not free ride. If one were to look around one would quickly see a large number of instances in which people were clearly free riding. Unions that receive the majority of votes from the labor force but cannot get a majority of workers to join and pay dues until the unions achieve the closed shop are a common example. Most people who approve of war X (let us say, sending troops to Afghanistan) do not run out and join the army. They actually try to avoid being drafted. And so on and so forth. Even in our experiments about 25% of subjects free ride to a great extent, contributing much less than their share to the provision of the public good. And most people give less than they could to the public good. How many of us actually contribute what the United Fund tells us is our "fair share"?

The fact remains that we sometimes free ride and sometimes do not. Whether we do varies as a function of individual situation, individual character, the nature of the public good, and other unknown factors.

The theory of collective action identifies the central pressure for free riding. For the countervailing force, the traditional answer has been normative pressure. In our experiments the subjects cannot communicate, and therefore cannot use normative pressure on one another. This has led us to seek a more fundamental explanation—one that is *not* a side payment, as are normative approval and disapproval. Thus, in the following analysis we turn instead to the impact of altruism.

The Assumption of Altruism

The economist Kenneth Arrow (1975) suggests three motives for altruism that are hierarchical in nature. The most fundamental, and least complex, is the one to be used in this analysis: "The welfare of each individual will depend both on his own satisfactions and on the satisfactions obtained by others [Arrow, 1975, p. 17]." In other words, I assume that people receive rewards not only directly but also indirectly, through the rewards received by others. Economists have found that such an assumption complicates analysis and is difficult to work with. Nevertheless, the problems for formal economic theory need not constrain our attempts to derive an understanding of why cooperation occurs in defiance of the predictions from such theory.

It should be noted that the preceding definition of altruism is not behavioral in character. It does not require that individuals *do* anything for anyone else. Instead, it is a description of "potential," or attitude toward a set of prospective outcomes. In keeping with the general economic model, I will assume that individuals will behave in accordance with their attitudes—in the usual economic theory this means simply that individuals seek to maximize their rewards. I specify only that the individual's reward calculations includes some factor for rewards gained indirectly, through rewards to others. The assumption that altruism is part of self-interest is not the most commonly used; altruism is usually contrasted with self-interested behavior. However, this distinction is only definitional, and our definition corresponds to practice in most economic treatments, where "altruism" would be a "taste," or individual preference.

Assuming the interdependence of welfare is not foreign to the literature on cooperation (see, for example, Chapter 3, by McClintock and Van Avermaet, this volume), and it is certainly consonant with our everyday observations. Even economists admit that people are forever receiving gratifications indirectly through the happiness of their children. Thus, some economists have been driven by their fundamental model to accept extraordinary—to my mind mystical—"gene-survival," ethological rationales for such behavior. Economists are less willing to admit that we are rewarded through the happiness of our friends, acquaintances, and even strangers. Yet who among us does not light up at the sight of a starving refugee child devouring a bowl of rice or a cup of milk? Even the rewards gained by characters in fiction often reward us indirectly. The fact is that humans have an enormous capacity to identify with the pains and pleasures of others. This capacity, of course, is distributed over the population, being more characteristic of some than of others. Perhaps more important, humans identify differentially over the list of possible others; more with their own children (as a rule) and less with strangers, for example. Moreover, this diversity is not random but culturally structured.

To me, the notion of the interdependence of rewards reflects a more reasonable view of human psychology and development than does any conception that is primarily individualistic in nature. Although we learn our individualism and separateness early enough in life, we surely learn our dependence on others as soon or sooner. When others are happy we are made happy by them, and the relationship is reinforced daily or more frequently. Some of us are taught the lesson better than others. But it is important to understand that wanting others to be happy is not only a normative lesson—and it is surely that—but a functional requisite of human dependence in infancy and youth. In short, it is in the nature of the beast. When others in our environment are unhappy they tend to punish *us*, even when we are not the source of their unhappiness. Or, at least, they may remove some of our rewards. And when something good happens to them, they turn around and share with us or otherwise give of their pleasure. It becomes part of our basic pattern of response to want to see others happy, particularly the significant others to whose lives our own lives are linked.

At first glance, the importance of altruism for collective action seems obvious, almost necessary. If the logic arising from assumptions of implacably self-interested behavior produces free riding, then the answer to the problem is likely to be behavior that is not self-interested, or altruism. People are seen to cooperate, and to join collective action, because of their desire to help others.

However, the rather general observation that "people are doing it for each other" neither specifies the processes by which altruism affects collective action nor allows for a formal building of theory around the construct of altruism. It is these issues that the remainder of this chapter will address. In particular, we will look at three mechanisms linking altruism and collective action:

1. The effect of altruism on noticeability: This involves perhaps the most basic change in the analysis underlying the free rider hypothesis and is also the most general and complex in its results
2. The effect of altruism on the costs of side payments: A more direct and obvious effect, increasing the attractiveness of the mechanism usually considered most important in producing collective action
3. The effect of altruism on group size: A less obvious, but potentially important process

Altruism and Noticeability

One of the key elements in Olson's formulation of the problem of collective action is *noticeability* or *perceptibility*. In Olson's (1968) words; "The standard for determining whether a group will have the capacity to act . . . in its group interests is . . . whether the individual actions of any one or more members are noticeable to any other members of the group [p. 45]." Unfortunately, Olson does not anywhere define noticeability with any precision and, upon examination, the concept appears to have several significantly different dimensions. Nevertheless, at least one, and perhaps all, of these dimensions is or are crucial to the problem of collective action and suggest how altruism might affect the process.

Olson's discussion of noticeability is contained in his distinctions among three types of groups: *privileged, latent* and *intermediate*. In the first of these groups, collective goods are provided because there is some individual who benefits enough that he or she is willing to provide the goods himself or herself. For example, a very rich man with emphysema might subsidize all the gas stations in his town to sell unleaded gas more cheaply than leaded. A latent group may be thought of as the opposite of a privileged group, it is the kind of group we have been discussing up to this point. In latent groups, no individual profits enough to be willing to provide the public good unilaterally. The intermediate group is a somewhat complicated concept, but it is crucial for understanding noticeability. As in the latent group, no individual in an intermediate group profits sufficiently to want to provide the good himself or herself. However, unlike the contribution of the latent group member, the contribution of the intermediate group member may be "noticeable": that is, the contribution of one member has a perceptible effect on the welfare—the burdens and/or rewards—of other members. For example, the privately owned bus company might itself be able to reduce a town's air pollution 25% by changing to unleaded gas. Because of this, in deciding how to behave, at least some group members may consider how some other member will react.

As Fleishman (1978) has pointed out, Olson's typology actually rests on a melange of covert, undiscussed differences along dimensions that are interrelated in complex ways. Most important, it is not clear whether noticeability is defined primarily by effects on the amount or value of a good that is provided or by effects on the probability of providing some amount of a good. Thus, we might ask if an intermediate group is one in which a single person can noticeably raise the probability that the United Fund will reach its objective—that is, one that guarantees a minimum amount—or if it is a group in which an individual can contribute a certain amount (above whatever everyone else provides) that has a major impact on the welfare of many group members. In the former case the key group member might actually contribute nothing but only affect other group members' perceptions of the probability that the good will be provided.[2]

In most formal decision theory analyses of behavior, both value and probability must be considered simultaneously. The key to understanding choices between behaviors is the difference in the associated expected values, where expected value is defined as the product of the value to be produced and the probability that it will be produced. In Olson's discussion, probability is assumed to be virtually one. There is a determinate relation between behavior and realized values, with no stochastic component. Under these circumstances, noticeability becomes defined by effects on realized value rather than probability. In later analyses, such as that by Fireman and Gamson (1979), the probability component gets more attention. There, the issue becomes whether some specific value of a good will be realized, and definitions of noticeability therefore focus on the effects of behavior on the probability of that outcome.

Both of these simplifications have their drawbacks. In the analysis to follow I will assume that both value and probability are important components of noticeability. I will argue that altruism affects the provision of public goods primarily because it directly affects the value component of

---

[2] A second issue raised by Fleishman (1978) is the difference between efficacy and noticeability. On the one hand, efficacy refers to the *capacity* of an individual to substantially affect the amount of collective good provided, or the probability that the good will be provided. On the other hand, noticeability refers to the question of whether other individuals will "notice" one's behavior. The two concepts are obviously related. If one has no effect, one is not noticeable. If one has substantial efficacy, ones' actions will probably be noticed. On the other hand, it remains possible for an individual to have a *noticeable* effect but *not* to be very efficacious. One could, perhaps, change another's outcomes by some amount that is slightly more than the minimum that he would notice. However, this amount might still be quite small and could not be called major power over outcomes (efficacy).

noticeability. However, the fundamental source of the problem of free riding lies in the probability component. Thus, it is mostly under certain assumptions regarding the relationship between value and probability that altruism will produce more collective action.

The Probability of Provision and Free Riding

The argument to be developed will be helped if we use a relatively simple formalization along with the verbal discussion. The formalization, at the outset, will use the following elements:

$A =$ the actor

$V_a =$ the value of a unit of a given collective good (in dollars) (e.g., how much is one unit less of pollution worth?)

$N =$ the number of units of the collective good that is provided

$C_a =$ the amount of private goods (in dollars) contributed by the actor to the collective action that provides a collective good (e.g., how much extra does one spend to use unleaded gas?)

$P_C =$ the probability that a specific amount of the collective good (N) will be provided if A contributes a given amount of private good (C_a)

$P_0 =$ the probability that the same specific amount of the collective good (N) will be provided if the actor contributes nothing

$\Delta P =$ the difference between P_C and P_0, or $P_C - P_0$.

$E_a =$ the expected value to the actor

$\Delta E_a =$ the expected benefit to the actor of contributing to the collective action

It is important to note that there is a distinct possibility that any given amount of the collective good might be provided by the other group members even if the actor himself or herself contributes nothing to the collective effort. In terms of the elements just listed we can easily show that if the actor does not contribute to the collective good his expected value is

$$E_a = V_a \int N P_0 \, dN, \tag{9.1}$$

where N might be the amount of cleaned-up air, from none to an infinite amount. It should be noted that a different probability is associated with each value of N specified in this function. In other words, it may be more probable that 50 units of air will be cleaned by the other group members than that they will clean four million units of air.

If the actor does contribute, his expected value would be

$$E_a = V_a \int N P_{/C} \, dN - C_a \tag{9.2}$$

The difference between these two equations gives us the expected benefit from contributing to the collective action. If this term is negative or zero, it is obvious that the actor should not contribute. If it is positive, he should contribute. The resulting formula is

$$\Delta E_a = V_a \int N \, \Delta P \, dN - C_a \tag{9.3}$$

Since there is always some real cost to contributing (i.e., C_a is positive), it is clear that the term including ΔP must also be positive if the individual is to decide to contribute. The essence of the free rider problem, however, is that ΔP is generally very small. Fireman and Gamson (1979), in their influential analysis, simply assert that $P_c \simeq P_0$, that is, that the probability of provision of the public good is approximately the same regardless of whether A contributes or not. The basic problem is that individual actors have little, if any, effect on the amount of air pollution. The air will be pretty much as polluted as before if you switch gasolines but everyone else does not. Thus, the term containing ΔP is always zero, this argument goes, and ΔE_a equals $-C_a$. ΔE_a is thus usually negative, and it makes little sense to contribute.

The Primary Effect of Altruism

Altruism provides no easy solution to the analysis detailed above. This is because at its simplest level altruism cannot directly affect the probability that a given level of collective good will be provided (ΔP). Instead, altruism most clearly affects the value of a given level of collective good for the individual.

The definition of altruism given at the beginning of this chapter states that the actor receives some reward indirectly through direct rewards to others. We may indicate this possibility by defining:

$S_t =$ The altruism felt by A toward each other group member (a vector for each actor across all other members of the group)
$V_t =$ The value to each other group member of a unit of the collective good (a vector across others in the group)
$k\;\; =$ The number of other members in the group

We also define:

$$V_a' = V_a + \sum^{k} S_t V_t \tag{9.4}$$

The "total" value of a unit of the collective good to the actor, V_a', is the direct value (V_a), plus the *indirect* value through rewards to others and altruistic identification with these others $(S_t V_t)$.[3] This definition of the total value of the collective good contains all the cardinal elements of our definition of altruism. Thus, including altruism in the prior analysis of the expected benefit of contributing to the collective good we find

$$\Delta E_a = V_a' \int N \, \Delta P \, dN - C_a \tag{9.5}$$

$$= V_a \int N \, \Delta P \, dN + \sum^{K} S_t V_t \int N \, \Delta P \, dN - C_a$$

As the right-hand version of Eq. (9.5) shows, we have simply added a new term that represents the impact of altruism on the decision. Since there is a potential impact for every single other individual in the group with whom the actor has some altruistic identification, this altruism term might have a considerable effect on the decision. However, given our previous discussion of the probability term (ΔP), such is not the case. If ΔP is zero, the effect of altruism is zero. All terms representing this effect contain ΔP and are therefore multiplied by zero. Thus, any possible effect is negated.

Alternative Assumptions

Peculiarly, Olson, our exemplar in setting the problem of collective action, does not assume that the effect of individual contributions on the probability of provision of a collective good is approximately zero. Although he does not discuss the issue directly, consider again his analysis of "privileged" groups. Such groups are defined by the fact that they contain one or more individuals for whom the value of the collective good, V_a, exceeds the cost of its provision, C_a. When this occurs, according to Olson, such members do provide the good. There is no question of their being unable to provide the good. They are quite capable, it seems, of substantially changing the probability that the good will be provided; indeed, they can change it all the way to certainty, if need be.

As a matter of fact, conceptualizing the collective good as providable in virtually continuous amounts (as opposed to Fireman and Gamson's ap-

---

[3] This analysis draws heavily on the work of Fireman and Gamson (1979), who present a "solution" to the problem of collective action based on the individual's "solidarity with the group." This concept is a group level version of what we term altruistic identification with specific other members of the group. Unfortunately, the Fireman–Gamson analysis is formally incorrect. It relies heavily on a probability term that reflects the effects of *group* actions and a term for the "group stake" in the collective action. Such terms are inappropriate in what is otherwise an individual-level decision theory analysis. If these terms were rephrased to reflect, for example, A's stake in the group's stake in collective action—a legitimate term in an individual decision formula—they would not serve to solve the problem of collective action.

proach) makes the notion of "no effect" somewhat inappropriate. Any contribution must have some effect on provision, even if it is very small. In fact, it must change the probability of provision of every specific amount of the collective good. This may be seen by considering the curves in Figure 9.1. These curves picture some hypothetical distributions of the number of units of collective good provided and the cumulative probability that that number or more will be provided by the group, as seen by A. The two curves represent the cumulative probability that the given amount of the good or more will be provided if A contributes nothing ($C = O$), and if A contributes some given amount ($C > O$). Assuming total independence of decisions, the two curves are actually representative of a family of curves, each of which represents a different specific level of contribution by A.

Since A's contribution to the collective good is simply added to the summed contributions of all the others, it must increase, at least marginally, the probability of provision of every amount of the collective good. This means that the $C > O$ curve has what Hadar and Russell (1969) call "first-order stochastic dominance" over the $C = O$ distribution. That is, the cumulative probability of providing any given N (or more) with $C > O$ is greater than the probability of providing it with $C = O$, for all values of N. Thus, the "difference in probability" caused by A's contribution is the shaded area in Figure 9.1.

The relationship between A's expectations of the behavior of others and the logic of his or her own behavior is obviously complex. It can be shown

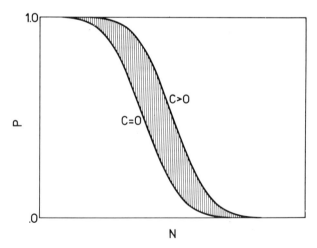

Figure 9.1. Cumulative probability (P) that N or more collective goods will be provided if A contributes nothing ($C = 0$) or something ($C > 0$).

that A's perception of his or her ability to influence the probability of the provision of different levels of the collective good depends particularly on his or her vision of the variance in the probability distribution of the behavior of the group members.[4] If A is fairly certain as to how much others will contribute—i.e., if the variance of A's expectations is low—he or she can have a very substantial effect on the probability distribution. If the variance of A's expectations is high, his or her effect will be quite small. For example, given certain distributional assumptions, if A is considering a contribution that would produce for himself as much as one standard deviation in his probable returns from others' contributions, he would change the cumulative probability of provision over the range of his envisioned levels of collective good by .38, a substantial effect. One tenth this contribution, however, would affect the envisioned probabilities only .04.

It seems not unreasonable to assume then, that A is able to have a non-zero, if not tremendous effect on the probability distribution for the provision of the collective good. Such effect need not be large for altruism to be able to exercise significant influence on noticeability and thus on the decision to contribute. This can be seen by returning to Eq. (9.5), above, where the effect of altruism is represented by the term $\sum^k S_t V_a \int N \, \Delta P \, dN$. We can see from this term that even if ΔP is comparatively small, altruism can easily lead to a decision to contribute to the public good. For example, let us assume that the value of the good to each other member of the group is identical to the value to the individual: for example, that everyone is equally interested in cleaner air. Then the "altruism" term may be calculated as $k\bar{S}_t V_a \int N \, \Delta P \, dN$ (where $\bar{S}_t = A$'s mean altruistic identification with other group members). If altruistic identification is very high, we could multiply

---

[4] Assume the original probability density functions from which the cumulative functions in Figure 9.1 are derived are normally distributed, and both have standard deviation σ. Further, define:

C' = the amount of collective good (N) directly produced by C (previously defined as A's contribution to the collective good)

Then,

$$\Delta P = \int_{-C'/2\sigma}^{C'/2\sigma} \frac{1}{2\pi} e^{-N^2/2} dN$$

This equation allows us to use normal probability tables to calculate ΔP for different values of C' and σ.

Obviously the key term in the equation is $C'/2\sigma$, which reflects the relationship between how much collective good A's contribution will generate and the deviation in contributions of other group members that A anticipates. As the deviation increases, A's impact on the *probabilities* (not the returns, per se) declines. If the deviation is small, A's impact is potentially large.

the value of the collective good to the individual by up to as much as the number of other persons in the group. Even with a small ΔP this might significantly increase the positive value to the individual for participating in collective action. Since $k\bar{S}_t$ is equal to the sum of the identification A has with all other members of the group, the effect can become large even when ΔP is fairly small. In short, because of altruism it might often be rational to invest in the collective good—depending on the number of others with whom one altruistically identifies, the strength of the identification, and the value to them (as well as oneself) of the good.

The Self-Reinforcing Cycle of Altruism

Interestingly, the last-mentioned factor influencing the decision, the value of the good to others, tends to be multiply related to altruism, which increases the effects of altruism greatly. In calculating the value of a collective good to some other group member we would begin by looking at his or her direct returns. However, we should also realize that we are not the only altruistic actors in the group. Thus, other individuals may be seen as having indirect, altruistic interests in the collective good. You might buy a family television set not only because you enjoy it, or because you enjoy seeing your spouse enjoy it, but because your spouse enjoys your own enjoyment, and you enjoy the pleasure he or she receives in that indirect fashion. In other words, rewards tend to reverberate through an interdependent, altruistic system, multiplying, or at least incrementally increasing in value at each step.

Furthermore, within a system of interdependent rewards, contributions by any given individual have the additional possible effect of increasing contributions by others through a process of signaling. Individuals who contribute to the collective good, and whose contributions are noticed by others, are also signaling that they value the good enough to make a "risky" contribution. If others have the welfare of that individual in their own welfare function, they are led to see that they can gain a substantial indirect reward by contributing themselves. This action, in turn, signals still others that there are at least two group members who value the good, perhaps provoking a veritable chain reaction.

In addition, a contribution is likely to invoke norms of reciprocity from others. Thus, if some other individual sees your contributions as partly or wholly due to your consideration of his or her welfare, rather than your own, that individual is likely to feel obliged to reciprocate, and contribute toward your welfare. Of course, he or she is also thereby contributing to everyone's welfare, so others may also respond by reciprocating.

Both of these processes mean that individuals can anticipate that contributions to the collective action may affect the behavior of other group members. Either because of signals, or reciprocity, a contribution by one tends to increase the contributions of others within an interdependent system of rewards. Thus, contributions may be seen as affecting the probability of provision well beyond the immediate impact of the amount you contribute, that is, the expected value of contributions is increased. Specifying such a self-reinforcing cycle of effect in formal terms may be difficult, but it is probably one of the most important facts linking social structure and altruistic commitment with provision of public goods.

Altruism and Side Payments

According to Olson, the fundamental way that public goods do get provided is through side payments. Individuals are given rewards for contributing to the collective good or punishments for not contributing, and both these rewards and punishments are themselves private goods, not intrinsic to the collective good. For example, individuals who contribute to building a public museum are given public praise, or plaques are displayed as a payment in prestige or gratitude; union members are allowed to purchase insurance at a discount; nonstriking fellow workers who cross picket lines are beaten up or threatened; pollutors are fined or jailed. Returning to our previous formulae, the trick is to work on the expected value of the private goods associated with contribution to the collective good. This part of the formula is not affected by the free riding problem and remains the key element in Olson's analysis after ΔP has been declared to be close to 0.

However, Froelich, and Oppenheimer (1970) have shown that the side payment solution to the free rider problem might not be a solution at all. Who, they ask, is going to pay the side payment, and why? For any given member of the group, making a side payment is identical to making a contribution to the public good. The individual uses some of his or her resources (realizes a cost) so as to increase the total amount contributed by the group toward providing the collective good. We have already seen that the formal economic analysis concludes that individuals should not thus contribute to collective goods but should try to free ride instead. By the same logic, nobody should want to beat up another worker, or pay for a plaque for somebody else. The "side paying" actor receives almost no direct return for the expenditure he thus realizes.

However, altruism may also significantly alter the situation within which side payments are used. This alteration could so substantially affect the cost of side payments that they become extraordinarily cheap, and totally bypass Froelich and Oppenheimer's objection to their use as a solution.[5]

The key problem with side payments is that they are costly. However, if the individual making the side payments actually has a stake in the welfare of the person to whom he or she is giving the side payment, then the cost of such payment can be reduced dramatically. In a sense, an interdependent welfare system is a system of low resistance to the flow of resources, where the flow contributes to an increase in the probability of collective action. For example, consider the situation facing someone trying to organize a collective picnic for a church group. This person might decide to give cookies and candy to all the children who help prepare the area for the picnic or who deliver circulars and notices. This side payment may in fact cost the person very little because he or she enjoys the pleasure the children get from the cookies and candy. These are children the person knows and values, and their pleasure brings him or her indirect rewards. The "cost" of the side payment becomes trivial in this case, because of altruism.

Closer to home, we see that parents find it very cheap to pay their children to do collectively needed chores, rather than give them allowances. Parents want the children to have the money, because they share the benefits of the children's enjoyment of the money.

Similarly, research has found that soldiers are best organized into small units where deep friendships develop, so as to maximize contributions to the collective action of fighting the enemy. In many ways, the risks taken by individual soldiers are seen to be side payments taken on behalf of their "buddies"—to save their lives or assure their safety—and not as contributions to the general war effort. The fact that the soldiers have buddies means that they have developed interdependent, altruistic welfare functions, and that the "contributions" they make are therefore seen as "cheap." Broadly speaking, the notion that primary groups bind individuals to the larger social structure is a version of the proposition that interpersonal commitment can induce contributions to broad collective goods.

The potential importance of such small-group commitments, when coupled with side payments, is made particularly clear if we consider a recent analysis by Schofield (1975). In a closely argued statement, Schofield concludes that the problem of collective action might be solved when small coalitions of individuals who can share payoffs through side payments are allowed to form. When one of these coalitions reaches a certain size, it can

---

[5] In a very insightful further analysis of this situation, Oliver (1980) has shown that the nature of the side payment *does* alter the payoff characteristics of the situation and may, in fact, provide some mechanisms for solving the problem of collective action. These mechanisms, though, have nothing to do with altruism.

use its side payments to continue to grow until it becomes a grand coalition of all individuals—that is, when it involves all individuals in providing the collective good. Although the analysis is very provocative, Schofield nowhere suggests the reason why, or basis on which, the small coalitions form in the first place. One answer might well be that the presence of altruism in the system, and the general distribution of interdependence, creates the basis for solidary coalitions. These coalitions then operate to gradually incorporate more and more people into the network and into the collective effort.

Increasing the Size of the Group through Altruism

The examples cited above involving children bring to mind a related process by which altruism might lead to collective action: increasing the size of the group. Consider a group of children who want to play hockey but have no skating rink. They consider building a hockey rink but obviously do not have the resources or organization to solve this collective goods problem.

At the same time, there is a second category of persons who do have such resources. However, they have no direct interest in a hockey rink. They neither skate nor enjoy watching others skate. According to the definition of group in our original discussion of the problem of collective action, members of this second category are *not* members of the group. In Olson's discussion it is precisely such interest in the collective good that defines group membership.

Despite the fact that they do not belong to the group, though, the persons who are in our second category often build hockey rinks in real life. That is because they are the parents of the children who wish to play hockey. Obviously, these parents do, indeed, have an interest in the hockey rink, or public good. But their interest is only indirect, because of altruism. Their interest arises wholly because of their commitment to the welfare of their children. They *become* group members through identification with the needs of others.

In this sense, then, altruism actually increases the size of the group. It makes available to the group additional resources that may (or may not) be contributed. For many collective activities such a broadening process may be crucial. The Irish Republican Army is said by some to depend on the commitments of Irish Americans for much of the IRA's resources, but Irish Americans will not become "free" if the British leave Northern Ireland. If boycotts of grapes and lettuce depended wholly on members of the farm workers' union they would not have been effective. They required the cooperation of altruistic nonfarm workers to make the boycott hurt the growers. Yet these nonfarm workers were actually helping to raise prices for themselves, if the farm workers they were helping received the public good of higher wages.

In formal terms, the notion of individuals being brought into the group through indirect interest in the public good suggests that the starting point for analysis might not be the group as Olson and others define it. Instead, we might wish to begin with some population of actors defined either by resources that might be applied to the collective action, or by participation in a broadly defined social network of mutually aware potential actors, or both. Group size, in Olson's sense of the amount of mobilized resources, is then a function of the total amount of mobilizable resources, that is, the size of the population and other factors. The relationship between group size and population size is itself specified, in part, by the level of altruism within the system. In general, the more altruism, the more individuals there are who will contribute to the public good without having direct interest in the public good.

Concluding Comments

Any look at the real world demonstrates that the problem of collective action is frequently "solved," at least to the extent of permitting some collective goods, if not an optimal amount, to be provided. The solution does not always depend on coercion. In fact, voluntary collective action seems endemic, except, of course, to people trying to get others to join.

Unproblematic collective action, which is almost invisible in its everyday occurrence, is founded mostly on the fact that people belong to groups and social networks and have personal, caring relationships with one another. These processes probably cannot be said to formally solve the formal problem of collective action with a simple cut through the Gordian knot. Nevertheless, they do suggest mechanisms through which the empirical reality can be fit to formal theory. In this paper we have discussed three such mechanisms: effects on noticeability, effects on the costs of side payments, and effects on group size.

Perhaps a more interesting question is one that lies beyond this initial analysis. If these mechanisms permit the emergence of collective action, can we specify the conditions under which we can expect the mechanisms—and which mechanism—to work? In particular, are there certain structural arrangements—particularly distributions of altruism—that are conducive to certain kinds of collective action but not to others? How might we typify such structural arrangements? For that matter, how might we typify the differences among concrete collective actions? In answering these questions we might explore the meaning of altruism and interpersonal commitment for social arrangements and social activity. We might get beyond exchange in explaining what happens.

Acknowledgments

Work on this research was supported by the Wisconsin Alumni Research Foundation. I would like to thank John Fleishman and Geraldine Alfano for their comments, and Arthur Goldberger, Donald Hester, Eugene Smolensky, and Michael Rothschild for their patience and instruction.

References

Alfano, G., & Marwell, G. Experiments on the provision of public goods III: Non-divisibility and free riding in "real" groups. *Social Psychology Quarterly*, 1980, *43*, 300–309.

Arrow, K. Gifts and exchanges. In E. S. Phelps (Ed.), *Altruism, morality and economic theory*. New York: Russell Sage Foundation, 1975.

Bohm, P. Estimating demands for a public good: An experiment. *European Economic Review*, 1972, *3*, 111–130.

Brubaker, E. R. Free ride, free revelation, or golden rule? *Journal of Law and Economics*, 1975, *18*, 147–161.

Brubaker, E. 13% golden rule, 16% free ride and 71% free revelation?: An experimental test of the free rider hypothesis. Unpublished manuscript, University of Wisconsin, 1979.

Dawes, R. M. Social dilemmas. *Annual Review of Psychology*, 1980, *31*, 169–193.

Fireman, B., & Gamson, W. A. Utilitarian logic in the resource mobilization perspective. In M. N. Zald and J. D. McCarthy (Eds.), *The dynamics of social movements*. Cambridge: Winthrop Publishers, Inc., 1979.

Fleishman, J. A. *Collective action as helping behavior: Effects of responsibility diffusion on contributions to a public good*. Unpublished doctoral dissertation, University of Wisconsin, 1978.

Froelich, N., and Oppenheimer, J. A. I get by with a little help from my friends. *World Politics*, 1970, *23*, 104–120.

Hadar, J., & Russell, W. R. Rules for ordering uncertain prospects. *The American Economic Review*, 1969, *59*, 25–34.

Hardin, G. R., The tragedy of the commons. *Science*, 1968, *162*, 1243–1248.

Marwell, G., & Ames, R. E. Experiments on the provision of public goods I: Resources, interest, group size, and the free rider problem. *American Journal of Sociology*, 1979, *84*, 1335–1360.

Marwell, G., & Ames, R. E. Economists free ride, does anyone else? Experiments on the provision of public goods IV. *Journal of Public Economics*, in press.

Marwell, G., & Ames, R. E. Experiments on the provision of public goods II: Provision points, stakes, experience and the free rider problem. *American Journal of Sociology*, 1980, *85*, 926–937.

Oliver, P. Rewards and punishments as selective incentives for collective action: Theoretical investigations. *American Journal of Sociology*, 1980, *85*, No. 6, 1356–1375.

Olson, M., Jr. *The logic of collective action: Public goods and the theory of groups.* New York: Schocken Books, 1968.

Platt, G. Social traps. *American Psychologist*, 1973, *28*, 741–651.

Schneider, F., & Pommerehne, W. W. *On the rationality of free-riding: An experiment.* Unpublished manuscript, University of Zurich, Zurich, 1979.

Schofield, N. A game theoretic analysis of Olson's game of collective action. *Journal of Conflict Resolution*, 1975, *19*, No. 3, 441–461.

Part II

HELPING BEHAVIOR

Chapter 10

Promotive Tension:

Theory and

Research[1]

HARVEY A. HORNSTEIN

During the time that Kurt Lewin lectured at the University of Berlin, more than 50 years ago, he and his students met regularly at the Schwedishe Cafe which was located near the university. It was here that Lewin one day entertainingly demonstrated the workings of a psychological principle that is central to the theoretical framework presented in this chapter.

As on any ordinary day, people ordered their coffee and cakes, and they talked. After some time the bill was requested. Although the waiter had not kept a written record, despite the time that had passed and the variety and number of items ordered, he provided a precise reckoning. This event might have been attributed to the individual skill of a competent waiter, but Lewin saw more in it. Thirty minutes later, when he called the waiter back and asked him to recount the tally, the waiter claimed it was impossible: "You have already paid the bill. I cannot be expected to remember."

Lewin's informal demonstration illustrated how a construct that he called *tension* operates in everyday life: As long as the waiter's goal of having the bill paid was unattained, goal-related tension remained aroused. This ten-

[1] Preparation of this chapter was supported by National Science Foundation Grant BNS-76-07697, "Experiments in the Social Psychology of Prosocial Behavior." The author is principal investigator of this grant.

229

sion caused the waiter to think about relevant issues: the items that were being ordered. And it would have caused him to seek payment at an appropriate moment. Once the bill was paid, however, goal attainment was complete, and the tension was dissipated. The items were no longer salient.[2]

Lewin reasoned that within individuals, tension corresponds to the existence of a psychological need or intention (sometimes called a quasi need). Once aroused it possesses two important dynamic properties (Deutsch, 1969): It is a state of a region or system that tries to change itself to become equal to the state of surrounding regions, and it involves forces at the boundary of the region. If in the psychological environment goal regions exist that are relevant to the tension, psychological forces may lead to actual locomotion as well as to thinking about goal-oriented activity.

Three categories of tension are identified as being the potential correspondents of psychological forces (Lewin, 1951): (a) tensions arising from own needs, such as the desire to attend a movie or have sexual intercourse; (b) tensions arising from induced needs, such as might result when a child's mother forces him or her to wear earmuffs; and (c) tensions arising from the need to satisfy impersonal demands that are matter-of-fact and situational, such as legal codes.

A fourth category of tension has been suggested by Hornstein (1972, 1976): *Promotive tension* is tension coordinated to *another's* needs or goals. Implicitly, Lewin (1951) acknowledged both the possibility and a principle consequence of promotive tension when he wrote,

> Forces may act on any part of the life space. Frequently the point of application is that region of the life space which corresponds to the own person. The child may, however, experience that the "doll wants to go to bed," or that "another child wants a certain toy." In these cases the points of application of the forces are regions in the life space of a child other than his own person. Such cases are common and play an important part, for example, in the problems of altruism [p. 260].

This chapter's next section focuses on the dynamic properties of promotive tension and is concerned with such questions as: Do people experience tension coordinated to *anothers* goals? Are there circumstances when one is aroused by *another's* needs almost as if they were one's own? I believe that these experiences do occur, and in order to support this claim I report research evidence that indicators of promotive tension display patterns that

---

[2] Although a clear consensus about the precise meaning of *tension* has never been achieved, it seems reasonable to claim that both Lewin and subsequent Lewinians are speaking about a psychological event—a kind of pressure or salience—rather than a physiological one. Correlates of a physiological nature are not explicitly rejected, but neither are they offered as essential defining characteristics of the construct. For confirmation readers are referred to Deutsch's (1969) classic exposition of field theory.

parallel those observed in classical research on the dynamic properties of tension systems that are aroused by own needs (Deutsch, 1949a, 1949b; Horwitz, 1953; Lewin, 1935, 1936, 1938, 1951; Lewis, 1944, Lewis & Franklin, 1944; Ovsiankina, 1928; Zeigarnik, 1927). The second and third major sections of the chapter report progress that we have made in investigating the social circumstances that affect promotive tension arousal.

Promotive Tension

Among the many hundreds of experiments stimulated by Lewin's ideas were a series concerned with the recall and resumption of interrupted activities (Lewis, 1944; Lewis & Franklin, 1944; Ovsiankina, 1928; Zeigarnik, 1927). The findings of these experiments make a number of suggestions: first, that the tendency to recall interrupted tasks is greater than the tendency to recall completed ones; second, that the tendency to resume interrupted tasks is greater than the tendency to resume completed ones; and third, that the tendency to recall interrupted tasks is greater when the task is interrupted near its end. These three conclusions are consistent with Lewin's notion that the strength of a psychological force increases as the psychological distance between a person and a valenced region decreases, and that, depending on direction, this strength can be graphically presented as an approach or avoidance gradient. Another conclusion suggested by these experiments is that the tendency to recall interrupted tasks is less when the tasks are completed by a *cooperating* partner, but is not affected if they are completed by a *noncooperatively* linked other.

These last findings (Lewis, 1944; Lewis and Franklin, 1944) are especially relevant to the issue under discussion. They suggest that tensions arising from own needs are reduced if someone else enters an appropriate goal region. Not *everyone* else, of course, but someone who is related in special ways, for example, a cooperating partner (see also Deutsch, 1949a, 1949b).

In a sense, the major concern of research on promotive tension has been and will continue to be the reverse of the one explored by Lewis and Franklin. Their work concerned the effects of social relationships on the *dissipation* of tension that was initially aroused by *one's own* goal-related activity. By contrast, research on promotive tension is concerned with the effects of social relationships on the *arousal* of tension as a consequence of *another's* goal-related activity. Two recent studies reported by Hornstein, Marton, Rupp, Sole, and Tartel (1980) provide an important example of this research. These studies are mirror images of the earlier work by Lewis and Franklin. The common dependent variable in these studies is the reported recall of *another's* completed and uncompleted tasks.

Subjects in both these studies watched another person's hands on a video screen as the other tried to complete a different puzzle in each of 12, 20-second work periods. They believed that they would subsequently work on a similar set of puzzles. The puzzles contained pictures of familiar objects, and subjects were made aware of what they would be, if completed: for example, teapot, scissors, and table. After the observation period ended and subjects witnessed the other person leave half the puzzle uncompleted, they were casually told, while equipment was presumably being reset for them, that we wanted to keep everyone's experience constant and asked to jot down the puzzles they remembered.

In the first study a subject's relationship to a bogus other was determined by varying the interdependence of payoffs for each completed puzzle. Different relationships were created: cooperative (subject and other earned 50¢ for each completed puzzle); competive (subject) lost 50¢ for one left uncompleted); and individualistic (subject and other were financially unaffected by each other's successes or failures). Accepting the assumption that one hopes to have cooperatively linked partners complete tasks on which they are working and to avoid having competitively linked other complete tasks on which they are working (Deutsch, 1949a, 1949b), this study tested the following hypothesis: A cooperative partner's interrupted tasks are recalled more frequently than his or her completed ones when the tasks' incompleteness is permanent; when it is temporary, differences in the recall of these two kinds of tasks occur less frequently. With competitively linked others, however, the reverse occurs: Interrupted tasks are recalled relatively more frequently when the incompleteness is temporary. If Lewis was examining Zeigarnik effects, then here we are examining "socially mediated Zeigarnik effects." The findings confirm the hypothesis, and by discounting an important alternative explanation, data from an additional control condition support the idea that promotive tension is mediating the pattern of effects observed in Table 10.1. One might argue that these data reflect differential attention of subjects to anothers' work. On this view, information, not recall, is producing the pattern. Following Lewin, Zeigarnik, and Lewis, an additional group of subjects in the cooperative nonresume condition were emphatically told that the study's principle objective was to measure their ability to recall the puzzles. (Of course, they learned this after observing the stimulated video material). Theoretically, this induction substitutes a new goal and should raise the salience of all items completed and uncompleted. Although the predisposition to recall uncompleted tasks had been greatest in this condition (60% of subjects showed a Zeigarnik effect), with this ego-involving goal set before them, only 32% of the subjects showed the Zeigarnik effect. Hence the pattern of recall evidenced in Table 10.1 reflects the motivational consequences of tension arousal coordinated

Table 10.1
Proportion of Subjects Showing Zeigarnik Effect for All Conditions (Percentages)[a]

	No ego pressure			Ego pressure
	Cooperative	Individualistic	Competitive	Cooperative
Resume	28	33	48	
	(25)	(15)	(25)	
Non resume	68	33	28	32
	(25)	(15)	(25)	(25)

Note: Ns are in parentheses.

[a] Zeigarnik quotient: $\dfrac{\text{uncompleted items recalled (Ru)}}{\text{completed items recalled (RC)}} > 1$

to another's goal related activity. The social relationships that existed differentially affected the salience of another's completed and uncompleted tasks, causing subjects to vary in the relative frequency with which such tasks were reported during the recall period.

These findings must be qualified. In this study the other's goal attainment in the cooperative and competitive conditions directly affected a subject's well-being. Thus, the findings cannot be introduced as evidence to support a claim that promotive tension is aroused when one has no stake whatsoever in another's goal attainment. In a replication of this experiment, however, these limiting conditions were removed by changing our independent variable manipulation. Subjects' relationships in the first experiment were determined by cooperative, competitive, and individualistic economic incentives. In this second experiment they were determined by their similarity or dissimilarity to a stranger on a bogus personality test. Using the same reasoning as before, we hypothesized that when subjects were confronted by dissimilar others, the opportunity for these others to *resume* work on uncompleted tasks was expected to heighten the occurrence of socially mediated Zeigarnik effects. The data strongly confirm the hypothesis. They are presented in Table 10.2. Once again, subjecting subjects to some pressure to report items makes an enormous difference. By taking the similar nonresume condition, where originally 73% of the subjects report more uncompleted than completed items, and telling subjects that "The main objective here is to recall as much as possible," we all but eradicate the occurrence of socially mediated Zeigarnik effects: Only 26% of subjects report more uncompleted than completed items. Clearly, this is a basis for arguing that the patterns of reporting in Tables 10.1 and 10.2 reflect differences in promotive tension arising from different social relationships.

The theoretical paradigm underlying these studies is germane to research on prosocial behavior: People often need assistance from others in order

Table 10.2
Subjects Showing Zeigarnik Effect for All Conditions (Percentages)[a]

	No ego pressure			Ego pressure
	Similar	No information	Dissimilar	Similar
Resume	20	33	53	
Non resume	73	40	26	26

Note: For all conditions, $N = 15$.

[a] Zeigarnik quotient: $\dfrac{\text{uncompleted items recalled (RU)}}{\text{completed items recalled (RC)}} > 1$

to achieve goals toward Which they are striving. An early application of these ideas can be found in a series of experiments by Hornstein and others (Hornstein, Masor, Sole, & Heilman, 1971; Hodgson, Hornstein, & Siegel, 1972) that had the double aim of further investigating dynamic properties of promotive tension and exploring its relationship to prosocial behavior.

In the first of these experiments (Hornstein et al., 1971) subjects were 175 pedestrians in Brooklyn, New York. Each of these people found two open envelopes belonging to a stranger. One envelope contained the stranger's pro- or anti-Israeli response to a "Harcourt Public Opinion Service" questionnaire, which contained a single question about the Middle-Eastern crisis. Pilot work demonstrated that pro-Israeli responses almost uniformly induced subjects in this population to hold positive sentiments toward the stranger and anti-Israeli responses induced them to hold negative sentiments. A second envelope contained a financial contribution to the "Institute for Research in Medicine." Information in this envelope indicated that it was either the second or the ninth in a series of 10 pledged contributions. Thus, a similar or dissimilar sender was either close to or far from completing a goal of 10 contributions to this fictitious institute.

It was hypothesized that the interrupted goal attainment of similar others would be completed (i.e., the Institute contribution would be mailed) more often when they were close to rather than far from completing their goal of ten contributions; for dissimilar others, nearness to goal was expected to be irrelevant, and overall returns would be comparatively lower. In essence, if promotive tension was mediating subjects' behavior for like others, then there should be evidence of an approach gradient. Data obtained in this experiment supported this hypothesis and confirmed our expectations of an approach gradient for helping.

This prediction assumed that the goal region was positively valenced for both the subject and the hapless stranger. As subsequent research demonstrated, contributions to medical research satisfied this assumption. Of course, Lewin's notions also provide a framework for predicting the effects of negatively valenced goal regions, an aim of a second experiment (Hodgson, Hornstein, & Siegel, 1972).

In this experiment, 475 subjects participated in a procedure similar to the earlier one with the exception that for half the subjects, a stranger was contributing to a foundation that was approved of by subjects, while for the other half he or she was contributing to one that was disapproved of by them.

The data replicated the earlier experiment by once again illustrating the existence of an approach gradient. Most important, the subjects also demonstrated promotive tension arousal corresponding to an avoidance gradient: They were actually more likely to help complete a liked other's attainment of goals of which they themselves disapproved when the other was *distant rather than close to goal completion.*

Data from these experiments provide a consistent demonstration of the way in which an individual's tension can be coordinated with the interrupted goal attainment of another. In the two laboratory experiments the frequency with which Zeigarnik effects occurred was clearly related to the social relationships that were experimentally established. And in the two field experiments, positive sentiment provided a basis for the arousal of promotive tension, while other factors, like a goal region's valence and the distance to it, determined the strength and direction of psychological forces operating on subjects.

Promotive Social Relationships

Lewin (1951) once commented, "Friendship as distinguished from enmity includes the readiness to accept and to back up the intention of the other person [p. 295]." The insight is germane to this inquiry, but imprecise. Amity and enmity have many causes. Time and social circumstance determine who is and who is not identified as "friend." Nonetheless, Lewin's insight is revealing and easily identified in everyday experience. On some occasions human beings experience a sense of community, a feeling of oneness with their fellows. As the famed sociologist Charles Horton Cooley (1909) once wrote, "Perhaps the simplest way of describing this wholeness is by saying it is a 'we'. . . .It involves the sort of sympathy and mutual identification for which 'we' is the natural expression."

Dichotomizing the world into groups of "we" and "they" reflects a process of social categorization. A common consequence of this process is discrimination, whereby a subset of the whole is identified as deserving preferential treatment. At least three sets of social conditions have been associated with the process of social categorization and discrimination:

1. *Social groupings with cooperative competitive goal structures.* The Sherifs (Sherif & Sherif, 1953; Sherif, White, Hood, & Sherif, 1961) demonstrated the effects of these structures in their classic "Robber's cave" experiment. Ingroup solidarity and hostile attitudes and stereotypes of outgroup members occurred under conditions of competition but diminished under conditions of cooperation. Similar results have been reported by other researchers (Bass & Dunteman, 1963; Blake & Mouton, 1962; Deutsch, 1973).

2. *Relationships in which individuals share a common social label.* In a series of experiments, Tajfel (1970; Tajfel, Flament, Billis, & Bundy, 1971) developed groups using trivial criteria that were either evaluative or nonevaluative in character. Regardless of whether subjects were in groups with evaluative labels, they discriminated in favor of ingroup members (see Ferguson & Kelley, 1964, for related findings). Tajfel claimed that in the absence of alternative guidelines for action, people will use available information to categorize others as a means of bringing order and coherence to a complex environment. Additional research by Rabbie, Wilkens, and Horwitz (Rabbie & Wilkens, 1968; Rabbie & Horwitz, 1969) and by Deutsch and his students (Deutsch, Thomas, & Garner, 1971; Chase, 1971) suggest qualifications of Tajfel's claim. Rabbie *et al.*, interpret their evidence as suggesting that group labeling per se is not a sufficient condition for discrimination. In these studies subjects discriminated only when they knew that they would share a common future that held positive promise. Studies by Deutsch and his students suggest that social discrimination does not occur when different labels exist unless the experimental world of the subject is *clearly* and unambiguously dichotomized into "we" and "they."

3. *Social situations in which individuals recognize that others share their attitudes or opinions.* In Hornstein's experiments, opinion similarity on an important topic and consequent interpersonal attraction were interpreted as being sufficient to provide a basis for promotive tension. The two, similarity and interpersonal attraction, were confounded, however. It is unclear whether both were operating in these experiments, or whether only one of the two was mediating the findings. Indeed, any question about which was operating may be meaningless, for Byrne (1969) has found that attraction to a stranger is linearly related to the proportion of similar attitudes attributed to him. An implication is that similarity and attraction together are a sufficient condition for the arousal of promotive tension. These issues were investigated in research by Sole, Marton, and Hornstein (1975).

Three studies were conducted employing experimental contexts similar to those used by Hornstein *et al.* (1971) and Hodgson *et al.* (1972). An unsuspecting pedestrian, "chanced" to find a packet of two envelopes which, it appeared, was "lost" by another person who had intended to mail them. As before, one envelope contained its owner's anonymous $2 contribution to a charity, and the other contained a sheet revealing the owner's opinions. In these three experiments, the owner expressed opinions on four issues. In the first experiment, the four issues were of uniformly *high importance* for subjects. In the second experiment they were of uniformly *low impor- tance.* The third experiment provided the subject with issues of *mixed im- portance*: two of high importance and two of low importance. Since four opinions were used, five levels of similarity of opinion could be created in each of the experiments: 0%, 25%, 50%, 75%, 100%. Prior to conducting the study, pretesting of residents from the same neighborhood at locations adjacent to the experimental sites allowed us to select opinion statements on which local opinion was uniform with respect to both the content of the issue and its importance.

Three major conclusions can be drawn from these experiments. First, in the initial experiment, when opinions were expressed on four issues of uniformly *high* importance, dissimilarity with the subject's opinion on any one of the four issues was sufficient to cause significantly lower rates of helping. In fact, one dissimilar opinion was as detrimental to the rate of helping as was total dissimilarity of opinion. The dramatic stepwise pattern of these data supported the idea that subjects divided their world and then granted help only to those strangers who were included in what can be described as their "we-group." A conclusion, based on these findings, but revised in light of subsequent ones is that *unclear boundaries, where others may belong to the subject's "we-group" along some dimensions and to one or more "they-groups" along others, are not likely to provide a basis for promotive tension.*

Second, agreement about issues of low importance seems to be critical only when that is all there is to agree about (as in the second experiment here, which employed four issues of uniformly low importance, or in Tajfel's laboratory procedure). Even then the effect is comparatively slight. In every- day affairs, people are not likely to act on behalf of another when their only bonds are rooted in a shared belief about inconsequential matters.

Third, attraction may be a common correlate of opinion similarity (Byrne, 1971) but is not a necessary condition for the formation of promotive social relationships. Corroboration of this statement is to be found by contrasting the return rates obtained in each of the experiments with other data from different groups of subjects in the same neighborhood. These subjects were shown the opinion statements of the bogus stranger. After learning that he agreed with their own views either 0%, 25%, 50%, 75%, or 100% of the time on issues of either high or low importance, they rated their attraction to the bogus other. In the first experiment the helping data's sharp stepwise pattern is in marked contrast to the attraction data's smooth, monotonic pattern. In the second experiment, increased agreement about trivial issues did not lead to increases in liking in this field situation (also see Banikiotes, Russell, & Linden, 1972), although it did affect levels of helping.

Similarity emerges as a critical variable determining the formation of promotive social relationships. But the role played by similarity between self and another in creating we-group ties depends in part on the nature of surrounding context.

Commonplace experience makes it plainly evident that the nature of social information which people use to judge their similarity to others changes as the social context changes. Each of us occupies many roles simultaneously. We are young or old, male or female, and we occupy some racial category and have political opinions, families, religious histories, and food preferences. The importance of these social cues and their salience is not rigidly fixed. They vary with time and social circumstance, so that we-group ties are constantly shifting. These issues were investigated in one of three experiments to be reported by Tucker, Holloway, Wagner, and Hornstein (in preparation). The experiments were all concerned with how social context altered the meaning and significance of information about another.

Subjects in this particular experiment happened on two bits of material lying on the street. One was a charity contribution, the other a report from a local public opinion poll, printed on a page from a local newsletter.

The public opinion poll material provided subjects with two pieces of information. First, they learned the results of a recent "neighborhood survey" which concluded that the "quality of life" in the neighborhood had either "improved" or "deteriorated" (social context manipulation). The "survey" offered specific information that preexperimental studies revealed had statistically significant effects on subjects' reported feelings about the neighborhood. Second, the public opinion poll material exposed the bogus respondent's opinions on three attitudinal statements. Extensive pretesting allowed responses to be varied, creating five conditions of subject stranger agreement: 100% agreement, 66.6% agreement, 33.3% agreement, 0% agreement, and no information about the stranger's opinions. This yielded a 3 × 5 factorial design with three conditions of social context (positive, negative, no information) and five conditions of subject–stranger agreement. There were 50 subjects in each condition. The data are presented in Table 10.3.

We predicted and found that when the social context was positive, subjects were more tolerant of differences, and provided help more frequently to those represented as *less similar* than they did when the social context was negative. Here the boundaries of "we" were drawn more narrowly. An

Table 10.3
Helping Behavior of Subjects in Different Social Context and Agreement Conditions
(Percentages)

Social context information	Percentage of subject–stranger agreement				
	0	33⅓	66½	100	No information
Positive	34	50	62	60	50
Negative	28	34	28	60	40
No information	36	32	34	54	60

examination of the diminution in helping between 100% and 66.6% agreement in the positive as compared to the negative social context conditions in Table 10.3 reveals the effect very clearly.

The data in the social context no information row represent a replication of Sole *et al.* (1975), and here, as before, there is a rapid drop-off in helping with anything less than 100% agreement with the stranger. Finally, the agreement no information column reveals that in the absence of information about the stranger, the rate of helping is calibrated to information about the surrounding community. This lends support to our view developed in the next section, that people act as if they were social actuaries, using this information to make inferences about total strangers.

The experiments just described, and others that follow as well, are concerned with what social conditions provide a basis for the arousal of promotive tension. Throughout our research there is evidence that promotive relationships are characterized by an absence of negative sentiment and a belief that others hold beliefs and values that are concordant with one's own beliefs, values, and self-interest (Hornstein, 1976). These issues are examined from a different perspective in this chapter's concluding section.

A Sense of Community

Reexamine the Tucker *et al.* (in preparation) findings in conditions where subjects had no information about the other, only information about the community-at-large. The finding that positive and negative information about the surrounding social context affected subjects' responses to a specific stranger about whom they had no information whatsoever has interesting theoretical and social implications. In modern society, people are frequently in situations in which they are required to make decisions affecting the lives of nameless, faceless others about whom they have no personal information whatsoever. With only a little introspection, we can easily see that each of us is capable of acting like an actuary who takes a sampling of the social universe and projects estimates of the extent to which its members subscribe to beliefs and values that are either concordant or antithetical to our own beliefs, values, and self-interests. It seems reasonable to assume that under some circumstances these estimates alter inferences about particular strangers and either foster or suppress the development of a promotive relationship. Further, it may be assumed that for each individual these estimates remain fairly stable until from time to time some especially persuasive bit of information causes shifts toward more favorable or unfavorable social conceptions (e.g., Murray, 1933; Wrightsman, 1964).

A series of experiments, stimulated by this view of humanity as composed of incorrigibly subjective pollsters, focused on how knowledge of remote social events affects promotive relationships and prosocial behavior. Before I report findings from these experiments I will summarize the essential details of the experimental procedures that we have used. These procedures vary slightly from experiment to experiment, but these are variations on a common theme.

Each subject is individually escorted to the door of the experimental room by an assistant, who first checks a bogus schedule sheet in order to determine the subject's "assigned" room and to create the illusion that more than one room is in use. While music plays from a radio located at the front of the room, a second assistant, the experimenter, meets each subject by the door, instructs him or her not to talk during the study and leads each to a cubicle–desk, partitioned so that a subject is able to see very little else besides the front of the room, the experimenter, and the radio. The experimenter then turns off the radio and plays tape-recorded instructions that explain the task in which the subject is going to engage.

After a brief delay, the experimenter announces, "We're a little early. We'll have to wait for the other room to be ready." The radio is then switched on and 60 seconds of music is followed by a news broadcast and then an additional 30 seconds of music, at which point a confederate enters and says, "The other room is ready." The experimenter turns off the radio and subjects engage in a task designed to obtain our dependent variable measure. After this task is completed, subjects are debriefed and paid equally for their participation.

Prior to the experiment, pretests are conducted on a number of stories in order to establish prosocial and antisocial news broadcasts. Potential stories are adapted from actual news reports and ranked by naive judges in a way that allows preselection of news stories that are clearly providing positive or negative social information.

In the first experiment in this series (Hornstein, LaKind, Frankel, & Manne, 1976), after hearing the news report, subjects played one round of a moderately high stakes ($1 and $2), two-choice, non-zero-sum game. The news stories were expected to affect a subject's views about strangers and, correspondingly, their relationship to him: That is, a "good" news story was expected to decrease the likelihood that subjects would perceive a stranger as someone who was promotively oriented toward them. A "bad" news story was expected to decrease the likelihood of strangers being perceived in this way, and subjects were not expected to exhibit or anticipate cooperative behavior. The relevant data are presented in Table 10.4.

The expectations were confirmed. Subjects who heard a prosocial newscast played the non-zero-sum game more cooperatively and had cooperative goals more often than those who heard an antisocial radio newscast.

In a second experiment, we were concerned with obtaining more direct evidence about the presumed mediator of this behavior. Specifically, we wanted to investigate our previously stated prediction that news events that symbolize "human goodness" cause subjects to hold inflated estimates of the distribution of promotive social dispositions among the general public, i.e., they believe that a relatively higher percentage of people subscribe to beliefs and values that concern the well-being of others and are therefore concordant with each subject's self-interest. On the other hand, news events that symbolize "inhumanity" cause inflated estimates about the percentage of people who subscribe to beliefs and values that are essentially antithetical to the well-being of others, including the subjects.

In this experiment, after overhearing the news report, subjects answered nine questions on an instrument called the "Population Estimate Questionnaire." This was, in reality, a substantially altered edition of a portion of Wrightsman's Philosophies of Human Nature Scale (1964), and included such questions as "What percentage of people are basically honest?" "What percentage of people would risk their own lives or limbs to help someone else?" Table 10.5 contains the data.

As you can see, subjects who heard a prosocial radio newscast, in contrast to those who heard an antisocial one, were more inclined toward believing

Table 10.4
Distribution of Responses in Different Newscast Conditions

Response	Newscast[a]		
	Prosocial	Antisocial	No news control
Competition	.09 (.18)	.28 (.50)	.23 (.50)
Cooperative	.43 (.82)	.28 (.50)	.23 (.50)
Mixed[b]	.48	.44	.54

[a] Twenty subjects in each condition. Parentheses enclose percentages of pure types who were cooperative or competitive.
[b] Includes those who chose cooperatively but expected the other to do otherwise or vice versa.

Table 10.5
Average Percentage of Responses Expressing Favorable View of Humanity to
Questions on the Population Estimates Questionnaire

	Newscast		
	Prosocial	Antisocial	No news control
Males	40.68	29.18	41.60
Females	48.96	40.36	a

[a] Subject availability and time constraints prevented data collection for a female control group.

that a relatively high percentage of people subscribed to beliefs and values which concerned them with the well-being of others (Hornstein, LaKind, Frankel, & Manne, 1976). Compared to males, females in this sample subscribed to a more favorable view of humanity and were clearly less affected by the newscasts: The difference for females between prosocial and antisocial conditions, as shown in Table 10.5, falls just short of the traditional .05 level of significance. For males, the differences are more dramatic and well within the range of statistically significant difference.

Social and Nonsocial Information

These data corroborate our assumption that information about the social universe alters perceptions of the public-at-large which, in turn, affects specific inferences about a particular stranger. The explanation of these data, however, rests on an untested assumption: that the *social content* of the remote event reported as news—that is, the fact that the outcome results from the action of a human agent—mediates the observed effect. People are harmed in the antisocial news conditions and benefited in the prosocial ones. Perhaps the outcomes alone caused the observed effects. Perhaps the same harm or benefit caused by nature would yield similar findings. Perhaps subjects are not making inferences about the social universe, based on their sampling of some human activity, but are simply becoming more or less pessimistic because of the character of the stories' outcomes.

Two studies (Holloway, Tucker, & Hornstein, 1977) investigated how one form of interpersonal behavior, cooperation–competition, is affected by social and nonsocial information conveyed in ordinary news reports about remote events. Subjects were exposed to one of four pretested "news" broadcasts and were then asked to play one round of a non-zero-sum game. In both studies, two of the broadcasts contained social information telling listeners about intentional human acts which caused a loss or a saving of lives. The second two broadcasts contained nonsocial information, reporting objectively equivalent consequences due to natural phenomena. In both experiments an interaction effect was evident: The frequency of cooperation and competition was more greatly affected by good and bad news containing social information than it was by good or bad news containing nonsocial information.

Affect and Cognition

Mood is another possible mediator of the effects observed in Hornstein *et al.* (1976) and in Holloway *et al.* (1977). Consequently, both experiments used the broadcasts but also had subjects complete the Nowlis Mood Adjective Checklist (MACL). Responses of subjects who heard the prosocial radio newscast were no different from those who heard the antisocial newscast. In comparison to other research using the Nowlis MACL, however, subjects in these experiments were not directed to listen to the news broadcast before receiving the checklist. A certain transparency may have been introduced in previous research when subjects were directed to attend to inputs before having their moods assessed. One is forced to wonder, would our experimental manipulation produce questionnaire evidence of mood change if the experimental instructions more closely paralleled those used by other researchers? In order to explore this possibility, a study was conducted using Aderman's (1972) instructions, with word changes to suit our content, which *specifically directed* subjects to attend to the news broadcast. Now the effect on mood became obvious (Hornstein *et al.*, 1976). Scores on all 12 clusters for both sexes indicate "better" moods after exposure to the "good" news broadcast, and many were statistically significant. On the basis of these findings it seems reasonable to conclude that previous findings involving direct measures of mood reflect the demand characteristics of the experiments.

Additional findings from Holloway *et al.* (1977) lend support to the idea that rather than mood it is social outlook, a cognitive variable that is mediating the effect that has been reported. Their findings indicate that neither social nor nonsocial information newscasts affected mood as measured by the Nowlis MACL. In contrast, the social outlook of subjects who behaved cooperatively was more positive than that of those who behaved competitively ($p < .01$), as measured by our revision of the Wrightsman scales. More importantly, the data demonstrate that social outlook is malleable and responsive to social but not nonsocial information: Analysis of variance of subjects' social outlooks produced a significant main effect for news, and simple effects analysis demonstrated that this effect occurred only in the social information condition.

These findings might tempt one to conclude that mood is unrelated to helping, but that seems excessive. Mood cannot be dismissed as a potential mediator of one's views about people. Intuition suggests that it is common for "good" moods to be associated with predispositions to evaluate the social community favorably and "bad" moods to be associated with the opposite. But only a little imagination is necessary to think of events that produce "bad" moods while simultaneously heightening favorable conceptions of humanity—some unexpectedly heroic efforts that end in tragedy, for example. Similarly, victories over an unusually ruthless and pervasive foe may produce "good" moods, but narrowed and comparatively unfavorable conceptions of humanity. To explore the relationships between mood and such beliefs about others, it is necessary to manipulate these two variables independently in a single investigation.

LaKind and Hornstein (in press) did just that, using Pensylvania homemakers as subjects. They created four stories that covaried social conception (favorable versus unfavorable) and mood (elated versus depressed). Two manipulation checks with separate groups of people verified the impact of these stories.

For their dependent measure they had different groups of subjects judge the guilt or innocence of defendants involved in hypothetical litigation. In accord with previous findings, the results indicate that social information and the changes in social outlook that it caused, were of primary importance in altering subjects' judgments about defendants. Subjects who heard positive social information in radio newscasts were more lenient in their judgments of defendants than were those who heard negative social information. Mood was not totally without consequence, however: Positive mood amplified the impact of social information, whatever its direction, whereas negative mood attenuated it.

These experiments place a theoretical premium on cognitive factors as determinants of promotive social relationships with total strangers. Positive social information enhances the development of such bonds, and negative social information discourages it. Historically, the idea has roots stretching several decades back. In his *Principles of Gestalt Psychology*, Koffka wrote, "visual space can only be understood as the product of field organization." The underlying theme fits, but let's change the words: "Social perception and contingent social behavior can only be understood as a product of information about the social context." Three separate studies explore this issue.

Social Context and Promotive Relationships

In her doctoral dissertation, Kaplan (1976) demonstrated how news of positive and negative social events affects judgments about another's status as "we" or "they." Using a procedure akin to one developed by Tajfel (1970), she gave subjects information about their tendency to over or underestimate the number of dots in a scatter plot. Subjects also learned that one of the two people with whom they would be working had a similar tendency, whereas the other had a dissimilar one. After exposure to this information, and to either the positive or negative social information newscast, subjects in two separate experiments had to judge the others' work on a task: box building. In one experiment they divided bonus money between the two others; in a second, they evaluated the others on a series of bipolar adjective scales.

After hearing negative social information, subjects were intolerant of differences. They discriminated sharply between similar and dissimilar others in both the written evaluations and the assignment of bonuses. In contrast, after hearing positive social information, they were more tolerant, and no such discrimination occurred. These issues were pursued in two studies to be reported by Tucker *et al.* (in preparation). Both studies used a procedure similar to Kaplan's. In one study subjects allocated bonuses to two others as in Kaplan's experiment, whereas in the second, they evaluated them on bipolar adjective scales. What was different about these studies is that the degree of difference between the two others was also varied.

Despite varying degrees of difference between the two others, the results were the same. After hearing negative social information, subjects discriminated in their allocation of money to similar and dissimilar others. This occurred even when the difference between them was minimal. After hearing positive social information, however, they allocated the money almost equally between the two.

A question arises: Did the social information alter subjects' perception of the others, causing them to "see" more or less difference, or did it leave perception untouched, altering instead their tolerance of difference? A second experiment investigated this by having subjects describe themselves and the others on a series of bipolar adjective scales after hearing either positive or negative social information newscasts. Changes in perception were clearly evident. After hearing negative social information, subjects' impressions of similar and dissimilar others diverged sharply, so that similar others were greatly favored. No such differences emerged after they heard positive social information. Once again the degree of difference between the others—in the way it was manipulated in this experiment—was irrelevant.

A crucial issue that emerges from this research is that in negative as opposed to positive social contexts people are concerned with identifying "who is similar" and "who is dissimilar." These subjects were unresponsive to differences between others and themselves. Fine discriminations were lost in the shadow of negative social information. Any disparity between others, large or small, was treated equivalently. Negative social information stimulated subjects to form gross categorizations, distinguishing those who were more similar from the rest.

These findings bear a striking resemblance to other findings in the conflict literature (Coser, 1956; Deutsch, 1969; Dion, 1973; Sherif *et al.*, 1961; Simmel, 1955). Outside threats have often been identified as the promoters of unexpected bedfellows. A noteworthy illustration of this general effect occurred in these two experiments in relation to a bogus other who was labeled "Perceptual Level 2." In one case he was the more similar of the two others, in a second case he was the more dissimilar one. Of course, he was the identical "person" in both instances—all that changed was his relationship to the second bogus other. After hearing negative, but not after hearing positive, social information the change from similar to dissimilar status condemned this other. He or she became one of *them*, and was mistreated accordingly.

Although these studies initially grew out of a theoretical concern with social conditions that affect the development of promotive relationships, it is clear that they continue moving toward making a statement that has theoretical as well as applied implications: News about the social world is not psychologically neutral. It is an important yet subtle source of influence on perceptions of self and assumptions about others. By changing one's general conception of people, news plays a critical role in shaping specific inferences about strangers. It acts as a bias, creating expectations that predispose us to classify complete strangers as *we* or *they*.

References

Aderman, D. Elation, depression and helping behavior. *Journal of Personality and Social Psychology*, 1972, 24, 91–101.

Banikiotes, P. G., Russell, J. M., & Linden, J. H. Interpersonal attraction in simulated and real interactions. *Journal of Personality and Social Psychology*, 1972, 23, 1, 1–17.

Bass, B. M., & Dunteman, G. Biases in the overevaluation of one's own group. Its allies and opponents. *Journal of Conflict Resolution*, 1963, 7, 16–20.

Billig, M. G. *Social categorization and intergroup relations.* Unpublished doctoral dissertation, University of Bristol, England, 1972.

Blake, R. R., & Mouton, J. S. Overevaluation of own group's product in intergroup competition. *Journal of Abnormal and Social Psychology*, 1962, 64, 237–238.

Byrne, D. Attitudes and attraction. In L. Berkowitz (Ed.), *Advances in experimental social psychology* (Vol. 4). New York: Academic Press, 1969.

Byrne, D. *The attraction paradigm.* New York: Academic Press, 1971.

Chase, M. *Categorization and affective arousal: Some behavioral and judgmental consequences.* Unpublished doctoral dissertation, Teachers College, Columbia University, 1971.

Cooley, C. H. *Social organization.* New York: Scribner, 1909.

Coser, L. *The function of social conflict.* New York: The Free Press, 1956.

Deutsch, M. A theory of cooperation and competition. *Human Relations*, 1949, *2*, 129–152. (a)

Deutsch, M. An experimental study of the effects of cooperation and competition upon group processes. *Human Relations*, 1949, *2*, 81–95. (b)

Deutsch, M. Field theory in social psychology. In G. Lindzey & E. Aronson (Eds.), *The handbook of social psychology* (2nd ed.). Reading, Mass.: Addison-Wesley, 1969.

Deutsch, M. *The resolution of conflict.* New Haven: Yale University Press, 1973.

Deutsch, M., Thomas, J. R. H., & Garner, K. A. *Social discrimination on the basis of category membership.* Unpublished manuscript, Teachers College, Columbia University, 1971.

Dion, K. L. Cohesiveness as a determinant of ingroup–outgroup bias. *Journal of Personality and Social Psychology*, 1973, *28*, 163–171.

Ferguson, C. K., & Kelley, H. H. Significant factors in overevaluation of own group's product. *Journal of Abnormal and Social Psychology*, 1964, *69*, 223–228.

Hodgson, S. A., Hornstein, H. A., & Siegel, E. Socially mediated Zeigarnik effects as a function of sentiment, valence and desire for goal attainment. *Journal of Experimental Social Psychology*, 1972, *8*, 5, 446–456.

Holloway, S., Tucker, L., & Hornstein, H. A. The effects of social and nonsocial information on interpersonal behavior of males: The news makes news. *Journal of Personality and Social Psychology*, 1977, *35*, 7, 514–522.

Hornstein, H. A. Social models and interpersonal helping behavior. In J. Macaulay & L. Berkowitz (Eds.), *Altruism and helping behavior.* New York: Academic Press, 1970. (a)

Hornstein, H. A. Experiments in the social psychology of prosocial behavior. Final report, National Science Foundation Grant No. 1715, 1970. (b)

Hornstein, H. A. Promotive tension: The basis of prosocial behavior from a Lewinian perspective. *Journal of Social Issues*, 1972, *28*, 2, 191–218.

Hornstein, H. A. *Cruelty and kindness: A new look at aggression and altruism.* Englewood Cliffs, N.J.: Prentice-Hall, 1976.

Hornstein, H. A., LaKind, E., Frankel, G., & Manne, S. The effects of knowledge about remote social events on prosocial behavior, social conception and mood. *Journal of Personality and Social Psychology*, 1976, *32*, 1038–1046.

Hornstein, H. A., Masor, H. N., Sole, K., & Heilman, M. Effects of sentiment and completion of a helping act on observer helping: A case for socially mediated Zeigarnik effects. *Journal of Personality and Social Psychology*, 1971, *17* 107–112

Hornstein, H. A., Marton, J., Rupp, A., Sole, K., & Tartell, R. The propensity to recall another's completed and uncompleted tasks as a consequence of varying social relationships. *Journal of Experimental Social Psychology*, 1980, *16*, 362–375.

Horwitz, M. The recall of interrupted group tasks: An experimental study of individual motivation in relation to group goals. *Human Relations*, 1953, *7*, 3–38.

Kaplan, S. The effects of news broadcasts on discriminating behavior toward similar and dissimilar others. (Doctoral dissertation, Teachers College, Columbia University, 1975). *Dissertation Abstracts*, 1976, *36*, 3123 B. (University Microfilms No. 75–77, 420.)

Koffka, K. *Principles of Gestalt psychology.* New York: Harcourt Brace, 1935.

LaKind, E., & Hornstein, H. A. The effects of mood and social outlook on hypothetical juridic decisions. *Journal of Applied Social Psychology*, 1979, *9*, 548–559.

Lewin, K. *A dynamic theory of personality.* New York: McGraw-Hill, 1935.

Lewin, K. *Principles of topological psychology.* New York: McGraw-Hill, 1936.

Lewin, K. The conceptual representation and measurement of psychological forces. *Contributions to Psychological Theory*, 1938, *1*, No. 4.

Lewin, K. *Field theory in social science.* New York: Harper, 1951.

Lewis, H. B. An experimental study of the role of the ego in work: I, The role of the ego in cooperative work. *Journal of Experimental Psychology*, 1944, *34*, 113–126.

Lewis, H. B., & Franklin, M. An experimental study of the role of the ego in work: II, The significance of task orientation in work. *Journal of Experimental Psychology*, 1944, *31*, 195–215.

Murray, H. A. The effects of fear upon the estimates of maliciousness of other personalities, *Journal of Social Psychology*, 1933, *4*, 310–328.

Ovsiankina, M. Die Wiederaufnahme von unterstbrochenen Handlungen. *Psychologische Forschung*, 1928, *11*, 302–379.

Rabbie, J., & Horwitz, M. Arousal of ingroup–outgroup bias by a chance win or loss. *Journal of Personality and Social Psychology*, 1969, *13*, 269–277.

Rabbie, J., & Wilkins, G. Intergroup competition and its effects on intra- and intergroup relationships. Unpublished report, 1968, University of Utrecht.

Sherif, M., & Sherif, C. *Groups in harmony and tension.* New York: Harper, 1953.

Sherif, M., Harvey, O. J., White, B. J., Hood, W. R., & Sherif, C. W. *Intergroup conflict and cooperation: The Robber's cave experiment.* Norman: University of Oklahoma Press, 1961.

Simmel, G. *Conflict.* New York: Free Press, 1955.

Sole, K., Marton, J., & Hornstein, H. A. Opinion similarity and helping: Three field experiments investigating the bases of promotive tension. *Journal of Experimental Social Psychology*, 1975, *11*, 1–13.

Tajfel, H. Experiments in intergroup discrimination. *Scientific American*, 1970, *223*, 96–102.

Tajfel, H., Flamant, C., Billig, M. G., & Bundy, R. P. Social categorization and intergroup behavior. *European Journal of Social Psychology*, 1971, *1 & 2*, 149–178.

Tucker, L., Holloway, S., Wagner, S., & Hornstein, H. A. The composition of we-groups as a function of positive and negative information about social events. Manuscript in preparation.

Wrightsman, L. Measurement of philosophies of human nature scale. *Psychological Reports*, 1964, *14*, 743–751.

Zeigarnik, G. Über den Behalten von erledigten und underledigten Handlungen. *Psychologische Forschung*, 1927, *9*, 1–85.

Chapter 11

The Justice Motive
in Human Relations
and the Economic
Model of Man:
A Radical Analysis
of Facts and Fictions[1]

MELVIN J. LERNER

A few observations form the outline of this chapter. The first of these is that most people, both social scientists and laypersons, accept what has been termed the economic model of man. This rather simple model portrays people as attempting to maximize their profits—desired outcomes less costs—in every endeavor. To the extent that people also use their intellectual abilities, the time frame is often extended so that the desire to gain pleasure and avoid pain is shaped into behavior that is governed by enlightened self-interest, that is, greater profit in the long run. But according to this model, in every case the essential rule of human behavior is the goal of maximizing one's profits (see, e.g., Thibaut & Kelley, 1959; Walster, Walster, & Berscheid 1978). In every situation not governed by rote habit, people will invariably elect the particular way of acting that they believe promises them the most pleasure at the least cost. And there are some who would insist that even "rote habits" have been stamped in by their prior association with pleasurable events (Homans, 1961).

The second observation is that, in fact, this economic model of man is

[1] The research reported here, conducted at the University of Waterloo, was supported by Grants to M. J. Lerner from the Canada Council (S-73-0194) and the Social Sciences and Humanities Research Council (410-77-0601-x2).

based on a distorted view of human motivation. There is considerable evidence that people organize their lives around the related themes of deserving and justice rather than simply the maximization of profits. Thus it seems that the image of what people care about that most people, including social scientists, hold is not only biased but essentially wrong.

Third, there are at least two reasons why, in spite of this evidence, the belief in the myth of economic man persists. One points to the institutional arrangements in our society and our social sciences that perpetuate the assumptions underlying the myth. The other portrays the myth as a functional defense for most people who feel they cannot afford to trust their own non-profit-oriented impulses in a world where they believe people must look out for themselves. They use the myth to justify not responding to their own "dangerous" impulses for justice and deserving in their relations with one another.

The Economic Model in the Social Sciences and Everyday Life

The Profit Motive in Contemporary Theories of Prosocial Behavior

COST-ACCOUNTING IN ALTRUISM

I will devote the least amount of space to presenting the evidence for the economic model. The assumption that people are governed basically, if not exclusively, by the desire to avoid pain and gain pleasure is taken as a truism within the human sciences. In general, any theoretical differences among social scientists center around the question of how people decide what gives them pleasure and pain and the role that developmental processes and prior experience play in shaping the way people go about the pursuit of maximizing their profits.

Most social scientists seem to agree that those human acts that appear on the surface to be relatively unprofitable for the actor are in fact designed by the individual's, or the social unit's, "intelligence" to be the most profitable course to follow. Presumably, prosocial, selfless, or altruistic behaviors are no less determined by the profit-maximizing rule than are acts that are patently self-interested, antisocial, or greedy. In any situation, the former rather than the latter occur when the person recognizes that the benefits to be derived from internally generated payoffs (negative ones, such as guilt for not being altruistic, or positive ones, such as pride or sense of superiority), together with the assessed external payoffs (positive ones, such as the anticipation of reciprocated benefits for helping, and negative ones, such as expected sanctions for failing to help), all add up to greater profit in the long run for helping. Differing proportions of guilt, expected reciprocity, social sanctions, etc., may of course elicit no help or even exploitation (Walster & Piliavin, 1972).

The person's intelligence functions to enable the widest scan of the alternatives and best assessment of the future consequences as well as to combine the painful and desirable weights in arriving at the final decision concerning the most profitable way to behave. In addition, the combination of many individuals' enlightened self-interest can lead to the creation of social units that adopt rules that curb members' appetites and enable them to coordinate their efforts for the best interest, or greatest profit, for all. As a result, many of the payoffs experienced and anticipated by the person are based on the internal representation of these social rules (Blau, 1964; Campbell, 1975).

Although I have not presented full documentation in support of each of these statements, I feel very comfortable in asserting at this point that there is no well recognized theory of prosocial or altruistic behavior that does not reflect these assumptions about human conduct, that is, that a profit-maximizing, cost-accounting homunculus guides the person's acts. For examples the reader should consult the chapters in this volume or other presentations of the most visible theories of prosocial behavior: see, for example, Aronfreed (1968), Bryan (1972), Campbell (1975), Hornstein (1976), Latané and Darley (1968, 1970), Rosenhan (1972), Schwartz (1975), Staub (1978), and Walster and Piliavin (1972).

THE RULE OF JUSTICE AS A DEVICE FOR PROFIT

For the most part, the theories that address directly the issue of the way considerations of justice or fairness appear in people's lives make the same set of assumptions about human motivation. The human concern with justice is described as the internalization and/or the awareness of the social conventions concerning rules of deserving. From this common perspective it is assumed that people follow rules of justice only as long as such rules are perceived to be the most profitable way to act in terms of the person's other goals (Walster, Walster, & Berscheid, 1978). Of course part of the profit is based on the internal representation of the relative costs and benefits associated with following the rules of justice, what has been called "self-concept distress," or dissonance (Leventhal, 1976b; Walster et al., 1978).

Also, it is assumed that this same instrumental orientation to rules of fairness appears in the particular form or rule of justice that a person applies in a given situation. These theories assume that the rule of justice that is elected in a given situation is determined by the particular goals of the person or the social unit in that context. For example, it is assumed that a justice of *equity*, based on relative contribution is employed when people are trying to maximize the productivity of the social unit. However, when harmonious relations among the members is the primary goal, people will apply a justice of *equality*. Presumably an equal allocation is less likely to elicit rancor and conflicts (Deutsch, 1975; Leventhal, 1976a,b; Sampson, 1975).

In other words, the rule of justice is an instrumental device to facilitate the person's or the social unit's acquisition of desired resources. And, of course, given this instrumentality, considerations of justice will be manipulated, blended, and even abandoned when acting "unjustly" is perceived to be the most profitable course of action. It is generally accepted that a profit-oriented homunculus guides the person's or society's decisions of what to consider "just" and when to follow its dictates (see, e.g., Campbell, 1975; Deutsch, 1975; Leventhal, 1976a, 1976b; Walster, Walster, & Berscheid, 1978).

Profit Motive in Everyday Encounters

It is not as easy to document the assertion that most members of our society accept this model of their own and others' motivation. I know of no set of available references or definitive survey data that would provide the required documentation. As an alternative I can suggest that it appears obvious from common observation—what most of us can see about us— that most people believe that in commercial transactions all participants must look out for themselves and that all are clearly in the business of advancing their own best interests. The "bottom line" of the profit and loss column clearly dictates the policies of companies and the futures of all employees; that is taken for granted as the natural way in which people should go about gaining and distributing resources.

What is less obvious, but not unfamiliar, to social analysts of our way of life is that as a result of our economic system, people begin to construe themselves and their relations to others in terms of resources to be developed, used, and exchanged for other desired resources (Fromm, 1955; Riesman, 1950; Sampson, 1975). In other words, we begin to see ourselves and others in instrumental terms. We view ourselves as a collection of wants and of resources that can be developed, exploited, or exchanged with others in order to meet those wants. We interact with others in ways that are designed to optimize our use of these resources—we want to get the most out of our time, effort, talents. And we assume everyone does that.

It was most startling to me, especially in view of what I assert later in this chapter, to recognize that our language and thinking habits naturally lead us to construe virtually all of our acts and relations in these instrumental, cost-accounting terms—even our most intimate relationships. For example, as a simple but rather frightening exercise, ask yourself why you are nice, loving, and generous to your spouse or children. With that question as the beginning, you can generate a dialogue that ends with "because to do otherwise would make me feel less good or cause me more pain and grief." Of course one can pose the alternative question, Why, do you believe, your spouse and children are nice, loving, and generous to you and spend time with you rather than with someone else? "Because they love me and care about me" is the natural answer which leads to the next question, Why do those feelings result in their being generous, friendly, etc.? The answer is "Because to do otherwise would make them unhappy or because it gives them more pleasure to act that way toward me." Question: "Does that mean if they did not find it more gratifying to themselves than some other available alternative, they would not stay with you, or be generous, caring, etc.?" Answer: "Of course." And that happens all the time or at least a great deal of the time, in relationships between friends, spouses, parents and their children, as well as business associates.

What could be more obvious? People spend time together because they believe it is the most valuable, desirable thing to do. To act otherwise would be sick or at least irrational. So, why do I buy my steak from Dominion rather than the A&P? Why do I teach psychology rather than sell cars? Why do I spend my money so that my children can invest their efforts and time in developing their talents and gaining credentials, etc.? Because I try to use my wits to increase my pleasure and reduce my pain—to maximize my outcomes. And that is exactly what everyone does.

So much for what are thought to be the simple facts of life. What I hope to demonstrate is that these assertions are *not at all simple*, nor are they *facts of life*. Indeed, they are probably wrong in all essential respects. The only exception results from the fact that because many people—social scientists and laypeople alike—*believe* that they and others think and act on this profit-maximizing basis, in specifiable and understandable circumstances, their behavior is influenced by these *beliefs*.

Evidence for the Preeminence of Justice in Human Relations

Sociocultural Perspective: Justice as the "Sacred Value"

The first point to recognize is that if one takes their behavior at face value, people rarely seem to act as if they are guided by the attempt to maximize their outcomes. There is overwhelming evidence that the theme of justice serves as the central organizing principle in most human endeavors. For example, if one takes a system-oriented, macro view of our culture, justice appears as the preeminent value—the "sacred" value in our secular society. In the service of justice, it is considered legitimate and at times desirable to sacrifice all other valued ends such as love, freedom, security, and family responsibilities. There is no other value in our society that has the power to legitimize the intentional sacrificing of human life. Whatever formal or informal juridical debates are mounted about how justice is to be best served in a given circumstance, there is no doubt that it is only *that judgment*, however it is arrived at, that *allows members of the society or their representatives to take another person's life, liberty, or pursuit of happiness.*

Our society's institutions also reflect the preeminent status of justice. Whatever other goals each serves, its structure is framed within rules of entitlement. Normative arrangements not only describe ways of acting for an occupant of a given position (status-role) but explicitly locate these expectations in terms of "who" is entitled to "what" from "whom." A failure to meet these obligations is construed as a violation of others' rights. This is as true within the normative structures of institutions such as family, education, and social welfare as it is within the structures of institutions more obviously designed to promote rules of just conduct, institutions designed for social control and for the organization of economic endeavors. The emphasis on meeting the legitimate, or just, needs of one's children or of those who are unable to care for themselves involves the same normatively based allegiance to rules of deserving that one finds in the framing of our legal system and the contractual arrangements for working productively with one another. The major institutional arrangements in our society reflect the tacit dialogue: "Of course we take care of the needy and the vulnerable; we must arrange to work productively together, educate and nurture our young, and control those who would disrupt our lives, but it must all be done in a way that is fair, just, equitable for all concerned."

The Theme of Deserving in Individual Processes

Given the preeminent position of justice in the normative systems of our society, it is no surprise to find considerable evidence that it plays a similarly central role in the lives of most individuals. Although, as described earlier, social scientists typically construe the person as employing rules of justice and deserving as means of facilitating the acquisition of other presumably more desired resources, the best evidence available indicates that for the most part, people do not act that way. In fact, the relationship appears to be quite opposite. Rather than the attempt to maximize outcomes determining how people use rules of deserving, considerations of deserving and justice actually shape what people consider to be a "desired outcome." This shaping occurs at two critical points in the person's goal acquisition.

DESERVING DEFINES THE VALUE OF A "RESOURCE"

One critical point in goal acquisition is the person's evaluation of a given resource. The body of literature associated with the concept of "relative deprivation" demonstrates that there is virtually no amount or kind of resource that will be judged a desired outcome if people believe it is less than they deserve. No amount of wealth, status, or health is sufficient or satisfactory if people believe they are entitled to more. Typically, but not exclusively, this judgment is arrived at by comparison of one's outcomes with a standard, which is usually what others have who are judged to be similar in relevant "inputs." It also appears that people can accept virtually any degree of deprivation and scarcity with equanimity if they believe it is not less than they deserve. (See Crosby, 1976, for a summary of relevant literature.)

JUSTICE IN THE EVALUATION OF OTHERS

There is a persuasive body of evidence, both experimental and anecdotal, that people rely on standards of deserving in evaluating and responding to the fate of others. We are upset if others have more or less then they deserve but satisfied if we believe their fate, regardless of its degree of deprivation or well-being, is deserved. In fact, we are sufficiently concerned with seeing to it that other people's fates match what they deserve that we may engage in cognitive distortions to persuade ourselves, after the fact, that there is an appropriate fit (Lerner, 1980; Lerner & Miller, 1978; Walster, Walster, & Berscheid, 1978).

The experimental evidence of these cognitive distortions is probably not as persuasive as the everyday examples in our own lives or in the mass media. One such incident was reported in a Toronto newspaper on November 7, 1977. A woman, Francine Hughes, "poured gasoline under her sleeping husband's bed and ignited it." She apparently knew what she was doing because she subsequently drove to the county jail, where she told the deputies that "I did it. I did it. I burned him up." Obviously, this was a horrendous act. The image of the man being burned to death as the result of her planned efforts is sufficient to elicit both enormous sympathy for him and demands for her punishment. Can you imagine the suffering and terror associated with dying that way? The horror he must have experienced if he awakened while being burned alive? And she did that to him, knowing all the while what would happen. However, a jury acquitted her of first-degree murder. Why? Some of the reasons are to be found in the background to the "torch-slaying." I will not describe all the details, but the following quotation should be sufficient to elicit the responses I want to illustrate. Examine your own feelings as you read these excerpts from the newspaper story:

> Neighbours and Mrs. Hughes testified Mr. Hughes locked her outside overnight in her pyjamas, beat her in public, kicked the baby in the face and let the family dog freeze to death.
>
> Desperate to improve her life and salvage her self-respect, Mrs. Hughes started to attend business school. A psychiatrist said that when Mr. Hughes forced her to burn her books on March 9, he made her kill part of herself.
>
> The fight that ended in his death started because Mrs. Hughes returned late from school and planned to fix TV dinners. Two Ingham County sheriff's deputies who were called to the house say Mr. Hughes threatened to kill her.
>
> The deputies left when things cooled down, but the fight soon resumed. Mr. Hughes dumped the food on the floor, made her clean it up, dumped it on the floor again and smeared it on her body and in her hair.
>
> He ordered Mrs. Hughes to fix him some sandwiches, forced her to have sex with him and fell asleep. . . .

The main point I wish to make here is that whatever reactions were generated in you by the details of this tragedy, your feelings and thoughts about Mr. and Mrs. Hughes will revolve around the issue of "who" deserves "what" by virtue of what they did or failed to do.

THE NEED TO SEE ONE'S OWN FATE AS JUST

There is also fairly persuasive evidence that people will alter perceptions of their own performance and self-worth to match their fates, even those imposed on them simply by happenstance. For example, Apsler and Friedman (1975) found evidence for the self-attribution of inferior performance as a result of arbitrarily imposed deprivation. The young men in Rubin and Peplau's (1973) study, who discovered that by virtue of the lottery, they were most likely to be drafted, revealed a measurably lowered self-esteem. Only temporarily, one hopes. Comer and Laird (1975) demonstrated that being assigned the task of eating a worm had relatively enduring effects on a person's self-concept. Approximately two-thirds of their subjects showed subsequent measurable changes in their self-concept. These changes were of sufficient duration that if subjects were released from the obligation to "eat the worm" they voluntarily elected the same fate or one that was equally undesirable in a presumed "next" situation.

By far the most dramatic evidence for the defining role of justice in determining the way people view their fate was reported in a study of 29 young accident victims who were either paraplegic or quadraplegic (Bulman & Wortman, 1977). Over the six months that had passed since their accidents, all but three of these victims had found a way to see their fate as relatively acceptable. They employed different ways of doing this; some victims discovered that it "was the best thing that could have happened." The majority came to view their fate as not unjust by achieving or reclaiming a religious perspective: "These things are always planned by a supreme power"; "I see God's trying to put me in situations, to help me learn about Him and myself." A few saw their fates as direct retribution for past misdeeds: "I deserved it for a lot of different reasons. You reap what you sow; I just believe that." The essential point is that in one way or another, they redefined their being crippled for life so that they came to view it as either not a deprived state or not an unjust fate. And, in fact, a subsequent study reported that these same patients expected their state of happiness in the next five years to be as high as a sample of the general public and a sample of people with similar backgrounds who had won $50,000 or more in a lottery (Brickman, Coates, & Janoff-Bulman, 1978).

Apparently the victims believed their suffering and deprivation would be compensated for by other more spiritual benefits that had already begun and would continue to occur. If being crippled for life has its compensation in spiritual gains or is deserved because of prior misdeeds, then it is tolerable, acceptable, maybe even desirable! The Brickman *et al.* study also provided some evidence that those people who had won hundreds of thousands of dollars—some who had won a million—were not appreciably happier than the run-of-the-mill folks with whom they were compared. Interestingly, over half felt they deserved the money they had won.

The main point to be made here is that it seems patently inverted to assume that people employ normative rules of deserving in order to gain desired resources when in fact people depend upon those rules of deserving to determine whether a resource is, in fact, desirable, or even acceptable. One's fate, a resource, has value to the extent to which it meets the person's assessment of what is deserved. The evidence is clear: Rules of deserving play a central role in the person's decisions about what resources are desirable.

DESERVING GUIDES THE ACQUISITION OF RESOURCES

Once having recognized the critical role justice plays in defining the desirableness of a given resource, it should be no surprise to discover that people actually design their attempts to acquire "desired resources" around considerations of deserving, that is, in terms of judgments concerning what they deserve or are capable of deserving. Certainly, since the persuasive field experiments reported by Adams (1965), social psychologists have recognized that people will often alter their efforts, in order to see to it that their pay does not exceed what they are entitled to receive. If necessary, to achieve their just fate they will incur additional costs by virtue of their legitimate "inputs" (Adams, 1965). Later research by "equity theorists" has provided further documentation that people are upset if they receive more than they are entitled to have in virtually any form of interpersonal exchange and that they will voluntarily engage in activities to prevent or reduce any such discrepancy, even at the cost of usually desired resources.

This evidence, however, is typically cast within the equity framework which interprets this voluntarily self-limiting or cost-incurring behavior as an enlightened or disguised attempt by the person to maximize his outcomes—if not immediately then ultimately (Lawler, 1971; Leventhal, 1976a,b; Walster, Walster, & Berscheid, 1978). Walster *et al.* (1978), in the most complete statement of equity theory available, quite explicitly propose that people will abandon the commitment to equity if they beleive there are other more profitable ways to act:

> Proposition 1: Corollary 1: So long as individuals perceive they can maximize their outcomes by behaving equitably, they will do so. Should they perceive that they can maximize their outcomes by behaving inequitably they will do so [p. 16].

Later on we will discuss these assumptions in more detail; however, it should be obvious that they seem to contradict the commonly available evidence that given the extent to which people often voluntarily give up their most desired resources, including safety of life and limb, to see that justice prevails in their world. For example, the actions of those who voluntarily joined the civil rights workers in their demonstrations must be construed and redefined by equity theory in terms of some other internal agenda. Whereas the obvious fact of the matter is that these volunteers cared more about justice than they did their own security and well-being, their own lives. Certainly, in times of war and disasters people typically act in ways that seem to contradict "Proposition I, Corollary 1." And in their everyday encounters they appear to design their own activities so that they get what they deserve, no more, no less. We will return to these issues.

An obvious question at this point must be, if evidence for the centrality of the theme of justice in human affairs is directly available to the layman and social scientist, why does the myth of the economic man persist? The answers are somewhat but not totally different for the layman and the social scientist. Let us look first at the social sciences.

The Momentum Generated by the Economic Model in Social Psychology: Typical Examples

Setting aside the historical issues of how it all happened initially, there is no doubt that at least in North America the psychology of social behavior was most directly influenced by the learning theories that portrayed people's behavior as guided by some variant of the law of effect and the biological perspectives that saw man as seeking either tension reduction or some optimal level of tension. Who would doubt that people seek pleasure and try to avoid pain? People will repeat acts associated with pleasure and change those that lead to pain. Similarly they will use their intelligence to find the most efficient (least painful) ways to achieve the most pleasure, etc. Assumptions such as these have achieved the level of truisms and as such they have begun to shape what social scientists do and how they interpret what they see happening.

Bystander Literature: Generating an Answer That Ignores the Question

An interesting example of this is an entire area of investigation in which an "answer" was generated that had little to do with the initial "question." It all began with the murder of Catherine Genovese. She was attacked repeatedly in the streets for approximately 35 minutes late one night as she screamed for help. When the police were finally called they arrived within two minutes. The next morning at least 38 people confessed witnessing some part of the terrible scene from their windows. Yet for 35 minutes, no one called the police.

Latané and Darley (1968, 1970) began a line of research on bystander intervention that revealed that people are less likely to intervene to help in an emergency when they can diffuse the responsibility to act and thus reduce the potential sanction, or costs, for not intervening. Also, if bystanders are confused about the meaning of the event they are less likely to intervene primarily because they do not want to incur the costly risk of making fools of themselves. The results of various experiments show that if bystanders are with friends rather than strangers or if they have the opportunity to communicate their impressions of what is happening to one another, then the costs will be low and they will intervene. Also, if there is any possibility of their being harmed or involved in costly efforts on behalf of the victim they are less likely to intervene. All of the research has confirmed this cost-accounting model of the conditions under which bystanders will try to help (Bar-Tal, 1976; Latané & Darley, 1970; Staub, 1978; Walster & Piliavin, 1972).

Surprisingly, the cost-accounting theoretical model and the findings that have been generated explicitly to answer the question of why people did not intervene in the Catherine Genovese incident and others of that sort have not been applied directly to an analysis of that event. If one engages in that exercise it becomes apparent that according to the best prediction derived from the research literature, there would have been a flood of telephone calls to the police shortly after the first cries of "Oh my God, he stabbed me: Please help me! Please help me!" An anonymous call to the police would have entailed no risk or "cost" whatsoever to the bystander. Even if others had called as well there would have been no risk of being seen as acting foolishly. Nor would there have been any chance that someone could retaliate. And, certainly one could assume that at 3:15 a.m. most of the people witnessing the event from their windows were either alone or with someone toward whom they felt at least friendly.

The main point to be made here is that according to the subsequent *bystander intervention* theory and findings, the Catherine Genovese incident contained the very conditions that lead to minimal cost for intervening and greater cost for not intervening—and yet not one of the 38 or more witnesses made an anonymous call for 35 minutes. As far as I know, none of the bystander research investigators have related their theory and findings to this puzzle. The reason for this, I would guess, is that it never crossed their minds to do that. And the reason for that is because the assumptions of the theoretical explanation were accepted as a truism to begin with.

The Genovese incident provided the occasion for the application of the assumption that people react to every situation by a cost–benefit analysis of the options open to them. But in fact the assumption does not seem to fit very well. Certainly, I recognize that it can be made to fit with a bit of strain, but it might strike you as at least a slightly intriguing example.

Interpreting Equality as Self-Interest Plus Equity

It may be easier to illustrate the extent to which the assumption of our economic model guides what social scientists "see" by referring to an early study that examined the appearance of equity considerations in children's behavior (Leventhal & Anderson, 1970). In that experiment, kindergarten-age children pasted either 15 or 5 stars on a sheet and were led to believe that their "partner," another child of the same sex and age, had completed either 5 or 15. These performances yielded them 20 prize stickers which the children were to divide between themselves and their fictitious partner. How did they actually allocate these 20 prize stickers?

The results showed that when girls believed both they and their partners did 5 units, they kept an average of 10.69 of the 20 prize stickers for themselves. When both subjects and partners supposedly did 15, the mean number kept was 10.19. When the child did 5 and the other 15, the mean kept was 10.12 and when the child did 15 and the other 5 the mean was 10.31. The boys yielded slightly different data. When the boys were led to believe they did 15 and the other 5, they kept 12.70; when the relative productivity was reversed, the mean number kept was 11.05. When they both did the same (5 or 15), the mean numbers kept were 10.55 and 10.25. How would you interpret this array of means? According to Leventhal and Anderson one finds in these data evidence for a blending of concern with both equity, and self-interest.

What is, of course, remarkable about these data is that the vast majority of these children, who had been told by the experimenter that they and the "other child" were actually partners in the task, were remarkably consistent in ignoring the relative performances and in dividing the prizes awarded to their "teams" equally. The only slight deviations from this occurred in the two conditions in which the boys performed differentially. But even so there was remarkably little evidence of self-interest. At the extreme, these "selfish" boys kept an average of 12.70 of the 20 stickers and the next greatest deviation from an even split yielded the mean of 11.05! The overwhelmingly obvious finding of this experiment is that the children appeared *strongly committed to an equal allocation* between themselves and their partners, *regardless of both self-interest* and *relative performance at the task!*

Later research added support confirming the children's commitment to an equal allocation between team members (Lerner, 1974; Nelson & Dweck, 1977). Yet this seemingly obvious finding was overlooked by Leventhal and Anderson (1970) in favor of the more complex and less apparent interpretation involving a blending of the opposing tendencies to be selfish and follow equity. Why? Conceivably the investigators and the reviewers were prepared to see the findings in terms of those assumptions. Of course, that may not be the reason but that interpretation does fit the general point that we in the social sciences are no less prone than the laymen to see evidence "out there" that fits our assumptions. In this case, the bedrock assumption is that people are motivated to maximize their outcomes in every situation either by directly self-serving acts or by the intelligent use of social stratagems to maximize their outcomes over a longer time perspective.

Methodological Traps in Contemporary Equity Research

One does not need to look very far to find considerable published data that directly confirms the economic model of man. For the most part, the large body of literature that has been generated in and around equity and exchange theory strongly confirms the assumption that people will choose and bargain for, if necessary, that arrangement that maximizes their own outcomes (see Berkowitz & Walster, 1976; Leventhal, 1976a, 1976b; and

Walster, Walster, & Berscheid, 1978, for summaries of the typical findings and references).

There is good reason, however, to believe that these findings that form the core of the relevant literature about interpersonal relations are biased in a systematic fashion. The main source of this bias derives from the combined effect of two aspects of the procedures commonly employed in these equity–exchange studies. One of these is the use of a business or industrial setting to frame the experimental setting. The subjects in these studies are led to believe they are involved in a simulation of some aspect of the world of commerce; for example, they are workers, supervisors, or representatives in a labor–management dispute. This procedure, of course, establishes the normative context of the subject's reactions. Second, the subjects are typically dealing with trivial outcomes that have no substantive value in any concrete sense. Either only a few dollars or less are at stake, or subjects are explicitly asked to role-play how they or others would allocate resources, pay, etc. In either case, whether the experimenter employs trivial amounts of money or gives explicit instructions to role-play, in order to generate a response in the experimental situation the subjects are required to use their imaginations to role-play and to predict how they would react were they actually functioning in a real business–industrial setting. That would not necessarily be a problem if subjects were able to make accurate predictions validly. The available evidence, however, indicates that their best predictions about how they and others would act if it all were real are biased in a systematic and, fortunately for us, understandable way.

The Reliance on "Marketplace" Norms

It is this array of data generated by subjects role-playing the norms of the business world that has provided the biased evidence for an economic model of human behavior. Let us look more closely at the evidence for this assertion.

Most people can describe the norms of the marketplace—the worlds of work and commerce—as a blending of "justified self-interest" and the desire to be fair: a fair day's pay for a fair day's work. Every investor wants a fair profit or return on his or her investment. However, if there is a windfall to be had, a special opportunity to be seized, or a scarce resource to be divided, anyone would be a fool not to look out for his or her own best interests. Let the buyer beware! In the world of business, even under the best of circumstances participants are supposed to see themselves in at least indirect or parallel competition. It is expected that all people will work within the rules of the "game" in their efforts to make the most money, get the promotion, get the largest share of the market, make the greatest profit for themselves.

This normative system is easy to discern even in noncommercial situations where there is a scarce, highly desired resource and the "contestants" have equal prior legitimate claim to it. In one experiment (Lerner & Lichtman, 1968) young women who had volunteered to participate in a study of human learning discovered that in each case either the subject or her partner would have to receive severe electric shocks while the other participant would be in a control condition, receiving no shocks or money. When, by virtue of a random draw subjects believed they were given their choice of conditions—experimental shock or control—approximately 90% chose the control. They later rated themselves as responsible for their own good fortune and for the fact that the other girl would be shocked, but they showed virtually no signs of guilt. As they expressed it, "Anyone would have taken the control condition. She would have, if she were given the choice."

When young men were put in a similar conflict, they showed considerable guilt and resentment if the choice they had won was between electric shocks or a neutral condition for themselves or the other young man. But if the choice was between electric shocks and earning a considerable amount of money, all subjects elected the money condition and showed no signs of remorse or guilt over the fact that the other person would be shocked severely. In another condition they also revealed virtually no resentment when they were led to believe that the other subject who had won the right to choose, via the lottery, had elected the money condition and placed them in jeopardy of receiving the severe shocks. (Of course, no shocks were actually given.) It was obviously seen by these young men as quite legitimate to "cause" others to suffer, if that happened in the legitimate pursuit of economic gain (Lerner, 1971b)!

A Typical Example of "Role-Playing" in a Work Simulation

FORCING THE FAKING SUBJECTS TO CONFESS THEIR GREED

If we examine the published literature in the equity area, we can see the biasing effects of trivial outcomes in a business or work context. One typical line of research employed young women to work in an industrial simulation task (Austin & Walster, 1974, 1975). After performing a simple task for a few moments they learned that the "other worker" (actually fictitious) had been given the chance to allocate their joint pay. They were also informed that they and the other worker had actually done equally well at the task. Subsequently they were led to believe that the other worker had allocated them either $1, $1.50 or $2.00 out of a total pay of $3, keeping the rest for herself. Finally, the subjects filled out an array of scales describing how happy, pleased, guilty, etc., they felt, how they felt about the other subject, how much they liked the other subject, how fair the allocation was, etc.

The results were dramatic. The subjects' ratings revealed that they were happiest and liked the other most when they received the $1.50, and equitable pay, according to their relative performances. They were markedly unhappy and disliked the other when they received only $1, less than they deserved, and somewhat more pleased when they were overcompensated, that is, given $2 by the other subject.

These findings presumably confirmed that the subjects' reactions to their pay was a blending of two motives: their desire to get their equitable share, what they actually earned, and the desire to get as much money as possible. Since they and the other worker did equally well at the task they each deserved half the pay, $1.50. Both $2 and $1 were inequitable, unearned, amounts and thus both generated a certain amount of dissatisfaction. But, the overcompensation ($2) was more acceptable than the $1 since it also included the greater monetary gratification. Any fool knows that $2 is better than $1, other things being equal!

Later, Rivera and Tedeschi (1976) reasoned that subjects in these experiments were actually faking their responses for the benefit of the experimenter. There was no equity motive involved at all. The subjects did not care about equity or fairness, but rather gave those ratings because of the public context of their responses. The subjects knew that people are supposed to express allegiance to norms of equity. So they faked their ratings to be in line with these norms. Privately, however, the more money they were given the happier they were!

To illustrate this analysis of the public versus private motives, Rivera and Tedeschi modified the Austin and Walster procedure (1974, 1975) slightly. They used a third subject (actually a confederate) as the supervisor who allocated total pay of $1 between the two workers (subjects) who had performed equally well at a brief anagrams task. They varied both the amount allocated to the subject and the conditions under which the subjects responded to their fate. In some conditions the subjects were given 50¢ of the dollar (a fair allocation based on equal production); in others they were given 75¢; in still others they were allocated almost the entire dollar, or 90¢. Cross-cutting this variable, the subjects either responded publicly on rating scales, as in the earlier Austin and Walster experiments, or they responded to the same questions by turning a dial, after they had been hooked up to what had been established as an unerring lie-detector (the bogus-pipeline procedure).

The results strongly confirmed both the earlier Austin and Walster findings and their bogus-pipeline predictions. In the public replication condition, the more money over 50¢ the subjects received, the less happiness, the more guilt, and the less liking for the supervisor they reported. Both the 75¢ and the 90¢ allocations were more than they deserved and so presumably, they pretended that getting more than was equitable bothered them. However, similar subjects, when hooked up to the bogus pipeline and "forced" to tell the truth, showed the opposite effect: significantly greater degrees of happiness and greater liking for the supervisor the more money they were given.

ROLE-PLAYING BY BOTH "EQUITABLE" AND "GREEDY" SUBJECTS

What might have occurred to the reader by this point is that in these experiments the allocations were trivial amounts of money for university students. It is difficult to imagine that these students would be measurably happier or less happy about the difference of 50¢, or as in the Rivera and Tedeschi study, the difference between getting 50¢ and 90¢ versus 75¢. Obviously, in order for any of these experiments to have yielded significant findings the subjects had to pretend that these trivial amounts of money represented something else! In other words, as good subjects they were role-playing how they should and would react in this kind of situation if there were serious considerations at stake. In all likelihood, in both the Austin and Walster research and the Rivera and Tedeschi public-replication conditions the subjects were not dissembling but were actually guessing how they would feel if they were treated inequitably by being given more than they deserved and if it were not merely a few cents at stake. It is hard to believe that the young women were measurably happier when they received 90¢ rather than 75¢: The 15¢ as such could not have mattered that much to them.

If that is the case, then it is plausible that the subjects in the Rivera and Tedeschi bogus-pipeline procedure were also trying to be good subjects and were role-playing their part. What role was that? Our best hunch was that in this kind of normatively transparent situation, hooking people up to a "lie detector" carries the strong message that the experimenter is studying something the subjects would otherwise try to hide. If they were to be cooperative subjects, then, and if it is obvious that the normative response is to care about fairness, the bogus-pipeline procedure in effect tells them that the experimenter wants them to respond counter-normatively—to act as if they did not care about fairness. And that is why they express significantly greater pleasure the more "unearned" money they are given, trivial though the amounts were.

Some Experimental Demonstrations of the Normative Bases of Subjects' Responses

In two experiments designed to examine the dynamics involved in these situations we were able to obtain reasonably consistent findings. Although we had considerable difficulty generating the magnitude of the effects reported by Rivera and Tedeschi, we were able to replicate the essential pattern of their findings. In their public paper-and-pencil condition replicating Austin and Walster (1974, 1975), we found that the subjects who were given 90¢ were somewhat less pleased and less willing to work with the unfair allocator in the future than those who were given the 50¢ they had actually earned and deserved. As expected, this pattern was somewhat reversed when the young women responded under the constraints of the bogus pipeline.

However, as we predicted, other subjects in a paper-and-pencil condition who responded under conditions of anonymity also revealed the equity effect to some degree, that is, the more money the less liking for the "unfair" supervisor. Yet, other subjects who went through the procedure that established the "validity" of the bogus pipeline but responded with no constraints "to tell the truth" because of a supposed machine malfunction responded in ways that resembled the subjects who thought the lie detector was actually functioning.

These findings suggest that the ratings generated by both Austin and Walster (1974, 1975) and Rivera and Tedeschi (1976) using the paper-and-pencil procedure were *not* the result of the subjects' attempt to meet the public norms and hide their true feelings. And they also suggest that the bogus-pipeline procedure may yield counter-normative data *not* because the subjects are forced into revealing the truth of their private greed by the unerring lie detector, but rather because they are trying to be good subjects and portray a counter-normative response to their obviously unfair pay.

To illustrate further that the subjects in this prototypical experimental situation were responding to the normative expectations, we generated some additional conditions to elicit virtually opposite norms. To do this we altered the instructions to emphasize "justified self-interest" rather than "a fair day's pay for a fair day's work." We told our subjects that after working at the task they would have the chance to send a note to their supervisor trying to persuade her to give them the maximum amount of money. This experiment, like all the others discussed, employed female subjects; ostensibly, we were giving our subjects this opportunity because we were testing whether women could in fact function in and deal with the hard realities of the business world, where the participants must try to get the most for themselves.

After they sent their notes the subjects were allocated either the same pay as the other worker who did the same amount—50¢—or 90¢ out of the dollar. As in the previous experiment, half of the young women responded to their allocations by filling out the rating scales which the experimenter would see, while the other half went through the bogus-pipeline procedure.

We reasoned that if we changed the normative structure of the situation in this manner we should get virtually the opposite findings from the earlier studies. In the paper-and-pencil conditions the more money the subjects were given the happier they would be and the more they would like the supervisor. Also, if the bogus pipeline actually served to communicate the message to respond counter-normatively, then we should expect these subjects, who presumably know what these norms are, to respond in just the opposite manner. They should report less happiness and less liking for the allocator the more money they were given. Again, although not nearly as dramatic as we would have liked, the results of two separate efforts were consistent with these hypotheses (Lerner, Meindl, & Peachey, 1979).

What do these findings add up to then? If my survey of the equity literature is essentially correct, it has produced a body of findings that reflect the *attempts of role-playing subjects to express in their responses the norms which they believe are operative in the business world.* These norms combine two dominant orientations: Get as much as one can for oneself but stay within the bounds of fair competition—"honesty is the best policy," "a fair day's pay for a fair day's work," "a fair return on one's investment," etc. The net effect of this body of literature, then, is to confirm the model of human motivation that holds that people do care more or less about equity, but that this concern is blended with and dependent on the desire to maximize their own outcomes. The critical importance of the Rivera and Tedeschi experiment was that it highlighted the role-playing bases of the data generated in virtually all of the equity experiments.

But even if this analysis is correct, does that necessarily indicate that the findings are systematically biased? It is conceivable that although the subjects were role-playing they were nevertheless providing us with a valid portrayal of how they and others would actually respond in those situations. Is there evidence that there are systematic biases in the predictions people make about their behavior toward others?

Systematic Biases in Role-Playing Reactions

Familiar Examples: Reactions to Victims

An important systematic error was revealed in the way people react as witnesses to the suffering of innocent victims. Most people are upset by the sight or awareness of an innocent victim and under some specifiable circumstances they condemn the victim as a function of the degree of the victim's undeserved suffering presumably as a way of coping with their own stress. Of course, not everyone does that, all the time, but it is a sufficiently common and predictable reaction that one can find measurable signs of this reaction among a greater or lesser proportion of observers (Lerner & Miller, 1978; Lerner, 1980). It is also true that witnesses of the same event who are informed that the scene is merely simulated are unable to predict the responses of those who believe they are actually witnessing undeserved suffering. Their predictions follow our norms very closely: They predict not condemnation of innocent victims but rather that they and others would uniformly exhibit increased compassion and concern as a function of the degree of undeserved suffering. That is not at all the way many of them respond, however, when they actually witness the victim's suffering (Lerner, 1971b; Simons & Piliavin, 1972).

The "Cynical" Bias of Role-Playing Subjects in the Business World

This presumed commitment to the theme of justice for others and the processes that link it to the person's own deserving provided the background for another highly germane example of systematic bias. For his doctoral thesis, Dale Miller (1975) examined the relationship between the person's commitment to deserving for himself and the way in which that commitment appears in the person's concern that others also have what they deserve.

At that point in our thinking we assumed that the person's concern for his own deserving takes precedence—that the person initially develops a "personal contract" with himself or herself to engage in goal acquisition by "deserving" what he or she desires. The child later recognizes and accepts the social fact that others are also attempting to gain what they deserve. At times, this can lead to conflicts or occasions for collective and integrated activities that are mutually beneficial. In any event, we assumed that children come to care about justice for others because it is recognized to be functional for maintaining their own deserving.

By implication, then, a priority is established whereby people genuinely care about justice for others, but this concern will appear in transactions only if and when the person's own deserving is met. The conflict, then, for contemporary man is not between one's own wants and the demands of others but between one's own deserving and justice for others (Lerner, 1971c). If this is true, we would expect people to engage in justice-motivated activities if and when their own deserving is not in jeopardy.

To examine these ideas Miller (1975, 1977) presented male university students, after they had completed an initial period of rather pleasant work, with the opportunity to sign up for additional work sessions doing the same sort of pleasant task. In the experiment he varied the amount of money subjects were offered for each work session and whether or not some of their pay would be allocated to help a very needy and worthy family that was not eligible for aid from any other sources. The solicitation occurred in the form of a mimeographed sheet they were given in the ostensible privacy of the secretary's office, where they went to get their pay for the first session. The description of the victims was a straightforward but nevertheless somewhat moving and persuasive account of a family in genuine need through no fault of its own. It also contained information about what various amounts of money would purchase for them.

The findings were fairly clear and straightforward (see Table 11.1). When the young men were offered $2 for each session on the average they signed up for 7.25 sessions. If, however, one of those dollars was to be given to the needy family they were considerably less interested in working, signing up for an average of 3.67 sessions. If the pay was a dollar greater ($3 rather than $2 per session) for themselves and there was no mention of the family, that did not provide a measurably greater incentive than the $2. Both amounts were within the range of fair pay and so the subjects signed up for 7.58 sessions. If, however, that additional dollar was to be allocated to the family then they were considerably more motivated to work, signing up for about 50% more sessions (11.91) than when they could keep the $3 for themselves.

Table 11.1
Mean Number of One-Hour Sessions Elected

Total pay	Pay allocation to family	
	$0	$1
$2	7.25	3.67
$3	7.58	11.91

Source: Adapted from Miller (1975, 1977).

Apparently awarding the needy family one of the two dollars would require the young men to have less than they believed they deserved for their work. If, however, they were able to get a "fair" rate of pay of $2 and have the additional dollar go to reduce an injustice to others, that provided a strong incentive for them to work. The incentive then to help the needy family was considerably stronger than the chance to keep the additional dollar for themselves—to maximize their profits!

What makes these findings even more relevant for our purposes are the data generated by asking similar young men to predict how they or others would react in one of these conditions. When asked to give their best predictions—under conditions of complete anonymity—they generated a pattern that was systematically different from the way people actually behave. This time it was not a benevolent bias, but rather revealed the relatively cynical view that people hold about the way they and others act when it comes to the world of work and commerce. The normative expectations were that they and others would be most motivated by the chance to earn the greatest amount of money—for themselves. In fact, it appeared that, if anything, they thought that the chance to earn money for the needy family would work as a disincentive—cutting into their profits (see Table 11.2). There is every reason to believe that these were genuine predictions reflecting their confident estimates of what motivates themselves and others.

If one is at all persuaded by this array of findings then an interesting but ironic conclusion begins to appear: *Not only are people strongly committed to living by rules of deserving and justice but they believe that they and others are essentially in the business of trying to maximize their own outcomes—those are the normative expectations.* If that is so, it would help to explain why having subjects role-playing their reactions would lead to systematically biased findings in the equity research. What remains, however, to be dealt with is why people maintain this relatively cynical and presumably inaccurate image of what people care about.

Table 11.2
Predicted Mean Number of Hours Elected

	Pay allocation to family	
Total pay	$0	$1
$2	11.33	4.60
$3	15.70	8.30

Source: Adapted from Miller (1975).

Reasons for the Persistence of the Myth of "Economic" Man

Historical Legacy: Law and Business Ethics

Without going into great detail in this chapter, I would like to offer two possible reasons for the persistence of the cynical myth in the population at large. One of these points to the historical legacy of two major parts of our society. The most obvious is the social-Darwinian ideology and institutional practices that appear in the economic sector. The "free enterprise," capitalist economy may itself be a contemporary fiction, given the increasing consolidation of controlling power in the hands of relatively few multinational corporations and the complex intertwining of the public with the private sectors of the economy. What remains current and viable is the imagery and values of the free enterprise mythology in the public dialogue. After all, what else distinguishes us members of the "free world" from "them"? Presumably, by allowing all people to pursue their own interests freely—their goal of making as much profit as possible—we have generated the most powerful economy in the world. The private pursuit of profit is not only the mother of invention and efficiency, it is the means for producing capital that can be used to create jobs, etc. But, most important, the pursuit of profit is at the same time the expression and protector of that which we hold most dear—our individual freedom to make what we wish, or can, of our lives. To the extent that this kind of thinking appears in our culture it is no surprise that people think we are all motivated by self-interest.

In addition, all phases of our legal institutions designed to maintain social control and social integration serve to perpetuate the assumption that people need to be controlled, that otherwise they would do something harmful or at least undesirably selfish. And, obviously, the way to control people and see to it that they behave decently and act cooperatively is by setting up systems of laws, and arranging for systems of penalties to be inflicted on those who commit infractions. It is rather fascinating to consider our legal institutions from the perspective of some of our attribution theories. Consider for a moment what the children growing up in our society must come to believe, as they gradually become aware of the vast resources our society devotes to insuring that people act decently toward one another—the police, the system of courts, the legal profession, procedures for detection, institutions for incarceration, the enormous number of laws, by-laws, regulations, and contractual arrangements that apply to virtually every aspect of people's lives. That includes even the closest relationships, such as those between husband and wife, parents and children. There are "laws" that require that parents take care of their children and that husbands and wives do not harm each other. No concerted cooperative effort of any consequence among adults is engaged in without a contractual legal device that "requires" that the participants not act unilaterally and establishes that if and when that happens, the others have means of restitution.

The two implicit but devastatingly clear questions that must arise at some level of children's awareness are: Why would people invest so much in legal institutions that require people to act decently and cooperatively if they did not know that people are essentially selfish, if not dangerous? And given all the legal devices that require and insure that people act decently, how can I ever learn whether one could actually trust people to behave decently on their own without any threat of external sanctions?

What I am suggesting here is that even if it were not for many of the inequities and injustices that appear in the functioning of our legal institutions (Nader, 1975), their very structure and infusion into every part of our civilized life perpetuates the image that people are essentially selfish and need to be controlled for the benefit of all (see Lerner, 1976, and Peachey & Lerner, 1981, for a fuller discussion of these points).

Self-Protective Function of the "Myth"

FEAR OF OUR IMPULSES TO HELP VICTIMS

The other main reason this myth persists is that at this time in our society people believe they cannot afford to trust their own impulses and feelings. There exists, I believe, what the sociologists have termed a special state of "pluralistic ignorance" in which each of us recognizes that we are emotionally quite vulnerable to signs of innocent suffering and deprivation. However, if we alone, as individuals, followed our impulses when we became aware of a hungry child, a defenseless woman, an exploited and beaten father, a physical or emotional cripple, we would be impelled to come to their aid until we had no more than they, given all the innocent victims in our society. If we followed, "believed in," our feelings that would be tantamount to voluntarily entering into the "world of victims" where no one can get what he or she deserves. On the other hand, our society makes it very easy to erect defenses against those impulses, at least partial ones. These defenses involve adopting institutional devices or cultural supports to keep ourselves and those we care about separate from the world of victims.

The cultural norms enable us to believe we must take care of our own kind first and that after that, we will do our share as good citizens to help "them"—the needy ones. The ideology that portrays everyone as essentially in the business of maximizing his or her own outcomes legitimizes these norms of "justified self-interest." The tragic aspect of this reaction is that although the norms of justified self-interest and the model of economic man enable each of us to avoid reacting to the needs of the victims, the impulses we defend against could generate a common motivational base for concerted social action that would increase the general level of well-being in our society. And there is reason to believe that does happen from time to time, but in strangely convoluted ways.

According to this analysis, people are most likely to react on the basis of their genuinely felt desire to help innocent victims, if in so doing they are still able to maintain their system of defenses against their own persistent feelings of concern for all those who suffer unjustly. That may help to explain why a clearly unique instance of victimization is more likely to elicit help than the same degree of need if it appears in one of many such victims. The single family stranded without means in one's town is inundated with spontaneous offers of help—but what if the family stayed in the town and their needs did not abate?

More typically, this defensive reaction to our own vulnerability elicited by victims' needs leads us to invoke the very normative system that keeps us alienated from one another. Commonly, we find that in order to help victims we must pretend to ourselves and them that we are actually doing it for our own best interests—we are really attempting to maximize our own outcomes. The public dialogue associated with the establishment of welfare programs takes the clear form of portraying the consequences of these programs as being in the best interests of taxpayers, as providing the greatest profit for them in the long run.

That may or may not actually be the case, but what I am proposing here is that this construction of the concerted attempt to eliminate suffering and deprivation is most acceptable to the people if it is portrayed as no more humanitarian than any other commercial transaction. But that seems rather bizarre. I am suggesting that people would rather portray their acts of help as crass, self-interested enterprises in order to disguise to themselves and others their truly genuine concern for the welfare of victims in our society.

A DEMONSTRATION OF THE "EXCHANGE FICTION"

We did two related field experiments to illustrate this process (Holmes, Lerner, & Miller, 1974). Both experiments involved the selling of decorator candles to members of the community in a door-to-door campaign. In Study 1's "exchange" condition, people approached were told either that the profits from the sales would be used to purchase uniforms and equipment for the local Little League baseball team or that the profits would provide needed facilities for the emotionally handicapped and/or crippled children in the community. In the control conditions when people were asked for *donations* to either of these causes they gave very little. However, if they were given the chance to *buy* the rather expensive candles the results were remarkably different. Again, the "uniforms" elicited few if any purchases; however, the candles assumed an extremely great value to the purchaser when associated with helping the genuinely needy victims (see Table 11.3). On the average, people bought approximately two candles.

If they cared about the "victims," why did the people not simply donate the money when solicited? If they cared about the candles, why did the people not buy them regardless of the "cause"? Why did they buy so many when the profits would help the victims? The answer we proposed is that, of course, the people cared about the victims but would not allow themselves to express this concern in their actions unless it was set in a context that enabled them to pretend to themselves, mainly that they were in fact not responding to victims' needs but that they were buying a candle. We called this defense the use of the *exchange fiction*.

This defense was also revealed in a second experiment in which we varied the strength of the emotional appeal and the degree of victimization from minimal—the baseball uniforms—to moderate—a program to help the perceptually handicapped improve their everyday skills—to fairly severe—a program to avoid an impending "tragedy" if the area's emotionally handicapped children were not given immediate remedial help. Again, none of these appeals were very effective in getting people to respond when they were simply asked for donations. However, when couched in the form of a commercial transaction—again buying the candles—the more severe the deprivation and the greater the need, the greater the willingness to "buy" a candle. (See Table 11.4.)

The findings of these experiments illustrate two important points. To

Table 11.3
Average Donations and Proportion of Persons Contributing: Study I

	Solicitation procedure				
	Donation		Altruist's price	Fair price	Bargain price
Condition	$1	$3			
Low need					
Amount (cents)	31.25	25.00	27.27	27.27	30.00
Proportion	0.25	0.08	0.09	0.09	0.10
High need					
Amount (cents)	41.97	50.00	120.00	150.00	184.62
Proportion	0.40	0.17	0.40	0.50	0.62

Source: Adapted from Holmes, Lerner, and Miller (1974).

Table 11.4
Average Donations and Proportion of Persons Contributing: Study II

Condition	Level of deserving			Marginal means
	Low	Moderate	High	
Donation				
Amount (cents)	14.47	34.06	40.50	28.78
Proportion	0.16	0.44	0.44	0.33
Exchange				
Amount (cents)	38.46	33.33	131.25	66.89
Proportion	0.23	0.17	0.69	0.35
Marginal means				
Amount (cents)	24.22	33.75	79.39	
Proportion	0.19	0.32	0.54	

Source: Adapted from Holmes, Lerner, and Miller (1974).

begin with, *people are highly responsive to the needs of others. They genuinely want to help innocent victims of suffering and deprivation.* However, they also seem impelled to disguise this motivation in ways that enable them to maintain a relatively distant image of their relation to these innocent victims in their society. One experiment revealed that young men held a cynically distorted expectation that they and others would be less willing to work if some of their pay went to help a deprived family (Miller, 1975). In the other experiments the subjects seemed impelled to disguise their desire to help victims by engaging in the "safe" pretense that they were not actually helping someone. They were merely engaged in a commercial transaction—the purchase of decorator candles (Holmes, Lerner, & Miller, 1974).

But I thought there were moral credits to be gained in our culture by being an altruist, helping needy victims. Why would it not have been more of an incentive to allow the people to be altruists and donate the money to the needy victims? The answer I am suggesting here is that because the potential donors, most of us, believe we live in a society where people are essentially out for themselves—everyone is trying to maximize his or her own profits. Given that kind of society, if I give in to the inner feeling, the desire, to help innocent victims then God knows what will become of me and my family!

Some Concluding Thoughts on Facts and Fictions

As I stated at the beginning of this chapter, I think the evidence is rather clear. The economic model of man is a tragically persistent, distorted image of human motivation that portrays each of us as continually engaged in the attempts to maximize our "profits." The main evidence that supports this model has been generated by the appearance of these "economic" norms in the belief system of subjects who participated in essentially role-playing—that is, norm-expressing—exercises under the guise of social psychological experiments. Unfortunately these norms are also taken as cultural truisms by most people in predicting their own and others' behavior outside the experimental situations.

In spite of the prevalence of these "economic" norms in our society there is nevertheless an even more persuasive body of evidence that most people are, in fact, psychologically committed to deserving their own outcomes and justice for others. This commitment to deserving is not a social derivative or private strategy for "maximizing one's outcomes" that is set aside if and when it appears less profitable than some other response. But rather, this commitment forms the core of the person's relation to the environment. Unfortunately, this is not the occasion to describe in more complete detail the social psychology of this "justice motive." That can be found in other sources (Lerner, 1977; Lerner & Whitehead, 1980). I hope that what I have accomplished here is sufficient to bring into serious question the economic model of man and the body of literature that has been generated in and around that set of assumptions.

References

Adams, J. S. Inequity in social exchange. In L. Berkowitz (Ed.), *Advances in experimental social psychology* (Vol. 2). New York: Academic Press, 1965.

Apsler, R., & Friedman, H. Chance outcomes and the just world: A comparison of observers and recipients. *Journal of Personality and Social Psychology*, 1975, *31*, 884–894.

Aronfreed, J. *Conduct and conscience*. New York: Academic Press, 1968.

Austin, G., & Walster, E. Participants' reaction to "equity with the world." *Journal of Experimental Social Psychology*, 1974, *10*, 528–548.

Austin, G., & Walster, E. "Equity with the world": An investigation of the transrelational effects of equity and inequity. *Sociometry*, 1975, *38*, 474–496.

Bar-Tal, D. *Prosocial behavior: Theory and research*. Washington: Hemisphere Publishing Co., 1976.

Berkowitz, L., & Walster, E. (Eds.) Equity theory: Toward a general theory of social action. *Advances in experimental social psychology* (Vol. 9), New York: Academic Press, 1976.

Blau, P. M. *Exchange and power in social life*. New York: John Wiley & Sons, 1964.

Brickman, P., Coates, D., & Janoff-Bulman, R. Lottery winners and accident victims: Is happiness relative? *Journal of Personality and Social Psychology*, 1978, *36*, 917–928.

Bryan, J. H. Why children help: A review. *Journal of Social Issues*, 1972, *28*, 87–104.

Bulman, R. J., & Wortman, C. B. Attributions of blame and coping in the "real world": Severe accident victims react to their lot. *Journal of Personality and Social Psychology*, 1977, *35*, 351–363.

Campbell, D. On the conflicts between biological and social evolution and between psychology and moral tradition. *American Psychologist*, 1975, *30*, 1103–1127.

Comer, R., & Laird, J. D. Choosing to suffer as a consequence of expecting to suffer: Why do people do it? *Journal of Personality and Social Psychology*, 1975, *32*, 92–101.

Crosby, F. A model of egoistical relative deprivation. *Psychological Review*, 1976, *83*, 85–113.

Deutsch, M. Equity, equality, and need: What determines which value will be used as the basis of distributive justice? *Journal of Social Issues*, 1975, *31*(3), 137–149.

Fromm, E. *The sane society*. New York: Rinehart, 1955.

Homans, G. C. *Social behavior: Its elementary forms*. New York: Harcourt, Brace, 1961.

Holmes, J. G., Lerner, M. J., & Miller, D. T. *Symbolic threat in helping situations: The "exchange fiction."* Unpublished manuscript, University of Waterloo, 1974.

Hornstein, H. A. *Cruelty and kindness: A new look at aggression and altruism*. Englewood Cliffs, New Jersey: Prentice-Hall, 1976.

Latané, B., & Darley, J. M. Group inhibition of bystander intervention. *Journal of Personality and Social Psychology*, 1968, *10*, 214–221.

Latané, B., & Darley, J. M. *The unresponsive bystander: Why doesn't he help?* New York: Appleton-Crofts, 1970.

Lawler, E. E., III *Pay and organizational effectiveness: A psychological view*. New York: McGraw-Hill, 1971.

Lerner, M. J. Justice, guilt, and veridical perception. *Journal of Personality and Social Psychology*, 1971, *20*, 127–135. (a)

Lerner, M. J. Justified self-interest and the responsibility for suffering: A replication and extension. *Journal of Human Relations*, 1971, *19*, 550–559. (b)

Lerner, M. J. *Deserving vs. justice: A contemporary dilemma*. Research Report No. 24, University of Waterloo, 1971. (c)

Lerner, M. J. The justice motive: Equity and parity among children. *Journal of Personality and Social Psychology*, 1974, *29*, 539–550.

Lerner, M. J. *The law as a social trap*. Culture Learning Institute Report. East-West Center, August 1976.

Lerner, M. J. The justice motive in social behaviour: Some hypotheses as to its origins and forms. *Journal of Personality*, 1977, *45*, 1–52.

Lerner, M. J. *The belief in a just world: The fundamental delusion*, New York: Plenum, 1980.

Lerner, M. J., & Lichtman, R. R. Effects of perceived norms on attitudes and altruistic behavior toward a dependent other. *Journal of Personality and Social Psychology*, 1968, *9*, 226–232.

Lerner, M. J., Meindl, J., & Peachey, D. An experimental analysis of the source of confusing inferences in the Equity literature: Problems generated by subjects trying to "role-play" their reactions to serious consequences. Paper presented at Canadian Psychological Association meetings in Montreal, June 1979.

Lerner, M. J., & Miller, D. T. Just world research and the attribution process: Looking back and ahead. *Psychological Bulletin*, 1978, *85*, 1030–1051.

Lerner, M. J., & Whitehead, L. A. Procedural justice viewed in the contest of Justice Motive Theory. In G. Mikula (Ed.), *Justice in social interaction*. Bern: Huber, 1980. New York: Springer Verlag, 1980.

Leventhal, G. S. Fairness in social relationships. In J. W. Thibaut, J. T. Spence, & R. C. Carson (Eds.), *Contemporary topics in social psychology*. Morristown, N. J.: General Learning Press, 1976. (a)

Leventhal, G. S. The distribution of rewards and resources in groups and organizations. In L. Berkowitz and E. Walster (Eds.), *Advances in experimental social psychology* (Vol. 9), New York: Academic Press, 1976. (b)

Leventhal, G. S., & Anderson, D. Self-interest and the maintenance of equity. *Journal of Personality and Social Psychology*, 1970, *15*, 57–62.

Miller, D. T. *Personal deserving versus justice for others.* An exploration of the justice motive. Unpublished doctoral dissertation, University of Waterloo, 1975.

Miller, D. T. Personal deserving versus justice for others: An exploration of the Justice Motive. *Journal of Experimental Social Psychology,* 1977, *13,* 1–13. (b)

Nader, L. Forums for justice: A cross-cultural perspective. *Journal of Social Issues,* 1975, *31,* 151–170.

Nelson, S. A., & Dweck, C. S. Motivation and competence as determinants of young children's reward allocation. *Developmental Psychology,* 1977, *13,* 192–197.

Peachey, D., & Lerner, M. J. Law as a social trap: problems and possibilities for the future. In Lerner, M. J. and Lerner, S. C. (Eds.). *Justice motive in social behavior: Adapting to times of scarcity and change.* New York: Plenum, 1981.

Riesman, D. *The Lonely Crowd: A Study of the Changing American Character.* New Haven: Yale University Press, 1950.

Rivera, A. N., & Tedeschi, J. T. Public versus private reactions to positive inequity. *Journal of Personality and Social Psychology,* 1976, *34,* 895–900.

Rosenhan, D. L. Learning theory and prosocial behavior. *Journal of Social Issues,* 1972, *28,* 151–164.

Rubin, Z., and Peplau, A. Belief in a just world and reaction to another's lot: A study of participants in the national draft lottery. *Journal of Social Issues,* 1973, *29,* 73–93.

Sampson, E. E. On justice as social equality. *Journal of Social Issues,* 1975, *31*(3), 46–64.

Schwartz, S. The justice of need and the activation of humanitarian norms. *Journal of Social Issues,* 1975, *31,* 111–136.

Simons, C., & Piliavin, J. A. The effect of deception on reactions to a victim. *Journal of Personality and Social Psychology,* 1972, *21,* 56–60.

Staub, E. *Positive social behavior and morality* (Vols. 1 and 2). New York: Academic Press, 1978.

Thibaut, J., & Kelley, H. H. *The social psychology of groups.* New York: John Wiley & Sons, 1959.

Walster, E., & Piliavin, J. A. Equity and the innocent bystander. *Journal of Social Issues,* 1972, *28*(3), 165–190.

Walster, K., & Walster, G. W. Equity and social justice. *Journal of Social Issues,* 1975, *31*(3), 21–44.

Walster, E., Walster, G. W., & Berscheid, E. *Equity: Theory and research.* Boston: Allyn and Bacon, 1978.

Chapter 12

Responsive Bystanders:

The Process

of Intervention[1]

JANE ALLYN PILIAVIN

JOHN F. DOVIDIO

SAMUEL L. GAERTNER

RUSSELL D. CLARK III

This chapter will present a model of the process by which bystanders come to intervene in the emergencies, crises, and problems of others. Why is it desirable to have such a model? In a volume dealing with positive social behaviors it is hardly necessary to justify the study of any type of prosocial action. Clearly, intervening in the problems, crises, and emergencies of others is positive social behavior that contributes to the overall good of a society. In some cases, such behavior is dramatically effective: Serious injuries are averted and lives are saved. Even when the help is of a more mundane sort, however, intervention to help "strangers" improves the quality of life. It momentarily changes our image of others from that of nameless, faceless shapes in the crowd to that of neighbors and friends. It adds a little *gemeinschaft* to our generally *gesellschaft* society and brings the two participants involved in the helping interaction momentarily into a personal relationship. Thus an understanding of the factors that contribute to in-

[1] We would like to acknowledge the support, provided by the National Science Foundation (Grants # GS-1901, GS-27053, GS-32335) to Jane Allyn Piliavin and Irving M. Piliavin and by the Office of Naval Research, Division of Organizational Effectiveness (Contracts N00014-70-A-0113-003 and N00014-76-C-0062) to Samuel L. Gaertner, that made possible much of the authors' research reported in this chapter.

COOPERATION AND HELPING BEHAVIOR
Theories and Research

creasing or decreasing the likelihood of intervention can help us (to the extent that they are manipulable) to improve in some way the quality of life we experience.

More specifically, though, why do we choose to focus on *process*? There are at least three critical reasons. First, we believe that outcome is strongly affected by the nature of process. Thus, if we are committed to increasing the incidence of safe, effective intervention in crises, we must understand the process. Second, the increasingly prevalent view among social scientists is that one cannot really speak of the beginning, the end, the cause, or the effect in human behavior. There is an ongoing stream of physiological and psychological events on which we superimpose new stimuli or into which a natural event inserts itself. The response to the event will be strongly influenced by what the individual is feeling, thinking, and doing at the time. Finally, it is unrealistic to expect unidirectional, simple causation; feedback effects must be considered the rule rather than the exception. Thus we find it difficult to think solely in input–outcome terms and have had to come to consider the problem of process.

The emphasis on process has led us to concentrate on the determinants of intervention in problems, crises, and emergencies rather than attempting to provide a general model of prosocial behavior. It is our belief that it is not productive to attempt to apply one model to all prosocial behaviors because (*a*) the motivation for different aspects of prosocial behavior may be quite different, and (*b*) the decision making that precedes the behavior differs across categories. In other words, we are dealing with different *processes* when we are dealing with intervention in the momentary problems of others, on the one hand, and with volunteer work, cooperation among children, or choosing to enter a "helping profession" as one's life work, on the other. Thus, our main focus is on the determinants of intervention by an "innocent" bystander who has no professional "stake" or expertise.

We distinguish among three subcategories of helping situations—problem, crisis, and emergency—on the basis of the dimensions of both severity of consequences to the person in need and dependency on outside assistance. The first dimension can go all the way from inconvenience, lost time, and mild annoyance to severe injury or probable death. The second dimension is related both to the nature of the situation (e.g., dropped groceries, stalled car, assault) and to characteristics of the victim that determine his or her ability to cope (e.g., age, sex, infirmity). We feel that our model is applicable to what we have defined as *problem, crisis,* and *emergency* situations, and we will try to use those terms consistently and in that order to indicate rough areas along these continua of relative severity of consequences and dependency on others.

The Arousal:Cost–Reward Model

The model to be presented here has gone through many versions, revisions, and incarnations. It was first presented "as a heuristic device" in a 1969 article entitled "Good Samaritanism: An underground phenomenon?," by I. M. Piliavin, J. Rodin, and J. A. Piliavin and was further developed in an unpublished manuscript by J. A. Piliavin and I. M. Piliavin in 1973.[2] In its present form (see Piliavin, Dovidio, Gaertner, & Clark, 1981) it consists of five propositions, or postulates, and a number of less formalized statements regarding the ways in which the relationships stated in the postulates are, in turn, related to each other. The five postulates are as follows:

Proposition I: Observation of an emergency arouses a bystander.

I–a. The degree of arousal is a monotonic positive function of the perceived severity of the emergency.

I–b. The degree of arousal is a monotonic positive function of the clarity of the emergency.

I–c. The degree of arousal is a monotonic negative function of the physical distance between the bystander and the emergency.

I–d. The degree of arousal is a monotonic positive function of the bystander's similarity to and emotional involvement with the victim.

I–e. The degree of arousal is a monotonic positive function of the length of the observer's exposure to the emergency, if no intervention occurs.

Proposition II: In general, the arousal occasioned by observation of an emergency and attributed to the emergency becomes more unpleasant as it increases, and the bystander is therefore motivated to reduce it.

Proposition III: The bystander will choose that response to an emergency that will most rapidly and most completely reduce the arousal, incurring in the process as few net costs (costs minus rewards) as possible.

Proposition IV: There will be (a) special circumstances that give rise to and (b) specific personality types who engage in rapid, impulsive, noncalculative, "irrational" helping or escape behavior following observation of an emergency.

Proposition V: On termination of contact with an emergency, the bystander's arousal will decrease monotonically with time, whether or not the victim

---

[2] The authorship of the model at this stage of development is best put as the "Piliavins *et al.*" model, if names must be attached. Acknowledgment is made of the major role played by I. M. Piliavin in the initial development of the model and the significant contributions of J. Rodin to the model and the early research on which it was based.

receives help. The rate of reduction will be a direct function of the proportion of initial distress cues to which the bystander is no longer exposed either physically or psychologically.[3]

There are conceptually two separate aspects to the model. There is the arousal process in response to the crisis or emergency, which is essentially an emotional response. Then there is the cost–reward calculation leading to a decision, which is basically a cognitive process. Although these two aspects of the model are conceptually distinct, it is important to keep in mind that operationally they are confounded. Many of the same features of situations and persons that lead to higher arousal also affect the perceived costs and rewards of various courses of action. Furthermore, the perception that the costs of taking action are high can feed back and increase the arousal experienced by the bystander. Finally, the perception of arousal can itself lead to effects on the judgment of costs and rewards.

In presenting the model and the support that we perceive exists for it, we will move through the postulates, beginning with those that deal with arousal. We will then discuss the impact of costs and rewards on helping. Finally, we will move to a discussion of the many complications that arise when one considers the problems of interaction of emotional response and cost calculations. In particular, we will deal briefly with the social context of helping and "impulsive" helping. We cannot in a single chapter provide all of the support that we believe now exists for the model. The interested reader should consult Piliavin, Dovidio, Gaertner, and Clark (1981) for an extended discussion.

Arousal in Response to the Emergencies of Others

The term *arousal* has been widely used and often misused in social psychology. Earlier presentations of our model have shared the same vagueness and underspecification that most social psychologists, accepting the Schachter (1964) model of emotion, have displayed. At this point, however, we will be much more precise in what we mean by arousal. It is now commonly accepted by psychophysiologists (e.g., Lacey & Lacey, 1970, 1973; Lynn, 1966; Routtenberg, 1968; Sokolov, 1963) that there are two arousal systems that operate in some ways antagonistically and in other ways cooperatively in regulating the organism's alertness, responsiveness to environmental stimuli, and readiness for action. In this brief presentation, we shall give only the barest outline of how these two systems differ. Essentially, two patterns

---

[3] Postulate V exists mainly for the purpose of closure. There would appear to be no way to test the basic statement; testing the "proportion of cues" portion would be possible, though difficult. We will not discuss this postulate further in this chapter.

of response can occur to a change in external stimulation (such as is involved when a problem, crisis, or emergency occurs). Sokolov (1963) calls these the *orienting response* and the *defense reaction*. The orienting response occurs to novel stimuli of moderate intensity. It habituates rapidly, and physiologically it is characterized by heart rate *decrease*, positive feedback to the reticular activating system and thence to the cortex (leading to increased attention to incoming stimuli), an increase in skin conductance, peripheral vasoconstriction, and pupillary *dilation*. According to Lynn (1966), it is accompanied by an "agreeable rise in excitement and interest" but not by any sympathetic nervous system involvement. The defense reaction, on the other hand, occurs to sudden and/or intense stimuli, whether novel or not. It hardly habituates at all, and physiologically it is characterized by heart rate *increase*, negative feedback to the reticular activating system and the cortex (leading to a blocking of much external stimlulation), signals to the limbic system and the sympathetic nervous system to prepare for "fight or flight," an increase in skin conductance, peripheral vasoconstriction, and pupillary *constriction*. Subjectively, the defense reaction is experienced as negative.

The arousal referred to in Postulates I and II of the model is clearly of the defense reaction kind; it is this pattern of arousal that we expect to be strongly related to intervention in crises and emergencies. The orienting response may also be related to some helping behaviors. Briefly, it seems to relate to state (attentional) and cognitive (cost) factors. Because of considerations of space, however, we will not discuss the relationship between the orienting response and intervention further in this chapter; for additional detail and discussion, see Piliavin, Dovidio, Gaertner, and Clark (1981). In this section we will very briefly present the evidence linking observation of others' emergencies to a *defense reaction*, as defined above, and then demonstrate that the degree of such arousal is indeed predictive of intervention in emergencies.

The literature on vicarious arousal generated by witnessing the distress of another is supportive of Proposition I of the model. A consistent pattern emerges on both indirect measures of arousal such as reaction time (e.g., DiLollo & Berger, 1965; Weiss, Buchanan, Alstatt, & Lombardo, 1971) and direct physiological measures of arousal (Craig & Lowery, 1969; Gaertner & Dovidio, 1977; Krebs, 1975; Lazarus, 1966). Individuals *are* aroused by the distress of another. This vicarious arousal is generally similar to but less intense than the arousal caused by a more direct threat to self.

Proposition I of the model also states that severity, clarity, time, distance, and involvement with the victim are directly related to degree of arousal. The evidence, where it exists, is largely supportive of these subhypotheses. The findings associated with the effect of severity on bystander arousal are most substantial. For both indirect (e.g., Berger, 1962; DiLollo & Berger, 1965) and direct (e.g., Geer & Jarmecky, 1973; Lazarus, 1966) measures of arousal, situations of greater severity consistently create higher levels of bystander arousal. Similarly, emergencies of greater clarity generate higher levels of arousal (e.g., Byeff, 1970; Sterling, 1977). In addition, there is evidence indicating that arousal increases as the length of the observer's exposure to the emergency increases, if no intervention occurs (Gaertner & Dovidio, 1977; Gaertner, Dovidio, & Johnson, 1979).

Similarity and feelings of attachment to the victim were also proposed to increase bystander arousal in response to the distress of another. Using the extreme example, it is difficult to deny that an emergency occurring to one's own child would be more arousing than the same emergency involving a total stranger. Nevertheless, research demonstrating an effect of attachment to a victim on bystander arousal is surprisingly infrequent. The little evidence that exists, though, supports the hypothesis that closer relationships with the victim increase a bystander's level of arousal (Krebs, 1975; Stotland, 1974). This effect becomes less pronounced, however, in very clear, serious emergencies. For example, for bystanders who witnessed an emergency alone, Gaertner and Dovidio (1977) found no significant difference in the amount of arousal generated by the plight of victims who were racially similar (white) or racially dissimilar (black) to the bystander.

Feelings of involvement with a victim may be inhibited or facilitated by situational as well as interpersonal factors. For example, when a bystander witnesses an emergency alone, he or she bears 100% of the responsibility for intervening; when more than one bystander can help, responsibility may be diffused. Thus, an individual believing that others can help may be less emotionally involved with the victim. Consistent with this reasoning, Gaertner and Dovidio (1977) found that bystanders who believed that others were present were less aroused by an emergency than bystanders who believed that they were the only witness. Bystanders who had the opportunity to diffuse responsibility in an emergency involving a racially dissimilar (black) victim showed a particularly low level of arousal. Thus, empirical evidence generally supports the proposed relationship between involvement with the victim and subsequent arousal generated by the victim's distress.

Finally, although physical proximity to a victim theoretically could affect a bystander's level of arousal, either by increasing the clarity or perceived severity of the emergency or by increasing involvement with the victim, there is no published literature relating arousal and distance from the victim. Nevertheless, the empirical evidence relating severity, clarity, and involvement to arousal continues to suggest a direct relationship between proximity and arousal.

Arousal and Bystander Responsiveness

The second proposition of the model states that, in general, the arousal occasioned by the observation of an emergency is unpleasant and the bystander is therefore motivated to reduce it. There is, in fact, substantial indirect evidence as well as more recent, direct evidence supporting this proposition. For example, the same factors that are directly related to bystander arousal are also directly related to bystander intervention. The effects of the severity (e.g., Ashton & Severy, 1976; Staub & Baer, 1974) and the clarity (e.g., Clark & Word, 1972, 1974; Yakimovitch & Saltz, 1971) of an emergency on helping behavior are well documented. Clearer and more severe situations generate higher levels of intervention. Increased proximity to the victim (e.g., Staub & Baer, 1974) also facilitates helping behavior. Finally, several researchers have demonstrated that greater involvement with a victim based on feelings of "we-ness" (e.g., Hornstein, Masor, Sole, & Heilman, 1971), similarity (e.g., Karabenick, Lerner, & Beecher, 1973), attraction (e.g., Gross, Wallston, & Piliavin, 1975), and personal responsibility (e.g., Darley & Latané, 1968) produce higher rates of helpfulness.

More directly, studies that have measured both arousal and helping behavior consistently demonstrate a relationship. Greater levels of arousal, measured by self-report (e.g., Clark & Word, 1974; Gaertner & Dovidio, 1977) or by GSR (e.g., Byeff, 1970; Piliavin, Piliavin, & Trudell, 1974) or by heart rate (e.g., Gaertner & Dovidio, 1977; Gaertner, Dovidio, & Johnson, 1979), are associated with faster rates of intervention. Furthermore, when a bystander is the only witness to an emergency in which there are low costs for intervention, the correlations between physiological arousal and speed of helping typically range from .45 to .77.

Increasingly, we are accumulating evidence that demonstrates that arousal is not merely associated with helping but that it can, in fact, motivate bystander intervention, as proposed in the original model. Weiss and his colleagues (Weiss et al. 1971; Weiss, Boyer, Lombardo, & Stich, 1973), for example, showed that vicarious arousal can activate instrumental responses that relieve the suffering of victims. Weiss concluded that the findings strongly support the notion that an aversive state is aroused by the suffering of another (due to electric shock), and that this state behaves like other drive states in motivating a person to relieve another's distress.

Additional research demonstrates that the *attribution of one's arousal* to the other's distress is a *critical* factor affecting a bystander's motivation to intervene in an emergency. When Gaertner and Dovidio (1977) persuaded subjects to misattribute to a placebo (described as having side effects associated with autonomic arousal) arousal that was generated by an ambiguous emergency, helping behavior was inhibited. When Sterling (1977) provided an opportunity for prior, irrelevant arousal to be attributed to an unambiguous emergency, bystander intervention was facilitated. These attribution-related effects have also been observed in less emergency-like situations. Harris and Huang (1973) found that subjects who had the opportunity to attribute arousal to noise described as having arousing side effects were less likely to help a victim with an injured knee. In a less immediate situation, Coke, Batson, and McDavis (1978) found that subjects who were administered a placebo described as having side effects of autonomic arousal volunteered less time for baby-sitting to a student who lost her parents in an accident.

The experiments investigating the effects of attribution of arousal on helping behavior also suggest that, depending on the nature of the situation, arousal may sometimes be interpreted as one emotion, sometimes as a quite different emotion. In severe, life-threatening situations, subjects respond with upset and alarm (Gaertner & Dovidio, 1977); in less critical, less intense problem situations, arousal interpreted as empathic concern (e.g., empathic, warm, concerned, softhearted, and compassionate) seems to motivate helping behavior (Coke et al. 1978). Thus, as we have come to consider a broader range of phenomena beyond emergency events, we have also come to consider a broader range of emotional experience—from promotive tension (see Hornstein, 1972, and Chapter 10 in this book), on the one hand, to an intense defense reaction, on the other.

The earliest (1969) version of the arousal:cost–reward model proposed that emergency helping is a selfish attempt to reduce unpleasant arousal, generated by another's victimization, in a manner that maximizes the bystander's own benefits and minimizes accompanying costs. Helping was not conceived to be a purely altruistically oriented attempt to reduce another's distress. The present model, while not excluding egoistic intent, also allows for more sympathetic motives for intervening, such that the needs of another can become undifferentiated from one's own. The needs of another can become coordinated with those of the bystander or become incorporated into the bystander's self-interest, although this does not necessarily happen.[4] To the extent that arousal is interpreted as alarm and concern for another person, rather than personal distress and upset, and the salience of empathic considerations associated with the victim's plight (e.g., the victim is suffering) exceed personal cost considerations, the motive for helping has a sympathetic rather than a selfish tone. Nevertheless, despite apparent vari-

---

[4] The process by which individuals incorporate the needs of another into their own self-interest also receives attention in other chapters of this book. Specifically, Hornstein's theory of promotive tension (Chapter 10), McClintock's theory of social values (Chapter 3), and Pruitt's theory of integrative agreement (Chapter 7) address this issue, as does the Grzelak–Radzicki concept of *multi-component of utility*.

ations in emotional content, the process by which another's need promotes helping seems dynamically similar across a variety of situations. In both emergency and nonemergency situations, arousal attributed to the distress of another has motivating properties independent of any solely cognitive factors.

Cost–Reward Considerations

The third proposition of the model states that the bystander will choose the response to an emergency that will most rapidly and most completely reduce his or her arousal, incurring in the process as few net costs (costs minus rewards) as possible. The application of the "economic man" model in the area of helping behavior has been quite common, and the evidence for the effects of the presence of costs for and costs for not intervening in emergencies on the likelihood of intervention is strong. We have set up, in our model, two general categories of potential costs and rewards for the bystander: (a) those that are contingent on his or her making a direct helping response and, (b) those that would result were the victim to receive no assistance from any source.

The first category, personal costs *for* helping, involves negative outcomes imposed directly on the benefactor and includes (but is not restricted to) physical danger, effort, embarrassment, disgust, feelings of inadequacy if one fails, and the value of rewards foregone because of one's taking the time to help. Briefly, the effect of disgust (or potential disgust) as a deterrent has been shown by Piliavin, Rodin, and Piliavin (1969), Piliavin and Piliavin (1972), Piliavin, Piliavin, and Rodin (1975), and Samerotte and Harris (1976), using manipulations of physical deformities, drunkenness, and the presence of blood on a victim. Possible physical harm has been shown to deter helping by Midlarsky and Midlarsky (1973), McGovern (1976), Piliavin, Piliavin, and Trudell (1974), Shotland and Straw (1976), and Borofsky, Stollak, and Messé (1971). These studies employed electric shock or potential physical attack by an individual who was already victimizing someone else. Effort and loss of time have been shown to deter helping by Darley and Batson (1973) and by Batson, Cochran, Biederman, Blosser, Ryan, and Vogt (1978). Space precludes our listing all of the other studies that have found effects of monetary costs, potential social sanctions for intervention, and the effects of potential rewards for helping. The evidence, with few exceptions, is very heavily on the side of the proposition that costs for helping deter intervention.

The second category of costs, namely, costs attendant on the bystander's knowledge that the victim has received no help, conceptually contains two subcategories. First there are "personal costs" for not helping, that is, negative outcomes imposed directly on the bystander for failure to intervene. These include self-blame for one's inaction, public censure, recriminations from the victim, and in some countries even prosecution as a criminal. The second subcategory of costs for the victim receiving no help is unrelated to bystanders' actions on behalf of the victim, but depends solely on their knowledge that the victim is continuing to suffer. In particular, these "empathy costs" involve internalizing the need or suffering of the victim and include continued unpleasant arousal related to the perceived distress of the victim.

Our expectations regarding the effects of costs for the victim receiving no help will depend on the level of costs for helping. As can be seen in Table 12.1, when costs *for* helping are low to moderate, helping should increase as costs for the victim's receiving no help increase. With high costs for helping, however, victims are predicted to receive indirect help or no help at all. In the latter case, the arousal engendered by observing the victim's distress will likely be handled through derogation of the victim or other reinterpretations of the situation as "not an emergency," or one that is not one's responsibility.

Since most of the research does not involve extremely high levels of costs for helping, we expect to find, in general, that as costs for the victim's receiving no help increase, helping will also increase. In general, the literature supports that expectation. Bickman and Kamzan (1973) and Field (1974), for example, manipulated victim "deservingness" and found more aid for the "deserving." Focusing responsibility on a bystander or letting him or her know that he or she is under surveillance should increase personal costs for the victim's receiving no help. This has been found to increase

Table 12.1
Predicted Modal Responses of Moderately Aroused Observer as a Joint Function of Costs for Direct Help and Costs for No Help to Victim

		Costs for direct help	
		Low	High
Costs for no help to victim	High	Direct intervention	Indirect intervention or → / Redefinition of the situation, disparagement of victim, etc., which lowers cost for no help, allowing ↓
	Low	Variable: will be a function largely of perceived norms in situation	Leaving the scene, ignoring, denial

intervention by Tilker (1970), Satow (1975), and Enzle and Harvey (1977), all in nonemergencies, and by Moriarty (1975), Shaffer, Rogel, and Hendrick (1975), and Schwartz and BenDavid (1976) in emergency situations. However, distortions and denials are found rather than increased intervention in some studies (e.g., Latané & Darley, 1970, pp. 81–85; Staub, 1970); no clearcut effects have been found in a number of other studies (e.g., Bickman & Rosenbaum, 1977; Konečni & Ebbesen, 1975; Ross, 1971; Schwartz & Gottlieb, 1976; 1980). The studies showing distortion or no clear effects, though, seem to involve relatively higher costs *for* helping. Thus, the impact of the costs for *not helping* may depend on the costs *for helping*.

HIGH COSTS FOR HELPING AND HIGH COSTS FOR NOT HELPING

The upper right-hand cell of the simplified two by two presentation of the cost–reward matrix (Table 12.1) is of particular interest, because it is the most like the emergencies of real life. Our initial prediction (in the 1973 version of the model) was that indirect helping would be the most likely response in the high–high cell. To our knowledge 14 studies have explicitly examined the incidence of direct as compared to indirect helping.[5] The situations in all of these studies are clearly crises or emergencies that could be described as having a range of costs *for helping* and high costs for the victim's receiving *no help*. Based on the results of these studies, we now believe that, given a bystander's *initial* perception of high costs both for helping and for the victim's receiving no help, the first likely response is typically one of cognitive reinterpretation. In particular, the bystander, whose attention is focused largely on the plight of the victim, first attempts to reduce the perceived costs for not helping. Similar to the process proposed by Lazarus (1968) concerning coping with perceived threat, reinterpreting the costs for not helping relieves the bystander's dilemma in a way that effectively reduces the bystander's unpleasant arousal state. Lowering the costs for not helping may be accomplished by redefining the situation as one in which help is unnecessary (e.g., "The situation is not *really* serious"), diffusing responsibility (e.g., "Someone else will intervene"), or derogating the victim (e.g., "He got what he deserved"). With high costs for helping and lowered costs for not helping, bystanders are less likely to intervene.

Indeed, there is research that suggests that cognitive reinterpretation is more likely to occur in emergencies when the costs for helping are high than when they are low. Piliavin, Piliavin, and Trudell (1974) found that subjects presented with a high cost "thief" emergency were more likely to question the reality of the event than were subjects exposed to a low cost "fallen woman" accident. Piliavin, Piliavin, and Rodin (1975) observed

[5] For further details and discussion, see Piliavin, Dovidio, Gaertner, and Clark, 1981.

greater diffusion of responsibility when a victim had a large facial birthmark than when the victim had no stigma. Similarly, in an experiment by Gaertner and Dovidio (1977, Study 1) white bystanders were more likely to diffuse responsibility when the victim was black than when the victim was white. Also, several investigators (e.g., Chaikin & Darley, 1973; Lerner, 1970, 1971; Stokols & Schopler, 1973) have found that subjects who cannot intervene will denigrate an apparently "innocent" victim.

It is possible, however, that a bystander in the high–high dilemma will be unable effectively to reinterpret costs. For example, an only witness to a victim trapped in a blazing building would not likely misinterpret the severity of the situation nor would the bystander likely risk certain injury by entering the fire. It is under these conditions—continued high costs for helping and high costs for the victim's receiving no help—that indirect help becomes likely. It is critical, though, that the bystander *perceive* that indirect help is possible. Given the prominent nature of the emergency event in the bystander's attentional field, bystanders may fail to consider this option unless the mechanism for indirect assistance (e.g., a firebox) is also prominent.

Consideration of how cognitive reinterpretation can affect bystander response underscores two important aspects of our model. Specifically, (a) we explicitly consider cyclical, iterative processing effects, and (b) we emphasize the notion that arousal and cost–reward considerations are not independent. In particular, if the search to resolve the high–high cost dilemma is satisfied by cognitive reinterpretation, the conclusion reached by the bystander is most likely to be one that not only lowers the costs for the victim's receiving no help, but lowers them partially through reduction of unpleasant arousal.

THE SOCIAL CONTEXT OF BYSTANDER RESPONSIVENESS

The very large body of research demonstrating the effect of social factors (e.g., the presence of others or the nature of the bystander–victim relationship) on the speed and likelihood of intervention can also be discussed in terms of cost considerations. For example, the commonly found decrease in intervention when others are thought or seen to be present—the *bystander effect*—may be translated into cost factors. The presence or believed presence of others, though, may also affect arousal factors.

The presence or presumed presence of others can affect bystander responsiveness through three different processes. First, the believed presence of others who might intervene may allow an individual to diffuse both responsibility for helping and guilt and blame for not helping (Darley & Latané, 1968). Diffusion effects, then, generally reduce the personal costs for not helping and thus inhibit intervention. Consistent with this formulation, several studies have demonstrated that simply the believed presence of other capable bystanders can reduce helping (e.g., Bickman, 1972; Darley & Latané, 1968; Horowitz, 1971; Schwartz & Clausen, 1970; Schwartz & Gottlieb, 1976). When other bystanders are believed to be present and their response cannot be monitored, it is possible for the bystander to come to think that someone else will intervene or already has helped. Such a belief should also lead to a decrease in arousal, since the victim's distress is being relieved by another. Thus, the inhibition of helping associated with diffusion may be mediated by both cost and arousal factors.

Of the many studies that have obtained a *diffusion effect* only one measured arousal (Gaertner & Dovidio, 1977). The results strongly suggest the importance of arousal processes. In particular, bystanders who overheard the emergency alone showed greater heart-rate increases than did subjects who believed that others were present. Furthermore, it was demonstrated in a pair of regression analyses that the diffusion effect was mediated in part by arousal. When entered into the regression equation *before* the arousal measure, the manipulation of the presence of others accounted for 16% of the variance in latency of response; when entered *after* the arousal measure, it accounted for only 4.6%, a nonsignificant amount of variance. We are not claiming here that the diffusion of responsibility effect is *nothing but* an effect of decreased arousal. We *are* saying that the cognitive processes leading to the judgment that one's responsibility for intervening is less than total lead to a decrease in arousal. This decrease in arousal then leads to slower intervention, in addition to whatever decreases are caused by more purely cognitive processes.

Information provided by the reactions of other witnesses to a relatively ambiguous emergency is a second way in which the presence of others can affect bystander responsiveness. For example, analogous to Sherif's (1936) classic study of informational social influence, the passivity of other bystanders can lead a potential benefactor to believe that the situation is not severe and thus can reduce the likelihood of intervention. Indeed, research has consistently demonstrated that the face-to-face presence of nonresponsive confederates substantially reduces intervention (e.g., Latané & Darley, 1970; Latané & Rodin, 1969; Ross, 1971; Smith, Smythe, & Lien, 1972; Wilson, 1976). Similarly, active and involved witnesses can lead a bystander to believe that a situation is relatively more serious, and therefore increase helping (e.g., Bickman, 1972; Staub, 1974; Wilson, 1976).

If one effect of the face-to-face presence of others is due to differential perceptions of the clarity and severity of the emergency, then it is possible that both personal costs for not helping and empathic costs for the victim's receiving no help may be affected. To the extent that the behavior of others leads a bystander to interpret the situation as less critical, he or she should feel less social pressure to intervene and should anticipate less blame for not helping. Thus, personal costs for not helping would be lower. In addition, empathic costs should also be reduced. That is, it is likely that a decrease in arousal accompanies the no-help-needed conclusion frequently reached by subjects in the face-to-face presence of passive others. Indeed, anecdotal evidence from the series of studies conducted by Latané and Darley indicated that subjects, on defining the situation as nonserious, exhibited little emotional concern.

The only direct evidence we have for decreased arousal among bystanders exposed to a relatively ambiguous emergency in the presence of other bystanders comes from Byeff (1970). In the Byeff investigation, some subjects were the sole bystander to an accidental fall, whereas other subjects were presented with the emergency in face-to-face pairs. Given that in the alone condition only about half (47%) the subjects intervened, we would judge the emergency to be ambiguous. The results, consistent with previous research, revealed a social inhibition effect on intervention in the "together" condition. In addition, together subjects also exhibited less emotional arousal (as indexed by the height of the first GSR peak following the accident) than "alone" subjects. Thus, decreased arousal and decreased intervention coincided ($r = .40$).

Concern for the evaluation of others, frequently termed *normative social influence* (Deutsch & Gerard, 1955), is a third social process that can critically affect bystander responsiveness. Normative social influence can either facilitate or inhibit intervention, depending on the bystander's belief about what others consider to be normatively appropriate. For example, a group of uniformly nonresponsive bystanders may establish a norm of nonintervention. The costs *for helping* will thereby be increased. In many of the studies involving the face-to-face presence of bystanders (Latané & Dabbs, 1975; Latané & Rodin, 1969; Ross & Braband, 1973; Smith, Vanderbilt, & Callen, 1973), both normative and informational social influence may have been operating to inhibit helping behavior. However, Schwartz, and Gottlieb (1976), in a study designed to isolate normative influences, found that when a bystander believed that others expected socially responsible behavior, intervention was facilitated.

Again, we have only one study of normative social influence that measured arousal. Gaertner, Dovidio, and Johnson (1979) showed, to subjects who were either alone or in the presence of three nonresponsive confederates, a very clear emergency (to minimize informational social influence), in which a stack of chairs fell on the victim. The expected decrease in the speed of intervention occurred in the presence of other bystanders. Furthermore, there was a parallel increase in heart rate among those who witnessed the emergency with nonresponsive others. Most critically for our hypothesis, there was a highly significant positive correlation between heart rate and intervention for subjects who were alone; the reverse was found among bystanders in groups. Thus, increased arousal due only to the emergency led to increased intervention; arousal beyond that level, and attributable to normative pressures, led to a decrease in intervention.

Hornstein and his colleagues (Hodgson, Hornstein, & LaKind, 1972; Hornstein, 1972, 1976; Hornstein, Masor, Sole, & Heilman, 1971; Sole, Martin, & Hornstein, 1975) have explored the social context of helping from a theoretical perspective different from the one we have presented. Applying an extension of the Lewinian tension system construct (see Hornstein's chapter in this volume (Chapter 10) for more detail). Hornstein and his colleagues propose that people often help one another in order to reduce *promotive tension*, defined as tension aroused by the awareness of another's interrupted goal attainment. That is, our own need state can become coordinated to that of another, which then motivates behavior intended to reduce this tension. It is proposed that perceived similarity to the other, which increases interpersonal attractiveness and which also may increase the feeling of "we-ness," must characterize the relationship with the other person before promotive tension can be aroused.

Consistent with Hornstein *et al.*'s theoretical framework, several researchers have demonstrated that greater feelings of involvement with the victim based on feelings of "we-ness" (e.g., Hornstein *et al.*, 1971; Sole *et al.*, 1975), similarity (e.g., Baron, 1971; Karabenick, Lerner, & Beecher, 1973; Ehlert, Ehlert, & Merrens, 1973), and attractiveness (e.g., Benson, Karabenick, & Lerner, 1976; Gross, Wallston, and Piliavin, 1975), consistently increases bystander intervention in nonemergency situations. These factors may also affect both cost considerations and arousal factors. As emotional involvement, a sense of "we-ness," similarity, or attraction to the victim increases, the benefits associated with helping as well as the costs for not helping, both personal and empathic, are proposed to increase monotonically. Furthermore, the costs for helping should be less for similar than for dissimilar victims if only because the bystander would be more confident of the consequences associated with interacting with a similar victim. The empathic costs for not helping dissimilar victims should also be lower, given that the bystander may be less concerned for the victim's well-being, while personal costs for not helping might also be lower since the social censure for not intervening may be expected to be less.

SUMMARY

The presence of other bystanders as well as the interpersonal relationship between the bystander and the victim appear to affect *both* the values within the cost–reward matrix *and* the bystander's level of emotional arousal. Furthermore, the pattern of findings across several studies suggests that arousal and cost-benefit factors may not be sequential and orthogonal determinants of bystander behavior. Rather, they may be involved in a feedback network in which each affects the value of the other. For example, for bystanders believing that others are present, the rationalization that someone else has already intervened reduces the perceived costs for not helping and may subsequently reduce bystander arousal. Thus, although the parameters of these interrelationships are not yet fully understood, there is sufficient evidence to warrant consideration of these possibilities in future research.

Impulsive Helping

The fourth fundamental proposition of the model asserts that there will be certain *specifiable* circumstances that give rise to a rapid, impulsive, "irrational" response. The impulsive behavior of subjects is a rapid, driven, almost reflexive response that appears to be insensitive to potential costs in the situation. In some of our earlier studies, variations in costs for helping (e.g., Clark & Word, 1974) and in costs for not helping (e.g., Piliavin, Rodin, & Piliavin, 1969) seemed to have little effect on bystander response.

The circumstances under which we initially observed *impulsive* helping seemed to be those in which high levels of arousal were immediately engendered in the bystander. In attempting to specify situational characteristics that should trigger impulsive helping, then, we first looked at the subpropositions of Proposition I of the model. These state that severity, clarity, physical proximity to the victim, and emotional involvement with and similarity to the victim all increase arousal experienced by the bystander. Generally consistent with our theoretical framework, a review of the experiments in which impulsive (defined as over 85% help with intervention in less than 15 seconds) or nonimpulsive helping occurred revealed several identifying characteristics of impulse-generating situations.[6] One variable appears particularly strongly related to impulsive helping. This is the clarity of the situation, operationally defined as the victim being visible or as someone clearly defining the situation as an emergency. Similar to clarity, reality—defined as a characteristic of studies done in a field setting or having as their victims people from outside the experiment—was also significantly related to impulsive intervention. Although we are convinced that severity is also an important factor, we were unable to find a sufficiently clear criterion to judge severity across different situations. Thus, we had to omit

---

[6] For further details and discussion, see Piliavin, Dovidio, Gaertner, and Clark, 1981.

this variable from our analysis. Finally, the relationship between the bystander and the victim, based on whether or not bystanders had any prior experience with the victim, was also correlated with impulsive helping. Several other factors, such as loudness of the event, physical posture of the bystander, and sex of the bystander showed no consistent relationship.

It is probably not coincidental that the same factors that facilitate impulsive helping have also been demonstrated to be related to greater levels of bystander arousal. It is likely that the high levels of arousal interfere with broad and "rational" consideration of costs. For example, a number of years ago Easterbrook (1959) demonstrated that, in a very basic physiological sense, under high levels of arousal the focus of attention of subjects was narrowed. Peripheral stimuli, therefore, were not considered in the determination of subjects' responses. Other researchers (e.g., Broadbent, 1971) have also concluded that organisms in an aroused state devote a higher proportion of time to the intake of information from dominant as compared to relatively minor sources. A unique aspect of very clear, serious emergencies is that they are both attention-getting and highly arousing. The victim's plight becomes the "dominant source" on which bystanders focus. Cost considerations become peripheral and are not attended to. Thus, the impulsive behavior that may appear irrational to an uninvolved bystander who considers all the apparent costs and rewards may be quite "rational" to a bystander attending primarily to the victim's plight.

Pictorial Presentation of the Model

For at least some people, a picture is worth a thousand words. We will now present pictorially our concept of the processes that occur. Specifically, we will use a path analysis format in which we will show what we believe to be the relationships among several categories of variables in the determination of bystander response. We hope this form of presentation will clarify the model more fully than words alone. Figure 12.1 represents a path diagram of the interrelationships considered in our model. One criticism that may be offered is that we consider so many predictor variables and place so much emphasis on process that the model is useless for prediction. However, our attempt has not been primarily to present a predictive model in the usual sense. We have instead attempted to develop a model that is designed to explain a variety of phenomena, to help researchers understand a complex area of behavior, and to suggest aspects of the phenomenon that have not yet been explored and are not well understood. Certainly prediction is part of this, but it is by no means all of it. Thus, in our presentation of the model we have attempted to organize and to

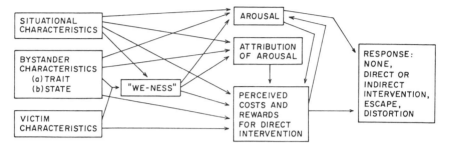

Figure 12.1. Arousal: Cost–reward model.

integrate past research, to suggest new ideas, to open new areas of inquiry, and to encourage orderly theoretical development of the area of helping behavior.

Does the complexity and the iterative nature of the present model make it impossible to use for predictive purposes, however? We think not. It merely requires that the user (*a*) attend to more features of the situation, the bystander, and the victim than formerly thought necessary and (*b*) be willing to state expectations probabilistically and contingently, depending on the occurrence or nonoccurrence of certain intervening processes, whose likelihood of occurrence can also be estimated. The overall model as depicted in Figure 12.1, then, may not serve particularly well for predictive purposes because of the highly inclusive, processual nature of the presentation. However, abstraction of certain aspects of the model can readily lead to direct, nonambiguous predictions. For example, in a very simple experiment, clarity of an emergency (in which the subject is the only bystander) can be manipulated. Diagrammatically, the potential effects associated with this manipulation are shown in Figure 12.2. Increased clarity of the emergency should lead to increased arousal. Increased clarity should also increase (both directly and indirectly) the costs for the victim's receiving no help. In the clearer emergency, the bystander would anticipate more guilt, blame, and

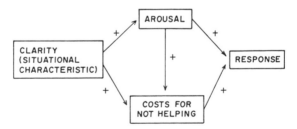

Figure 12.2. Arousal: Cost–reward model: Effects of clarity.

censure for not intervening. Thus, personal costs for not helping are directly affected. In addition, to the extent that the greater arousal generated by the clearer emergency is experienced by the bystander as unpleasant, empathic costs for the victim's receiving no help would be greater. Clarity, therefore, also indirectly increases the costs for not helping, mediated by the unpleasant emotional state. These processes, taken together, suggest that clarity should have a strong facilitative effect on bystander intervention.

Another example of research that demonstrates how the current model can be applied—a study in which more elements are present—is the Gaertner and Dovidio (1977) study involving race of victim (a victim characteristic) and the presence or absence of other witnesses to the emergency (a situational characteristic). As shown in Figure 12.3, being alone with the potential victim is postulated to lead to the perception of "we-ness," regardless of race of the victim (an illustration of the situational characteristics → we-ness path). Being of the same race as the victim (in this case both white) is also postulated to lead to judgments of "we-ness" (an illustration of the victim characteristics + bystander characteristics → we-ness path). "We-ness" then leads to increased arousal as well as increased costs of the victim's receiving no help. Greater degrees of arousal also can lead to the perception of greater seriousness and therefore to perceived even higher costs of nonintervention (the path from arousal to costs); similarly, perceived high costs for nonintervention can lead to increased arousal through the addition of feelings of moral obligation (Schwartz, 1977) on top of empathic arousal. Not only can the order of obtained outcomes for the conditions of the Gaertner and Dovidio study be predicted with the use of this overall path model, the intervening links can also be tested.

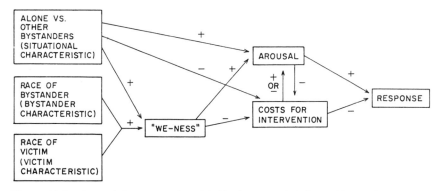

Figure 12.3. Arousal: Cost–reward model: Varying race of victim and bystander and presence of additional bystanders.

Relationship to Other Models

Several theorists working on the same problem should indeed reach some of the same conclusions. Thus, there should be similarities as well as dissimilarities between our model and other models. For example, both the Latané and Darley model and the Schwartz model of helping see the helping act as the final outcome of a decision-making process, as does our model. The event that provides the opportunity for intervention or for the performance of helping behavior is a stimulus, in many ways no different from many other occurrences, that is perceived by a bystander as requiring his or her attention. The decision-making process is then begun. Latané and Darley presented their version of this process in their 1970 book. Essentially, their model involves a decision tree, a sequence of decisions that must be made, if an individual is to intervene in another's crisis, problem, or emergency. They suggest that bystanders move from one decision to the next, except that some cycling may take place. They also suggest the possibility of blocking or becoming "transfixed at the decision point." These suggestions are made speculatively in the last chapter of their book, and no one to our knowledge has taken up these suggestions to the extent of actually trying to probe into the nature of the decision process in emergency helping. Conceptualizing the problem as a decision, however, is rather generally agreed upon.

Schwartz (1977; see also Chapter 14 in this book) has modified and expanded the Latané and Darley decision-tree model. Three major changes from the Latané and Darley model are embodied in Schwartz's version. First, Schwartz goes into much greater detail in his discussion of the steps. Second, his model explicitly allows for cycling or reevaluations of earlier steps in the sequence. Finally, the Schwartz model provides for a specific motivational construct—feelings of moral obligation—that gives the bystander a reason to intervene. The Latané and Darley model presented the framework for the decision process without postulating one specific motivation that might lead people to proceed through the specified steps. They suggested a number of motivational constructs; however, they did not incorporate one into the actual model. In the Schwartz model, the feeling of moral obligation is the primary motivation behind helping in a crisis. Feelings of moral obligation are or are not aroused by the helping opportunity, and the reward for action is increased self-evaluation as a result of adherence to one's moral standards.

Although we also conceptualize the helping act as the outcome of a decision process, our model has more in common with the general framework for decision-making recently presented by Janis and Mann (1977) than it does with the Latané and Darley or Schwartz (1977) models. Janis and

Mann make an important distinction between "hot" cognitions (Abelson, 1963) and the "cool," calculated approach to problem solving usually recommended and generally assumed as the model for all kinds of decision making. By "hot" cognitive processes they mean thinking that is accompanied by emotional arousal. Given our assumption that observation of the problems, crises, and emergencies of others leads to emotional arousal in the observer, the Janis and Mann model, which explicitly builds in the effect of emotion, seems ideally suited to the intervention situation.

In general, the Janis and Mann model of emergency decision-making has much in common with our model and other models of bystander intervention. It involves four basic questions a person confronted with a danger or warning asks him or herself:

1. Are the risks serious if I do nothing?
2. Are the risks serious if I do take the most available protective action?
3. Is it realistic to hope to find a better means?
4. Is there sufficient time to search and deliberate?

The Janis and Mann model presents several important insights that are quite consistent with our own approach. First, these authors assume that in most emergency situations, decisions are not based on purely intellectual deliberation. Instead, the four basic questions in their model are "posed and answered on the basis of a very hasty surmise, sometimes limited to split-second perceptions of what is happening and what might happen [Janis & Mann, 1977, p. 54]." Furthermore, the answers to these questions do not necessarily occur in the sequence shown, and some or all of the questions and answers might occur with great rapidity as visual images, rather than in verbal form. This aspect of their model has obvious relevance to our analysis of impulsive helping.

In addition, Janis and Mann hypothesize that simply being faced with a consequential decision leads to stress and arousal. Thus, by itself, the feeling of insufficient time to make a decision can create arousal and consequently affect the nature of the decision process. The final major contribution of the Janis and Mann approach is related to this postulated impact of the need for a decision on stress and arousal. Because it is the perception of alternatives and the perception of sufficiency of time that are critical rather than some "objective" reality, person variables are very important for the process and outcome of emergency decisions. "State" variables such as level of arousal at the time of the emergency, trait variables such as self-confidence, past experience, and/or specific training in similar situations all moderate the impact of such highly stressful, high time-pressure decision situations.

Integration of our model with other models may also be accomplished through a reconceptualization based on the Lewinian notion of *resultant force*. Emergency situations (as contrasted with a descending series of crises, problems, and mundane help-requiring situations) are typically characterized by high costs for intervention. It is seldom dangerous to pick up dropped groceries or to donate to the Salvation Army. Intervening in a rape or an armed robbery, on the other hand, involves a high level of personal cost. Thus the forces opposing such intervention are great. In order for a helping act to occur, the force propelling the individual to the act must be stronger than the forces opposing the act. Unpleasant, high arousal associated with the distress of the other (that is, perceived as empathic arousal) is the strongest instigator to intervention (*a*) because of its immediacy and negative feeling tone and (*b*) because the most efficient and immediate way to relieve one's own distress is to alleviate the distress of the other. As the level of arousal decreases, the force leading the individual to "locomote" toward the victim is decreased. Given the same level of costs associated with intervention, then, helping will be less likely as arousal decreases.

On the other hand, with relatively low-cost forms of helping, such as returning "lost" letters or contributing money to charity, the strong emotion aroused in a defense reaction is not necessary to overcome the forces against taking the action. A relatively mild emotional response, such as Hornstein's postulated *promotive tension*, Schwartz's *feelings of moral obligation*, or Coke *et al.*'s (1978) *empathic arousal* should be sufficient to energize helping in low cost situations. It is even possible that other drives or motives, such as physical attraction to the victim or a desire to do something interesting can motivate helping, as long as the costs are low.

Conclusion

In this chapter we have attempted to develop a theoretical framework for bystander intervention and to provide support for our propositions. The result is a relatively complex model. Nevertheless, it must be realized that we are dealing with a complex problem. In the past twenty years, a large base of empirical work has been accumulated in the areas of emergency intervention and helping behavior. However, no comprehensive theory of the determinants of helping behavior exists. We have attempted with our model of emergency intervention to provide a first step in that direction. We hope that others will explore the theoretical and applied implications of our model, will compare and test the predictions that can be drawn from it and other approaches, and will attempt to extend it to other areas of prosocial behavior.

References

Abelson, R. P. Computer simulation of 'hot' cognition. In S. Tomkins and S. Messick (Eds.), *Computer simulation of personality*. New York: John Wiley & Sons, 1963.

Ashton, N. L., & Severy, L. J. Arousal and costs in bystander intervention. *Personality and Social Psychology Bulletin*, 1976, *2*, 268–272.

Baron, R. A. Magnitude of model's apparent pain and ability to aid the model as determinants of observer reaction time. *Psychonomic Science*, 1971, *21*, 196–197.

Batson, C. D., Cochran, P. J., Biederman, M. F., Blosser, J. L., Ryan, M. J., & Vogt, B. Failure to help when in a hurry: Callousness or conflict? *Personality and Social Psychology Bulletin*, 1978, *4*, 97–101.

Benson, P. L., Karabenick, S. A., & Lerner, R. M. Pretty pleases: The effect of physical attraction, race and sex on receiving help. *Journal of Experimental Social Psychology*, 1976, *12*, 409–415.

Berger, S. M. Conditioning through vicarious instigation. *Psychological Review*, 1962, *69*, 450–456.

Bickman, L. Social influence and diffusion of responsibility in an emergency. *Journal of Experimental Social Psychology*, 1972, *8*, 438–445.

Bickman, L., & Kamzan, M. The effect of race and need on helping behavior. *Journal of Social Psychology*, 1973, *89*, 73–77.

Bickman, L., & Rosenbaum, D. P. Crime reporting as a function of bystander encouragement, surveillance, and credibility. *Journal of Personality and Social Psychology*, 1977, *35*, 577–586.

Borofsky, G., Stollak, G., & Messé, L. Bystander reactions to physical assault: Sex differences in socially responsible behavior. *Journal of Experimental Social Psychology*, 1971, *7*, 313–318.

Broadbent, D. E. *Decision and stress*. New York: Academic Press, 1971.

Byeff, P. Helping behavior in audio and audio–video conditions. Senior honors thesis, University of Pennsylvania, 1970.

Chaikin, A. L., & Darley, J. M. Victim or perpetrator: Defensive attribution of responsibility and the need for order and justice. *Journal of Personality and Social Psychology*, 1973, *25*, 268–275.

Clark, R. D., III, & Word, L. E. Why don't bystanders help? Because of ambiguity? *Journal of Personality and Social Psychology*, 1972, *24*, 392–400.

Clark, R. D., III, & Word, L. E. Where is the apathetic bystander? Situational characteristics of the emergency. *Journal of Personality and Social Psychology*, 1974, *29*, 279–287.

Coke, J. S., Batson, C. D., & McDavis, K. Empathic mediation of helping: A two-stage model. *Journal of Personality and Social Psychology*, 1978, *36*, 752–766.

Craig, K. D., & Lowery, H. J. Heart-rate components of conditioned vicarious autonomic responses. *Journal of Personality and Social Psychology*, 1969, *11*, 381–387.

Darley, J. M., & Batson, C. D. "From Jerusalem to Jericho": A study of situational and dispositional variables in helping behavior. *Journal of Personality and Social Psychology*, 1973, *27*, 100–108.

Darley, J. M., & Latané, B. Bystander intervention in emergencies: Diffusion of responsibility. *Journal of Personality and Social Psychology*, 1968, *8*, 377–383.

Deutsch, M., & Gerard, H. A study of normative and informational social influence upon individual judgment. *Journal of Abnormal and Social Psychology*, 1955, *51*, 629–636.

DiLollo, V., & Berger, S. M. Effects of apparent pain in others on observer's reaction time. *Journal of Personality and Social Psychology*, 1965, *2*, 573–575.

Easterbrook, J. A. The effect of emotion on cue utilization and the organization of behavior. *Psychological Review*, 1959, *66*, 183–201.

Ehlert, J., Ehlert, N., & Merrens, M. The influence of ideological affiliation on helping behavior. *Journal of Social Psychology*, 1973, *89*, 315–316.

Enzle, M. E., & Harvey, M. D. Effects of a third-party requestor's surveillance and recipient awareness of request on helping. *Personality and Social Psychology Bulletin*, 1977, *3*, 421–424.

Field, M. Power and dependency: Legitimation of dependency conditions. *Journal of Social Psychology*, 1974, *92*, 31–37.

Gaertner, S. L., & Dovidio, J. F. The subtlety of white racism, arousal, and helping. *Journal of Personality and Social Psychology*, 1977, *35*, 691–707.

Gaertner, S. L., Dovidio, J. F., & Johnson, G. *Race of victim, non-responsive bystanders, and helping behavior.* Paper presented at the meeting of the American Psychological Association, New York City, August 1979.

Geer, J. H., & Jarmecky, L. The effect of being responsible for reducing another's pain on subjects' response and arousal. *Journal of Personality and Social Psychology*, 1973, *26*, 232–237.

Gross, A. E., Wallston, B. S., & Piliavin, I. M. Beneficiary attractiveness and cost as determinants of responses to routine requests for help. *Sociometry*, 1975, *38*, 131–140.

Harris, M. B., & Huang, L. C. Helping and the attribution process. *Journal of Social Psychology*, 1973, *90*, 291–297.

Hodgson, S. A., Hornstein, H. A., & LaKind, E. Socially mediated Zeigarnik effects as a function of sentiment, valence, and desire for goal attainment. *Journal of Experimental Social Psychology*, 1972, *8*, 446–456.

Hornstein, H. A. Promotive tension: The basis of prosocial behavior from a Lewinian perspective. *Journal of Social Issues*, 1972, *28*, 191–218.

Hornstein, H. A. *Cruelty and kindness: A new look at aggression and altruism.* Englewood Cliffs, New Jersey: Prentice-Hall, 1976.

Hornstein, H. A., Masor, H. N., Sole, K., & Heilman, M. Effects of sentiment and completion of a helping act on observer helping: A case for socially mediated Zeigarnik effects. *Journal of Personality and Social Psychology*, 1971, *17*, 107–112.

Horowitz, I. A. The effect of group norms on bystander intervention. *Journal of Social Psychology*, 1971, *83*, 265–273.

Janis, I. L., & Mann, L. *Decision making.* New York: The Free Press, 1977.

Karabenick, S. A., Lerner, R. M., & Beecher, M. D. Relation of political affiliation to helping behavior on election day, November 7, 1972. *Journal of Social Psychology*, 1973, *91*, 223–227.

Konečni, V. J., & Ebbesen, E. B. Effects of the presence of children on adults' helping behavior and compliance: Two field studies. *Journal of Social Psychology*, 1975, *97*, 181–193.

Krebs, D. Empathy and altruism. *Journal of Personality and Social Psychology*, 1975, *32*, 1134–1146.

Lacey, J. I., & Lacey, B. C. Some autonomic–central nervous system interrelationships. In P. Black (Ed.), *Physiological correlates of emotion.* New York: Academic Press, 1970.

Lacey, J. I., & Lacey, B. C. Experimental association and dissociation of phasic bradycardia and vertex-negative waves: A psychophysiological study of attention and response-intention. In W. C. McCallum and J. R. Knott (Eds.), *Event-related slow potentials of the brain.* New York: Elsevier, 1973.

Latané, B., & Dabbs, J. M., Jr. Sex, group size and helping in three cities. *Sociometry*, 1975, *38*, 180–194.

Latané, B., and Darley, J. M. *The unresponsive bystander: Why doesn't he help?* New York: Appleton-Century-Crofts, 1970.

Latané, B., and Rodin, J. A lady in distress: Inhibiting effects of friends and strangers on bystander intervention. *Journal of Experimental Social Psychology*, 1969, *5*, 189–202.

Lazarus, R. S. *Psychological stress and the coping process.* New York: McGraw-Hill Book Co., 1966.

Lazarus, R. S. Emotions and adaptation: Conceptual and empirical relations. In W. J. Arnold (Ed.), *Nebraska symposium on motivation.* Lincoln: University of Nebraska Press, 1968.

Lerner, M. J. The desire for justice and reaction to victim. In J. Macaulay and L. Berkowitz (Eds.), *Altruism and helping behavior.* New York: Academic Press, 1970.

Lerner, M. J. Justice, guilt, and veridical perception. *Journal of Personality and Social Psychology*, 1971, *20*, 127–135.

Lynn, R. *Attention, arousal, and the orientation reaction.* Oxford: Pergamon Press, 1966.

McGovern, L. P. Dispositional social anxiety and helping behavior under three conditions of threat. *Journal of Personality*, 1976, *44*, 84–97.

Midlarsky, E., & Midlarsky, M. Some determinants of aiding under experimentally induced stress. *Journal of Personality*, 1973, *41*, 305–327.

Moriarty, T. Crime, commitment and the responsive bystander: Two field experiments. *Journal of Personality and Social Psychology*, 1975, *31*, 370–376.

Piliavin, I. M., Piliavin, J. A., & Rodin, J. Costs, diffusion, and the stigmatized victim. *Journal of Personality and Social Psychology*, 1975, *32*, 429–438.

Piliavin, I. M., Rodin, J., & Piliavin, J. A. Good Samaritanism: An underground phenomenon? *Journal of Personality and Social Psychology*, 1969, *13*, 289–299.

Piliavin, J. A., Dovidio, J. F., Gaertner, S. L., & Clark, R. D., III. *Emergency intervention.* New York: Academic Press, 1981.

Piliavin, J. A., & Piliavin, I. M. The effect of blood on reactions to a victim. *Journal of Personality and Social Psychology*, 1972, *23*, 253–261.

Piliavin, J. A., & Piliavin, I. M. The Good Samaritan: Why does he help? Unpublished manuscript, 1973.

Piliavin, J. A., Piliavin, I. M., & Trudell, B. Incidental arousal, helping, and diffusion of responsibility. Unpublished data, University of Wisconsin, 1974.

Ross, A. S. Effect of increased responsibility on bystander intervention: The presence of children. *Journal of Personality and Social Psychology*, 1971, *19*, 306–310.

Ross, A. S., & Braband, J. Effect of increased responsibility on bystander intervention, II: The cue value of a blind person. *Journal of Personality and Social Psychology*, 1973, *25*, 254–258.

Routtenberg, A. The two-arousal hypothesis: Reticular formation and limbic system. *Psychological Review*, 1968, *75*, 51–79.

Samerotte, G. C., & Harris, M. B. Some factors influencing helping: The effects of a handicap, responsibility, and requesting help. *Journal of Social Psychology*, 1976, *98*, 39–45.

Satow, K. L. Social approval and helping. *Journal of Experimental Social Psychology*, 1975, *11*, 501–509.

Schachter, S. The interaction of cognitive and physiological determinants of emotional state. In L. Berkowitz (Ed.), *Advances in experimental social psychology* (Vol. 1). New York: Academic Press, 1964.

Schwartz, S. H. Normative influences on altruism. In L. Berkowitz (Ed.), *Advances in experimental social psychology* (Vol. 10). New York: Academic Press, 1977.

Schwartz, S. H., & BenDavid, A. Responsibility and helping in an emergency: Effects of blame, ability, and denial of responsibility. *Sociometry*, 1976, *39*, 406–415.

Schwartz, S. H., & Clausen, G. T. Responsibility, norms, and helping in an emergency. *Journal of Personality and Social Psychology*, 1970, *16*, 299–310.

Schwartz, S. H., & Gottlieb, A. Bystander reactions to a violent theft: Crime in Jerusalem. *Journal of Personality and Social Psychology*, 1976, *34*, 1188–1199.

Schwartz, S. H., & Gottlieb, A. Bystander anonymity and reactions to emergencies. *Journal of Personality and Social Psychology* 1980, *39*, 418–430.

Shaffer, D. R., Rogel, M., & Hendrick, C. Intervention in the library: The effect of increased responsibility on bystanders' willingness to prevent a theft. *Journal of Applied Social Psychology*, 1975, *5*, 303–319.

Sherif, M. *The psychology of social norms.* New York: Harper and Brothers, 1936.

Shotland, R. L., & Straw, M. K. Bystander response to an assault: When a man attacks a woman. *Journal of Personality and Social Psychology*, 1976, *34*, 990–999.

Smith, R. E., Smythe, L., & Lien, D. Inhibition of helping behavior by a similar or dissimilar nonreactive fellow bystander. *Journal of Personality and Social Psychology*, 1972, *23*, 414–419.

Smith, R. E., Vanderbilt, K., & Callen, M. B. Social comparison and bystander intervention in emergencies. *Journal of Applied Social Psychology*, 1973, *3*, 186–196.

Sokolov, E. N. *Perception and the conditioned reflex.* Oxford: Pergamon Press, 1963.

Sole, K., Marton, J., & Hornstein, H. A. Opinion similarity and helping: Three field experiments investigating the bases of promotive tension. *Journal of Experimental Social Psychology*, 1975, *11*, 1–13.

Staub, E. A child in distress: The effects of focusing responsibility on children on their attempts to help. *Developmental Psychology*, 1970, *2*, 152–154.

Staub, E. Helping a distressed person: Social, personality, and stimulus determinants. In L. Berkowitz (Ed.), *Advances in experimental social psychology* (Vol. 7). New York: Academic Press, 1974.

Staub, E., & Baer, R. S. Stimulus characteristics of a sufferer and difficulty of escape as determinants of helping. *Journal of Personality and Social Psychology*, 1974, *30*, 279–284.

Sterling, B. The effects of anger, ambiguity, and arousal on helping behavior (Doctoral Dissertation, University of Delaware, 1977). *Dissertation Abstracts International*, 1977, *38*(4), 1962.

Stokols, D., & Schopler, J. Reactions to victims under conditions of situational detachment: The effect of responsibility, severity, and expected future interaction. *Journal of Personality and Social Psychology*, 1973, *25*, 199–209.

Stotland, E. Exploratory investigations of empathy. In L. Berkowitz (Ed.), *Advances in experimental social psychology* (Vol. 7). New York: Academic Press, 1974.

Tilker, H. A. Socially responsible behavior as a function of observer responsibility and victim feedback. *Journal of Personality and Social Psychology*, 1970, *14*, 95–100.

Weiss, R. F., Buchanan, W., Altstatt, L., & Lombardo, J. P. Altruism is rewarding. *Science*, 1971, *171*, 1262–1263.

Weiss, R. F., Boyer, J. L., Lombardo, J. P., & Stich, M. H. Altruistic drive and altruistic reinforcement. *Journal of Personality and Social Psychology*, 1973, *25*, 390–400.

Wilson, J. P. Motivation, modeling, and altruism: A person × situation analysis. *Journal of Personality and Social Psychology*, 1976, *34*, 1078–1086.

Yakimovich, D., and Saltz, E. Helping behavior: The cry for help. *Psychonomic Science*, 1971, *23*, 390–400.

Chapter 13

The Help-Seeking

Process

ALAN E. GROSS
PEG A. MCMULLEN

One of the features of human society that distinguishes it from collections of more self-sufficient beasts is that interdependence is often required for survival and for fulfillment. In modern technological times, when few humans can provide everything for themselves, one form of interdependence is reflected in the evolution of a complex system for the division of labor and the exchange of labor, goods, and services. Most relationships within this economic system have been structured into organizations and institutions that facilitate the trading of these items, usually on a quid pro quo basis.

Although economic interdependencies are of great importance in industrialized North American society, another set of more interpersonal behaviors are at least equally important. These behaviors, which include giving and receiving help, are less likely than purely economic actions to be motivated by anticipated rewards; indeed a subset of these helping behaviors, often labeled *prosocial*, is characterized by people helping others for no obvious gain.

In this chapter, helping behavior is broadly construed to include any act of giving and receiving aid that is intended to alleviate suffering or to improve the quality of life. Benefits can be delivered by one person directly

COOPERATION AND HELPING BEHAVIOR
Theories and Research

to another, or they can be brokered through organizations or agencies; helping interactions can occur during a chance meeting or in the context of an intimate, ongoing social relationship such as marriage or parenting. Help can be obtained from friends, neighbors, strangers, or skilled experts, and motives for giving can range from voluntary altruism to the provision of service for a fee.

Helping interactions minimally involve a helper or service provider who controls resources and a potential recipient who can benefit from these resources. However, until a few years ago, almost all research dealing with helping relationships focused only on variables that facilitate or inhibit the actions of potential helpers (see Bar-Tal, 1976; Krebs, 1970; Macauley & Berkowitz, 1970; Rushton, 1980; Staub, 1978, 1979, for reviews of the literature on help giving). The recipients were virtually ignored, and their utilization of available services was simply taken for granted. It has been suggested that little effort is devoted to incorporating the psychology of the potential beneficiary into help delivery systems because it is often assumed that helpers and recipients will somehow automatically contact each other (Gross, Fisher, Nadler, Stiglitz, & Craig, 1979).

Perhaps because much of the earlier helping research was stimulated by concern about lack of bystander intervention in emergencies (Darley & Latané, 1970), it was assumed that if it could be determined why help was not offered, most problems of help delivery would be solved. In emergencies where victims' identities, plights, and what is required to aid them are relatively obvious, research focusing only on the helper was appropriate. In fact, concepts developed from this research (e.g., diffusion of responsibility) have proven useful in understanding helper behaviors. Nonetheless, generalizing from research on emergency and other helper-focused characteristics to research concerned with more routine helping where the recipient is an important element has extremely limited utility.

Psychology of the Help Recipient

A central assumption of this paper is that in order to understand helping relationships and to design effective and humane helping systems, theory and research must take into account the psychology of the recipient. Recipient attitudes and behaviors are as important to the successful functioning of most helping interactions as are those of the helper. Professional service providers have become increasingly aware that development of high-quality resources in itself is not enough to guarantee that help will actually reach those who need it. One indicator of the seriousness of this problem is that many services are underutilized by needy individuals (McKinlay, 1972).

In many helping relationships there is some complementarity between helper and recipient; therefore it may be helpful to begin this analysis by rephrasing some of the helper-focused questions, explanations, and models and reapplying them to recipient-focused theorizing and research. For example, Darley and Latané's (1970) award-winning book is titled *"The Unresponsive Bystander: Why Doesn't He Help?"*, but no counterpart volume, entitled something like *"The Unassertive Victims: Why Don't They Ask For Help?"* has yet been published. A number of helper-oriented papers have asked why people help for no obvious gain (altruism), and why they occasionally turn their backs on victims (bystander apathy), but few questions have been asked about why people do not avail themselves of useful services; why they sometimes don't ask for what they want or need even when costs appear minimal and resources are readily available. This last question is all the more puzzling and interesting because it implies that needy people often behave counter to their own self-interests.

At the theoretical level, help giving, especially altruism, has long intrigued philosophers, sociologists, and others. Many explanations have been offered to account for this prosocial behavior, ranging from a functional–evolutionary theory (Trivers, 1971) to a somewhat circular postulation of a social responsibility norm (Gouldner, 1960). When what is included in helping behavior is extended beyond individual relationships to institutionalized help-delivery systems, more cynical explanations have been suggested. For example, Gross, Wallston, and Piliavin (1980) argue that welfare agencies exist in part for the nonaltruistic purpose of handling the embarrassing problem of the poor in a rich society. Only recently has theoretical attention turned to help recipients and their reasons for seeking or avoiding help (e.g., Fisher, Nadler, & Whitcher, 1979; Gross, Wallston, & Piliavin, 1979).

Models of the Help-Seeking Process

Based on their analyses of the conditions affecting bystander intervention in emergency situations, Darley and Latané (1970) presented a simple model designed to approximate the process of deciding whether or not to help as it might occur in the potential helper's head. Examination and adaptation of this model for the recipient reveals striking parallels in the decision-making sequence experienced by individuals on either side of the helping relationship. Their model basically requires a person to answer yes to all three of the following questions before acting to help:

1. Does the victim have a problem that my help will alleviate?
2. Am I responsible for helping? (Should I help?)
3. Am I capable of successfully rendering aid?

The complementary questions that the potential recipient might ask before seeking help are:

1. Do I have a problem that help will alleviate?
2. Should I ask for help?
3. Who is most capable of providing the kind of aid I need?

This three-question model demonstrates that the choice of whether or not to seek help is not a simple dichotomy; however, a number of complexities that exceed the model's capacity soon become evident. Another more elaborate model for help-seeking decisions appears in Figure 13.1. This model is adapted and expanded from Piliavin's (1972) linear sequential model for help utilization, and it also includes some features from Shulman, Rosen, and Gross's (1976) model of how widows use resources, tactics, and strategies to cope with bereavement. The various activities and decision points in the model presented in Figure 13.1 can be discriminated from each other, and they can also be collapsed to the three general stages as shown in Figure 13.2. These general stages—perceiving a problem, deciding to seek help, and operationalizing strategies—are quite similar to the obverse of the Darley–Latané help-giving model noted above, and to Gurin, Veroff, and Feld's (1960) three-step process leading to self-referral: (a) defining a situation as a mental health problem, (b) deciding to seek help, and (c) selecting a specific source of help.[1]

Before proceeding, a few features and limitations of both forms of the model should be pointed out. The simplified sequence as drawn in Figure 13.2 indicates that it is first necessary to recognize or infer a problem, then to decide whether or not to seek aid, and only then to engage in activities aimed at solving the problem. However, it is unlikely that such a serial process approximates the tortuous route of many help-seeking decisions. In actuality, these separate stages, though analytically distinct, often interact experientially. Each subsequent step in the sequence is at least partly dependent on the manner in which preceding steps are resolved, and later stages often have an anticipatory effect on earlier stages. For example, it is quite possible for second- and third-stage considerations to influence and interact with each other. The specific source of help chosen in the third stage may often be associated with costs and benefits influencing whether

---

[1] A number of others have suggested similar stages in the help-seeking process. For example, Theodore (cited by McKinlay, 1972) proposed a stage model involving perception of conditions needing medical attention, willingness to treat such conditions, and ability to transform a perceived need into an actual demand for health care; Kadushin (1958–1959) described a five-step model for the decision to enter psychotherapy; and Kulka (1978) used the Gurin, Veroff, and Feld (1960) model to analyze help seeking in a massive survey study of how people cope with personal problems.

or not help is sought in the first place (second stage). Furthermore, in making a complex decision such as deciding to seek help, some stages may be reversed in order, cycled several times, or omitted altogether. For purposes of clarity, appropriate feedback loops and simultaneous processing connections are not shown for either model, but it is acknowledged that the decision process is not necessarily sequential and linear.

It should also be noted that neither model is intended as an exhaustive analog. Specifically, neither model, as illustrated, includes psychological processes presumed to be operating at decision junctures. Instead, these models are presented to provide a general framework for locating points in the process where psychosocial factors can critically affect decisions.

The remainder of this paper will be devoted to describing and discussing, within the framework of the help-seeking model, some of the psychosocial factors and processes that influence help-seeking decisions, and concepts and theories that aid in understanding these influences.

Perception of Problems

For any individual to decide ultimately to seek help, he or she must first recognize some *symptom* and define it as a *problem*, acknowledging that help is needed and/or appropriate for dealing with the problem. Each of us is steadily bombarded with a variety of stimuli and events over the course of our lifetimes. Some of these stimuli are powerful, others are subtle and difficult to discern. Some effects accrue over time, and others impinge upon us precipitously. Certain of these stimulus configurations are easily recognized as problematic by almost everyone, e.g., loss of a job, death of a loved one, severe physical symptoms, etc. However, there are a great many more conditions that are considered problematic by some individuals, though regarded as normal states by others.

Based on personal life experiences, cultural conditioning, and knowledge acquired regarding "normality," health and illness, each individual holds implicit ideas as to what physical, psychological, and social states are normal and what deviations from these norms are unusual (Mechanic, 1968). These ideas vary from person to person and group to group. Consequently, considerable variation exists as to the types and qualities of problems that receive attention and generate sufficient concern to seek help across individuals. The same conditions and feelings that signify a serious psychological problem to a white, middle class, older woman, for example, may be viewed as nonproblematic and quite normal by a black, working class, younger man.

A realistic view of the relationship between symptom experience and help

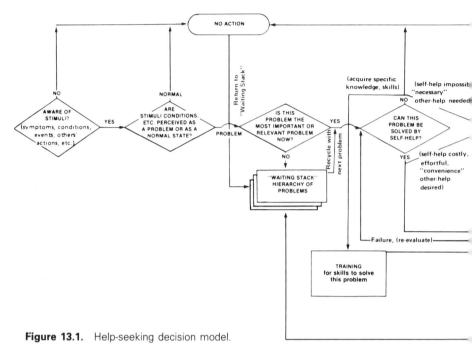

Figure 13.1. Help-seeking decision model.

seeking acknowledges that it would take different symptoms to bring various individuals to specified helpers and that the presence of similar symptoms among differing populations may lead to vastly divergent courses of action. Such a view is contrary to the "logical" and commonly held notion that objective symptom–problem characteristics are the primary determinants of help-seeking behaviors; that is, that those who seek help are those who need help and those who do not seek help do not need help. Although this rational association between symptom characteristics and the utilization of help may be sufficient to account for the help-seeking behaviors of persons with seriously disruptive problems, many researchers have documented the inadequacy of this explanation.

Numerous community health surveys and epidemiological studies have demonstrated that very high percentages of apparently healthy populations (i.e., those not seeking help) evidence some physical aberration or psychological disorder amenable to diagnosis and treatment. Zola (1966), for example, estimated that the proportion of *untreated* disorders in the population equals two-thirds to three-fourths of all existing conditions. In many cases, neither type of disorder nor the objective seriousness of symptoms experienced has been found to differentiate those who feel sick and seek treatment from those who do not (Hollingshead & Redlich, 1958; Koos,

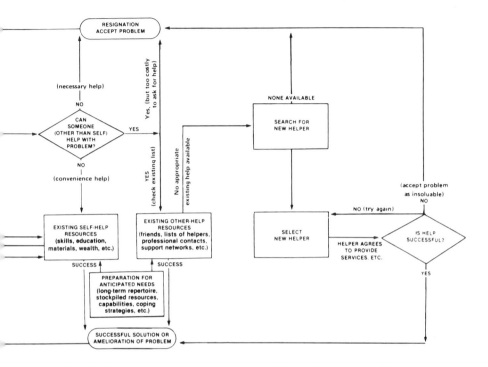

1954; Schenthal, 1960; for reviews see Stoeckle, Zola, & Davidson, 1963; Zola, 1966).

Thus, the mere recognition of some difficulty or unusual symptom is often insufficient to lead an individual to decide to take action and seek help. Unless the individual further identifies the condition as problematic or as potentially harmful, it is unlikely that outside help will be sought. This is consistent with the general rationale underlying various consciousness-raising techniques which assumes that individuals and populations often need to be sensitized to conditions that affect them adversely. For example, modern feminists have encouraged women to identify limited opportunity and other features associated with the traditional female role as problematic. As such consciousness-raisers recognize, awareness is the first step, and individuals must consider their present state to be problematic before they will be motivated to change it. It is not enough, however, to simply label a set of symptoms or a certain condition as a problem. Once identified as such, the problem must further be perceived as amenable to aid for the help-seeking process to be activated.

Given the evidence of such widespread individual differences in noticing and labeling problems, it is clear that important factors other than the mere presence of some objective disorder intervene in the making of a

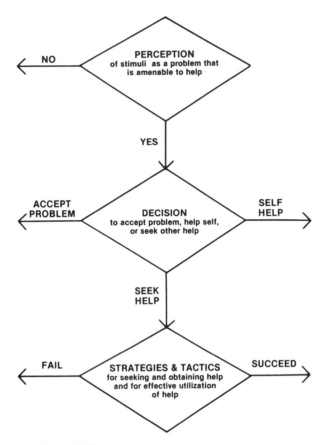

Figure 13.2. Stages in the help-seeking process.

decision to seek or not seek help in a particular situation. Most people experience some symptoms or problems almost continuously throughout their lives, and yet seek help relatively infrequently. Zola (1966) noting that very often "it is the 'fit' of certain signs with a society's major values which accounts for the degree of attention they receive [p. 618]," suggested that the particular symptoms or problems that are acted on by any individual are those defined as "relevant for action" by his or her important cultural, ethnic, or reference groups. Understanding the contextual relevance of any specific symptom–problem experience has been a recurrent theme throughout the literature on problem perception.

Many researchers have confirmed that subcultural patterns and values give substance to the manner in which problems are perceived, expressed, and judged worthy or unworthy of concern by various individuals. Such significant indices of one's major reference group identifications as social class, ethnicity, religious affiliation, age, and sex have all been related to variations in problem perception.

For example, there is evidence that the lower the social class, the less likely a given symptom will be perceived as requiring professional attention (Antonovsky & Hartman, 1974; Hollingshead & Redlich, 1958; Koos, 1954; McKinlay, 1972). Perhaps due to their differing relations with society's healthcare system, working class and white collar groups differ significantly in their concepts of health and illness. Symptoms that do not incapacitate are often ignored by blue-collar workers. Members of the middle and upper classes, however, are likely to regard less serious but unusual conditions as requiring attention simply by virtue of their existence (Rosenblatt & Suchman, 1964).

Likewise, subcultural components are influential even in determining one's response to the symptom of pain. Significant variation exists in the types of complaints (areas of the body affected) that different ethnic groups tend to present for treatment. Even with the same diagnosis, members of some ethnic groups acknowledge more pain, more diverse symptoms, and greater interference with their daily activities than members of other ethnic or racial backgrounds (Zborowski, 1958; Zola, 1964, 1966).

Regardless of their class or ethnic orientation, women have consistently been found to report greater distress and more of all kinds of symptoms than men (Chesler, 1971; Gurin, Veroff, & Feld, 1960; Kulka, 1978). Rather than representing an actual difference in the stresses and strains encountered by men and women, however, this difference between the sexes primarily reflects disparate cultural expectations regarding expressive control. In a culture that has traditionally ascribed strength and independence to the "masculine" role and weakness and dependence to the "feminine" role, it is small wonder that women find it easier than men to acknowledge various symptomatic feelings or behaviors. Since it is more culturally acceptable for females to be expressive about their difficulties, women would be expected to admit distress or discomfort more readily than men. Men, in fact, have frequently been found to underreport their symptoms (for reviews, see Kasl & Cobb, 1966; McKinlay, 1972). In one well-controlled study, it was observed that "men were more likely than women to decide that the frequency or intensity of certain symptoms was not sufficient to make them worth reporting, especially if it was possible to assume that the presence of these symptoms could be interpreted as a sign of weakness [Phillips & Segal, 1969, p. 70]."

Thus, the very definition of a certain situation or a particular bodily or emotional state as a "problem" is, in itself, part of a social process. Before deciding to ask for help, one must first recognize some condition as problematic and acknowledge that seeking help is an appropriate way of dealing with the problem. In most cases, it is not the content of the problem itself that is significant (except perhaps when extremely serious or disruptive), but the social context within which it occurs and within which it is perceived and understood. Often this understanding is heavily influenced by family, friends and other lay people in a person's social environment (Gottlieb, 1976; Gourash, 1978). Far from reflecting arbitrary or idiosyncratic processes, variations in problem perception represent all people's attempts to make sense of their problems within particular life contexts and prevailing social and cultural understandings and expectations.

Interpretations of problems and actions taken with respect to them are rooted in subcultural definitions of "health," "sickness," and "normality." Behaviors or actions that may appear deviant or dysfunctional when considered in isolation often emerge as realistic and logical choices when interpreted within the life context of the individual. One's cultural context affects not only the perception and interpretation of symptoms; it also conditions the alternative responses that are identified as ways of dealing with a problem.

The Decision to Seek Help

Once a problem is recognized, an individual in need faces difficult choices that more often than not involve assessment of costs. For those problems that are judged insoluble or extremely unlikely to be resolved, the unfortunate victim can only suffer and/or learn to accept and live with a continuing or inevitable problem. Fortunately, however, most problems can be alleviated by one's own actions or by receiving help from others. For these more optimistic problems, an individual can choose an appropriate means for coping.

Necessary and Convenient Help

Those problems that are amenable to help can be divided into two general classes: those that are impossible to solve by oneself and those that can be solved alone if sufficient time and effort are expended. Help is *necessary* for ameliorating the first class of problems but only *convenient* for the second class, which can be solved or completed independently in the absence of available help (see Figure 13.1). Among those problems requiring necessary help are conditions calling for special expertise (e.g., medical, mechanical); tasks requiring more than one individual (e.g., lifting a heavy object); and situations requiring an instrument to reach a goal that is not available to the needy individual (e.g., money to buy food, a car to travel to a hospital). Those problems benefiting from convenience help are generally found under conditions where assistance from one or more individuals will ease a task that could be accomplished by one individual but at a higher cost in effort or time; for example, a political worker might ask volunteers to help address and fold letters to save the time that would be spent in completing the entire mailing without help.

Even this seemingly basic determination of whether outside help is necessary or convenient, however, often involves subjective judgments and reflects individual differences in temperament and values. Most mothers would agree that high fevers are dangerous and necessitate professional medical attention. Some mothers will call the doctor when their child's temperature is only slightly above normal, however, whereas others may not feel it necessary to obtain outside medical assistance unless the fever reaches a much higher level. And among any group of students experiencing similar objective difficulties in their coursework, there will likely be wide variations in decisions as to when or whether outside help is necessary.

Therefore, before calculating costs and seeking help for a problem, a person must first acknowledge that a problem exists, and moreover that it is amenable to amelioration or help. Help from others is viewed as necessary for some problems and only convenient or desirable for others. If a problem is amenable to self-help, the costs of solving it independently without seeking convenient help are usually calculated in time and effort units; for example, "it will take me ten hours to do it myself." If a problem cannot be alleviated without help, the costs of not seeking necessary help are those associated with the continued presence and possible worsening of the problem. In both instances the costs of not seeking help can range from slight to considerable.

Psychological Costs of Seeking Help

We know from everyday observations as well as from survey and experimental data (e.g., McKinlay 1972) that many needy people do not seek help even when it is readily accessible. Because individuals are willing to forego help when the alternatives of tolerating problems or expending additional effort are costly, it can be deduced that the process of seeking aid in itself has inhibitory costs associated with it. Some of the costs and negative valences attached to help seeking are obvious—for example, traveling a great distance or paying large fees—but others are more subtle. The obvious costs are of more interest to economists than psychologists, but the less detectable costs related to intrapersonal and interpersonal factors are at the core of the help-seeking process. It is to these psychological costs of help seeking that we now turn.

Several general frameworks for evaluating these psychological costs have been proposed in recent years. Piliavin and Piliavin (1973) have presented a model for analyzing costs and benefits related to the help-giver's decision of whether or not to offer help, and this model is easily applied to the help-seeker's decision as well. As shown in Figure 13.3, costs can be attached to either seeking or not seeking help. The matrix assumes that the needy person calculates the appropriate cost ratios and then decides on a course of action. Although this model provides a general cost–benefit framework, it does not specify how various kinds of behaviors and perceptions related to help seeking are evaluated.

In a paper more specifically directed at understanding the avoidance–avoidance conflict between costs and rewards associated with help seeking, Wallston (1972, 1976) has proposed a model based on social learning theory that is intended to predict when individuals will seek necessary help in completing a competency-related task. The mediating cost concept in the needy person's avoidance–avoidance dilemma is embarrassment. Wallston suggests that embarrassment accrues from continued failure at solving a problem, but that publicly seeking help for the problem also creates embarrassment since it implies that an individual is not competent to complete the task independently. According to this reasoning, help seeking may alleviate the embarrassment of failure at the cost of embarrassment for appearing incompetent or inadequate. Wallston's model also incorporated the probability that a given act of help seeking will lead to success and/or embarrassment. In the model, the probability of attaining a given cost or reward is multiplied by the expected value of the effect. In an empirical test that partly corroborates her theory, Wallston (1976) found

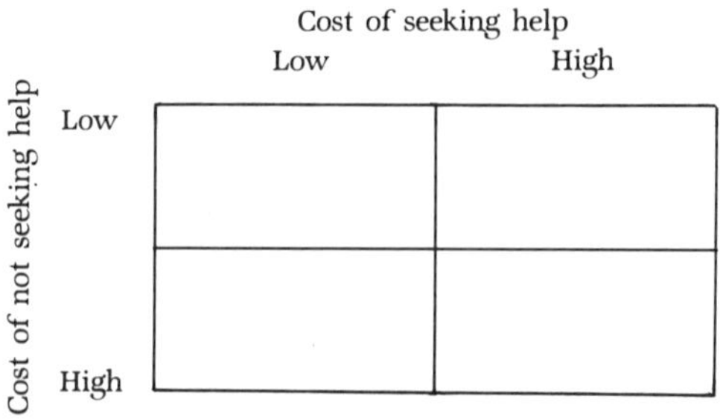

Cost of seeking help

		Low	High
Cost of not seeking help	Low		
	High		

Figure 13.3. Help-seeking cost matrix. Adapted from Piliavin and Piliavin (1973).

that subjects who eventually requested help on a task reported greatest embarrassment on the trial immediately prior to the help-request; and that subjects who never requested aid reported generally lower levels of embarrassment.

The importance of evaluating psychological costs is crucial to understanding help seeking, and several recently developed theoretical frameworks can be adapted to explain and elaborate this theme. Fisher, Nadler, and Whitcher (in press), for example, have presented a comprehensive theory in which all costs are presumed to be mediated by threat to the potential help-seeker's self-esteem. Greenberg (1980) has emphasized the negative effects of indebtedness resulting from interpersonal help seeking and receiving, and Gross, Wallston, and Piliavin (1979) summarized a number of studies that document high costs associated with seeking and receiving help in the context of reactance, attribution, and equity theories. These authors argue that negative feelings associated with seeking help are most likely to occur when people feel threatened with loss of esteem (threat to self-esteem) or freedom (reactance), interpret their help seeking as a sign of inadequacy (attribution), or feel uncomfortably indebted (equity).

Thus, it is clear that seeking help can be related to a number of negative effects or psychological costs. These potential costs can be classified into two general categories—personal costs related to self-esteem and self-concept, and social costs associated with interpersonal relationships and the perceptions of others. Several social psychological theories, especially attribution (Jones & Davis, 1965; Kelley, 1967) in the case of personal costs, and equity (Walster, Walster, & Berscheid, 1978; Adams, 1965) in the case of social costs, are useful in understanding why negative reactions to receiving help and inhibition about asking for help are so common in our society.

Personal Costs of Seeking Help

Perhaps the most important personal cost related to help-seeking is the damage to self-esteem that can occur when help-seekers interpret their own requests for aid as admissions of incompetence or inadequacy. Especially in a culture that values achievement and rugged independence, the act of asking for help often implies to individuals that they are failing to measure up to what they have been socialized to expect of themselves.

In their model for conceptualizing recipient reactions to aid, Fisher *et al.* (in press) cite nonconformity to this cultural ideal of self-sufficiency and the "inevitable" discomfort associated with the inequality and dependency inherent in the helping relationship as major sources of potential threat to self-esteem that may deter one from choosing to seek help.

It is important to note, however, that these particular cultural values have been considered "masculine" in North American society. Thus, although all members of this culture have been exposed to these ideals, it has been primarily the males who have been expected and pressured to emulate these standards of self-reliance (Brannon, 1976). Thus, the same cultural pressures that inhibit men from acknowledging problems and symptoms (see discussion of sex differences in the Perception of Problems section, this chapter) may create costs of asking for help that are higher for males than females in otherwise identical circumstances, and therefore fewer males than females may actually choose to seek help with their problems.

That a sex difference in actual help seeking exists has been well-documented in the literature. The utilization of a variety of medical, social, and mental health services has been directly related to sex, with women demonstrating higher utilization rates than men (e.g., Chesler, 1972; McKinlay, 1972; Phillips & Segal, 1969). Among the few laboratory studies that have included subjects of both sexes, women have consistently reported more positive attitudes toward help seeking than men (e.g., Fischer & Cohen, 1972; Fischer & Turner, 1970), and when responding to a variety of potential help-seeking situations, men reported significantly more often than women that they would not ask for help at all (DePaulo, 1978).

Findings such as these led McMullen (1980) to speculate that the behavior of "asking for help" has been included among the many activities and traits that are regarded as sex-typed in our culture. In her experimental investigation of the hypothesis that help seeking has been typed as "feminine," male and female subjects were asked to write stories about hypothetical male or female college students experiencing identical, common problems. They then rated their impressions of these same stimulus people under two conditions: when they decided to ask for help and when they chose to manage on their own. Overall, McMullen's results supported the hypothesized cultural double standard defining help seeking as appropriate for females and inappropriate for males. Female subjects included help seeking in their stories more than males and they were more positive toward help seeking in their evaluative ratings. That this response pattern is directly associated with underlying sex role norms was confirmed in that all subjects consistently rated the "ask for help" option as more feminine and less masculine than the "manage on own" option. Thus, it appears that seeking help may actually mean different things to males and females. In particular, males incur the heavy personal cost of deviating from "masculine" sex role standards when asking for help, while this same behavior for females is congruent with norms for appropriate "feminine" behavior.

Several recent papers (Fisher, Nadler, & Whitcher, in press; Gross, Wallston, & Piliavin, 1979; Tessler & Schwartz, 1972) have applied attribution theory concepts to understanding how help seeking can negatively affect self-esteem for both sexes. According to attribution theorists, humans are motivated to seek explanations for their own behavior. From this it follows that potential aid recipients are motivated to search for reasons to explain their requests for help.

When help seeking is not normative or cannot easily be attributed to external pressures, people in need tend to look for personal explanations. Although several positive explanations for help seeking are generally feasible, feelings of inadequacy and failure are commonly selected attributions. According to the Fisher, Nadler, and Whitcher (in press) model, such negative attributions threaten self-esteem, and that threat in turn has multiple effects, including derogation of the helper and the quality of the aid, and inhibition of subsequent help seeking (Nadler, Fisher, & Streufert, 1976).

Several studies support such attributional explanations for the phenomenon of help-seeking inhibition. For example, Broll, Gross, and Piliavin (1974) found that college students who were required to ask for help with a difficult logic problem received fewer units of necessary help than those who were able to accept regular offers of help. It was reasoned that the act of asking was inhibited for some participants because it was interpreted as an admission of inadequacy or incompetence. This finding was replicated in a field study demonstrating that welfare recipients received more units of aid when they were visited regularly by social workers than when they were required to initiate requests for service (Piliavin & Gross, 1977).

In addition, Tessler and Schwartz (1972) predicted and found that more help would be sought when students attributed responsibility for failure on a task to external factors rather than to themselves. Participants sought help sooner and more often in conditions where the task was described as so difficult that most people needed help to succeed (high normativeness treatment) than in conditions where the task appeared easy to accomplish (low normativeness, low difficulty treatment). Although there may be rare exceptions (Gerdes, 1973), in general help seeking has been inhibited in situations where there is potential for this behavior to be interpreted as demeaning or threatening to self-esteem.

Whether or not people attribute their own help seeking to personal inadequacy, another more social kind of negative attribution can create additional costs and inhibition. Help seekers may fear that other people will interpret their efforts at seeking help as a sign of incompetence and failure. For example, a person experiencing a problem may believe that it makes good sense to seek psychotherapy, but at the same time recognizes that friends, neighbors, and co-workers will interpret this act as a sign of weakness. In this example, clandestine or anonymous help seeking (Nadler &

Porat, 1978) may reduce costs; however, in many instances such covertness is impossible or attached to high inconvenience costs.

Conceptually, fear of others' negative attributions has social consequences and self-attribution has personal consequences; however, perceptions of others' feelings and attitudes toward the self can also have powerful effects on self-concept. As classic symbolic interaction theory proposes (Mead, 1934), self-concept develops and is maintained largely through interaction with significant others.

In one of the first analyses of the helping relationship that devotes almost equal time to the recipient, Brickman, Rabinowitz, Coates, Cohn, Kidder, and Karuza (1979) have developed a taxonomy of helping models that centers on attribution of responsibility to recipients for the origins and solutions of their problems. For example, according to this scheme, situations in which the help recipient is seen as responsible for both getting into and getting out of trouble are labeled the "moral model" and are characterized by self-help. These authors construct three other models using the remaining combinations of whether or not the recipient is responsible for the cause and/or remedy for a problem.

Although the Brickman et al. models have many implications for both helper and recipient sides of the helping interaction, what is most relevant to the help-seeking process is how attributions made by seekers, helpers, and others can affect potential help seekers. Very little research relevant to this question has yet been conducted; nonetheless, it is apparent that when needy people blame themselves for their present condition they are likely to be more hesitant to utilize services. This hypothesized inhibition could be affected by feelings of unworthiness or because potential helpers in the society have labeled the victims as undeserving. Obviously, inhibitions related to the origin of the problem can be changed by perceptions of responsibility for solutions. Although the effects of the interaction of these two kinds of attributions are not yet clear, the Brickman et al. models provide an intriguing perspective for conducting research focusing on help-seeking inhibition within an attributional framework. For example, Fisher and Farina (1979), and Farina, Fisher, Getter, and Fischer (1978) suggest that if a mental problem is viewed as a disease more than a social learning problem people may be more willing to seek help but less likely to involve themselves in the helping process.

Social Costs of Seeking Help

The personal costs discussed above are often potent inhibitors of help seeking; they are often invidious, dysfunctional, and ego deflating, and they usually operate at a level less than full awareness. On the other hand, social costs, which can also function as inhibitors, are much more likely to be consciously considered in making the decision of whether or not to seek help. Weighing and balancing of social costs for help-seeking decisions is frequently governed by common sense versions of equity theory (Adams, 1965; Walster, Walster, & Berscheid, 1978), especially indebtedness theory (Greenberg, 1980).

According to the indebtedness formulation, receipt of a benefit from another person creates an uncomfortable drive state of indebtedness that can be reduced or alleviated by repayment. Since potential recipients are often aware of this phenomenon, the unpleasant prospect of indebtedness can be calculated in a cost–benefit ratio prior to asking for aid. In many instances a needy person contemplating a help request is faced with two possible negative consequences: (a) the burden to repay perhaps at an inconvenient time if the debt is called in, and (b) guilt and other negative feelings associated with violating a strongly inculcated norm of reciprocity (Gouldner, 1960). Thus the social costs of receiving help involve either the obligation of repayment, or if no reciprocity is intended, the penalty, at least for middle-class North Americans, of attendant guilt feelings.

A number of laboratory studies offer support for the strength and extent of the quid pro quo norm. For example, college students tend to reciprocate in a manner that approximately equals what they have received (Wilke & Lanzetta, 1970; Gross & Latané, 1974); and Greenberg and Shapiro (1971) have shown that asking for help is inhibited when the potential recipient expects that it will be difficult or impossible to offer help in return. North American middle-class society abounds with evidence of the importance of equity in help seeking. Perhaps the richest source of this evidence is found in common everyday remarks such as "How can I ever repay you for this kindness?", and popular maxims such as "It is better to give than to receive."

Perceived Helper Costs

Help-seeking inhibition associated with accepting help without opportunity of equal repayment is relatively well documented, but another more subtle kind of equity calculation may also affect whether or not aid is sought. In addition to assessing or predicting their own equity state after obtaining help, recipients may also estimate the cost–reward balance for the potential helper. This perceived balance sheet for a helper's inputs and outcomes may determine whether or not a needy person is willing to obtain help from a given helper.

Specifically, it can be derived from equity theory that a recipient will feel less obligation to repay and hence less inhibition when (a) helper inputs measured in effort or cost are relatively low, and (*b*) when helper outcomes or rewards are relatively positive or high. According to this reasoning, recipient perceptions of helper costs and benefits can mediate the recipient's estimate of the equity in a potential helping relationship. If the helper's net outcomes are viewed as relatively positive—that is, if the helper will benefit from helping or at least will not incur heavy costs—help is more likely to be requested.

Several laboratory studies have been designed to investigate the effects of helper costs and benefits on help-seeking inhibition. Gross and Somersan (1974) assigned participants to a tedious long-division task but permitted them to delegate all or part of this chore to a confederate helper. In one study, fewer problems were shared with the helper when the helper's effort was high (hand calculation was necessary) than when effort was perceived as relatively easy (helper had access to an electronic calculator). In a second study using a similar task, participants assigned more problems or asked for help sooner when an actor posing as a helper could benefit by helping because he was paid by the job rather than by the hour. These studies support the notion that needy people are more willing to seek help when helper input is low and when helper outcomes are high. Under such conditions, according to Greenberg's (1980) indebtedness theory, the help seeker should feel less obligation to repay after help is received.

A more recent study conducted by DePaulo and Fisher (1980) confirms the importance of helper costs in the subjective calculation of the costs of asking for help. In this study, cost to the helper was operationalized according to what alternative activity for the helper would be interrupted if help was asked for and delivered. In high-cost situations, participants believed that they would be interrupting a graduate student helper's work on her dissertation; in low-cost conditions the helper was not engaged in any task at the time help was needed. As expected, participants in this study asked for less help when the helper was believed to be busy with her dissertation. Aside from the possibility that help-seeking inhibition occurred because of anticipated indebtedness, DePaulo and Fisher offer two additional explanations. They suggest that the needy participants may have empathized with the helper's feelings about not wanting to be disturbed, or that the help seeker may have feared a negative reaction after intruding on a busy helper.

Inferences from these data can be generalized to nonlaboratory settings as well. For example, college students usually are aware that professors are paid on an annual salary basis and that they do not receive direct financial benefits from assisting students. This knowledge of incremental net cost for potential helper professors may inhibit students from approaching them even during office hours. Even if help is sought, length of questions or visits may be abbreviated and the overall quality of help may be negatively affected. On the other hand, there should be less inhibition when approaching a professional helper who is paid by the unit of help offered, for example, a psychotherapist who is paid by the hour. Even less inhibition should be present when the potential helper wants to help, benefits from helping, or needs to help as part of a role or to maintain employment. For example, in some social agencies, counseling services, or recreation centers, staff jobs depend on the maintenance of a minimum case load or number of help users.

Summary and Conclusion

The foregoing analysis was designed to separate the help-seeking process into elements and stages (Figure 13.1), and then to focus on these elements in the context of social psychological theory with the aim of achieving better understanding of what facilitates and inhibits help-seeking. Most of the studies, concepts, and theories duscussed here are relevant to two critical stages in the process: (a) the perception of whether a situation is seen as a problem and if so whether the problem is amenable to help, and (b) given that a problem is recognized, the decision about whether to help oneself, seek help from others, or accept the problem. A third major stage involving selection and use of strategies and tactics for obtaining help (see Figure 13.2) was only briefly discussed in this paper, partly because this area is more applied than conceptual, and also because very little social psychology research has yet been completed in this area. Recent exceptions are Rosen and Shulman's (1978) intensive study of the coping and help-seeking tactics used by widows, and research indicating that class and other variables can affect help-seeking style (Asser, 1978).

Throughout the discussion we have pointed to places where social psychological theories, especially derivations of attribution and equity concepts, are relevant and useful in understanding the help-seeking process. Although direct applications are outside the scope of this chapter, we could not resist offering a few applied suggestions. Eventually these theories and concepts might be applied in designing interventions from two perspectives: (a) training help seekers to pursue their self-interest more assertively by recognizing and seeking useful help when it is needed or desired; (b) designing help-delivery systems that facilitate help seeking and service utilization.

Both of these perspectives are uncommon in that the preponderance of effort, both in theoretical understanding of the helping relationship and in applied design of delivery systems, has been derived from the viewpoint of the help giver. It is our hope that analyses such as this one will help remedy this unbalanced approach to helping relationships by sensitizing researchers and practitioners to the psychology of the potential help seeker.

Acknowledgment

We are indebted to Irving M. Piliavin, whose 1972 model for help utilization serves as the basis for the model presented in Figure 13.1 of this chapter. Thanks are due to Jeffrey D. Fisher, Susan K. Green and Barbara Strudler Wallston for useful comments.

References

Adams, J. S. Injustice in social exchange. In L. Berkowitz (Ed.), *Advances in experimental social psychology* (Vol. 2). New York: Academic Press, 1965.

Antonovsky, A., & Hartman, H. Delay in the detection of cancer: A review of the literature. *Health Education Monographs*, 1974, *2*, 98–128.

Asser, E. S. Social class and help-seeking behavior. *American Journal of Community Psychology*. 1978, *6*, 465–475.

Bar-Tal, D. *Prosocial behavior*. New York: John Wiley & Sons, 1976.

Brannon, R. The male sex role: Our culture's blueprint of manhood, and what it's done for us lately. In D. S. David & R. Brannon (Eds.), *The forty-nine percent majority. The male sex role*. Reading, Mass.: Addison-Wesley, 1976.

Brickman, P., Rabinowitz, V. C., Coates, D., Cohn, E., Kidder, L., & Karuza, J. *Helping*. Unpublished manuscript, University of Michigan, 1979.

Broll, L., Gross, A. E., & Piliavin, I. Effects of offered and requested help on help seeking and reactions to being helped. *Journal of Applied Social Psychology*, 1974, *4*, 244–258.

Chesler, P. *Women and madness*. New York: Avon Books, 1972.

Darley, J., & Latané, B. *The unresponsive bystander: Why doesn't he help?* New York: Appleton-Century-Crofts, 1970.

DePaulo, B. M. Help-seeking from the recipients' point of view. *JSAS Catalog of Selected Documents in Psychology*, 1978, *8*, 62. (Ms. No. 1721).

DePaulo, B. M., & Fisher, J. D. The costs of asking for help. *Basic and Applied Social Psychology*, 1980, *1*, 23–35.

Farina, A., Fisher, J. D., Getter, H., Fischer, E. H. Some consequences of changing people's views regarding the nature of mental illness. *Journal of Abnormal Psychology*. 1978, *87*, 272–279.

Fischer, E. H., & Cohen, S. L. Demographic correlates of attitudes toward seeking professional psychological help. *Journal of Consulting and Clinical Psychology*, 1972, *39*, 70–74.

Fischer, E. H., & Turner, J. L. Orientations to seeking professional help: Development and research utility of an attitude scale. *Journal of Consulting and Clinical Psychology*, 1970, *35*, 79–90.

Fisher, J. D., & Farina, A. Consequences of beliefs about the nature of mental disorders. *Journal of Abnormal Psychology*. 1979, *88*, 320–327.

Fisher, J. D., Nadler, A., & Whitcher, S. J. *Recipient reactions to aid: A conceptual review and a new theoretical framework. Psychological Bulletin, in press.*

Gerdes, J. *Attribution of responsibility for failure, stability of failure, achievement motivation, and help seeking*. Unpublished doctoral dissertation, Duke University, 1973.

Gottlieb, B. H. Lay influences in the utilization and provision of health services: A review. *Canadian Psychological Review*, 1976, *2*, 126–136.

Gouldner, A. W. The norm of reciprocity: A preliminary statement. *American Sociological Review*, 1960, *25*, 161–178.

Gourash, N. Help-seeking: A review of the literature. *American Journal of Community Psychology*, 1978, *6*, 413–423.

Greenberg, M. S. A theory of indebtedness. In K. J. Gergen, M. S. Greenberg, and R. S. Willis (Eds.), *Social exchange: Advances in theory and research*. New York: Plenum, 1980.

Greenberg, M. S., & Shapiro, S. P. Indebtedness: An adverse aspect of asking for and receiving help. *Sociometry*, 1971, *34*, 290–301.

Gross, A. E., Fisher, J. D., Nadler, A., Stiglitz, E., & Craig, C. Initiating contact with a women's counseling service: Some correlates of help-utilization. *Journal of Community Psychology*, 1979, *7*, 42–49.

Gross, A. E., & Latané, J. G. Receiving help, reciprocation, and interpersonal attraction. *Journal of Applied Social Psychology*, 1974, *4*, 210–223.

Gross, A. E., & Somersan, S. Helper effort as an inhibitor of help-seeking. Paper presented at the annual meeting of the Psychonomic Society, Boston 1974.

Gross, A. E., Wallston, B. S., & Piliavin, I. M. Reactance, attribution, equity, and the help recipient. *Journal of Applied Social Psychology*, 1979, *9*, 297–313.

Gross, A. E., Wallston, B. S., & Piliavin, I. M. The help-recipient's perspective. In D. H. Smith, J. Macauley, and Associates, *Participation in social and political activities*. San Francisco: Jossey-Bass, 1980, 355–369.

Gurin, G., Veroff, J., & Feld, S. *Americans view their mental health*. New York: Basic Books, 1960.

Hollingshead, A., & Redlich, F. *Social class and mental illness*. New York: John Wiley & Sons, 1958.

Jones, E. E., & Davis, K. E. From acts to dispositions: The attribution process in person perception. In L. Berkowitz (Ed.), *Advances in experimental social psychology* (Vol. 2). New York: Academic Press, 1965.

Kadushin, C. Individual decisions to undertake psychotherapy. *Administrative Science Quarterly*, 1958–1959, *3*, 379–411.

Kasl, S. V., & Cobb, S. Health behavior, illness behavior, and sick role behavior. *Archives of Environmental Health*, 1966, *12*, 246–267.

Kelley, H. H. Attribution theory in social psychology. In D. Levine (Ed.), *Nebraska Symposium on Motivation*. Lincoln: University of Nebraska Press, 1967.

Koos, E. L. *Health of Regionville*. New York: Columbia University Press, 1954.

Krebs, D. L. Altruism: An examination of the concept and a review of the literature. *Psychological Bulletin*, 1970, *73*, 258–302.

Kulka, R. A. *Seeking formal help for personal problems: 1957 and 1976*. Paper presented at the meeting of the American Psychological Association, Toronto, 1978.

Macauley, J. R., & Berkowitz, L. (Eds.) *Altruism and helping behavior*. New York: Academic Press, 1970.

McKinlay, J. B. Some approaches and problems in the study of the use of services: An overview. *Journal of Health and Social Behavior*, 1972, *13*, 115–152.

McMullen, P. A. *A sex role analysis of help-seeking behavior*. Unpublished doctoral dissertation, University of Missouri, St. Louis, 1980.

Mead, G. H. *Mind, self and society*. 1934. Reprint. Chicago: University of Chicago Press, 1962.

Mechanic, D. *Medical Sociology*. London: Collier-MacMillan, 1968.

Nadler, A., Fisher, J. D., & Streufert, S. When helping hurts: The effect of donor-recipient similarity and recipient self-esteem on reactions to aid. *Journal of Personality*, 1976, *44*, 392–409.

Nadler, A., & Porat, I. Names do not help: Effects of anonymity and locus of need attribution on help-seeking behavior. *Personality and Social Psychology Bulletin*, 1978, *4*, 624–626.

Phillips, D. L., & Segal, B. E. Sexual status and psychiatric symptoms. *American Sociological Review*, 1969, *34*, 58–72.

Piliavin, I. *A model of help utilization.* Paper presented at the meeting of the American Psychological Association, Honolulu, 1972.

Piliavin, I., & Gross, A. E. The effects of separation of services and income maintenance on AFDC recipients' perceptions and use of social services: Results of a field experiment. *Social Service Review*, 1977, *51*, 389–406.

Piliavin, J. A., & Piliavin, I. *The Good Samaritan: Why does he help?* Unpublished manuscript, University of Wisconsin, 1973.

Rosen, A., & Shulman, A. D. *Lifecycle related needs and interpersonal coping strategies of widows.* Paper presented at Gerontological Society Meetings, Dallas, 1978.

Rosenblatt, D., & Suchman, E. A. The underutilization of medical-care services by blue-collarites. In A. B. Shostak & W. Gomberg (Eds.), *Blue-collar world: Studies of the American worker.* Englewood Cliffs, N.J.: Prentice-Hall, 1964.

Rushton, J. P. *Altruism, Socialization, and Society.* Englewood Cliffs, N.J.: Prentice-Hall, 1980.

Schenthal, J. E. Multiphasic screening of the well patient. *Journal of the American Medical Association*, 1960, *172*, 51–64.

Shulman, A. D., Rosen, A., & Gross, A. E. *Needs and behavioral strategies of widows throughout the life cycle.* Research proposal funded by National Institute of Aging, 1976. St. Louis: Washington University.

Staub, E. *Positive social behavior and morality. Vol. 1: Social and personal influences.* New York: Academic Press, 1978.

Staub, E. *Positive social behavior and morality. Vol. 2: Socialization and development.* New York: Academic Press, 1979.

Stoeckle, J., Zola, I. K., & Davidson, G. E. On going to see the doctor: The contributions of the patient to the decision to seek medical aid. *Journal of Chronic Diseases*, 1963, *16*, 975–989.

Tessler, R. C., & Schwartz, S. H. Help-seeking, self-esteem, and achievement motivation: An attributional analysis. *Journal of Personality and Social Psychology*, 1972, *21*, 318–326.

Trivers, R. L. The evolution of reciprocal altruism. *The Quarterly Review of Biology.* 1971, *46*, 35–57.

Wallston, B. S. *The effects of sex role, self-esteem, and expectations of future interaction with an audience on help seeking.* Unpublished doctoral dissertation, University of Wisconsin, 1972.

Wallston, B. S. The effects of sex-role ideology, self-esteem and expected future interactions with an audience on male help-seeking. *Sex Roles*, 1976, *2*, 353–365.

Walster, E., Walster, G. W., & Berscheid, E. *Equity: Theory and research.* Boston: Allyn & Bacon, 1978.

Wilke, H., & Lanzetta, J. T. The obligation to help: The effects of amount of prior help on subsequent helping behavior. *Journal of Experimental Social Psychology.* 1970, *6*, 488–493.

Zborowski, M. Cultural components in response to pain. In E. G. Jaco (Ed.), *Patients, physicians, and illness.* Glencoe, Ill.: Free Press, 1958.

Zola, I. K. Illness behavior of the working: Implications and recommendations. In A. B. Shostak and W. Gomberg (Eds.), *Blue-collar world: Studies of the American worker.* Englewood Cliffs, N.J.: Prentice-Hall, 1964.

Zola, I. K. Culture and symptoms: An analysis of patients presenting complaints. *American Sociological Review*, 1966, *31*, 615–630.

Chapter 14

Helping and Cooperation: A Self-Based Motivational Model[1]

SHALOM H. SCHWARTZ

JUDITH A. HOWARD

The increase in studies of cooperation and helping illustrates the impact of current sociopolitical problems on the selection of topics for research. Alarming rates of population growth; critical shortages of energy resources and concomitant predictions of widespread food shortages; growing interdependence of nations in political, economic, and even athletic spheres—all these phenomena attest to the reality of an increasing need for cooperation. Paralleling this need for cooperation is an apparent decrease in the incidence of cooperative, prosocial responses in situations where help is clearly required. Although the Kitty Genovese murder may seem dated, the many summaries of the decade of the 1970s again decried spreading individual isolation and anonymity, moral apathy, and the increase of "blind" aggression against an increasingly unreachable sociopolitical system. Thus, according to these analyses, precisely when the need for cooperation and helping is intensifying, the occurrence of these behaviors is in rapid decline.

[1] Preparation of this manuscript was supported by NSF grant BNS 77-23287 to the first author.

COOPERATION AND HELPING BEHAVIOR
Theories and Research

Definitions

What are cooperation and helping and how are they related? Both involve human relationships characterized by dependence (Grzelak & Derlega, Chapter 1 of this book). The helping relationship has been characterized as involving the unilateral dependence of people in need on others perceived as able to help, whereas cooperation has been defined as a relationship of mutual dependence among actors. Because the implications of mutual dependence are rather different from those of unilateral dependence, cooperation and helping behavior have been viewed as theoretically distinct, and research on them has proceeded independently.

In contrast, we view both helping and cooperation as characterized by mutual dependence. Dependence generally involves relations in which the costs and benefits (rewards) that one party obtains from her or his own behavior are determined at least partly by the actions of another party. Mutual dependence means that the costs and benefits for all parties to a relationship are determined by their joint behavior. What distinguishes helping from cooperation in our view is the nature of the jointly determined costs and benefits rather than the nature of the dependence relation.

Marwell and Schmidt (1975) define cooperation as joint behavior that is directed toward a goal in which the participants have a common interest. Usually the reward is the same for both participants. The classic illustration of the research on cooperation is the prisoner's dilemma game (Luce & Raiffa, 1957), in which the outcomes, commonly operationalized as material benefits or losses, are a function of the behavior of both participants. Although the theory of cooperation does not limit rewards to those of a material nature, we will suggest that the emphasis on material rewards prevalent in the research on cooperation does distinguish helping from cooperation.

Helping typically entails a situation in which a person in need of aid is dependent on another to incur some costs in order to provide help. Associated with this characterization of helping is a view of the helper as active and in control of outcomes, and of the helpee as the passive, dependent recipient of outcomes. Thus the reward is experienced by the helpee alone, the costs (and decision control) by the helper alone.

Although accurate in a limited sense, this conception of helping is incomplete. The normative model of helping we present here identifies a more complex reward structure. We propose that both parties gain rewards and both experience costs, but their rewards and costs differ. The helper acts to gain psychological, social, and/or material rewards; the helpee gains material rewards. The helper typically incurs material or social costs, while the helpee incurs social or psychological costs. We will shortly distinguish altruism from other acts of helping on the basis of the rewards the helper seeks.

The costs and rewards of each actor in a helping situation are at least partly contingent on the actions of the others; hence the actors are mutually dependent. A man who offers to assist an infirm woman across the street, for example, is dependent on her not to victimize him. If she picks the helper's pocket, he will suffer not only material costs and foregoing of the pleasure of enhanced self-esteem but also the psychological stress of shaken faith both in humanity and in his own judgment, and possibly the barbs of social ridicule. Thus situations of helping are similar to those of cooperation in that both involve the interdependence typical of social interaction, including the investment of costs and receipt of benefits, by some or all people involved. It is the nature of the cost and reward distribution that distinguishes helping from cooperation.

The normative model of altruism and helping presented in this chapter elaborates the decision-making process underlying helping, spelling out the roles of cognitive awareness, abilities (resources), both internalized and external normative and nonnormative costs and benefits, and person and situational influences that are particularly relevant to helping. This analysis may illuminate discussions of analogous variables in the literature on cooperative decision making—that is, information, abilities, trust, risk, etc. (Marwell & Schmidt, 1975; Dawes, 1980). The understanding of cooperation might be enhanced by consideration of this normative approach to helping, particularly in its attention to the nature of psychological and moral rewards. Similarly, an understanding of altruism–helping may be improved through examination of the nature of the dependence that obtains in cooperative relationships.

Helping and altruism are not interchangeable concepts, although both refer to normatively guided behaviors. Norms are shared expectations about how we ought to act, enforced by the threat of sanctions or the promise of rewards. Helping is motivated by *social* norms, that is, group expectations backed by externally defined and imposed rewards and punishments. Altruism differs from helping in its self-based locus of normative motivation. Altruism is motivated by *personal* norms, situation-specific behavioral expectations generated from one's own internalized values, backed by self-administered sanctions and rewards.

If a doctor, for example, wearing a white coat and carrying a bag of medical instruments, aids a heart attack victim she encounters in a lunchtime crowd, motivated by the social norm that doctors should help disabled victims, she is offering *help*. This same doctor is viewed as behaving *altruistically* if, devoid of her professional costume, and sparked by her own internalized values dictating that she offer assistance, she leaves a concert to aid a victim. Thus, acts may be helpful regardless of the actor's internal motivation, but they are altruistic only when motivated by a self-based desire to help others. In sum, helping, altruism, and cooperation are distinguished from one another by the nature of the costs and benefits associated with the behavioral choice. Aspects of each type of behavior are considered within the normative decision-making model we will now present. Following this presentation, we will examine the relationship of the model to other theories of altruism and helping.

A Normative Model of Helping

Overview

This model describes a decision-making process through which personal and social norms mediate the influence of general values on altruistic and/ or helping behavior. This process includes five sequential stages illustrated in the following example. Two students, Art and Sally, receive letters requesting them to participate in a fund-raising drive for WORT, a local, listener-sponsored radio station. Art decides not to help, but Sally volunteers to distribute pamphlets for the station. Why?

ATTENTION

Perceptions about need, potential action, and ability derive from the particular aspects of the immediate situation to which people attend. For example, Sally may notice the paragraph describing need while Art passes over this paragraph, focusing instead on the sentence appealing for help. Alternatively, both may perceive need, recognize that canvassing would help, and feel capable of this action.

MOTIVATION

This set of perceptions may activate the individual's unique internal value system, generating specific personal norms—feelings of moral obligation to perform or refrain from particular acts. Thus, even if Art and Sally both think they can help, the implications of helping may generate quite different personal norms from their individual internalized systems of values. Art's complex structure of internalized values may lead him to view fund-raising activities as infringements on people's rights. Thus the personal norm he constructs in this situation may enjoin him to avoid imposing on his neighbors. Sally's perception of the situation may activate a different set of values. Her values may lead her to construct a specific self-expectation to volunteer in this situation, accompanied by feelings of moral obligation.

EVALUATION

The potential moral and nonmoral costs and benefits of engaging in specific behaviors are evaluated. Suppose both Art and Sally generate personal norms prescribing help. Nonetheless, in evaluating the pros and cons of behavior, Art may feel the moral benefits of saving the station clearly do not outweigh the social or material costs of canvassing, whereas Sally feels they do.

DEFENSE

This step follows if evaluation indicates that costs and benefits are relatively balanced. Since it is easier to distort our own perceptions than to control the material and social outcomes of action, defenses usually reduce conflict by weakening our own feelings of moral obligation. This is accomplished by redefining some element of the situation perceived in stages 1 or 2, that is, by changing perceptions about need, potential actions, ability, or the relevance of one's moral values. (The defector in a cooperation situation may construct similar rationales to justify taking a noncooperative action.) With this new definition, the person recycles through subsequent steps in the decision-making process until evaluation of costs and benefits points to a clearly preferable action (or to inaction).

For Art the anticipated costs of provoking his neighbors' annoyance and of the time and energy involved in canvassing may outweigh the moral benefits of self-affirmation and the moral costs of violating any sense of obligation. To defend against moral self-deprecation, Art may redefine the situation: The station is not really in dire straits; the canvassing won't raise enough money anyway. By denying the reality of need or efficacy of action, Art can ignore the appeal with minimal moral costs.

BEHAVIOR

Overt helping or inaction follows from the preceding evaluation. Art throws out the appeal letter, but Sally signs up to help; both feel satisfied with their decisions. Nonetheless, each may experience lingering dissatisfaction. Art's redefinition of the situation may not totally convince him that he has no moral obligation to help, and Sally may worry about the time she is committing.

In sum, our model describes a sequential process activated by the perception of need. This in turn generates value-based self-expectations for behavior and associated feelings of moral obligation. The moral and nonmoral costs and benefits of action are evaluated, producing either a behavioral decision or conflict. Conflict leads to defensive reactions that weaken feelings of moral obligation, facilitating attainment of a behavioral decision.

Although the example we have presented highlights cognitive processes, the model does not require conscious awareness. Consequently, people cannot be relied upon to report their relevant cognitions and emotions accurately. This raises the question whether the model is testable. As we elaborate the model, we will point to types of analyses suitable for establishing an empirical base for this view of normative decision making.

Elaborated Model

The decision maker's progress through the specific steps that occur in each stage of this model is influenced by situation and person variables that determine the initial activation of the internalized value structure, the perceived relevance of social norms, and the viability of defenses against feelings of obligation. For each stage in the model, important person and situation variables are identified, and available empirical evidence for their operation is cited. No single study has tested the full causal process represented in the complete model, but tests of connections among various parts have been reported (see Figure 14.1).

ATTENTION

During the attention stage, the actor becomes aware of those characteristics of the specific situation that determine whether a decision is needed. Perceptions of the situation determine the appropriateness of particular actions. If the need for a decision becomes apparent, and actions that address the need can be identified and executed, those actions defined as appropriate determine which internalized values are relevant. There are three steps in the attention stage.

Awareness of a Person in a State of Need   First, the person in need must be noticed; second, his or her state must be defined as needy. Becoming aware of need contradicts our general expectation that the welfare of those around us will be relatively satisfactory. The undesirable discrepancy between this expectation and the perceived present state of affairs motivates action to reduce this discrepancy. Thus the "motor" of this normative decision-making model, like other cognitive discrepancy models of motivation (e.g., Deci, 1975; Reykowski, 1975), is the need to reduce perceived discrepancies between actual and desired conditions.

Consistent with recent attention to the importance of salience effects (Taylor & Fiske, 1978), two situational factors, salience and clarity of need, influence both the initial noticing of need and the definition of the perceived need as serious. Spelling out the detailed needs of the family of a woman requiring a bone marrow transplant in a study by Schwartz (1970), for example, made need more salient and clear, eliciting more volunteering to

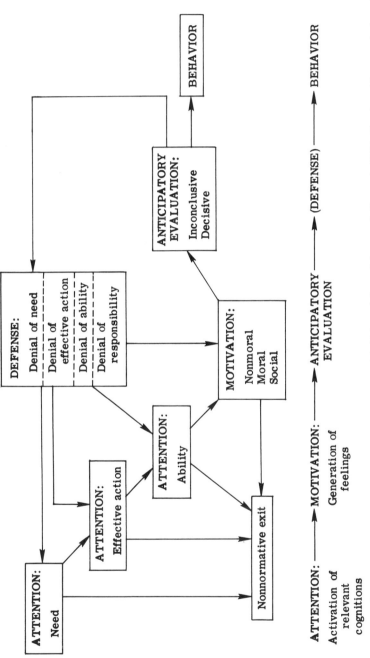

Figure 14.1 Cycling through a normative decision-making model. (Adapted from Schwartz & Howard, 1981. Reprinted by permission of Lawrence Erlbaum Associates.)

be a transplant donor. Dawes (1980) points out that limitations on cognitive abilities may prevent thorough comprehension of the real costs and benefits in a cooperation situation. These limitations may also impair cognitive processing in helping situations.

Situational cues also influence whether another's need will be defined as sufficiently serious to warrant remedial action. For example, passers-by are more likely to offer aid when a victim appears to collapse from a heart attack than from an injured knee, presumably because a heart attack is defined as more serious (Staub & Baer, 1974). The seriousness of perceived need also influences the evaluation and defense stages of the model. The success of attempts to justify one's mistaken interference in another's affairs increases, for example, if one can claim the victim's need appeared serious.

Individual differences in receptivity to situational need cues have also been found to influence the awareness of need and hence helping behavior. Awareness of the specific negative consequences for others of remaining in their current needy state is critical to this normative decision-making process, heightening the perceived discrepancy between actual and desired conditions. The Awareness of Consequences Scale (AC; Schwartz, 1968a) measures this tendency to become aware of the consequences for others of remaining in their current state. The scale, a test of insight into how people make choices, presents six story segments, each depicting a situation in which a person's decision may affect the welfare of others. The potential consequences of the person's decision for the others are not spelled out. Respondents are asked to describe the inner dialogue of the actor in each story as he decides what to do. Responses are coded for the extent to which the needs of others enter into the decision process.

In situations where the moral desirability of a behavior is widely accepted, AC is positively associated with that behavior. The higher their AC scores, for example, the more likely students were to be helpful and considerate toward their peers in residential groups ($r = .27$, Schwartz, 1968a). More interesting is evidence that awareness of a person in need is influenced by the interaction among situation and person factors (Schwartz, 1974). When the needs underlying a Head Start campaign were not spelled out, the volunteering behavior of college women was significantly correlated with their AC scores ($r = .34$). When serious need was described, AC did not influence helping behavior ($r = -.27$). Presumably the situational salience of need made women sufficiently aware, rendering superfluous any further impact of their individual tendency to become aware of need.

Identification of Actions That Might Relieve This Need   Once the awareness of a person in need is activated, particular actions that can relieve this need must be identified. Those situational factors that influence the awareness and definition of need also define the scope of relevant actions. If situational cues suggest that a collapsed person has suffered a heart attack, wrapping him in a blanket is seen as appropriate but rousing him to physical exercise is not. The necessity of choice among possible actions takes us to the next step in the normative decision-making model. The choice of actions determines which values will be activated. If no actions are recognized as appropriate, even after searching for a way the need might be relieved, the decision terminates. The actor does not proceed to generate personal norms or to assess social expectations or material outcomes.

Recognition of Own Ability to Engage in These Actions Once potentially helpful actions are recognized, internalized values become relevant only for those actions a person feels able to execute. If a woman with a heart condition witnessed the heart attack, for example, she might feel incapable of helping. Her failure to intervene would not have implications for her internalized moral values because no personal norms would be generated. Bystanders' perceived ability to help was manipulated directly in a study in which a woman was threatened by a dangerous rat (Schwartz & Ben David, 1976). Students who were persuaded they were unable to handle rats helped substantially less than those persuaded they were able to do so, presumably because relevant values were less likely to be activated in the low-ability group.

Perceived ability may also influence decision making during later steps in the model. Attributions of ability are associated with general feelings of competence, satisfaction, confidence (Weiner, Russell, & Lerman, 1978), and good mood (Rosenhan, Karylowski, Salorey, & Hargis, 1981). These feelings affect the anticipated social and physical costs of helping (Isen, Shalker, Clark, & Karp, 1978) and the evaluation of these costs. Students who believed themselves unable to handle the dangerous rat, for example, were more likely both to anticipate that they could deflect social criticism by claiming inability and to expect failure if they tried to intervene.

Thus far we have focused on the sequence of steps that activate perceptions required for normative decision-making. The individual actor may not generate each of these perceptions. The perceived severity of need may be insufficient to stimulate a search for appropriate actions. Alternatively, no such actions may be recognized, or relevant actions may be missing from the actor's repertoire. Unless each of these perceptions is activated in turn, the decision-making process ends prior to norm construction. The objective result is inaction. Unlike inaction at a later stage, however, this decision not to act is not based on internalized values.

GENERATION OF FEELINGS OF OBLIGATION

If a person perceives actions as relevant to another's need and feels capable of performing these actions, he or she considers their implications. We distinguish three types of implications: (a) physical, material, and nonmoral psychological implications that follow directly from the action; (b) implications for the actor's internalized moral values; (c) social implications, that is, outcomes dependent on the reactions of other people.

Every act requires some effort and time; thus there are always at least some physical and material costs of behavior. Many acts also have direct psychological consequences. Leaping into the sea to rescue a drowning stranger, for example, is dangerous (physical costs), will ruin one's clothes (material costs), and will provide a thrill (nonmoral psychological benefits). Although these nonmoral implications are not sharply delimited here because they are not uniquely important for a model of normative decision-making, people do weigh them together with normative considerations during the evaluation of costs and benefits. Our central concern is with the psychological implications that actions have for people's internalized moral value systems. Social implications are also important for a normative decision-making model insofar as people use perceived social norms as cues to the social responses that acts will elicit.

Internalized Moral Values and Personal Norms   Each person has a unique organized cognitive structure of values. Some values are particularly relevant to moral choices (e.g., compassion), whereas others are not (e.g., logic). These values vary from person to person in their importance to the self, their specificity, their interconnections, and their relationships to experience and to overt expression (Bem, 1970; Rokeach, 1973; Rosenberg, 1979; Schwartz, 1977). No two people have precisely the same value structure; hence, the value implications of engaging in a specific behavior vary across people.

Among the most important values for altruistic helping are equity and justice. Equity and justice are general social norms insofar as they are invoked as legitimate social expectations in order to induce compliant helping (Berkowitz & Walster, 1976; Lerner, 1981). But most social psychological analyses of the influences of equity and justice on individual behavior treat these as internalized values from which specific personal norms are generated in the behavioral situation (e.g., Greenberg, 1978).

A personal norm is constructed for each potential action focused on throughout the attention stage of the model. Personal norms are constructed by scanning the implications of these actions for one's relevant internalized values. In other words, the actor asks herself whether she is morally responsible for these actions in this situation, given her own general internalized values. Personal norms consist of both cognitive and affective components—a self-expectation for behavior and emotions associated with this expectation.

The more central to one's self-evaluation the values implicated by an action, the stronger the emotional arousal. Anticipated compliance elicits feelings of self-satisfaction, and anticipated inaction elicits feelings of self-deprecation. Thus the sanctions attached to personal norms are based in the self-concept. Because the stimuli that activate the scanning of internalized values are situationally variable, the personal norms generated are momentary rather than enduring standards. Whereas values are relatively enduring preferences for general outcomes or modes of behavior, personal norms are situation-specific reflections of the cognitive and affective implications of a person's values for specific actions.

Because personal norms are conceptualized as constructed in the choice situation, measuring personal norms in advance of behavioral choice is problematic. Measuring relatively stable underlying values may reveal little about personal norms. We cannot know what feelings of obligation will actually be generated from a person's unique complex of values unless we know what aspects of a situation are attended to and what specific actions are considered. Thus we ask people to describe the degree of moral obligation they would feel if faced with specified behavioral choices.[2]

Although personal norms may be constructed for any value-relevant behavior, they have been studied primarily with reference to unusual, non-recurrent actions (e.g., organ donation, volunteering to tutor blind children). This invalidates the alternative explanation that a relationship between personal norms and behavior emerges through the construction of norms that appear consistent with and justify prior behavior.

Social Norms   If the perceptions activated in the attention stage of the model point to general social expectations for particular actions, these perceived social norms may also influence the behavioral decision. Here the actor asks himself whether he is responsible for action in terms of social norms. Like personal norms, social norms have a cognitive component—an awareness of a social standard for behavior—and an affective component—feelings of shame, fear, pride, etc., in anticipation of others' reactions to the behavior. Both the informal and formal sanctions associated with such norms are based on social rather than internalized values. People comply with social norms to maximize socially mediated external reinforcements.

---

[2] The validity of this procedure depends on the extent to which respondents actually project themselves into the hypothetical situations described in the personal norm items. A typical format is: "The following questions ask whether you personally would feel a moral obligation to be a transplant donor under various circumstances. Do you think that this is something you ought to do or something you ought not do? . . . If a close relative of yours needed a bone marrow transplant and you were a suitable donor, would you feel a moral obligation to donate bone marrow?"

Social norms are influential only when the actor believes that a relevant social group shares a behavioral expectation and when he attends to that shared expectation while reaching the decision.

Measuring social norms entails determining whether the actor perceives that others share specific expectations for behavior in a given situation. We therefore measure *perceived* social norms by asking about the social obligations people believe that others would apply to them in concrete situations. The typical format asks "how the people whose opinions you value most would react if you discussed with them whether you should perform act X in circumstances Y. *Regardless of your personal views*, would these people think that this is something you ought to do or something you ought not do?"

Empirical Evidence   Evidence that behavior is dependent on the personal norms constructed from internalized values is provided by significant correlations between personal norms and a variety of subsequent behaviors: volunteering to donate bone marrow ($r = .24$, Schwartz, 1973), pledging to take university class notes for Army Reservists ($r = .26$, Rothstein, 1974), donating blood ($r = .43$, Pomazal, 1974; $r = .24$, Zuckerman & Reis, 1978), volunteering to tutor blind children ($r = .26$, Schwartz, 1978), volunteering time for elderly welfare recipients ($r = .30$, Schwartz & Fleishman, 1978). Evidence for the influence of perceived social norms is both weaker and less diverse. A significant correlation has been observed with volunteering time for elderly welfare recipients ($r = .15$). Positive but nonsignificant correlations were found with donating blood ($r = .09$ in both studies), with volunteering to donate bone marrow ($r = .12$), and with everyday considerateness and helpfulness ($r = .09$, data from a study reported in Schwartz, 1968a).

While many of these correlations are significant, they are not particularly strong, consistent with the assumption of the normative decision-making model that the strength of the association between norms and behavior depends on the moderating effects of attention conditions. Evidence for such moderating effects was obtained in the study of everyday helpfulness and considerateness among peers (Schwartz, 1968a). As expected, personal norms were substantially correlated with behavior for students who tend to take note spontaneously of others' need ($r = .44$, high AC quartile), but not for those who tend to overlook others' need ($r = -.01$, low AC quartile).

There was also some indication that awareness of consequences moderates the impact of perceived social norms. Behavior correlated significantly with perceived social norms for the high AC quartile ($r = .27$) but not for the low AC quartile ($r = -.05$). Thus whether people consider the relevance of social norms for their potential actions may also be a function of the individual tendency to take note spontaneously of others' need.

ANTICIPATORY EVALUATION

Subsequent to identification of the material, moral, and social outcomes implied by specific helping behaviors, the anticipated costs and benefits of these outcomes are evaluated. Both situation and person factors influence the assessment of costs and benefits. Thus the salience of social costs and benefits may be increased by a situational cue such as the presence of referent others (Ewens & Ehrlich, 1972). Anticipated physical costs of intervention may be increased, for example, by witnessing a rescuer injured in a fire.

Among person factors that affect the evaluation of moral outcomes is the centrality of the values implicated in a behavior. The impact of a personal norm on a behavior is stronger for people whose self-evaluation is closely tied to the values from which the personal norm is constructed. Thus the correlation between personal norms for considerateness and everyday considerateness behavior was significantly stronger for students who ranked considerateness as one of their most central values ($r = .32$) than for students who viewed it as less central ($r = .04$, Schwartz, 1977).

Minimal physical costs of effort and time are inherent in any action, but the presence of social and moral implications is less certain. There are behaviors that have no moral relevance for some people; because these behaviors are unrelated to internalized values, no personal norms are constructed. In the absence of internalized moral implications, social and material costs and benefits may have considerable influence on behavioral decisions.

The interaction of social and moral implications is illustrated in a study of volunteering to aid elderly welfare recipients in need (Schwartz & Fleishman, 1978). An appeal for help invoked the social expectation that women should offer aid, but varied the legitimacy of this expectation by describing the need as due either to the elderly persons' lack of trustworthiness or to arbitrary events beyond their control. Women who had indicated feelings of moral obligation either to aid elderly persons or to oppose such aid responded consistently with their premeasured personal norms, regardless of the legitimacy of need: For these women the moral costs and benefits outweighed the social. On the other hand, women who had reported no personal norm regarding this issue were significantly influenced by the legitimacy of need, volunteering twice as much when the social expectation invoked was legitimate rather than illegitimate.

The outcome of the evaluation of anticipated costs and benefits determines which step in the model ensues. If moral and nonmoral considerations favor the same helping action, a decision is reached and the defense step is skipped. If the various costs and benefits of available actions are evaluated as relatively balanced, however, and the outcomes of these actions are not trivial, conflict is experienced. The decision is delayed while the person tries to reduce the conflict.

DEFENSE

The most common method for reducing decisional conflict is to weaken one's feelings of moral obligation through redefining the situation. The preferred defense is to redefine one's own perceptions and interpretations, because physical and social outcomes of action are less believably redefined. Four types of denial, each implied by one of the earlier steps in the model, can reduce feelings of obligation: denial of need, denial of effective actions, denial of ability, and denial of responsibility. The actor cycles back through the decision-making process in order to generate a new definition of the situation that may facilitate a clear-cut behavioral decision. Where the new cycle begins depends on the form of denial employed (see Figure 14.1).

Denial of Need   The first step in the model is awareness of a person in need. Faced with the costs of acting on a recognized need, a person may reexamine the situation defensively to find cues that permit denial of the need or at least a reduction in its perceived severity. Thus people who feel they should donate bone marrow but fear the physical pain of a transplant may seek a rationale for denying the recipient's need.

Ambiguity of need cues and individual insensitivity to such cues enhance the probability of effective denial. An actor who totally denies the reality of need in this second pass through the decision-making process can exit from this process without incurring moral costs. If the perceived severity of need is only weakened, decision making continues through the subsequent steps. The reduction in perceived severity of need may lead, however, to weaker personal norms or to a lower estimate of moral or social costs. The new cost–benefit ratio may permit a clear decision not to help.

Denial of Effective Action   If need is perceived as serious enough to merit attention, the actor may defend against the conflict by concluding that the action would not be effective. Bystanders may conclude that intervening to protect a woman from a beating by her husband will not work. Instead, another line of action may be defined as more appropriate (e.g., calling the police). This action may then be evaluated in subsequent steps in the decision-making process. Choice of eventual action to be undertaken is a function of the relative conflict aroused by evaluation of the set of social, physical, and moral implications associated with each of the possible actions.

Denial of Personal Ability   Another mode of defense is to deny one's ability or competence to perform the necessary actions. If redefinition of need points to new effective actions, the actor may now simply conclude that he lacks the requisite abilities. Or, defensive recycling may commence with reevaluation of the actor's personal competence. In a current study, for example, we have been amazed at the number of women whose arthritis renders them unable to distribute pamphlets. This mode of defense is especially effective for deflecting the social costs of ignoring social norms invoked in appeals.

Denial of Responsibility   The final mode of defense is denial of responsibility to conform with normative obligations. That is, actors reject their liability for violating the personal or social norms activated in the motivation stage, claiming that under the circumstances the norms do not apply to them. As with the other defenses, both person and situation variables influence the use of responsibility denial.

The Responsibility Denial Scale (RD; Schwartz, 1968b; Schwartz & Howard, 1980) measures the individual tendency to accept or reject rationales that reduce personal responsibility for the interpersonal consequences of one's actions. The scale consists of 28 items using a 4-point agree–disagree format. Agreement that "when a person is nasty to me, I feel very little responsibility to treat him well," for example, is taken as responsibility denial. Agreement that "professional obligations can never justify neglecting the welfare of others" is taken as responsibility acceptance.

Responsibility denial has mediated the personal norm–behavior relationship in several studies. Personal norms were not correlated with volunteering to donate bone marrow among Wisconsin women high on RD ($r = .01$), for example, but the correlation was substantial for women low on RD ($r = .44$, Schwartz, 1973). Thus those likely to deny their responsibility do not behave consistently with their feelings of moral obligation, while those who accept personal responsibility do behave consistently.

The same pattern of mediation by responsibility denial has been observed for everyday helpfulness and considerateness (Schwartz, 1968b), for volunteering to aid elderly welfare recipients (Schwartz & Fleishman, 1979), and for volunteering to tutor blind children (Schwartz & Howard, 1979). Responsibility denial does not mediate the impact of perceived social norms on behavior, however, probably because denying responsibility to oneself fails to reduce the anticipated costs of violating social expectations (Schwartz & Fleishman, 1979).

Situational factors also influence the success of responsibility denial. Any factor that initially increases the salience of a person's special liability for the fate of a needy other also increases the difficulty of subsequently denying responsibility. Students helped the woman endangered by an escaped rat significantly more if they were directly blamed for causing the escape than if it was the woman's own fault (Schwartz & BenDavid, 1976). Presumably those blamed for the accident were less able to deny personal responsibility for its consequences.

Salience of responsibility should also mediate the relationship between personal norms and behavior, since it should block responsibility denial. In the only test of this mediating effect, however, the results were opposite to those predicted. This anomalous finding has stimulated refinements to the theory, discussed below.

In sum, decisional conflict produced by evaluating the anticipated costs and benefits of an action elicits defenses against the feelings of moral obligation to perform that action. If these defenses succeed, actors may either exit from the system before new personal norms are constructed, or they may construct new personal norms and reach a behavioral decision on the basis of the reevaluated social, material, and moral outcomes. If further conflict is generated, recycling through the decision-making process may continue. Repeated iterations are unlikely, however, because the passage of time leads eventually to changes that end the process: Need may intensify or dissipate, or attention may be drawn elsewhere by new stimuli.

BEHAVIOR

Once a behavioral decision is reached, the helping act is or is not performed. This model points to a continuing process of reciprocal determinism among person, environment, and behavior (Bandura, 1978). Both behavioral action and inaction modify the situation and thus may change its meaning. New needs may become salient, new actions may be recognized, perceived responsibility may shift. Dissatisfactions may linger because decisions rarely permit avoidance of all costs. Thus a new sequence of decision making may occur. Moreover, the outcomes of the behavior enacted may change the structure of internalized values and perceived social norms and the assessment of physical and material costs. Consequently, future behavior in apparently similar situations may differ considerably from past behavior.

Boomerang Effects

The empirical data presented suggest that situation and person factors conducive to norm activation increase the association between personal norms and behavior. Although most of the available findings support this key hypothesis of the normative decision-making model, anomalous results have also been obtained. Specifically, in the presence of factors presumed *most* conducive to activating norms favoring helping, decreased rates of helping behavior have sometimes been obtained. We term this a *boomerang* effect. Much of our current research examines this effect.

A boomerang effect was first found in the study of bone marrow donation. Personal norms and behavior were significantly associated in all conditions but the high responsibility/high salience of need condition, the one most conducive to norm activation. Although this is the only study with a boomerang effect in which personal norms were measured, two other studies produced similar results. In one (Schwartz, 1970), the volunteering rate increased when the salience of need was increased from low to moderate among people told there was a 1/25 chance they would provide an adequate match for a bone marrow transplant, but volunteering boomeranged to its lowest level when need was most salient. A similar unexpected finding was obtained in the bake sale study (Schwartz, 1974): When exposed to high seriousness of need, students with the highest scores on the spontaneous tendency to attend to others' need (AC) volunteered significantly less than those with moderate and low AC scores.

Given the worthy causes involved in these two studies, we can safely assume that most participants felt some moral obligation to volunteer. The unexpected drops in volunteering therefore suggest that personal norms had the least impact on behavior in precisely those circumstances hypothesized to be most conducive to norm activation.

Three plausible explanations suggest that the boomerang effect is associated with a loss of internal value-based motivation to behave altruistically. The explanations are complementary; all are consistent with the process of personal norm construction presented here. First, when an appeal is framed in a highly pressuring manner (e.g., by including excessive or dramatic statements of need), the target of the appeal may become suspicious of the motives of the person seeking help or of the true severity of need. This suspicion may elicit denial of need, so that feelings of moral obligation are not generated and helping behavior is therefore reduced.

A second explanation maintains that the perception of manipulativeness in an appeal elicits reactance, stimulating a need to retain behavioral freedom by resisting the pressure to help (Brehm, 1966). Even though subjects accept the reality of need, their feelings of reactance may lead them to exercise behavioral freedom by refusing to volunteer. More generally, complying with an appeal may produce nonmoral psychological costs that weigh against the moral benefits of acting on one's feelings of moral obligation. Moreover, the threat to behavioral freedom is strongest for people with positive personal norms: Because they stand to benefit most from self-affirmation, they experience the strongest reactance.

A third explanation of boomerang effects suggests that external pressures to provide aid undermine the internalized motivation to perform altruistic actions. We have argued that the benefit of altruistic acts is affirmation of one's internalized values. Making salient external reasons to engage in helping behaviors may deprive otherwise internally motivated actors of the opportunity to see themselves as guided by their own values. People exposed to conditions that heighten the salience of external reasons for helping (e.g., social pressure, money) may actually help, but their help may be a function of external rewards rather than of internalized values. If personal norms tap one form of intrinsic motivation, as is implicit in the internalized value approach, their influence on behavior should decrease when pronormative behavior is induced by external rewards (cf. Deci, 1975; Lepper & Greene, 1978).

Other Models of Helping and Altruism

Explanations of helping are broader than those of altruism, incorporating motivations presumably unrelated to moral values. Helping theories have emphasized either physiological arousal, cognitive discrepancies, or social norms. The normative model we have presented subsumes all of these motivations, although arousal receives minimal attention. Similarly, the cognitive and normative explanations of helping are more relevant to theories of cooperation than is the arousal explanation. Models of cooperation usually refer to arousal linked to the real or anticipated defection of potential cooperators, whereas the type of arousal typically referred to in theories of helping is physiological distress. Consider now the relationship of our model to other models of helping.

Arousal

Piliavin and her associates (Chapter 12) propose an arousal explanation of helping in emergencies. Piliavin suggests that observation of an emergency arouses the bystander physiologically, the degree of arousal depending on the perceived severity of the emergency, the distance between the observer and the victim, their perceived similarity, and the length of time elapsed since initial observation. The arousal is thought to grow more distressing as it increases. Observers are motivated to help in order to reduce their own distressing arousal.

This arousal explanation may be adequate for rapidly developing emergencies where the complex information-processing inherent in our model may not occur. Where considerations of social, material, moral, and nonmoral psychological costs and benefits do enter the decision-making process, the arousal of physiological distress plays another role. This arousal directly influences anticipatory evaluations of psychological outcomes, potentially energizing feelings that are subjectively labeled moral or social obligations.

Hornstein (Chapter 10) proposes that helping is traceable to a different type of arousal, one he calls *promotive tension*. Promotive tension is generated when one becomes aware that another with whom one identifies wishes to reach a goal valued by oneself. Awareness of the other's need produces an aversive, drive-like state of arousal, a kind of interpersonal Zeigarnik effect. The closer the relationship, the stronger the tension and the greater the likelihood of helping.

That the decision to help is influenced both by the psychological distance between the potential helper and the person in need and by the importance for the helper of the goal in question suggests that the helper's own values are relevant to the arousal of promotive tension. Hornstein's concept of promotive tension may be one aspect of the affective component of personal norms in our model. To the extent that promotive tension is aroused only when the potential helper shares the other's goals, however, the helping action is not truly altruistic. The passerby who sends on a lost letter she finds only if the contribution it contains is for a cause she herself supports is acting at least partly out of self-interest.

Batson (Coke, Batson, & McDavis, 1978) distinguishes two types of arousal that may influence helping. The first, *personal distress*, is equivalent to the Piliavin concept of arousal. Personal distress motivates acts intended to reduce one's own discomfort, regardless of their helpfulness for others. The second, *empathic concern*, is tied to the welfare of the other. Batson suggests that only empathic concern mediates altruism, because it motivates acts intended to reduce the other's suffering. From the viewpoint of our model, personal distress is one affective component of anticipated material or nonmoral psychological outcomes of action, whereas empathic concern is an affective component of personal norms that refer to the welfare of others. We propose that empathic concern is elicited only when awareness of another's need has implications for one's own internalized values.

Cognition

Cognitive theories of helping maintain that awareness of another's need causes inconsistency in one's cognitive system; this inconsistency is removed by providing help. Reykowski (Chapter 15) posits that there are fully developed stable representations of external social objects (other people) in one's cognitive system. These representations include conceptions of normal states as well as conceptions of ideal or expected states. When the input of ongoing perceptions points to a discrepancy between the current state of the other's welfare and the expected or ideal state, cognitive inconsistency is experienced. This motivates action intended to reduce the inconsistency—helping.

The motivational strength of the inconsistency depends on one's ego strength; the position of the representations in one's cognitive structure (e.g., close friends are presumably more centrally located); the state of competing representations, such as the balance between one's own existing and ideal states; and one's evaluation of the goal desired by the other. Reykowski's model is quite consistent with the motivational aspects of our own, if we assume that the inconsistency between existing and ideal states arouses self-based motivation to reduce the perceived need as a function of one's internalized values.

Lerner (1975, 1981) proposes a cognitive model of helping based on the idea that people believe in a just world, one in which people get what they deserve. Observing someone subject to an apparently undeserved fate (e.g., suffering or deprivation) shakes our confidence in our own invulnerability to a similar fate. To restore our own confidence, we may undertake behavior intended to reestablish justice in the state of the other. Lerner's concept of justice appears to function as an internalized value. This value activates nonmoral psychological motivation—a desire to ward off threatening doubts about one's own fate. Aid to the other is therefore helping rather than altruism.

The "justice motive" is relevant to altruism only when, with socialization, commitment to justice for others may become independent of nonmoral goals: Justice becomes an important value for the person in itself. In this form, justice is implicated in the motivation stage of our model. The perception that need produced a state of injustice correctable through helping actions may lead to the construction of morally relevant personal norms—based in part on the justice value—and hence to altruistic behavior.

Social Norms

Social normative theories view helping as a function of pressure to comply with shared group expectations about appropriate behavior that are backed by social sanctions and rewards. Berkowitz (1972) postulates the existence of a widespread norm of social responsibility that dictates helping those who are dependent on us. People in western societies generally believe that failure to help dependent others elicits social disapprobation, while helping brings social approval. Walster, Walster, and Berscheid (1973) suggest that a generally accepted norm of equity motivates helping. For example, people who perceive they are inequitably advantaged in a relationship may help the disadvantaged and restore equity in order to avoid social condemnation for being exploitive and win social approval for being considerate.

Our model encompasses social normative explanations, pointing both to conditions likely to activate social norms as sources of motivation and to the complex of other sources of motivation with which social norms combine. The social emphasis refers to potential externally mediated rewards and costs. But general social norms such as equity and responsibility may be internalized during socialization, becoming values of importance for self-evaluation (Greenberg, 1978). The implications of potential helping behaviors for these values may therefore lead to construction of personal norms, reflecting self-based motivation. In this case the helping may also be altruistic.

Cooperation and Helping

The Nature of Rewards

The relevance to cooperation of the normative model of helping behavior has received little attention in the discussion above. This section reviews this connection between cooperation and helping where relevant. In the course of this discussion our model is applied to an understanding of cooperation, elaborating the nature of rewards, and in particular the role of psychological costs and benefits. Cooperation is conceptualized here as the product of a behavioral decision-making process, analogous to the decision-making view of altruism–helping.

Marwell and Schmidt (1975) characterize the cooperation literature as focusing on individual characteristics of participants and on situational influences such as setting, task characteristics, and reward conditions. They also identify other relevant independent variables that entail interactions between the person and situation, such as the perceived equity of the behavior–reward relationships, the degree of interpersonal risk involved, and the possibility of trust. These latter variables go beyond concern with material outcomes to the impact of social and moral considerations. The prediction and understanding of cooperation would be facilitated by a theory that integrated these types of variables.

Although the normative model presented above was developed to explain altruism and helping, certain aspects of the model might be suitable to a theory of cooperation. In particular, the elaborate analysis of the cognitive evaluation of social, moral, psychological, and material benefits of behavior may be relevant. Much research on cooperation has emphasized material payoffs. To understand the undermining of cooperation by perceived inequity, however, we must attend to psychological, moral, and social costs and benefits. Participants in a relationship may refrain from cooperation even when a calculation of absolute material benefits would dictate cooperative behavior. Anticipated group sanctions for violating equity norms, moral self-deprecation for perpetuating an unjust distribution of resources, and psychological discomfort for allowing oneself to be exploited may all militate against cooperation in inequitable relationships. Conversely, cooperation may be elicited in equitable relationships because of the moral, social, and psychological benefits of promoting equity even in the face of material loss.

The degree of interpersonal risk as a factor in cooperation refers directly to potential material benefits or costs. In calculating risks, however, people must estimate the likelihood of cooperation or defection by others. These estimates are undoubtedly affected by assumptions regarding the moral, social, and material gains and losses others will incur. Gouldner (1960) has suggested that the norm of reciprocity is one basis for engaging in the risks of cooperation because it increases the perceived likelihood of mutual benefits over time. Thus the normative climate may enhance or impair trust. Note too that people can afford greater material risks if they anticipate the compensation of social and moral benefits for cooperating. Of course, fear of the social and psychological costs of appearing foolishly naive may also discourage cooperation.

Social Dilemmas

Dawes (1980) discusses a particularly interesting subset of the cooperation literature—that dealing with social dilemmas. A social dilemma is a situation in which each individual receives a higher payoff (reward) for a socially defecting, noncooperative choice than for cooperation no matter what others do, but where all individuals are better off if all cooperate than if all defect. People who ignore requests to conserve water during the summer can enjoy their green lawns, for example, without appreciably depleting the general water supply; yet if all use water this freely, all will suffer when rationing is imposed.

Helping is typically directed to specific needy recipients whose current state is inferior to that of the potential helper. In social dilemmas potential cooperators are themselves members of the recipient group; they are not necessarily better off than any of the other members. From a motivational viewpoint, however, behavioral choice in the social dilemma is quite similar to that in potential altruism settings. The actor who cooperates, like the actor who behaves altruistically, is contributing to the welfare of others with tangible material cost to the self. In a social dilemma, the potential material gain to the single cooperator from contributing to or preserving public goods is usually small and uncertain; thus, this source of motivation must be unimportant, just as it is in altruism.

Dawes proposes three variables as particularly important influences on cooperation in social dilemmas: knowledge, morality, and trust. By knowledge he refers to cognitive awareness and understanding of the utilities of all relevant rewards and/or costs—not just those associated with material factors, but also those associated with altruism, conscience, etc. Under the rubric of knowledge Dawes is apparently trying to capture much of both the process and content elaborated in the attention, motivation, and anticipatory evaluation stages of our model of helping. Like us, he singles out internalized moral values as especially relevant to the type of decision of concern.

Dawes (1980) hypothesizes that if people are to cooperate they must first "think about and come to understand the nature of the dilemma, so that moral, normative and altruistic concerns as well as external payoffs can influence behavior [p. 170]." Both the nature of this cognitive evaluation process and some of the person and situation variables that may influence it are suggested in our model. Dawes further hypothesizes that cooperation in a social dilemma requires that people "have some reason for believing that others will not defect," some basis for trust. The contribution of the normative climate to trust has already been noted. Lack of trust discourages cooperation not only because it directly affects the subjective probability of material loss, but also because it facilitates defense against the moral costs of defecting.

All the types of defense identified in our model of helping are relevant to the understanding of social dilemmas, but two are especially germane. Noncooperation is most often supported by denial of the possibility for effective action ("No restraint on my part will really prevent an oil shortage, a worldwide famine, or runaway inflation") and by denial of personal or social responsibility ("Why should I exercise restraint if no one else does?") The various person and situation variables that have been shown to promote or block the use of such defenses against helping also merit consideration for explaining cooperation.

Dawes speculates, for example, that defection in social dilemmas is fostered by diffusion of the harm over many people and anonymity of the single actor. Support for these speculations comes from findings regarding closely related concepts in the helping literature. Diffusion of harm parallels diffusion of responsibility, a defense that reduces intervention in emergencies as the number of bystanders increases (Latané & Darley, 1970). Such responsibility denial may deflect both the potential moral costs of self-deprecation and the perceived social costs of group condemnation. Regarding anonymity, Schwartz and Gottlieb (1980) have found that bystander helping drops when the actor's presence is unknown to others. Anonymous bystanders are less likely both to think about social expectations for helping and to feel that moral responsibility is focused on them.

Altruism and Cooperation: An Exchange

The preceding discussion notes parallel developments in the literatures on cooperation and helping. In concluding, we suggest several points with potential for further exchange. First, our model postulates that both social and personal normative influences on helping are activated only when people attend to and define the choice situations in terms of the other's need, the consequences for the other of actions taken on his or her behalf, and their own ability and responsibility. Numerous situational variables (e.g., salience of need and of responsibility) that promote both attention processes and normative definitions have indeed been found to foster helping. Dawes (1980) proposes that increased salience of factors connected with moral influences should enhance cooperation. Are the situational variables that might increase the salience of moral responsibility for cooperation analogous to those variables that do so for helping?

Second, the cooperation literature has not distinguished between the influences of both social and personal norms on prosocial behavior. Research on helping attests to the utility of this distinction. There is strong evidence that behavior is dependent on personal norms constructed from internalized values (Pomazal, 1974; Rothstein, 1974; Schwartz, 1973), but evidence for the influence of perceived social norms is weaker (Pomazal, 1974; Schwartz, 1973; Schwartz & Fleishman, 1979). This distinction may prove relevant to the comprehension of cooperation, particularly where cooperation occurs even when the social costs for defection are low.

Third, our model of helping points to the multifaceted nature of the definition of behavioral choices and the consequent evaluation of several different types of costs and benefits. Specifying the social and psychological costs and benefits of cooperation or defection in concrete situations, in addition to the material payoffs, might facilitate more precise predictions of behavior. The limited information-processing typical of decision makers tends to restrict attention to the most salient outcomes, however, and in cooperation settings material outcomes are likely to be particularly salient, in the absence of specially designed communications (Dawes, 1980). Consideration of specific payoffs also highlights another important difference between cooperation and helping: Defection improves material payoffs, whereas the choice not to help generally leads only to the avoidance of material losses. The implications of this difference between aggrandizing one's material resources and staving off their depletion require further study.

Other questions are suggested in considering possible contributions of the normative model of helping to the understanding of cooperation. Are those individual differences identified as influential for altruism (responsibility denial, awareness of consequences, personal norms) also relevant to cooperation? Our unpublished data on the influence of responsibility denial on cooperation in a prisoner's dilemma game suggest an affirmative answer. Would those factors found to elicit boomerangs—leading to unexpected reduction in helping—also reduce the likelihood of cooperation? All three proposed explanations for boomerang effects—mistrust, reactance, and undermining of internalized motivation—might well provide insight into failures of attempts to induce cooperation in social dilemmas.

There are undoubtedly also many insights in the cooperation literature that would prove useful to the understanding of altruism. The research on cooperation has paid particular attention to the influence of interpersonal risk, trust, and the role of uncertainty in decision making. Inasmuch as the decision to help is typically made with some degree of uncertainty regarding outcomes and involves material as well as psychological risks, this cooperation research is undoubtedly relevant.

Bilder (1979) has elaborated many factors that serve to strengthen or undermine trust in cooperation among nations. While analogues of some of these factors have been examined in the helping literature (e.g., the perceived motives of the interactants, the fairness of the reallocation of resources), analogues of other factors deserve consideration (e.g., the recipients' ability to use the help effectively, the complexity of the performance that establishes the purported need). Findings regarding trust are particularly important to clarify the reasons for boomerang effects in helping. Trust may also play a central role in the definition of the parameters of need and of the costs and benefits of helping.

One emphasis in the cooperation literature virtually unexplored in research on helping is the importance of interpersonal negotiation in reaching behavioral choices. We have argued that mutual interdependence prevails in helping as well as in cooperation situations. The costs and benefits experienced by a helper are at least partly determined by the definitions of the situation agreed upon by the helpee and by the use the latter makes of the help. Is the helper's action generous or niggardly, altruistic or duty-bound, socially desirable or undesirable, courageous or foolish? Answers to these questions are negotiated in interaction between helpers, helpees, and often third parties as well. The rich cooperation literature on bargaining and communication may suggest which variables influence negotiation in helping settings and in what ways.

References

Bandura, A. The self in reciprocal determinism. *American Psychologist*, 1978, *33*, 344–358.

Bem, D. *Beliefs, attitudes and human affairs*. Belmont, California: Brooks/Cole, 1970.

Berkowitz, L. Social norms, feelings and other factors affecting helping and altruism. In L. Berkowitz (Ed.), *Advances in experimental social psychology* (Vol. 6). New York: Academic Press, 1972.

Berkowitz, L., & Walster, E. (Eds.) *Advances in experimental social psychology* (Vol. 9). New York: Academic Press, 1976.

Bilder, R. B. *The role of trust in international agreement*. Unpublished manuscript, University of Wisconsin–Madison, 1979.

Brehm, J. W. *A theory of psychological reactance*. New York: Academic Press, 1966.

Coke, J. S., Batson, C. D., & McDavis, K. Empathic mediation of helping: A two-stage model. *Journal of Personality and Social Psychology*, 1978, *36*, 752–766.

Dawes, R. M. Social dilemmas. *Annual Review of Psychology*, 1980, *31*, 169–193.

Deci, E. L. *Intrinsic motivation*. New York: Plenum Press, 1975.

Ewens, W. L., & Ehrlich, H. J. Reference–other support and ethnic attitudes as predictors of intergroup behavior. *Sociological Quarterly*, 1972, *13*, 348–360.

Gouldner, A. W. The norm of reciprocity: A preliminary statement. *American Sociological Review*, 1960, *25*, 161–178.

Greenberg, J. Effects of reward value and retaliative power on allocation decisions: Justice, generosity, or greed? *Journal of Personality and Social Psychology*, 1978, *36*, 367–379.

Isen, A. M., Shalker, T. E., Clark, M., & Karp, L. Affect, accessibility of material in memory, and behavior: A cognitive loop? *Journal of Personality and Social Psychology*, 1978, *36*, 1–12.

Latané, B., & Darley, J. M. *The unresponsive bystander: Why doesn't he help?* New York: Appleton, 1970.

Lepper, N. R., & Greene, D. (Eds.), *The hidden costs of reward*. Hillsdale, N.J.: Lawrence Erlbaum, 1978.

Lerner, M. J. The justice motive in social behavior: Introduction. *Journal of Social Issues*, 1975, *31*, 1–19.

Lerner, M. J. Justice and altruism. In J. P. Rushton and R. M. Sorrentino (Eds.), *Altruism and helping behavior*. Hillsdale, N.J.: Lawrence Erlbaum, 1981.

Luce, R. D., & Raiffa, H. *Games and decisions*. New York: John Wiley & Sons, 1957.

Marwell, G., & Schmidt, D. R. *Cooperation: An experimental analysis*. New York: Academic Press, 1975.

Pomazal, R. J. *Attitudes, normative beliefs, and altruism: Help for helping behavior*. Unpublished doctoral dissertation, University of Illinois, 1974.

Reykowski, J. Prosocial orientation and self-structure. In J. Reykowski (Ed.), *Studies on the mechanisms of prosocial behavior*. Warsaw: Warsaw University Press, 1975.

Rokeach, M. *The nature of human values*. New York: Free Press, 1973.

Rosenberg, M. *Conceiving the self*. New York: Basic Books, 1979.

Rosenhan, D. L., Karylowski, J., Salorey, P., & Hargis, K. Emotion and altruism. In J. P. Rushton and R. M. Sorrentino (Eds.), *Altruism and helping behavior*. Hillsdale, N.J.: Lawrence Erlbaum, 1981.

Rothstein, H. R. *Attitudes and behavior: The effects of perceived payoffs and facilitating intrapersonal conditions*. Unpublished master's thesis, Hebrew University of Jerusalem, 1974.

Schwartz, S. H. Awareness of consequences and the influence of moral norms on interpersonal behavior. *Sociometry*, 1968, *31*, 355–369. (a)

Schwartz, S. H. Words, deeds, and the perception of consequences and responsibility in action situations. *Journal of Personality and Social Psychology*, 1968, *10*, 232–242. (b)

Schwartz, S. H. Elicitation of moral obligation and self-sacrificing behavior. *Journal of Personality and Social Psychology*, 1970, *15*, 283–293.

Schwartz, S. H. Normative explanations of helping behavior: A critique, proposal, and empirical test. *Journal of Experimental Social Psychology*, 1973, *9*, 349–364.

Schwartz, S. H. Awareness of interpersonal consequences, responsibility denial and volunteering. *Journal of Personality and Social Psychology*, 1974, *30*, 57–63.

Schwartz, S. H. Normative influences on altruism. In L. Berkowitz (Ed.), *Advances in experimental social psychology* (Vol. 10). New York: Academic Press, 1977.

Schwartz, S. H. Temporal stability as a moderator of the attitude–behavior relationship. *Journal of Personality and Social Psychology*, 1978, *36*, 715–725.

Schwartz, S. H., & Ben David, A. Responsibility and helping in an emergency: Effects of blame, ability and denial of responsibility. *Sociometry*, 1976, *39*, 406–415.

Schwartz, S. H., & Fleishman, J. A. Personal norms and the mediation of legitimacy effects on helping. *Social Psychology*, 1978, *41*, 306–315.

Schwartz, S. H., & Fleishman, J. A. *Personal norms as a distinctive attitudinal variable.* Unpublished manuscript, University of Wisconsin—Madison, 1979.

Schwartz, S. H., & Gottlieb, A. Bystander anonymity and reactions to emergencies. *Journal of Personality and Social Psychology*, 1980, *39*, 418–430.

Schwartz, S. H., & Howard, J. A. *Explanations of the moderating effect of responsibility denial on the personal-norm behavior relationship.* Social Psychology Quarterly, 1980, *43*, 441–446.

Schwartz, S. H., & Howard, J. A. A normative decision-making model of altruism. In J. P. Rushton & R. M. Sorrentino (Eds.), *Altruism and helping behavior.* Hillsdale, N.J.: Erlbaum, 1981.

Staub, E., & Baer, R. S., Jr. Stimulus characteristics of a sufferer and difficulty of escape as determinants of helping. *Journal of Personality and Social Psychology*, 1974, *30*, 279–284.

Taylor, S. E., & Fiske, S. T. Salience, attention, and attribution: Top of the head phenomena. In L. Berkowitz (Ed.), *Advances in experimental social psychology* (Vol. 11). New York: Academic Press, 1978.

Walster, E., Walster, G. W., & Berscheid, E. New directions in equity research. *Journal of Personality and Social Psychology*, 1973, *25*, 151–176.

Weiner, B., Russell, D., & Lerman, D. Affective consequences of causal ascriptions. In J. H. Harvey, W. Ickes, & R. F. Kidd, *New directions in attribution research* (Vol. 2). Hillsdale, N.J.: Lawrence Erlbaum, 1978.

Zuckerman, M., & Reis, H. T. Comparison of three models for predicting altruistic behavior. *Journal of Personality and Social Psychology*, 1978, *36*, 498–510.

Chapter 15

Motivation of

Prosocial Behavior[1]

JANUSZ REYKOWSKI

For decades research has concentrated primarily on the individualistic aspects of social behavior. An implicit assumption of many studies is that human beings try to maximize their well-being. Due to the specific conditions of their growth and development, people may develop different criteria of well being and different techniques of achieving it in a given social environment. Psychologists have sought to describe these criteria and the processes involved in the acquisition of different techniques of dealing with the social environment, studying such phenomena as power seeking, achievement orientation, need for approval, Machiavellianism, competitive attitudes, compliance, risk taking, role playing, etc. Recently, social scientists have paid attention to the fact that people do a great deal for the benefit of others. Studies of *positive forms of social behavior* (a term used by Wispé, 1972, and Staub, 1978)—that is, helping, sharing, cooperating, sympathizing, empathizing—have flourished in the last 15 years in many countries (Wispé, 1979). Books dealing with these behaviors have been published not only in the United States (Hornstein, 1976; Latané & Darley, 1970; Macaulay

[1] The paper is part of Project 11.8, sponsored by the Polish Academy of Sciences. I acknowledge the valuable editorial assistance of Valerian J. Derlega in preparing this chapter.

& Berkowitz, 1970; Mussen & Eisenberg-Berg, 1977; Staub, 1978, 1979; Wispé, 1972, 1978) but in other countries as well, including West Germany (Lück, 1975, 1977 and Israel (Bar-Tal, 1976). In Poland several books and monographs have been written on this topic (Jarymowicz, 1979; Karylowski, 1975a,b; Kiciński, 1978; Potocka-Hoser, 1971; Reykowski, 1972, 1975, 1978, 1979). In the Soviet Union there is a long tradition of research on this phenomenon. Social motivation, especially as a collectivistic orientation (i.e., a relatively stable motivational system that directs a behavior toward protection and enhancement of the interests of the social group or collective), is an important area of study in Soviet psychology (Bozowich, 1968; Pietrowsky, 1975, 1977; Schorochova & Platonov, 1975).

The main question in studies on prosocial behavior is: How is it possible that people undertake action that is directed toward the protection, maintenance, and enhancement of the well-being of others, of social objects—that is, people, groups, institutions—different from themselves? (The term *external social object* will be used to refer to social objects different from the self.) In other words, what are the mechanisms underlying prosocial action?

Two major strategies have been used to answer this question. The first strategy, deeply rooted in the American tradition of pragmatism, aims to describe and measure internal and external variables that are associated with the occurrence of prosocial acts. Based on this empirical strategy, prosocial behavior has been found to depend on characteristics of the target person or recipient (such as race, physical appearance, dress, social position); characteristics of the situation (such as number of witnesses, noise, social requirements); the momentary state of a subject (his or her mood or recent experience of success or failure); personality characteristics of the subject (his or her values, needs, attitudes, traits); psychological relationship between subject and recipient (friendship, rivalry, sympathy); physical relationship between subject and recipient (distance); costs involved in prosocial action; the needs of the recipient; the psychological processes activated in the situation, and so forth.

One has the suspicion, after a close scrutiny of these results, that everything is associated with prosocial behavior. In fact it is probably difficult to find variables that are not, directly or indirectly, related to the phenomenon. No wonder. Prosocial behavior, like any other form of social behavior, is controlled by a complex regulatory system. And any factor that can change the state of such a system must have some impact on all the system's regulatory functions.

Would it not, therefore, be more interesting and more productive to look for factors that under no conditions are associated with prosocial acts? Although this approach might be more parsimonious, nobody would recommend it. Instead, we advocate a strategy of searching for crucial factors that may have a decisive role in the occurrence of prosocial action. This approach requires careful theoretical analysis.

In fact this is an essential characteristic of the second strategy used in studies of prosocial behavior, which emphasizes theory construction. Authors who have chosen this approach attempt to build elaborate models to account for underlying mechanisms that are responsible for the interrelation of many variables (e.g., Schwartz, 1970, 1976, 1977; Staub, 1978, 1979). But the critical question not answered by these models is, Why are people interested at all in a state of affairs that produces any benefits for someone external to themselves; where does the motivation for prosocial action come from?

This question is not implicitly individualistic. Asking it, we are not implying that caring for oneself is a "natural" state of affairs and caring for others requires a special explanation. As a matter of fact, an explanation is required for the former phenomenon as well as for the latter. However, in this chapter we are concentrating on the second issue, that is, on the question of motivation for prosocial behavior.

Motivation and Value Attribution

The question about the motivation for prosocial acts assumes that behavior is goal oriented and that a positive state of the external social object becomes a goal of an action (i.e., the person is pursuing a prosocial goal). This assumption is not always met, however. In some cases prosocial behavior may take the form of a reflexive act, such as impulsive helping (Piliavin, 1976; also see Piliavin, Dovidio, Gaertner, & Clark, Chapter 12 in the present volume), rather like the immediate response to a trivial request: for instance, "What time is it?" "Is this car going uptown or downtown?" (Latané & Darley, 1970). Reflexive acts can be interpreted as the expression of ready-made response tendencies coordinated with the specific requirements of a situation. But in most cases the prosocial action assumes that the subject is deliberately choosing a specific direction of an action aimed at realizing "a prosocial goal." What makes a person choose goals of this kind?

The precondition for choosing any goal is the attribution of value to given objects, actions, or states of affairs. In the case of prosocial action, a value is attributed to a social object (in this case a person is interested in the well being of someone), or to specific forms of behavior (e.g., helping, sharing) or to a specific state (e.g., justice).

Value attribution may derive from different sources. Two of these are the most widely recognized, namely: An object or activity or state may be valued on the basis of its need-gratification characteristics or its instrumental role in need gratification. Thus, the value of an object (act or state) is learned or discovered (in the latter case, higher mental functions are assumed to be operating). These are *utilitarian* values.

An object (activity or state) may be valued as a consequence of the assimilation of rules and principles formulated by society. Social groups establish norms that define what, when, and to what extent objects, acts, or states should be respected. Every member of society acquires these norms, although to different degrees. Persons may obey either because they have internalized the norms or out of deference to societal demands. These are *normative* values.

In the case of utilitarian values, motivation is aroused whenever a person perceives that his or her interests can be protected or enhanced by prosocial activity. It may also be aroused when the interests of an object regarded as useful for the self are at stake. Since in this case the self-interests are the source of motivation and the motivation has self-protective or self-expanding functions, it may be called *ipsocentric*. The strength of this motivation depends primarily on how important the given event seems to be for the self.

In the case where normative values are involved, associations between norms and self-esteem provide a basis of motivation. According to some authors, adhering to normative demands may be a condition for a positive attitude toward oneself (e.g., Schwartz, 1976). Here the strength of motivation depends on the degree of involvement of one's self-esteem.[2] The degree of involvement of one's self-esteem seems to be related to the importance of a given object (or state, or act). Importance is defined by society in the framework of its normative system. This form of motivation has been called *endocentric* by Karylowski (1979; see also Chapter 17 in this book).

These two motivational mechanisms, based on two different value attribution processes, have different functional characteristics. The difference can be illustrated by some empirical findings we have obtained in one study (Paspalanowa, 1979). College students in Sofia, Bulgaria, had been selected for a study on helping behavior by means of a peer rating technique: In one group were students perceived as "prosocial"; in the other were those perceived as "egocentric." On a later occasion the students were approached by a stranger who solicited their help to perform an unattractive social task. It was found, contrary to expectations, that a greater proportion of egocentric

---

[2] There are also normative systems that are not associated with the self. Norms can be organized into a complex cognitive organization and can have motivational potential of their own. This issue is discussed further a bit later in the chapter.

than prosocial subjects offered help (36.4% and 21.6%, respectively, $\chi^2 = 3.61$, $p \approx .05$).

To explain this finding we need to say more about the selected group and the situation. Egocentric subjects were selected on the basis of items that identified people who had strong competitive attitudes and who openly sought prestige in their group. Such strivings could be easily gratified by demonstrating one's readiness to perform some morally valuable act. The circumstances surrounding a declaration of help gave subjects an opportunity to show their moral superiority over the rest of the group. It may not be unreasonable, therefore, to infer that ipsocentric motivation was responsible for the prosocial actions of the egocentric subjects.

But what about the subjects classified as prosocial? Why did only 20% of this group display helpfulness? Let us consider other important features of the study. It should be noted that all subjects completed a questionnaire about the desirability of helping fellow students in various situations. As might be expected, more than 90% of respondents supported the principle of helping on all questions. The students were promised that the results of the survey would be made known to them. In fact, they obtained this information only a few minutes before they were confronted with the request for help. Half of the subjects received the true information that an overwhelming majority supported the principle of helping (helping approved group). The other half received false information. They were told that less than 50% of the respondents supported the principle of helping (helping disapproved).

Results indicated that information about group norms had more impact on the helping behavior of subjects in the prosocial than in the egocentric group. In the prosocial group the helping approved situation was associated with significantly more offers of help than the helping disapproved situation ($\chi^2 = 4.98$, $p < .05$). In the egocentric group there was no significant difference between offers of help in the helping approved and the helping disapproved conditions. In other words, subjects who were perceived by their fellow students as prosocial were much more influenced by the expectations of their peers than students perceived as egocentric. The value of helping behavior for subjects in the prosocial group seems to have been determined by group norms. These subjects were oriented toward meeting the normative expectations of their own group. The prosocial subjects seemed to demonstrate direct dependence on the norm-defining behavior of the group.

The relationship between group expectation and an individual's social behavior may operate in an indirect manner when normative expectations become internalized and immediate control is located inside instead of outside of a person. In such a case helping motivation is generated by personal norms. In many situations, however, compliance with group expectations is a major motive for prosocial action. Motives of this kind can be looked upon as intermediate between ipsocentric and endocentric motivation.

Our description of endocentric and ipsocentric motivation does not give a full account of the motivational bases of prosocial behavior. New perspectives on the nature of value formation have emerged from the expansion of the so-called cognitive approach in the last two decades (Zajonc, 1968). According to this approach, the mental apparatus can be described as a multidimensional space (or system) representing physical and social objects and their relations. The system has generative potentiality, that is, its elements as well as its organization have properties that are not only reflective but creative too.

In our view this system operates at two levels. One level is based on iconic ("pictorial") and linguistic symbols. It represents the actual state of affairs (objects, situations, processes) and its infinite transformations. The transformations take the form of a constant flow of associations, concepts, and images or, in a more advanced state, a form of operations (in the Piagetian sense of the term), e.g., counting, logical reasoning. Due to these processes the individual is able to move symbolically in time (thinking about the past or future) and in space (imagining objects and events in remote places), and to recombine elements as in fantasy, goal setting, planning, and programming.

The second level of cognitive organization, encoding an experience in *deep structures*, has a different quality. It consists of stable, highly elaborate organizations that are a product of all constancies in human experience. At the level of deep structures, significant objects (people, institutions, things) and their stable interrelationships are recorded. The basic order of nature and basic principles of social life have their representations here too. The self is also represented on this level. The self-structure can be regarded as a specific organization, being a product of the accumulation and processing of information concerning the person himself or herself. (This way of looking at the self has become increasingly popular; see Smith, 1978).

The organization that exists at "surface" and at "deep" levels deals with the same reality but in different ways. A person may have an image of the face and the posture of his or her father, that is, a knowledge of the father's physical and psychological characteristics. The person may think about the father, imagine him, talk about him with someone, or plan to help him. But in doing all that the person is dealing with the superficial, external layer of something that is deeply rooted and interwoven with his or her own self, namely the interiorized father-figure that is part of an internal system.

Objects encoded at the level of deep structures have value properties.

There are two different principles of value attribution that apply to the objects represented at this level.

First, such objects have a *personal* value for the subject because they are part of a system of meaning that is used to define and evaluate oneself. Maintaining a relationship with these objects is necessary to preserve one's self-concept and self-esteem. In many cases, the feeling of control of one's own fate also depends on such a relationship. Typically, a spouse, the closest members of one's family, or a very close friend possess this kind of value to a high degree. To a lesser extent this value is attributed to all those who are part of an individual's personal world.

Second, objects encoded in deep structures have a value property because their representations have been developed in a highly complex structure that functions according to the *principle of equilibrium* (Piaget, 1966). Maintaining the equilibrium of such structures is necessary for the proper functioning of the whole system. The structures contain the representation of the normal state of an object, that is, the standards representing its normal location, functioning, and other characteristics.[3] These standards, which are embedded in the structures, can be regarded as the criteria of equilibrium, since a deviation from them produces an equilibration process that has been described in many studies. Early studies of the relationship between perception and emotion (Hebb, 1949), cognitive dissonance (Festinger, 1957, 1958), motivation inherent in information processing (Hunt, 1965), and achievement motivation (McClelland, Atkinson, Clark, & Lowell, 1953), have shown that the discrepancy between cognitive standards and incoming information (from outside or inside) arouses a state of tension and a tendency to restore a "proper state of affairs" (Lukaszewski, 1971, 1974). The discrepancy instigates a person to an action that is directed at the maintenance, protection, and development of an object if it is represented at the level of deep structures. It means that the object is a value for a person since he is interested in its well-being. But the value of an object *is not* an effect of evaluating operations coming from outside of an object. This is an *intrinsic kind of value* attributed to the "nature" of an object; its identity implies its value.

The value-attributing mechanisms described above give rise to two different forms of motivation. If the object is represented in the system as a highly complex structure, the sheer discrepancy between information about the real or possible state of an object and standards of its normal or desirable state will evoke motivation. This is an *intrinsic prosocial motivation*. The

---

[3] Some standards embedded in objects represent "an ideal state," that is, a state that has not been achieved as yet. To meet these standards a person has to undertake action that brings about some developmental change.

strength of this motivation depends on the degree of discrepancy and, in addition, on the position of the given structure in the system. We assume that cognitive structures differ with respect to their motivational potential. Structures having a more central position in a system have higher value and thus generate stronger motivation.

Personal value is attributed to objects that are located in close psychological proximity to the self, which makes possible a process that can be described as *generalization of personal standards* (Karylowski, 1975a,b; Reykowski, 1975, 1977, 1979; Reykowski & Smolenska, 1980). This process involves comparing the situation of another person with standards of well-being that are operating for oneself. In other words, it is a tendency to react to a state of another person because one's own needs, preferences, and desires are transferred to him or her. The strength of this kind of motivation is a function of the psychological distance of the given person from one-self.

One additional point should be mentioned. The process of motivational arousal described above, involving a discrepancy between a real state of affairs and one's standards, is universal, that is, it operates with all objects represented in the cognitive system. But the discrepancy does not necessarily generate motivation that has significant impact on behavior in all cases. It has such impact only if the object is regarded as a value. Our analysis suggests that there are at least four different sources of value attribution. We further suggest that these sources affect the nature of motivation underlying prosocial behavior.

Consequences of Different Motivational Mechanisms

We assume that prosocial action is aroused whenever the needs and interests of objects that have been assigned value by a subject are involved.[4] Of course, an ability to perceive those needs and interests correctly and a conviction that one is able to deal properly with those needs are of primary importance for prosocial behavior (Schwartz, 1970; Staub, 1978, 1979). But we are further assuming that important characteristics of the prosocial action depend on the type of motivational mechanisms involved.

For each motivational mechanism there is a specific pattern of conditions

---

[4] Some forms of prosocial behavior are not object oriented; a person may perform an action that is not aimed at any specific object. This classification, therefore, does not exhaust all types of motivation for prosocial behavior. Due to the lack of space the present analysis is limited to object-oriented forms of prosocial behavior.

that instigates or inhibits it. Behavioral acts controlled by different mechanisms have different functional characteristics (see Table 15.1). These conditions may actualize either motivation that originates from representations of social objects (intrinsic prosocial motivation) or motivation that originates from the self (endocentric and ipsocentric motivation), or motivation that stems from some relationship between both sources (motivation based upon generalization of personal standards). Now we will concentrate on describing the specific role of the self-structure in the functioning of these motivational mechanisms. The role is different for different mechanisms. We suggest that in the case of intrinsic prosocial motivation self-involvement may be a source of inhibitory forces, whereas for other forms of motivation self-involvement may be a precondition for their activation. The self-structure thus plays an important part in the occurrence of prosocial behavior. In the remaining part of the chapter the double role of the self-structure will be discussed.

Self as a Source of Inhibitory Forces

Some researchers have noted that prosocial action can be suppressed by factors that produce self-concern or self-concentration (e.g., Berkowitz, 1970, 1972). One can therefore argue that to enhance prosocial motivation we should deal with self-concentration. This poses a question: What are the sources of self-concentration? Based on our earlier studies (Reykowski, 1972, 1975) we think that it may be produced either by physical stress or by some specific states of a self-structure. Two different causes of self-concentration originate within the self: (a) Factors that produce a state of tension and *uncertainty* concerning one's own value, competence, identity, or attribution of low value to the self (low self-esteem), may be a source of self-concentration; (b) Self-concentration may be a consequence of the self's high position in the individual's system of values. The self in this case becomes an object of very high importance (high self-esteem). Other social objects are placed in positions of relatively low importance. (The states of the self that we have mentioned—uncertainty concerning the self, low self-esteem, high self-esteem—can be either situational, transient characteristics or more or less stable, dispositional features of a person.)

We hypothesize that high as well as low self-esteem increases self-concentration, while intermediate self-esteem produces a moderate level of self-concentration. Some support for this prediction has been found. For instance, self-concentration scores (as measured by a special Test of Associative Egocentrism; Szustrowa, 1976) are higher among people with positive and negative self-evaluation than among subjects with moderate self-evaluation

Table 15.1
Comparison of Four Motivational Mechanisms of Prosocial Behavior

Ipsocentric	Endocentric	Intrinsic	Generalization of personal standards
	Condition of initiation		
Expectation that in a given situation a prosocial act will lead to some social reward (praise, material gain, fame, etc.) or will prevent social punishment.	Actualization of relevant norm.	Perception of social need.	Perception of need of object perceived as psychologically close.
	Anticipatory outcome		
Personal gain (protection of own interest).	Increment of self-esteem or avoidance of its decrement.	Information that social interest is taken care of (according to standards embedded in object's representation).	Information that object's interest is taken care of (according to personal standards).
	Facilitating conditions		
Increased demand for rewards mediated by prosocial behavior or increased fear of loss of reward if prosocial act is not performed.	Concentration on a moral aspect of own behavior and moral aspect of the self.	Concentration on the state of external social object (ESO).	Moderate concentration on personal standards: short psychological distance of an object from the self.

	Inhibitory conditions		
Possibility of personal loss or harm due to involvement in prosocial action.	Concentration on those aspects of self that are not related to prosocial norms (as result of stress, deprivation, striving for achievement, etc.).	Self-concentration. Realizing that ESO is able to satisfy its needs by other means. High disproportion between possible gain of ESO and possible personal loss (low partner's profit—high personal costs).	Salient characteristics differentiating an object from the self.

Qualitative characteristics of an act

Low level of interest in real needs of ESO. Low degree of accuracy of offered help.	Same as Ipsocentric.	High level of interest in real need of ESO. High degree of accuracy of offered help.	High level of interest in real need of ESO. Degree of accuracy depending on a degree of similarity of ESO to the self.

(Szustrowa, 1972). (The term *self-evaluation* refers to judgments about oneself that are either positive or negative.) There is also evidence of a curvilinear relationship between some forms of prosocial behavior and self-esteem. We have found that low and high self-esteem people are less pro-social than those with moderate self-esteem (Kowalczewska, 1972).

In the domain of interpersonal communication it has been found (Grzes-iuk, 1979) that the ability to consider the partner's view and coordinate it with one's own view is higher among persons at a medium level of self-esteem than among those at high and low levels. High and low self-esteem persons are either more egocentric in communication (being relatively insensitive to a partner's communication needs) or "allocentric" (willing to subordinate their own communication needs to suit their partner's interests).

The above reasoning has some implications for the problem of enhancing prosocial behavior. Apparently an increase in self-esteem might lower self-concentration among people with low self-esteem but raise self-concentration among people with high self-esteem (or, at least, not evoke any noticeable changes). This notion has been, indirectly, tested by Jarymowicz (1979) in an extensive program of research with high school pupils. Jary-mowicz compared the effect of procedures aimed at increasing self-esteem among pupils with low self-esteem, those uncertain about self-esteem (based on a discrepancy between evaluation by the self and by others), and those with relatively stable self-esteem (based on agreement between evaluation by the self and by others).

This program to raise self-esteem was constructed so that subjects had an opportunity to obtain specially designed information from three sources: peers, authority, and their own performance. Jarymowicz found that this procedure had a marked impact on perceptual sensitivity to the needs and interests of others as measured by a specially prepared technique (using film characters as an object of observation), but only for the low and uncertain self-esteem groups. No changes were observed in the stable self-esteem group (Jarymowicz, 1979).[5]

If procedures aimed at changing self-esteem have a long-term effect, the corresponding changes in behavior should be permanent as well. This was observed by Malinowska (1978), who studied the effects of an interpersonal training program for managers 3 months after the program's completion. It should be added, however, that significant changes in behavior in a

---

[5] It should be mentioned that although perceptual sensitivity to needs of others was rather low among subjects from the low and uncertain self-esteem groups, the motivation to help, as measured by declaration of participation in helping activity, was high among those from the low self-esteem group. Apparently poor orientation to the needs of others does not preclude a tendency to act prosocially, since this action may be instigated by motivation coming from other sources.

prosocial direction (as evaluated by superiors and subordinates) occurred only if the changes in self-esteem were associated with an improvement in perspective-taking skills (as measured by a Role Taking Test; Feffer & Schnall, 1976). This finding indicates that an increment in self-esteem does not always result in increased prosocial tendencies. In fact, it is even possible that procedures that raise self-esteem can suppress prosocial behavior if self-esteem was originally high. Hamer (1978), who studied women who had been selected for their initial high self-esteem, found information that boosted self-esteem had a detrimental effect on subjects' willingness to react with approval to requests for help.

This last finding suggests that self-concentration may have impact not only on perceptual processes but on evaluative processes as well. The tendency to devaluate the needs of others, even if they are clearly articulated, can be related to a high value attributed to oneself and to all those events that are related to the self (e.g., the time and effort required for prosocial activity can be overestimated). This tendency to attribute a high value to oneself may be a consequence of self-concentration. It is well known that objects are overestimated when they are in the center of attention—this overestimation refers to size as well as to value (Flavell, 1963).

We may expect that if attention is directed to the self, the value attributed to the self may increase and the value of other objects not related to oneself may decrease, which, in turn, would interfere with prosocial behavior. In fact, Karylowski (1979) has shown that if a subject looks at himself or herself in a mirror (which supposedly directs attention to oneself) during an action that can bring some profit for oneself and for a partner, output in behalf of a partner decreases while effort for one's own benefit does not change. Apparently, the interests of others become less important under these conditions. But, according to our reasoning, the motivation for a prosocial act can originate in the representation of a social object; therefore, a concentration on the object should enhance prosocial behavior. In other words, this behavior can be enhanced not only by lowering self-concentration but also by heightening concentration on external social objects. This concentration can be increased in various ways. One possible way is by induction, which involves explaining the consequences of an act for the other person's well being and making salient the other's needs and situation (Hoffman, 1970; Staub, 1978). It is also possible to increase prosocial behavior by concentrating a subject's attention on the normative requirements of a situation. It has been shown that observing someone who reacts positively to the needs of others (gives money to a charity) or, on the other hand, who acts contrary to a social norm (refuses to donate money to a charity) may activate prosocial behavior (Macaulay, 1970).

Increasing concentration on normative requirements can also be produced by a specific task. For instance, norms can become more salient if a subject has to analyze them. This procedure has been used by Jarymowicz (1979) to enhance prosocial behavior among people with predominantly egocentric attitudes. She found that subjects who had to find arguments against egocentric beliefs (experimental group) obtained higher scores on measures of sensitivity to the needs of others than subjects who were not involved in this activity (control group).

Results of this kind are sometimes interpreted in terms of the relationship between a norm's salience and activation of behavioral patterns; that is, actions associated with a given norm may increase as a consequence of attention paid to the norm itself. But this interpretation can be challenged by the results of the Jarymowicz study. Jarymowicz found that dealing with egocentric and prosocial norms not only increased willingness to participate in helping activities but affected one's perceptual processes (perceiving needs of others) and the planning of prosocial action. Norm activation, therefore, may not be regarded as a mere actualization of some behavioral patterns. It seems, instead, to operate by producing changes in the tuning of regulatory mechanisms.

In summary, it can be said that:

1. Self-concentration is associated with a low level of intrinsically motivated prosocial activity, since it influences the amount of value attributed to the self and to the external social object. This does not imply that other forms of motivation for prosocial acts have to be affected by self-concentration.
2. Self-concentration is influenced by different states of the self-structure. Depending on the initial state of the self, the same procedures may cause an increment or decrement of self-concentration.
3. Self-concentration can be counteracted by factors that induce concentration upon external objects.

Self-structure as a Source of Motivation for Prosocial Behavior

In agreement with other theories (see Berkowitz, 1970, 1972) and common sense, we are assuming that self-concentration suppresses prosocial behavior. We have also presented some data showing that changes in self-concentration influence prosocial motivation.

The assumption seems to be self evident: If a person is attending to himself or herself, by definition, presumably, the person is not attending to someone else. But the issue is not as obvious as it seems to appear. It is quite possible that the suppression of prosocial behavior by self concern is occurring under certain conditions only. To specify these conditions we must first try to understand why this "suppression effect" occurs at all. Possible explanations for this inhibitory effect may be sought in the limited capacity of attention: If a person concentrates attention upon the self there is no room in his or her mind to do anything else (Wicklund, 1975). This is not necessarily true, however.

People who are concerned about themselves very often are quite sensitive to all those external events that can possibly affect their well being. It is not the perceptual activity that is interfered with in such a case. Rather, self-concentration has some impact on the processing of information about other people. Sensitivity to cues concerning other people as separate psychological entities seems to be lowered by situational as well as dispositional self-concentration. In this case the intrinsic form of prosocial motivation should be impaired, since perception of someone's need is a precondition for this motivation (see Table 15.1). But what about other forms of motivation to prosocial behavior?

According to the model we have presented, the self-structure can be involved in the regulation of prosocial behavior. Self-concentration may have quite different consequences for motivation of prosocial behavior that originates in a self-structure. We can describe three different ways of inducing this motivation.

One possible way is based on the actualization of personal norms. The term *personal norm* refers to the action programs that are defined by society (or a social group) as desirable or necessary and incorporated into the self as prerequisites for self-esteem. Personal norms may also take the form of opinions about the value of given objects (or objects of a given class). It should be added that besides personal norms, a person can develop an individual normative system—a complex cognitive organization that is relatively independent of the self but that exercises some control over the self. Kohlberg's (1964) postconventional stage of moral development is an example of this form of normative organization. If the normative system is autonomous in relation to the self, the preservation of the system rather than the protection of self-esteem becomes the main motivational force. The action tendencies that are consistent with the system are preferred over those that are directed toward self-esteem enhancement or defense.

But personal norms are related to the self. We expect that concentration of attention on normative aspects of the self should facilitate prosocial behavior based on endocentric motivation (Karylowski, 1978, 1979). The generality of the statement presented in the section on "Self as a Source of Inhibitory Forces" concerning the role of self-concentration should be qualified. Some forms of self-concentration—namely concentration on one's own moral standards and their importance for self-esteem—can have positive impact on prosocial behavior. We developed procedures to test this idea in a study by Hamer (1978) with highly egocentric women. Hamer led her subjects to believe that on the basis of previous testing they had a high potential for being helpful. This procedure apparently concentrated attention on the self but primarily on its normative (moral) aspect, which facilitated prosocial behavior.

Other results that support this line of reasoning were obtained by Karylowski. He found that procedures that concentrated attention on the self (by means of a mirror) did not produce any decline of prosocial behavior when applied to persons for whom the norm of helpfulness had a very high ranking in their hierarchy of values. Presumably it was a very salient norm for them.

A second way of involving the self in the regulation of prosocial behavior is by eliciting a feeling of closeness to the person in need. Several studies show that there is a bias in the evaluation of people who are perceived as similar to oneself (Shaver, 1970; Ledzińska, 1974). The direction of bias depends on one's self-esteem: People with high self-esteem have a tendency to exaggerate the achievements of those similar to themselves and to underestimate their short comings, but people with low self-esteem do the reverse. Low self-esteem individuals underestimate the achievements of those similar to themselves (Karylowski, 1975b).

Similarity influences helping. Young people who were working on a task to earn money for themselves and for an unidentified partner increased their output for their partner after they learned the partner had interests similar to them (Karylowski, 1975b), or they worked more for those whose actual activity and plans for the future were similar to their own (Smoleńska, 1979). The phenomenon of attraction to similar persons (Byrne, 1969) does not account for an observed relationship: Attraction to a similar person is related to self-acceptance. People with low self-acceptance are less attracted to similar persons than people with high self-acceptance, but self-acceptance has no effect on helping behavior (Smoleńska, 1979). People evaluated as not attractive obtain more help when they are similar to the self.

One explanation for prosocial behavior toward people located near the self in cognitive space is based on the phenomenon of generalization of personal standards of well-being to those objects (Reykowski, 1977; Reykowski & Smoleńska, in press). Some degree of concentration on personal standards (probably not too strong) might contribute to the greater effectiveness of this mechanism. In fact, Smoleńska (1979) has found that people who received high scores in egocentrism (as measured by the Associative Egocentrism Test; Szustrowa, 1976) were much more sensitive to the difference in similarity of their partners than people with low scores. The amount of effort for a similar person was substantially higher than for a dissimilar person. Subjects with low egocentrism scores reacted much less to this difference.

A third way of involving the self in the regulation of prosocial behavior—by means of external reward or punishment—is common to everyday life. In studies with children we have found that this way of inducing prosocial behavior has a detrimental effect on the cognitive analysis of a situation in which someone needs help (Kochańska, 1980). In Kochańska's experiment one group of children was externally rewarded for helping (the children received chocolate bars), while another group had an intrinsic reward (they were informed about the positive effects of their helping). In a separate test all subjects had an opportunity to obtain information about children in a hospital and to select toys for them. It was found that externally rewarded subjects were much less interested in obtaining this information and they selected toys for others that were inappropriate, given the age, sex and health status (e.g., being immobilized or having serious visual impairment) of the would-be recipients.

In conclusion, it can be said that:

1. The self plays a mediating role in the regulation of prosocial behavior.
2. Involvement of the self in the regulation of prosocial behavior can be achieved via different procedures: by making salient either personal norms, personal standards of well-being in relation to persons closely related to the self, or personal interests.
3. The mediating function of the self may be enhanced by self-concentration. A person may concentrate on various aspects of self which, in turn, arouses different kinds of prosocial motivation.

Final Remarks

According to an old Latin proverb, "Si duo faciunt idem non est idem." (If two persons are doing the same thing, it is not the same thing.) Acts that, according to their social meaning, are classified as prosocial may differ substantially in nature. Behaviors may be caused and controlled by different factors and by mechanisms that in turn are a function of various criteria or value attributions assigned to the external social object.

People differ in their rules of value attribution with respect to an external social object. The same object (or category of objects) may have different values for various people, producing different kinds of motivation. For instance, it may be expected that self-centered persons react to the needs and interests of their peers on a different basis than less self-centered persons. This has been shown empirically in a study of pupils from special high schools for talented children. Smoleńska (1975) found that these children were more egocentric than pupils from regular schools but, at the same time, that they were more sensitive to cues concerning the similarity of persons than their peers from other schools. Apparently, in these children, mechanisms for the generalization of personal standards were much easier to activate than in the children from regular schools.

Nowak (1977) constructed a paper and pencil test for measuring dominant criteria for value attribution.[6] Subjects were presented with a series of descriptions of everyday situations and asked for their reactions. The answers were classified by means of a specially developed scoring system. Results indicated that there was a substantial correlation between a person's dominant criterion of value attribution and his or her way of reacting to situations involving the problems and interests of other people.

But it would be misleading to say that people are using the criteria of value attribution consistently. The Latin proverb quoted above can be extended: The same act by the same person in different situations may not have the same meaning. In fact, Szumotalska (1978) has found that a person can have different rules of value attribution for different people in his or her social surroundings.

The major conclusion of this chapter is that the value attribution process plays a crucial role in controlling prosocial behavior. An understanding of this process as well as of its origin seems to be a major challenge for the study of prosocial behavior.

References

Bar-Tal, D. *Prosocial behavior.* New York: John Wiley & Sons, 1976.

Berkowitz, L. The self, selfishness and altruism. In J. Macaulay & L. Berkowitz (Eds.), *Altruism and helping behavior.* New York: Academic Press, 1970.

Berkowitz, L. Social norms, feelings, and other factors affecting helping and altruism. In L. Berkowitz (Ed.), *Advances in experimental social psychology* (Vol. 6). New York: Academic Press, 1972.

Byrne, D. Attitudes and attraction. In L. Berkowitz (Ed.), *Advances in experimental social psychology* (Vol. 4). New York: Academic Press, 1969.

Bozowich, L. L. *Licznost i jejo formirowanije w detskom wozrastie.* Moscow: Proswieszczenije, 1968.

Feffer, M., & Schnall, M. *Role taking test: Scoring criteria.* Washington: Library of Congress, 1976.

Festinger, L. *A theory of cognitive dissonance.* Stanford: Stanford University Press, 1957.

Festinger, L. The motivating effect of cognitive dissonance. In G. Lindzey (Ed.), *Assessment of human motives.* New York: Rinehart, 1958.

---

[6] Applying factor analysis to the test data, Nowak (1977) obtained factors that can be interpreted satisfactorily in terms of the value attribution mechanisms I have described.

Flavell, J. *The developmental psychology of Jean Piaget.* Princeton, New Jersey: D. Van Nostrand, 1963.

Grzesiuk, L. *Style komunikacji interpersonalnej.* Warsaw: Uniwersytetu Warszawskiego, 1979.

Hamer, H. Wywoływanie motywacji do działań prospolecznych u kobiet aktywnie egocentrycznych. In J. Reykowski (Ed.), *Teoria osobowości a zachowania prospoleczne.* Warsaw: IFiS PAN, 1978.

Hebb, D. O. *The organization of behavior.* New York: John Wiley & Sons, 1949.

Hoffman, M. L. Moral development. In P. H. Mussen (Ed.), *Carmichael's manual of child psychology* (Vol. 2). New York: John Wiley & Sons, 1970.

Hornstein, H. *Cruelty and kindness.* Englewood Cliffs, New Jersey: Prentice-Hall, 1976.

Hunt, J. McV. Intrinsic motivation and its role in psychological development. In D. Levine (Ed.), *Nebraska symposium on motivation.* Lincoln: University of Nebraska Press, 1965.

Jarymowicz, M. *Modyfikowanie wyobrażeń dotyczących "ja" dla zwiekszenia gotowości do zachowań prospolecznych.* Breslau: Ossolineum, 1979.

Karylowski, J. *Z badań nad mechanizmami pozytywnych ustosunkowań interpersonalnych.* Breslau: Ossolineum, 1975. (a)

Karylowski, J. Evaluation of others' acts as a function of self-other similarity and self-esteem. In J. Reykowski (Ed.), *Studies on the mechanisms of prosocial behavior.* Warsaw: Warsaw University Press, 1975. (b)

Karylowski, J. Explaining altruistic behavior: A review. *Polish Psychological Bulletin,* 1977, *8,* 27–35.

Karylowski, J. O dwóch typach mechanizmów regulacji czynności prospolecznych: zaangażowanie osobiste vs. zaangażowanie pozaosobiste. In J. Reykowski (Ed.), *Teoria osobowości a zachowania prospoleczne.* Warsaw: Wyd. IFiS. 1978.

Karylowski, J. Self-focused attention, prosocial norms and prosocial behavior. *Polish Psychological Bulletin,* 1979, *10,* 57–66.

Kiciński, K. *Egoizm i problem zachowań prospolecznych.* Warsaw: Uniwersytetu Warszawskiego, 1978.

Kochańska, G. Experimental formation of cognitive and helping social motivation in children. *Polish Psychological Bulletin,* 1980, *11,* 75–87.

Kohlberg, L. Development of moral character and moral ideology. In M. Hoffman & L. W. Hoffman (Eds.), *Review of child development research.* New York: Russell Sage Foundation, 1964.

Kowalczewska, J. *Zależność miedzy postawami wobec "ja" i nastawieniami wobec innych a tendencja do podejmowania zachowan allocentrycznych.* Unpublished master's thesis, Warsaw University, 1972.

Latané, B., & Darley, J. *The unresponsive bystander: Why doesn't he help?* New York: Appleton-Century-Crofts, 1970.

Ledzińska, M. *Zależność miedzy ocena etyczna zachowania a pozycja spoleczna ocenianej osoby.* Unpublished master's thesis, Warsaw University, 1974.

Lück, H. E. *Prosoziales Verhalten.* Cologne: Kiepenheuer und Witsch, 1975.

Lück, H. E. (Ed.) *Mitleid-Vertrauen-Verantwortung.* Stuttgart: Ernst Klett Verlag, 1977.

Lukaszewski, W. Niezgodność informacji i aktywność. *Przeglad Psychologiczny,* 1971, *21.*

Lukaszewski, W. *Osobowość, struktura i funkcje regulacyjne.* Warsaw: PWN, 1974.

Macaulay, J. A skill for charity. In J. Macaulay & L. Berkowitz (Eds.), *Altruism and helping behavior.* New York: Academic Press, 1970.

Macaulay, J. R., & Berkowitz, L. (Eds.) *Altruism and helping behavior.* New York: Academic Press, 1970.

Malinowska, M. *Zmiany w gotowości do zachowań prospolecznych pod wpływem treningu interpersonalnego.* Unpublished doctoral dissertation, Warsaw University, 1978.

McClelland, D., Atkinson, J. W., Clark, R. A., & Lowell, E. L. *The achievement motive*. New York: Appleton-Century-Crofts, 1953.

Mussen, P., & Eisenberg-Berg, N. *Roots of caring, sharing and helping*. San Francisco: W. H. Freeman, 1977.

Nowak, A. *Zależność miedzy stylami prospoleczności a kryteriami nadawania wartości innemu człowiekowi*. Unpublished master's thesis, Warsaw University, 1977.

Paspalanowa, E. *Niektóre czynniki osobowościowe warunkujace wpływ norm moralnych grupy na zachowanie prospoleczne*. Unpublished doctoral dissertation, Warsaw University, 1979.

Piaget, J. *Studia z psychologii dziecka*. Warsaw: PWN, 1966.

Pietrowski, A. W. *K postrojeniju socjalno-psihologitcheskich teorii kolektiva*. *Voprosy Filozofii*, 1975, *12*.

Pietrowski, A. W. *Psikhologiceskaja teoria grup i kolektivov na novom etapie*. *Voprosy Psikhologii*, 1977, *5*, 48–61.

Piliavin, J. A. *Impulsive helping, arousal and diffusion of responsibility*. Paper presented at the 21st Congress of Psychology, Paris, 1976.

Potocka-Hoser, A. *Wyznaczniki postawy altruistycznej*. Warsaw: PWN, 1971.

Reykowski, J. Position of self-structure in a cognitive system and prosocial orientation. *Dialectic and Humanism*, 1966, *5*, 19–30.

Reykowski, J. Introduction. Studia z psychologii osobowości. *Zeszyty Naukowe Uniwersytetu Warszawskiego*, 1972, *1*, 2–11.

Reykowski, J. Prosocial orientation and self-structure. In J. Reykowski (Ed.), *Studies on the mechanisms of prosocial behavior*. Warsaw: Warsaw University Press, 1975.

Reykowski, J. Cognitive development and prosocial behavior. *Polish Psychological Bulletin*, 1977, *8*, 35–43.

Reykowski, J. *Teoria osobowości a zachowanie prospoleczne*. Warsaw: PWN, 1978.

Reykowski, J. *Motywacja, postawy prospoleczne a osobowość*. Warsaw: PWN, 1979.

Reykowski, J., & Smoleńska, M. Z. Personality mechanisms of prosocial behavior. *Polish Psychological Bulletin*, in press.

Schorochova, E. W., & Platonov, K. K. (Eds.) *Kolektiv i litchnost*. Moscow: Nauka, 1975.

Shaver, K. G. Defensive attribution: Effects of severity and relevance on the responsibility assigned for an accident. *Journal of Personality and Social Psychology*, 1970, *14*, 101–114.

Schwartz, S. H. Moral decision making and behavior. In J. Macaulay & L. Berkowitz (Eds.), *Altruism and helping behavior*. New York: Academic Press, 1970.

Schwartz, S. H. Aktywizacja osobistych standardów normatywnych a zachowanie prospoleczne. *Studia Psychologiczne*, 1976, *15*, 5–33.

Schwartz, S. H. Normative influences on altruism. In L. Berkowitz (Ed.), *Advances in experimental social psychology* (Vol. 10). New York: Academic Press, 1977.

Smith, M. B. Perspectives on selfhood. *American Psychologist*, 1978, *33*, 1053–1063.

Smoleńska, M. Z. Self-other similarity and the allo- and egocentric behavior of gifted adolescents. In J. Reykowski (Ed.), *Studies on the mechanisms of prosocial behavior*. Warsaw: Warsaw University Press, 1975.

Smoleńska, M. Z. *Dystans psychologiczny partnera a działanie na jego rzecz*. Unpublished doctoral dissertation, Warsaw University, 1979.

Staub, E. *Positive social behavior and morality: Social and personal influences* (Vol. 1). New York: Academic Press, 1978.

Staub, E. *Positive social behavior and morality: Socialization and development* (Vol. 2). New York: Academic Press, 1979.

Szumotalska, E. *Wzajemne spostrzeganie siebie przez partnerów w zwiazku heteroseksualnym. Style kodowania partnerów a wlasciwosci zwiazku*. Unpublished master's thesis, Warsaw University, 1978.

Szustrowa, T. Zdolność do dzialania na rzecz celów pozaosobistych a niektóre wlaściwości rodzinnego treningu wychowawczego. *Zeszyty Naukowe Uniwersytetu Warszawskiego*, 1972, *1*, 12–77.

Szustrowa, T. Sytuacyjne i osobowościowe determinanty zachowania prospolecznego w sytuacji naglego sypadku. *Psychologia Wychowawcza*, 1975, *6*, 381–397.

Szustrowa, T. Test of egocentric associations. *Polish Psychological Bulletin*, 1976, *1*, 263–267.

Wicklund, R. Objective self-awareness. In L. Berkowitz (Ed.), *Advances in experimental social psychology* (Vol. 9). New York: Academic Press, 1975.

Wispé, L. (Ed.) Positive forms of social behavior. *Journal of Social Issues*, 1972, *28* (3).

Wispé, L. (Ed.) *Altruism, sympathy and helping*. New York: Academic Press, 1978.

Wispé, L. Pozytywne i negatywne zorientowanie badan psychologicznych a sytuacja spoleczna. *Studia Psychologiczne*, 1979, *18*, 5–19.

Zajonc, R. B. Cognitive theories in social psychology. In G. Lindzey & E. Aronson (Eds.), *The handbook of social psychology* (Vol. 1). Reading, Mass.: Addison-Wesley, 1968.

Chapter 16

Cognitive Basis

for the Development

of Altruistic

Behavior[1]

DANIEL BAR-TAL

RUTH SHARABANY

AMIRAN RAVIV

In the last decade, research on helping behavior has become a major area of interest for social scientists. Most of the research has concentrated on the search for situational variables that affect helping behavior; little has been said, however, about the development of such behavior. The present chapter, although it analyzes the components of altruism—especially as they are related to aspects of cognitive, social-perspective, and moral development—suggests that helping behavior develops in stages. In each stage, we believe, motivating factors on which helping behavior is based differ, and only in the last stage can helping acts be considered altruistic.

Defining an Altruistic Act

During the last decade dozens of studies investigating altruistic behavior have been conducted; nevertheless, there is still some disagreement con-

[1] This chapter is based on a presentation at the biennial conference of the International Society for the Study of Behavior Development, Pavia, Italy, 1977. The authors would like to thank Yaakov Bar-Zohar and Rachel Lazarowitz for their helpful comments on the earlier version of this manuscript.

377

cerning the definition of altruism. For example, Midlarsky (1968) has defined altruism "as a subcategory of aiding, referring to helpful actions which incur some cost to the individual but bring either very little or nothing by way of gain, relative to the magnitude of the investment [p. 229]." Bryan and Test (1967) view altruism as "those acts wherein individuals share or sacrifice a presumed positive reinforcer for no apparent social or material gain [p. 400]." Similarly, Walster and Piliavin (1972) argue that "altruistic behavior is generally thought of as behavior that benefits another rather than the self" —as something that is done "out of the goodness of one's heart [p. 166]." These definitions imply that altruistic behavior is self-initiated and aimed at benefiting another person, without expectation of external rewards.

Other psychologists have stated other specific conditions necessary for the emergence of altruism. Aronfreed (1970), Cohen (1972), and Hoffman (1975) have all emphasized that empathy is an essential condition for altruistic behavior. Only help that is performed as a result of empathic reaction to another's experience can be called altruistic. Leeds (1963) presented three essential conditions for altruistic behavior: (a) the act must be treated as an end in itself, (b) it must be elicited voluntarily, and (c) it must be judged by others as "doing good."

In spite of the disagreement as to a definition of altruistic behavior, most psychologists agree that three minimal conditions must be met if an act is to qualify as altruistic. First, there must be intention to benefit another; second, the act must be initiated by the person voluntarily; and third, it must be performed for its own end only, without expectation of reward from external sources (Bar-Tal, 1976; Berkowitz, 1972; Krebs, 1970). The authors of the present paper accept these delineated conditions and consider them necessary and sufficient to consider a helping act altruistic. According to the accepted conditions, helping behavior carried out as a result of obligation, indebtedness, restitution, the expectation of quid pro quo, or the expectation of external rewards cannot be called altruistic, even if it may benefit another person and is initiated intentionally and voluntarily. It is only on the basis of knowledge of the motives that led to the act that one can determine whether or not the behavior can be considered altruistic. Therefore, the leading questions in research on altruism should be, Why do individuals help others and, why do individuals differ in their helping behavior?

Psychologists have studied the helping behavior of children and adults both in the laboratory and in simulated real-life situations. Usually subjects have been placed in situations in which a person was in need of help, investigators observing whether subjects offer help and how rapidly. Whenever individuals helped, the researchers assumed that the behavior was altruistic. That is, researchers assumed that subjects' behavior was aimed at benefiting another and was initiated voluntarily for its own end only and that subjects did not expect external rewards. However, very few studies have actually attempted to investigate why individuals carry out helping acts (see, e.g., Krebs, 1970; Rushton, 1976). Most of the research, although it discusses altruism, has actually dealt with helping behavior only. The essence of altruism has very rarely been brought under examination.

Individuals help others for many different reasons. These reasons can vary from wanting to comply to wanting to exert authority; they may be based on self-interest or on a belief in moral principles. Moreover, reasons for helping appear to change with age. That is, although children help others at very early ages, the reasons why they help often differ from those of adults. In principle, at least, adults are capable of initiating altruistic acts; the motivating factors behind young children's helping behavior, however, do not allow us to interpret their behavior as altruistic. The present chapter advances this postulate by suggesting that helping behavior develops through stages that are closely related to the cognitive, social-perspective, and moral development of the individual. In each stage, we believe, individuals carry out helping behavior for different reasons.

Altruistic Behavior and Cognitive, Social-Perspective, and Moral Development

We have specified three conditions that define an altruistic act: (a) The act must be initiated voluntarily; (b) the helper's intention must be to benefit another; and (c) the act must be performed for its own end only, when the helper does not expect external rewards. We have also postulated that altruistic behavior develops through stages and that young children are incapable of performing helping behavior that meets the conditions of altruistic behavior. In this section, aspects of cognitive, social-perspective, and moral development that are related to the capability of performing an altruistic act will be examined. The purpose of this examination is to strengthen our claim that the capacity to perform a truly altruistic act is a developmental achievement.

Cognitive Development and Altruistic Behavior

It has been suggested that the stages of cognitive development, as conceptualized by Piaget, represent basic capacities (Kohlberg, 1969, 1976). As children develop through these stages, they change from organisms that are dependent solely on their senses and motor activities to understand the world about them, to individuals capable of complex thinking with great flexibility of thought and abstract reasoning. In the early stages of cognitive development children's thinking is characterized by egocentrism, "centration," primitive understanding of causality, inability to deal with quantitative relationships, inability to consider a variety of alternatives to act, and inability to understand the importance of one's own intentions in behavior. It is suggested that because of these limitations, children in their early stages of cognitive development have limited capabilities of performing an altruistic act. Several cognitive capacities are necessary in order to perform such an act. Individuals must be able to consider the various alternatives for action, to predict the consequence of a helping act, to consider equitable exchange, and to understand the meaning and importance of intentions. These skills develop during the first decade and a half of an individual's life, and we can assume that the development of each of these skills might qualitatively influence the conditions under which the individual would perform a helping act.

An additional limitation related to cognitive development that may prevent young children from performing altruistic acts is their inability to defer gratification. Research has shown that the ability to defer immediate and concrete gratifications in favor of more valued long-range satisfactions develops through the years. In a series of studies, Mischel (1965) has demonstrated that delay of gratification responses tends to increase with age. An altruistic act is based on a definite delay of immediate and concrete gratification. It may be that because young children are incapable of deferring such gratification, there is little likelihood that they would perform altruistic acts.

Social-Perspective Development and Altruistic Behavior

Social-perspective development deals mainly with the development of perceptions and feelings toward another person. Social perspective, like cognitive capacity, develops through stages, and it is related to cognitive development; however, it involves social interaction and includes some emotional components (Flavell, 1968; Selman, 1976). Theories of social perspective suggest that the individual goes through a number of changes in his development. First, the child is characterized by egocentrism; that is, the response to another person is self-centered and undifferentiated. Later, the child recognizes the fact that others have inner states, independent of the child's, and the child develops the ability to consider another person's perspectives. On reaching this stage, the child is able to perform a helping act that will at least be relevant to the needs of the recipient. Finally, the young person achieves a sense of continuity of the identity of objects and of other people so that he or she recognizes that these identities go beyond the immediate situation. At this point, young people cannot only take other people's roles and assess their feelings or needs but can generalize and construct a concept of others' general life experience. It is likely that an individual in this stage can respond to the needs of others without expecting an immediate reward. It is argued that without the ability to take another person's view, without the ability to recognize another person's needs, and without the ability to feel concern for another person's welfare, the individual is incapable of carrying out an altruistic act.

Accompanying the stage-by-stage perceptual development of a sense of another is an evolving capacity for empathy (Hoffman, 1975). During their early years, children do not discriminate between stimuli that come from their own body and those that come from outside; therefore they are incapable of knowing that another person might be in distress. Only when children acquire a sense of "other" as separate and different from themselves, can they recognize other persons in distress. Such recognition of another person's distress gradually develops into a more reciprocal, sympathetic concern for other people in need. Shantz (1975), reviewing the empirical evidence, has suggested that "accurate empathy concerning simple emotions is achieved by preschool children when tht situation of the other person is familiar to the child and/or the other person is substantially similar to the child. Accurate understanding of these same emotions is not usually attained until middle or late childhood when the situations and people judged have low similarity and low familiarity to the child [p. 281]." A number of psychologists claim (e.g., Aronfreed, 1970; Hoffman, 1975; Piliavin & Piliavin, 1972) that empathy is a necessary condition for altruistic behavior. Only sympathetic concern for others in need can motivate people to initiate an altruistic act. However, children at early ages do not feel sympathetic concern.

Moral Development and Altruistic Behavior

According to the principles of moral development as conceptualized by Piaget (1932) and Kohlberg (1969), children's moral orientation is qualitatively different from adults', and moral judgment develops through a sequence of stages. On analyzing the stages of moral development, it is possible to recognize the following changes in an individual's moral orientation: (a) a change from an external morality, which is based on results, to an internal morality, which is based on evaluation of intentions; (b) a change from a reward–punishment orientation to an orientation that focuses on authority and conventional requirements; and (c) a change from external considerations of the moral situation to an internalization of abstract principles of justice that are based on the welfare of others in a social contract or the categorized intuition of whether an act is right or wrong. These principles of moral development indicate that young children are incapable of performing an altruistic act, for, according to the above principles, the moral orientation of young children is guided by external demands, directed toward specific rewards or avoidance of punishment, linked to specific contexts, and characterized by unilateral consideration of moral rules (see Baldwin & Baldwin, 1970). It is again assumed, however, that as an individual's moral orientation changes there may also be qualitative changes with regard to conditions that would bring on the initiation of helping acts.

Helping Behavior, Age, and Cognitive, Social-Perspective, and Moral Development

The suggestion that helping behavior develops in stages is based on two types of empirical evidence: (a) helping behavior increases with age; and (b) helping behavior is positively related to cognitive, social-perspective, and moral development.

Helping Behavior and Age

The finding that helping behavior steadily increases with age during the first years of life has been confirmed by several experiments. For example, in a recent experiment, Green and Schneider (1974) investigated age differences in altruistic behavior in three situations. The subjects were 100 boys from 4 age groups: 5–6, 7–8, 9–10, and 13–14. The three situations involved sharing candy, helping to pick up "accidentally" dropped pencils, and volunteering to work for poor children. The results of the study indicated that sharing candy increased with age and helping to pick up pencils increased until ages 9–10, when virtually all the boys helped, but that volunteering was unrelated to age. The experimenters explained the latter finding by suggesting that the younger children—and even the youngest children tended to volunteer—could not "fully appreciate the implication that the expression of intention to help has for their future behavior [Green & Schneider, 1974, p. 250]." Other studies (e.g., Handlon & Gross, 1959; Midlarsky & Bryan, 1972), also obtained results indicating that age and helping behavior are positively related.

One possible explanation of Green and Schneider's results is that helping behavior is related to development. The initiation of helping acts depends on the level of children's cognitive, social-perspective, and moral development. Thus young children cannot behave altruistically because of their conceptual and cognitive limitations. We have already suggested that children must reach a certain level of moral development in order to be able to carry out altruistic acts (Bar-Tal, 1976; Bryan & London, 1970; Krebs, 1970; Rosenhan, 1972; Rushton, 1976).

Helping Behavior and Cognitive, Social-Perspective, and Moral Development

Several empirical studies have investigated the relationship between cognitive, social-perspective, and moral development and helping behavior. These investigations have taken the form of correlational research. For example, a study by Rubin and Schneider (1973) focused on the relationships among moral judgment, lack of egocentrism, and helping behavior. The experimenters measured separately the communicative skill (or lack of egocentrism), moral judgment, and helping behavior of 7-year-old children. Helping behavior was measured in two different situations. In the first situation, each child was asked to donate boxes of candy to a group of poor children. In the second situation, each child had an opportunity to help a younger child put tickets into small piles. The results of the study showed that the number of candy boxes donated to poor children was positively related to both a low degree of egocentrism ($r = .31$), and moral judgment ($r = .31$). Also, the number of ticket piles completed for the younger child was significantly related to both egocentrism ($r = .44$) and moral judgment ($r = .40$). The results indicate that as children acquire more "decentration" skills and develop higher levels of moral judgment, they are more able to initiate helping behavior.

Similarly, Dreman (1976), Emler and Rushton (1974), and Rushton (1975) also found that the moral judgment of children was positively related to helping behavior. In this vein, Lazarowitz, Stephan, and Friedman (1976) investigated the effect of an individual's stage of moral judgment and exposure to different levels of moral justification on helping behavior. The results of this study indicate that although individuals at lower stages of moral development are unaffected by presented moral reasoning that is several stages above their own, individuals at the higher stages helped as a function of exposure to different statements of moral justification. That is, individuals who do not comprehend the reasoning do not and cannot react accordingly.

Furthermore, there is evidence that a relationship exists between understanding the conservation of liquid quantity and sharing behavior (Larsen & Kellogg, 1974). In addition, a significant positive correlation has been found to exist between role-taking ability and helping behavior (Krebs &

Sturrup, 1974). The results of the first study show that helping behavior is related to cognitive development and the results of the second study indicate that helping behavior is related to social-perspective development.

A remark should be made about the aforementioned studies. Although the authors refer in their articles to altruistic behavior, there is no verification that these helping acts were in fact altruistic.

A study by Baldwin and Baldwin (1970) is of particular interest for the thesis of this chapter. This study sheds some light on the relationship between moral development and helping behavior. In their experiment, Baldwin and Baldwin presented their subjects with 10 stories. In each story, two helping situations were presented and the subjects were asked to judge in which situation the helper was kinder. The 10 stories included descriptions of the following aspects of helping behavior: intentional help versus unintentional help; choice versus no choice in giving help; spontaneous help versus obedience; help involving high cost versus help involving low cost; helping a guest versus not helping a guest; helping versus exchange; helping versus bribery; helping versus reciprocity; helping versus equalizing benefits; and high versus low locus of need of the helpee. The stories were presented to groups of subjects who ranged from 4-year-olds to young adults. The results of this study showed significant differences between age groups. More specifically, "by second grade children understand the importance of intentionality and the role of self-interest as it appears in a trade [p. 39]." By fourth grade, children understand the meaning of choice, obedience, cost of help, obligation to a guest, and bribery. "It is not until eighth grade that the problem of returning a favor is responded to in an adultlike fashion, and there is still a significant change between eighth grade and adults in the responses to the situation of equalizing benefits [p. 39]." These results indicate that the concept of kindness develops with age. Thus, it seems possible to infer that if children of different ages judge the meaning of a kind act differently, children of different ages will also give qualitatively different reasons for performing helping behavior.

In sum, if we accept the analysis that developmental limitations prevent individuals from performing altruistic acts, we can assume that helping behavior develops in stages. The developmental stages of helping behavior are presented in the next section.

The Developmental Stages of Helping Behavior

This chapter suggests that there are six stages in the development of helping behavior, each related to cognitive, social-perspective, and moral development. In the sixth stage, helping behavior finally fulfills all the conditions defining an altruistic act. In the earlier stages, individuals do help; however, their helping behavior cannot be considered altruistic.

Stage 1: Compliance and Concrete, Defined Reinforcement

In the first stage the individual carries out a helping act because a request or command has been accompanied by an obvious promise of a concrete reward or an explicit threat of a punishment. The helping behavior is guided at this stage by the experience of pain or pleasure without any sense of responsibility, duty, or even respect of authority. In this stage children have an egocentric perspective, that is, they do not realize that others feel and think differently from them. This is a stage of behavior guided by concrete and defined rewards and punishments. Children who help to put their toys away because their mothers have told them to do so and have promised them candy exemplify behavior in the first stage.

Stage 2: Compliance

In this stage the individual carries out the helping act in order to comply with authority. The individual does not initiate helping behavior but obeys the requests or commands of others superior to him or her in power or prestige. In the second stage the child realizes that people may feel and think differently. A helping act at this stage is motivated by the need to gain approval and avoid punishment. At this stage the individual does not need a concrete reinforcement because he or she recognizes the power of authority. However, the reinforcement remains defined: approval or disapproval. For example, at this stage, children report that they helped because their mother told them to do so.

Stage 3: Internal Initiative and Concrete Reward

In the third stage the individual voluntarily initiates help; however, the initiation is contingent on receiving a concrete and defined reward in return. In this stage children are able to define their needs. Their orientation is egoistic, and their actions are motivated by the desire for benefit or reward in order to satisfy their own needs. Helping acts at this stage are carried out only if the person perceives the opportunity to receive an immediate and concrete reward in return. For example, a child may help in this stage by giving his or her toy to another child in exchange for receiving ice cream.

Stage 4: Normative Behavior

At this stage the individual carries out helping acts in order to comply with societal demands. The individual knows that certain kinds of behavior are expected and that conformity to these behavioral norms is followed by positive sanctions, whereas violation of the norms is followed by negative sanctions. The requirements of the society are external to people in this stage. They help because they are expected to do so, and they want to be good people in others' eyes. This orientation encompasses the desire to receive approval and please others. The expected reward for helping is nonconcrete but defined.

In this fourth stage the child is able to take the role of the person in need and to feel sympathetic distress. Helping acts at this stage are justified by expressing reasons such as, "I helped because my mother will like my behavior," "I helped because people will like me," or "I helped because good people help others."

It should be pointed out that a number of psychologists have suggested that helping behavior is guided by prescriptions of social norms (e.g., Berkowitz, 1972; Staub, 1972). The specific examples of proposed norms are the *norm of giving* and the *norm of social responsibility*. Leeds (1963) proposed the existence of the norm of giving, which states that "one should want to give, not because he may anticipate returns but for its own value [p. 229]." Leeds maintained that the norm of giving is only partially institutionalized. A person who has internalized this norm has a "need-disposition to give." Berkowitz and his associates (e.g., Berkowitz & Connor, 1966; Berkowitz & Daniels, 1963) suggested the existence of the social responsibility norm which prescribes that an individual should help those who depend on him and need his assistance. People who internalize the norm of social responsibility "act on behalf of others, not for material gain or social approval, but for their own self-approval, for the self-administered rewards arising from doing what is 'right' [Goranson & Berkowitz, 1966, p. 228]."

Stage 5: Generalized Reciprocity

In this stage, the helping behavior of individuals is guided by universal principles of exchange. People recognize a regulated system in the world that controls helping behavior. They help, believing that one day when they are in need, they will be helped in return. This is a reciprocal social agreement based on an abstract contract: The expected reward is nonconcrete and undefined. The individual in this stage internalizes the rules of the society and helps in order to avoid creating a breakdown in the system.

Two theoreticians have explicitly referred to the system of generalized reciprocity. Gouldner (1960) has discussed principles of exchange by postulating the presence of a universal norm of reciprocity which states: "(1) People should help those who have helped them, and (2) people should not injure those who have helped them [p. 171]." This norm, according to Gouldner, has an important function in stabilizing human relations in society. It "engenders motives for returning benefits even when power differences might invite exploitation. The norm thus safeguards powerful people against the temptation of their own status; it motivates and regulates reciprocity as an exchange pattern, serving to inhibit the emergence of exploitive relations [Gouldner, 1960, p. 174]." This norm serves as a starting mechanism for human interactions. A person who initiates a helping act is confident that the recipient will reciprocate one day: "When internalized by both parties, the norm obliges the one who received a benefit first to repay it at some time; it thus provides some realistic grounds for confidence, in the one who first parts with his valuable, that he will be repaid [Gouldner, 1960, p. 177]." Such a norm regulates social exchanges and contributes to social stability. Gouldner (1960) however adds that "the norm of reciprocity cannot apply full force in relations with children" [p. 178], whose behavior is still guided by other principles.

Trivers (1971) calls a helping act in the fifth stage *reciprocal altruism.* The individual carries out a helping act even when detrimental to himself or herself because there is always a chance that the helpee will help the helper in the future. Trivers uses a rescue model to show that in the long run it is more beneficial for the individual to help than not to help. When individuals help, they have greater probabilatity to survive than when they do not help because one day somebody will also help them. Thus, Trivers (1971) concluded that "the benefits of human altruism are to be seen as coming directly from reciprocity [p. 47]."

Stage 6: Altruistic Behavior

In this stage, an individual initiates the helping act voluntarily, for its own end only, and to benefit another, and he does not expect external rewards. Most psychologists agree that helping behavior at this stage is altruistic (e.g., Bar-Tal, 1976; Krebs, 1970; Macaulay & Berkowitz, 1970). The individual's helping act at this stage is self-chosen and based on moral principles. The individual is concerned about another's welfare, can assess another's needs, and experiences sympathy when another is in need. Although the individual does not expect any benefits in return for helping, he or she feels self-rewarded. He or she may have feelings of self-satisfaction and sense a rise in his or her self-esteem.

Summary

The stages described above can be differentiated on the basis of two dimensions. The first dimension differentiates helping behavior carried out in order to comply with external authority A_1 as opposed to self-initiated helping behavior A_2. The second dimension differentiates helping behavior according to the kind of reinforcement expected following the helping act. There are four kinds of reinforcements: external, concrete, and defined reinforcement B_1; external, nonconcrete, and defined reinforcement B_2; external, nonconcrete, and undefined reinforcement B_3; and self-reinforcement B_4.

On the basis of the two dimensions, the stages of altruistic development can be represented as follows:

$$\text{Stage } 1 = A_1B_1$$
$$\text{Stage } 2 = A_1B_2$$
$$\text{Stage } 3 = A_2B_1$$
$$\text{Stage } 4 = A_2B_2$$
$$\text{Stage } 5 = A_2B_3$$
$$\text{Stage } 6 = A_2B_4$$

Empirical Evidence

A number of experiments provide evidence in support of our theory of developmental helping-behavior stages. These studies can be classified into two types: first, studies that present hypothetical situations involving helping acts and ask subjects to discuss their readiness to help in such situations and their reasons for assuming they would perform these helping acts; second, studies in which subjects perform a helping act and then are asked why they performed it. In both types of studies the categorization of the subjects' answers indicates that there are differential responses and that the nature of the responses is related to age.

In the first of two experiments, children of various age groups were presented with stories describing hypothetical helping situations. In a study by Raviv, Bar-Tal, and Amir (1977), 306 children from the second (7–8-year-olds), fifth (10–11-year-olds) and eighth (13–14-year-olds) grades were presented with 6 stories describing how one child helps another. The helping act in each story reflected one of the six "exchange resources" suggested by Foa (1971): love, service, goods, information, money, and status. In each story, the subjects were asked why the child helped. The responses were first classified into two categories: (*a*) self-initiation (the child in the story initiated the helping act himself or herself); (*b*) compliance with external authority (another person induced the child to help). The responses showed that 90% of the acts were seen as self-initiated.

Subjects' responses were also categorized according to the three levels of reward that could be expected in return for the helping act (external reward, internal reward, no reward). A significant relationship was found between age of subject and the level of expected reward across the six stories ($\chi^2(4)$ = 91.6, $p < .001$). A close look at the numbers indicates that the frequency of answers in the internal reward category increased with age. Of the answers in this category, 23% were given by the second graders, 28% by fifth graders, and 43% by eighth graders. The frequencies of answers in the external reward category were somewhat different. Of these answers, 50% were given by second graders, 17% by fifth graders, and 33% by eighth graders. In the category of no reward, 31% of the answers were given by second graders, 39% by fifth graders, and 30% by eighth graders. The authors explained these results by suggesting that the answers in the category of no reward reflect, in this particular study, an expression of Stage 4 (normative behavior). The content analysis of the responses in the latter category showed that the children knew that a helping act was expected, and therefore that the no reward answers probably indicated social desirability (Stage 4). This explanation is reinforced by the content analysis of the answers in the category of external reward: Whereas in the second grade, children expected an immediate, concrete, external reward (Stage 3), in the eighth grade, children expected nonconcrete and undefined reinforcement (Stage 5). These results showed that although the majority of the youngest children voluntarily initiated a helping act, they also expected either a concrete, defined external reward (Stage 3) or a nonconcrete, defined external reward (Stage 4) for their behavior. In contrast, the majority of the oldest children expected either a nonconcrete, undefined external reward (Stage 5) or internal reward (Stage 6). The majority of children from the middle group gave answers corresponding to expected responses from children at Stages 4 and 5.

A study by Bar-Tal, Raviv, and Shavit (1977) compared the expressed motives for helping behavior between kindergarten children (ages 4–5½) and grade school children (ages 7–8½) in a kibbutz and a city. Children were presented with three pictures, each describing two children, one of them in a state of need. In one picture, one child looked enviously at the other child's ice cream; in the second one, a child fell and was hurt; and in the third picture, a child's pencils dropped on the floor. The subjects were asked whether the second child would help or share and why he or she would help or share. Whereas 95% of the children thought that the second child would help or share, the responses to the second question varied according to age. These answers can be categorized according to the stages of helping-behavior development presented in this chapter with one difference: There were seven stages instead of six. That is, Stage 5 was divided into two levels: (a) expectation of specific reciprocity and (b) generalized reciprocity.

This study's 2 × 2 × 2 × 3 factorial design was composed of the between factors of age, sex, and place of residence (kibbutz or city) and a within factor of the story (3 different pictures). Analysis of variance yielded only a strong main effect for age (F (1,79) = 53.78, p < .001), and an interaction effect between sex and place of residence (F (1,79) = 3.6, p < .05). The data indicated that whereas the answers of the kindergarten children corresponded to Stage 3 (internal initiative and concrete reward) and Stage 4 (normative behavior) of altruistic development, the answers of grade school children corresponded to Stage 4 and Stage 5a (specific reciprocity) of helping-behavior development.

Although the results of the studies reviewed do provide support for our theory of altruistic development, conclusions should be drawn with caution. In the experiments reviewed, subjects did not actually perform helping acts; they only expressed intentions.

In the next three reported experiments children of various ages were given the opportunity to share with another child and, after the interaction, they were asked why they behaved as they did.

Levin and Greenberg (1977) investigated the development of reasoning about sharing in a situation in which children had the opportunity to share pretzels with other children and were then asked to explain why they either shared or did not share. The subjects consisted of 80 children from kindergarten, second, fourth, and sixth grades. The results of this study indicated that there is a positive relationship between age and the number of pretzels shared. In addition, the responses of the subjects to the question as to why they shared were categorized into five levels: (a) generosity due to immediate automatic reward; (b) generosity due to "good boy–good girl" morality; (c) conditional generosity; (d) generosity due to empathy; and (e) functional generosity due to the value of positive justice. It should be pointed out that the first level corresponds to our proposed Stage 3, the second and third levels correspond to our proposed Stage 4, the fourth level corresponds to Stage 6, and the fifth level corresponds to our Stages 5 and 6. The findings showed that the expressed justification for sharing was related positively to age. Whereas the majority of the kindergarten and second grade children expected an immediate reward for their sharing act, the majority of fourth and sixth grade children shared because they recognized the importance of societal demands. Finally, the researchers also found a positive relationship between the number of pretzels given and the level of justification expressed.

In a study by Ugurel-Semin (1952), children between the ages of 7 and 11 were required to divide an unequal number of nuts between themselves and another child. After sharing, the children were asked why they divided the nuts as they did. The children's responses were classified into seven major categories: egocentrism; sociocentrism (obedience to moral and religious rules and customs); awareness of social reaction (fear or shame of public opinion); superficial reciprocity; deeper and enlarged reciprocity; altruism; and justice. According to Ugurel-Semin, the seven listed categories represent levels of moral judgment. The first category corresponds to our proposed Stage 3, the second and third categories correspond to our Stage 4, the fourth and fifth categories correspond to our Stage 5, the sixth and seventh category corresponds to our Stage 6. The results of this study showed that children justify sharing differently at different ages; the older the children the higher the level of justification they used. In addition, the results showed that there is a positive relationship between level of moral judgment and the percentage of children who behaved generously (keeping fewer nuts for themselves).

In a study by Dreman and Greenbaum (1973), kindergarten children (5–6-year-olds) were asked to share candies with their classmates. Those children who agreed to share were asked to indicate reasons for their behavior. The answers were coded into four categories: (*a*) altruism—"the donor wants the recipient to be happy; no interpersonal profit or loss is supposedly involved"; (*b*) social responsibility—"the donor feels obligated to give to the dependent recipient because of prevailing social norms"; (*c*) ingroup—"the donor feels obligated to help people he likes because assumedly he wants to perpetuate the friendship and/or repay friends for past services remembered"; and (*d*) reciprocity—"the donor feels obligated to help because of immediate services rendered or the possibility of future interpersonal reward [Dreman & Greenbaum, 1973, pp. 65–66]." The results of this study showed that the majority of the children (43.3%) explained their sharing by expressing societal requirements (either social responsibility or ingroup rules), and that only 17.5% of the children shared for altruistic reasons. In addition, the results indicated a significant relationship between the expressed reasoning and actual sharing. That is, the mean number of candies shared increased in each successive content category from reciprocity to altruism. The authors concluded that "the relationships between actual sharing behavior and verbal justifications for sharing are complex and may change with age or cognitive development [Dreman & Greenbaum, 1973, p. 67]."

In sum, although not all the reviewed experiments classified the motives of children according to the proposed stages of development of altruistic behavior, the results of the experiments clearly indicate that the reasons behind the helping acts of children change as they grow older. Furthermore, when individuals reach higher levels of helping-behavior development, they actually render more helping behavior.

Conclusions

The proposed theory of helping-behavior development makes a number of contributions to the understanding of child development. First, in contrast to other theories of development, it deals mainly with behavior and not with reasoning, perception, or affection. That is, while other theories (e.g., Kohlberg, 1969) first analyze the development of reasoning, perception, or judgment and then discuss its possible relationship to behavior, the present theory focuses on the behavior first and then discusses the reasons behind the act.

Second, while we are taking into account the levels of cognitive, social-perspective, and moral development as necessary sources for the performance of an altruistic act, we argue that in order to actualize the potential cognitive, social, and affective growth, there is need to apply certain social learning principles. Although cognitive theories mention the mechanisms that encourage the transition from cognitive readiness to performance, these mechanisms have not been presented in an explicit manner. As a result, few attempts to go beyond cognition into actual moral behavior were made in the literature. The present theory, by incorporating particular principles of social learning, tries to define the changes in behavior that occur between the stages of development. For example, we examine the characteristics of the reinforcement, which changes from a very concrete, defined, and immediate one to an abstract, undefined, and delayed one. In this vein, it should be noted that Mischel and Mischel (1976) view the outcome elements in moral judgment in a progressive way from the concrete and immediate to the more abstract. They claim that the element of outcome persists even in the highest levels of moral judgment. The more advanced stages are distinct from the earlier ones in that the self is now seen as the source of evaluation, the terms are more abstract, and the outcomes that are considered are neither immediate nor concrete.

Third, the present theory integrates the relationship between helping behavior and cognitive, social-perspective, and moral development into a coherent framework. It suggests that the development of high quality helping behavior is contingent on the development of a high level of cognition, social perspective, and morality. Within these domains individuals develop skills that are necessary for performance in the advanced stages of helping behavior.

Fourth, the present chapter specifies the stages of development of one specific type of moral behavior. Moral behavior consists of a general category of behaviors which includes positive acts such as helping, sharing, and sacrificing as well as avoidance of negative acts such as cheating or exploiting. Lickona (1976) pointed out that "different levels of moral principles permit different kinds of actions [p. 5]." The present theory discusses the specific relationship between helping behavior and cognitive, social-perspective, and moral development. It is possible that other moral behaviors such as honesty, or resistance to temptation require different skills and that therefore the stages of their development are different.

Finally, the relationship between the development of helping behavior and the likelihood of performing helping acts in different situations must be clarified. As was stated, individuals in all stages of helping-behavior development are capable of carrying out helping behavior. However, the reasons why they carry it out differ from one stage of development to another. Only in the sixth stage of development are individuals capable of performing an altruistic act. This is not to say that individuals perform helping behavior in all situations or even that individuals in Stage 6 will act altruistically under all circumstances. Helping behavior is greatly affected by situational conditions. In this vein, Gergen, Gergen, and Meter (1972), who investigated the stability of helping behavior, have pointed out that "what is needed, then, is a trait disposition approach that fully takes into account the nature of the situation and the helping behavior required [p. 118]." This approach corresponds to recent theorizing that suggests that performances are affected by a variety of stimulus conditions and, as a result, people tend to show considerable variability in their behavior even across seemingly similar situations. Knowledge of individual differences often tells us little unless it is combined with information about the conditions and situational variables that influence the behavior (Mischel, 1968, 1973). Thus, in our case, knowledge of the stage of altruistic development might indicate why the individual performed a helping act. In addition, the knowledge of the stage might indicate the likelihood of performing a helping act. (The latter assumption is based on the evidence that the higher the stage of development the more helping acts are performed.) However, the knowledge of the stage of helping development does not indicate when the individual will help in a particular context.

It should also be noted that the achievement of a high stage of helping development does not preclude the possibility of performing helping acts at a lower level of development. That is, individuals at the sixth stage may perform helping acts as a result of their expectation of future reciprocity from the recipient. However, the theory postulates that individuals at the lower stages of helping development are incapable of performing helping acts from higher stages.

In sum, we have presented a description of the concomitant growth of individuals' helping behavior occurring through a sequence of defined stages. At present, there is a need for additional research to validate proposed stages of development and for research investigating variables that affect development from one stage to another. Such research is necessary in order to understand individual differences in helping behavior and the differential effect of situational conditions on an individual's behavior. This direction of research can complement greatly the existing amount of data investigating the effect of personal and situational variables on helping behavior.

References

Aronfreed, J. The socialization of altruistic and sympathetic behavior: Some theoretical and experimental analyses. In J. Macaulay & L. Berkowitz (Eds.), *Altruism and helping behavior*. New York: Academic Press, 1970.

Baldwin, C. P., & Baldwin, A. L. Children's judgements of kindness. *Child Development*, 1970, *41*, 29–47.

Bar-Tal, D. *Prosocial behavior: Theory and research*. New York: Halsted Press, 1976.

Bar-Tal, D., Raviv, A., & Shavit, N. *Motives for helping behavior of kindergarten and school children in kibbutz and city*. Unpublished manuscript, Tel-Aviv University, 1977.

Berkowitz, L. Social norms, feelings, and other factors affecting helping and altruism. In L. Berkowitz (Ed.), *Advances in experimental social psychology* (Vol. 6). New York: Academic Press, 1972.

Berkowitz, L., & Connor, W. H. Success, failure and social responsibility. *Journal of Personality and Social Psychology*, 1966, *4*, 664–669.

Berkowitz, L., & Daniels, L. R. Responsibility and dependency. *Journal of Abnormal and Social Psychology*, 1963, *66*, 429–436.

Bryan, J. H., & London, P. Altruistic behavior by children. *Psychological Bulletin*, 1970, *73*, 200–211.

Bryan, J. H., & Test, M. A. Models and helping: Materialistic studies in aiding behavior. *Journal of Personality and Social Psychology*, 1967, *6*, 400–407.

Cohen, R. Altruism: Human, cultural, or what? *Journal of Social Issues*, 1972, *28*(3), 39–57.

Dreman, S. B. Sharing behavior in Israeli school children: Cognitive and social learning factors. *Child Development*, 1976, *47*, 186–194.

Dreman, S. B., & Greenbaum, C. W. Altruism or reciprocity: Sharing behavior in Israeli kindergarten children. *Child Development*, 1973, *44*, 61–68.

Emler, M. P., & Rushton, J. P. Cognitive–developmental factors in children's generosity. *British Journal of Social and Clinical Psychology*, 1974, *13*, 277–281.

Flavell, J. H . *The development of role–taking and communication skills in children*, New York: John Wiley & Son's 1968.

Foa, U. Interpersonal and economic resources. *Science*, 1971, *171*, 345–351.

Gergen, K. J., Gergen, J. M., & Meter, K. Individual orientation to prosocial behavior. *Journal of Social Issues*, 1972, *28*(3), 105–130.

Goranson, R. E., & Berkowitz, L. Reciprocity and responsibility reactions to prior help. *Journal of Personality and Social Psychology*, 1966, *3*, 227–232.

Gouldner, A. W. The norm of reciprocity: A preliminary statement. *American Sociological Review*, 1960, *25*, 161–178.

Green, F. P., & Schneider, F. W. Age differences in the behavior of boys on three measures of altruism. *Child Development*, 1974, *45*, 248–251.

Handlon, B. J., & Gross, P. The development of sharing behavior. *Journal of Abnormal and Social Psychology*, 1959, *59*, 425–428.

Hoffman, M. L. Developmental synthesis of affect and cognition and its implications for altruistic motivation. *Development Psychology*, 1975, *11*, 607–622.

Kohlberg, L. Stage and sequence: The cognitive–development approach to socialization. In D. Goslin (Ed.), *Handbook of socialization theory and research*. Chicago: Rand McNally, 1969.

Kohlberg, L. Moral development form the standpoint of a general psychological theory. In T. Lickona (Ed.), *Moral development and behavior: Theory, research, and social issues*. New York: Holt, Rinehart and Winston, 1976.

Krebs, D. L. Altruism: An examination of the concept and a review of the literature. *Psychological Bulletin*, 1970, *73*, 258–302.

Krebs, D., & Sturrup, B. Role-taking ability and altruistic behavior in elementary school children. *Personality and Social Psychology Bulletin*, 1974, *1*, 407–409.

Larsen, G. Y., & Kellogg, J. A developmental study of the relation between conservation and sharing behavior. *Child Development*, 1974, *45*, 849–851.

Lazarowitz, R., Stephan, W. G., & Friedman, T. Effects of moral justifications and moral reasoning on altruism. *Developmental Psychology*, 1976, *12*, 353–354.

Leeds, R. Altruism and the norm of giving. *Merrill-Palmer Quarterly*, 1963, *9*, 229–240.

Levin, I., & Greenberg, R. *The development of reasoning about sharing and its relation to sharing behavior*. Unpublished manuscript, Tel-Aviv University, 1977.

Lickona, T. (Ed.), *Moral development and behavior: Theory, research, and social issues*. New York: Holt, Rinehart and Winston, 1976.

Macaulay, J. R., & Berkowitz, L. (Eds.), *Altruism and helping behavior*. New York: Academic Press, 1970.

Midlarsky, E. Aiding responses: An analysis and review. *Merrill-Palmer Quarterly*, 1968, *14*, 229–260.

Midlarsky, E., & Bryan, J. H. Affect expressions and children's imitative altruism. *Journal of Experimental Research in Personality*, 1972, *6*, 195–203.

Mischel, W. Theory and research on the antecedents of self-imposed delay of reward. In B. A. Maher (Ed.), *Progress in experimental personality research* (Vol. 2). New York: Academic Press, 1965.

Mischel, W. *Personality and assessment*. New York: John Wiley & Sons, 1968.

Mischel, W. Toward a cognitive social learning reconceptualization of personality. *Psychological Review*, 1973, *80*, 252–283.

Mischel, W., & Mischel, H. B. A cognitive social-learning approach to morality and self-regulation. In T. Lickona (Ed.), *Moral development and behavior: Theory, research, and social issues*. New York: Holt, Rinehart and Winston, 1976.

Piaget, J. *The moral judgement of the child*. London: K. Paul, Trench, Trubner, & Co., 1932.

Piliavin, J. A., & Piliavin, I. M. The effect of blood on reactions to a victim. *Journal of Personality and Social Psychology*, 1972, *23*, 353–361.

Raviv, A., Bar-Tal, D., & Amir, O. *The development of motives for helping behavior and its relationship to moral judgement*. Unpublished manuscript, Tel-Aviv University, 1977.

Rosenhan, D. L. Learning theory and prosocial behavior. *Journal of Social Issues*, 1972, *28*(3), 151–163.

Rubin, K. H., & Schneider, F. W. The relationship between moral judgement, egocentrism, and altruistic behavior. *Child Development*, 1973, *44*, 661–665.

Rushton, J. P. Generosity in children: Immediate and long-term effects of modeling, preaching, and moral judgement. *Journal of Personality and Social Psychology*, 1975, *31*, 459–466.

Rushton, J. P. Socialization and the altruistic behavior of children. *Psychological Bulletin*, 1976, *83*, 898–913.

Selman, R. L. Social-cognitive understanding: A guide to educational and clinical practice. In T. Lickona (Ed.), *Moral development and behavior: Theory, research, and social issues.* New York: Holt, Rinehart and Winston, 1976.

Shantz, C. U. The development of social cognition. In E. M. Hetherington (Ed.), *Review of child development research* (Vol. 5). Chicago: The University of Chicago Press, 1975.

Staub, E. Instigation to goodness: The role of social norms and interpersonal influence. *Journal of Social Issues*, 1972, *28*(3), 131–150.

Trivers, R. L. The evolution of reciprocal altruism. *The Quarterly Review of Biology*, 1971, *46*, 35–57.

Ugurel-Semin, R. Moral behavior and judgement of children. *Journal of Abnormal and Social Psychology*, 1952, *47*, 463–474.

Walster, E., & Piliavin, J. A. Equity and the innocent bystander. *Journal of Social Issues*, 1972, *28*(3), 165–189.

Chapter 17

Two Types of Altruistic Behavior: Doing Good to Feel Good or to Make the Other Feel Good[1]

JERZY KARYLOWSKI

Altruistic behavior must be a challenging phenomenon for theories in social psychology that are based on reinforcement mechanisms. The concept of reinforcement, fundamental to so many theories of learning seems to fail when it comes to explaining altruistic behavior (see, e.g., Rosenhan, 1972). In order to explain altruistic behavior the concept has to be extended so that it takes into account internal reinforcement. This may easily lead to a vicious circle: Since behavior is exhibited, it must be reinforced in some way, and since there is no evidence of any external reinforcements, there must be an internal one. An explanation of altruistic behavior that would avoid such tautologies requires more specific hypotheses or assumptions concerning the nature of the internal reinforcement in question.

In recent years, some attempts have been made to describe different internal mechanisms underlying altruistic behavior (see Karylowski, 1977a, and Staub, 1978, for reviews). However, there is no convincing empirical evidence that these mechanisms can be separated from each other. In the majority of cases, the results of studies that have focused on one particular

[1] The research reported in this chapter was done at the University of Warsaw as part of project 11.8 sponsored by the Polish Academy of Sciences. Preparation of the chapter was facilitated by an American Council of Learned Societies Fellowship.

mechanism could have been explained by other mechanisms. Given these circumstances, a rough classification of internal mechanisms underlying altruism might be a useful starting point for research. We propose to base this classification on the *source of gratification*.

Endocentric and Exocentric Sources of Altruistic Motivation

We will exclude from our analysis pseudo-altruistic behavior, which is controlled either by anticipations of external reinforcement (in the form of material rewards and punishments, or social approval) or by nonspecific sources of motivation for helping (i.e., need for stimulation). In the analysis of altruistic behavior, only two sources of gratification seem plausible. One source deals with the maintenance or heightening of one's positive self-image; the second source deals with the improvement of the conditions of another person in need, or the prevention of those conditions from getting worse. In other words, we assume that helping another person can be either pseudo-altruistic or altruistic. Altruistic behavior is motivated either by a desire for bringing about changes in the self (i.e., improving one's self-image) or by a desire for altering something in the external world (i.e., improving the partner's conditions). The first source of motivation is called *endocentric altruism*, in which attention is focused not so much on a partner as on the self, or, more precisely, on the self's moral aspect. The second source of motivation is called *exocentric altruism*, in which attention is focused on the external world, that is, on a partner.

Different situational factors contribute to activating either endocentric or exocentric sources of altruism. All factors that focus attention on the self (especially, but not only, on its moral aspect) should increase the relative share of endocentric elements in altruistic behavior, whereas those factors that focus on the environment should increase the share of exocentric elements (see Karylowski, 1979, for some relevant data).

Certainly, any given behavior is due in part to both types of altruistic motivation as well as to elements of pseudo-altruistic motivation that are present. Nevertheless, the various mechanisms of altruistic behavior as proposed in different theories can be classified into one of our categories. And even with respect to a single behavior or, especially with respect to altruistic behavior typical of a given individual, it is possible to speak of the relative dominance of one type of motivation over another. We believe that such statements may have some interesting empirical implications. But before proceeding with our analysis, let us consider how the existing theoretical and research literature fits into the endocentric and exocentric categories.

Approaches developed by Berkowitz (Berkowitz, 1972; Berkowitz & Daniels, 1963) and especially by Schwartz (Schwartz, 1970, 1977; Schwartz & Howard, 1981; see also Chapter 14 in this volume) seem to fit into the endocentric category. Berkowitz and Schwartz assume that, as part of one's self-concept, one may have certain kinds of self-expectations that, in particular situations, require altruistic actions. To quote Schwartz (1977), "Anticipation of or actual conformity to self-expectation results in pride, enhanced self-esteem, security, or other favorable self-evaluations; violations or its anticipation produce guilt, self-depreciation, loss of self-esteem, or other negative self-evaluations [p. 231]." In this case, therefore, altruistic behavior may be seen as "motivated by the desire to act in ways consistent with one's values so as to enhance or preserve one's sense of self-worth and avoid self-concept distress [Schwartz, 1977, p. 226]."

These altruistic self-expectations may consist either of internalized social norms (e.g., Berkowitz & Daniels, 1963) or they may be generated by the individual himself/herself on the basis of more general norms and values (e.g., Schwartz, 1977). There is some evidence on the kinds of social norms (in terms of content) that can lead to altruistic behavior. These norms can be divided into two groups according to the external end-state whose attainment they prescribe. The first kind can be called *norms of aiding*. The norm of *social responsibility* (Berkowitz & Daniels, 1963) and the norm of *giving* (Leeds, 1963) are both examples of such norms. In general, these norms simply prescribe that one should aid dependent others who are in need. The second kind, *norms of justice*, are represented, for instance, by the norm of *equity* (Walster, Walster, & Berscheid, 1978) or by the norm of *reciprocity* (Gouldner, 1960), and they prescribe that one should act justly, which may mean aiding those who deserve it.

The major characteristic of endocentric approaches to altruistic behavior is the assumption that what is reinforcing for the helper is not simply the actual occurrence of certain changes in the external world (i.e., improvement of partner's condition) but the very fact that this change has been caused by the action of the helper himself. On the other hand, exocentric approaches assume that improvement of the partner's condition may possess inherent gratification value for the observer, regardless of whether it has been caused by him or not.

An example of such an exocentric approach is the model, deriving from the Lewinian tradition, proposed by Hornstein (1972, 1976; see also Chapter 10 in the present volume). The central concept here is *promotive tension*, defined as a "tension coordinated to another's goal attainment [Hornstein, 1972, p. 193]." This motivational factor can form the groundwork for altruistic behavior. The following conditions must be fulfilled for promotive tension to appear:

1. The subject must be aware that someone else desires to locomote toward a goal that is positively valenced by the subject himself or herself or away from a goal that is negatively valenced by the subject.
2. The subject and the other person are linked by a promotive social relationship (one in which other people are thought of as "we" and not as "they").

A somewhat similar model, though of a more specific nature (since it concerns only situations of emergency), has been proposed by Piliavin & Piliavin (1973; Piliavin, Dovidio, Gaertner, & Clark, 1981; see also Chapter 12 in the present volume). The Piliavin model has two basic propositions:

1. The observation of an emergency that happens to someone else arouses the bystander. The degree of arousal is a function of (a) perceived severity of the emergency, (b) physical distance between the bystander and the emergency, (c) perceived similarity and/or emotional attachment to the victim, and (d) length of time that has elapsed since the emergency without help having been received by the victim.
2. In general, the arousal occasioned by observation of an emergency becomes more unpleasant as it increases and the bystander is therefore motivated to reduce it.

This certainly provides a motivational basis for altruistic behavior, but whether such behavior actually occurs is also determined by the various costs perceived to exist in the situation.

The most important feature in the explanation of altruistic behavior in both the Piliavin and Hornstein models is that awareness of another person in need has an aversive, drive-like component. However, neither model accounts fully for why this is so. In this respect both models seem to be descriptive rather than explanatory.

Among the exocentric explanations that are more explicit about the source of motivation, two distinct subtypes seem distinguishable: cognitive and affective. These proposed explanations assume that awareness of another person in need causes either inconsistency in the individual's cognitive system (to be more precise, in his cognitive representations of external social objects), or some form of conditioned or unconditioned emotional response.

Systematic discussion of these explanations should begin with the cognitive subtype, since it is an obvious analogue of *endocentric* explanations, which we have already discussed. Let us consider the viewpoints of Lerner and Reykowski.

As in the case of the endocentric explanations, which had to do with the regulatory role of self-expectations, so in Lerner's (1977; Lerner, Miller, & Holmes, 1976; see also Chapter 11 in this volume) approach this role is played by a certain kind of expectation regarding the external world. It takes the form of believing in a just world or, in other words, that in the world (environment) in which the subject lives each person's fate corresponds to what he deserves. Lerner argues that expectations of this kind can result from the maturing of cognitive structures and that they do not require specific learning. Once they are present, any evidence that the environment of the subject is so constructed that someone does not get what he deserves can constitute a motivational basis for altruistic behavior. As in the case of the regulatory role of self-expectations, equilibrium can also be attained here by means of symbolic operations, through reinterpretation of the situation. This is especially likely when improvement of the situation of an underbenefited person would inevitably entail the subject's being deprived of what is in justice due to him. One method to restore equilibrium symbolically may be to adopt the belief that there is more than one world and that though the world in which the victim lives is unjust, the world in which the subject lives has remained a just one. This is naturally made easier if the degree of self–other similarity is slight. Here, therefore, we have a clue to the relationship between perceived similarity and helping described in the Piliavin and Hornstein models.

A similar though more general explanation of altruistic behavior is proposed by Reykowski (1976, 1977, 1979; see also Chapter 15 in this volume). Reykowski draws attention to the fact that certain social objects in the external world can, like the self, have well-developed and stable cognitive representations in the individual's cognitive system. A close friend, people in general, or even Lerner's "just world," can be good examples of such objects. As in the case of the self, these representations can be twofold: representations of normal states or representations of expected (ideal) states. Reykowski argues that each such stable cognitive representation works according to homeostatic principles, that is, it shows a tendency to maintain equilibrium. When incoming information is inconsistent with anticipations or expectations, disequilibrium occurs. This may provide a motivational basis for behavior designed to effect the necessary changes in the external world. Such behavior may be of an altruistic nature. It should be noted, however, that the mechanism postulated by Reykowski may not always generate altruistic behavior. It may, for instance, precipitate aggressive behavior. This depends on the nature of the content of the cognitive representations of a given social object.

This difficulty in predicting when altruistic behavior occurs can be at least partly overcome by taking account of the following notion: Invoking the Pavlovian (1960) concept of stimulus generalization, Reykowski suggests that if we perceive another person as very similar to us, information about the person's state can be directly confronted with our anticipations and expectations regarding ourselves. Inconsistency may result in disequilibrium, which may provide a motivational basis for altruistic behavior. In keeping with the generalization gradient notion, there should be a stronger motivation for altruistic behavior, the greater the perceived self–other similarity.

This similarity gradient notion dovetails nicely with both the Piliavin and (in principle) the Hornstein models. It is true that for Reykowski perceived self–other similarity is a continuous variable (generalization gradient), while for Hornstein it is a dichotomous variable (others perceived as "we" or "they"). However, the difference does not seem critical. It is probable that in some conditions (e.g., when similarity involves emotionally highly charged dimensions) these variables function as a dichotomous variable and in others as a continuous one (cf. Sole, Morton, & Hornstein, 1975).

Reykowski's explanation (which invokes the concept of generalization) seems to converge with the Hornstein model in another respect. A characteristic of altruistic behavior as explained by Reykowski is that the subject acts for the benefit of another person only insofar as this enables the latter to approach a goal (or state) that the subject would regard as desirable in his case also. A similar requirement or condition is contained in the Hornstein model.

Other explanations that treat altruistic behavior as controlled by anticipation of improvement in the situation of another person are represented by the affective approaches. These approaches see the motivational factor energizing behavior as some form of unconditioned or conditioned emotional response to cues (including social ones) that indicate the affective state of another person. We shall consider the explanations proposed by Aronfreed and Hoffman.

Aronfreed (1970) notes that in the course of socialization, social cues that transmit information about the experience of others are often linked to closely related events whose affective value is directly experienced by the subject. As a result of the temporal association that occurs here, "the cues which transmit the experience of others will acquire their own independent value for the elicitation of [corresponding] changes in the child's affectivity, under conditions which are no longer perceived by the child as signals of other events which it will experience directly [Aronfreed, 1970, p. 111]." This is, therefore, a case of classical conditioning. At the same time instrumental conditioning also comes into play. For altruistic behavior is reinforced by empathic experience of the effect of such behavior on others. Some experimental findings (Aronfreed & Pascal, cited in Aronfreed, 1970) indicate that this kind of classical and instrumental conditioning can in fact lead to altruistic behavior, though the permanence of this effect remains an open question.

There are, on the other hand, adherents to the view that empathic emotional responses to expressive cues reflecting another's distress may be (Hebb, 1971; Hoffman, 1975; MacLean, 1973; Trivers, 1971; Wynne-Edwards, 1962). But, regardless of whether we are dealing with unconditioned responses, they undergo substantial modifications in the course of a person's cognitive development and become an element in a more complex mechanism of behavior. The basic change is that empathic responses cease to be controlled solely by currently perceived cues but may also be controlled by cognitive representations of the present and anticipated states of another person (Coke, Batson, & McDavis, 1978). An interesting description of the development process occurring here has been presented by Hoffman (1975, 1977). It is worth noting that although he proceeds from totally different premises than Reykowski's, Hoffman arrives at a similar conclusion: that one of the basic determinants of altruistic behavior is the presence in the individual's cognitive system of mature (developed) cognitive representations of other people. This variable or construct performs a different role, however, for each theorist. Whereas Reykowski sees it as controlling behavior rather directly, Hoffman sees it acting as a modifying variable, the energizing factor always being an unconditioned or conditioned empathic emotional response.

Development of Motivational Sources of Altruistic Behavior

The development of endocentric versus exocentric sources of altruistic behavior may be promoted by different socialization techniques. It seems plausible that certain techniques that strongly focus the attention of the child on himself or herself might promote development of endocentric sources while inhibiting development of exocentric ones.

1. The manipulation of love (that is, love withdrawal and conditional love) is one technique that may promote the development of endocentric sources of altruism but not promote, or possibly even inhibit, the development of exocentric ones. At first, parents play the role of arbiters and dispensers of love and deference. A child's behavior in moral dilemmas provides an opportunity for parents to make a global evaluation of him or her in moral terms and to decide whether or not the child deserves deference and love. Later, processes of internalization and autonomization take place. In normal socialization the child gradually takes over the role of the parents in evaluating his or her own behavior. However, the tendency to perceive situations involving moral dilemmas as a sort of "defiance" of the self remains unchanged. This may in turn have a debilitating effect on the

ability to focus on a partner (compare Wicklund's, 1975, notion of the antagonism between self-focused attention and outward-focused attention).

Although previous studies find that frequent use of love withdrawal inhibits expression of hostility (Hoffman, 1963; Hoffman & Saltzstein, 1967) and promotes resistance to temptation (Burton, Maccoby, & Allinsmith, 1961), the tendency to confess (Hoffman & Saltzstein, 1967; Sears, Maccoby, & Levine, 1957), and guilt intensity (Hoffman & Saltzstein, 1967), no positive relationship between love withdrawal and altruism ("consideration for others") has been found. In one study (Hoffman, 1963) in which consideration for others was measured as giving unsolicited help to another child in distress and/or using influence techniques that show awareness of the other child's needs, no relationship was found. In another study (Hoffman & Saltzstein, 1967), children identified by their peers as most likely to "care about other children's feelings" and "defend a child being made fun of by the group" were found to have mothers who used love withdrawal even *less* often than a nonaltruistic group. However, given that the relative share of exocentric motives is probably much higher in cases of consideration for others (as measured in those studies) than for any other index of morality mentioned above, this pattern of results should not be surprising. In fact, another study by Hoffman (1970) found that children whose moral judgment responses show rigid adherence to institutional norms report more frequent use of love withdrawal by their mothers than do children (presumably more exocentric) whose responses show more concern for the human consequences of behavior.

2. Attaching positive or negative labels to a child (depending on his behavior in a given situation) is another socialization technique that may promote the development of endocentric sources of altruism but inhibit the development of exocentric ones. Particular note should be given to indefinite, open forms of evaluative labeling (e.g., "Bad kids behave in such a way," instead of "You're a bad kid"), as they suggest to the children that negative or positive evaluations they receive may easily change if only they change his behavior. As in the case of using love as a tool for manipulation, it is assumed that the initially external source of evaluation is gradually internalized, so that finally the child alone starts to label himself or herself positively or negatively, depending on his or her own behavior, actual or anticipated.

3. Focusing children's attention on consistencies or inconsistencies between their behavior and the demands of their social roles—for example, the role of a "child" or a "girl"—may function like indefinite labeling. In this case, however, the evaluative consequences for the "self" are more implicit or even nonexistent. For instance, a girl may experience an unpleasant "I am not being myself" feeling when behaving in a way she was

told (and believes) girls do not behave even if she does not feel that being a girl is more desirable than being a boy. One could say that while evaluative labeling promotes development of prosocial behavior motivated by the tendency to avoid inconsistency between actual behavior and *ideal* self, the latter technique mostly appeals to the *real* self. It provides ties between the child's behavior and vital elements of his or her self-description (in terms of social roles).

4. The development of endocentric sources of altruism is also facilitated by persuading a child to apologize. Apologizing is aimed at eliminating the negative effects of an act that affect the doer (thus exonerating her or him from guilty feelings) rather than the negative consequences for the victim, whose position possibly remains the same.

5. Reparation can also be an effective way of getting rid of guilty feelings, but its goal is aimed at improving a partner's situation. We can assume that asking a child to make reparation for his or her behavior conveys a message that what is important is not misbehavior itself, but its negative consequences for others and, most of all, the elimination of these consequences. As opposed to asking a child to apologize, persuading him or her to make reparation should promote the development of exocentric altruism.

6. Finally, the development of exocentric sources should also be favored by indicating what consequences a child's behavior has for a partner (so-called other-oriented induction).

Measurement of Endocentric versus Exocentric Altruism: The Prosocial Motivation Inventory

We assume that activation of exocentric sources will usually be accompanied by *conscious* focusing on the partner and his or her states, needs, and feelings, both present and anticipated. On the other hand, an activation of endocentric sources might be characterized by preoccupation with questions like, "What kind of person am I?", "Am I good and moral enough to help?", with images of moral satisfaction one might experience after the deed, and, perhaps, images of guilt and "not-myself feelings" one would experience by not helping.

The technique that we devised for measuring endocentric versus exocentric motivation (called the *Prosocial Motivation Inventory*) has a semi-projective character.[2] It consists of seven short stories. A female student is always the main character. The stories present situations in which a girl faces a moral

[2] This measure was developed in collaboration with two students, Hanna Gorska and Maria Wasiak.

dilemma, that is, she has to decide whether to help another person or not. In each case helping involves some psychological costs for the girl, and there is little opportunity of finding any substantial external reinforcement. Each story is followed by a different list of 24 items that are reasons for or against helping the person. Table 17.1 presents a sample story and a list of items. Items that encourage helping are always listed at the left side of the answer-form. Half (or six) of those pro-helping items focus on the moral aspect of the self (endocentric sources of altruism), while the other half focus on the partner's state (exocentric sources of altruism). Items of both help-favoring sets are arranged in random order. The items at the right side of the answer-form and in Table 17.1 are all arguments against helping and serve as filler items.[3]

Subjects are told to identify with the potential helper and to choose in each story 5 to 10 items, that they considered the most representative of the thoughts and feelings of the person in the situation.

The difference between the number of endocentric choices minus the number of exocentric choices provides a measure of the subject's tendency to focus on the moral aspect of the self (endocentrism) as compared to the tendency to focus on a partner (exocentrism).[4] The measure is based on standardized frequencies (z-scores) of subjects' choices before being actually subtracted from each other.

This technique has moderate internal consistency (split-half reliability with Spearman-Brown correction is .650; $N = 120$) with good stability over time (test–retest correlation after 2 years is .611; $N = 42$). It does not correlate significantly with the Marlowe-Crowne scale measuring need for social approval; for two different samples of $N = 132$ and $N = 56$ the correlation is $r = .135$ and $r = .112$ respectively.[5,6]

---

[3] There were two reasons for including such filler items: (a) The pilot studies had shown that they made the task look more natural; and (b) the clear dichotomy (pro- versus anti-helping arguments) is strongly loaded on the social desirability dimension. This might be expected to decrease further the effect of social desirability on choice of items within the pro-helping list.

[4] We decided to measure one bipolar variable instead of two, separate single variables, mainly for technical reasons. We suspected that measurement of the two separate variables would be highly contaminated with social approval and that this difficulty could be overcome with a single variable technique, since both poles are loaded on social approval.

[5] In the case of the first sample we were looking for a curvilinear correlation too. But there was no significant correlation at all.

[6] All the data reported here are for samples of female students between the ages of 16 and 19 who exhibited at least a moderate tendency for altruistic behavior (as reported by their peers).

Table 17.1
Prosocial Motivation Inventory (Sample Story)

Beth felt happy on her way home. She had been studying with her friend for two days for tomorrow's test and she was looking forward to relaxing and watching the last episode of a TV show she had been watching for weeks. Tonight, all the problems of the serial's heroes were supposed to be settled.

There were only a few people on the bus at this time of day, and Beth was probably the only person who, between bus stops, noticed a panicky young dog running aimlessly around. Obviously, the dog was lost, but there was nothing one could do.

However, Beth noticed an upset little girl near the next bus stop. The teary-eyed girl stood at a corner, scanning up and down the street. She held a leash in her hand, which made Beth even more certain that this girl was the owner of the lost dog. Beth could get off the bus and tell the little girl that she had seen her dog just a moment before, but then she would have to wait for the next bus for at least 20 minutes since the buses were running infrequently at this time of the day.

I think I'll get off and help the girl find the dog:

She must be terribly worried about her pet, she shouldn't be left all alone in her state.

I wouldn't forgive myself for staying in the bus. (x)

She's waiting for someone to help her, she's so poor.

If I don't help her, that will prove my complete callousness. (x)

I won't be able to ease my conscience if I don't do it. (x)

I can imagine what she feels right now.

She's so sad and helpless.

It would be easy not to get off. (x)

The thought that I can give up my own pleasure for another person is worth more than watching TV. (x)

I'll feel OK with my principles. (x)

I can imagine her happiness when she finds out where the dog is.

It will be nice to see their mutual happiness when they find each other.

I think I'll stay in the bus:

I've worked so hard, I want to get home as fast as possible.

A stupid dog that gets lost irritates me.

I don't want to get off and then wait half an hour for the next bus.

The brat should watch her own dog better; she deserves to look for it herself.

The dog's not far away; they'll run into each other.

I want to watch TV.

I'm tired and I need a rest.

The girl can ask somebody else to help her; why should I be the person?

Sometimes you have to think about yourself.

I can't see any reason for making such sacrifices.

The girl will calm down for sure and should do well without anybody's help.

A person should pay for her mistakes all by herself.

Note: Endocentric items are marked with an "x". The remaining items on the left hand side are exocentric. The items on the right hand side were fillers.

Empirical Evidence for Child Rearing Antecedents of Endocentric and Exocentric Motivation

Recently we conducted a study to test the hypotheses suggested earlier about developmental antecedents of prosocial behavior.[7] The data collection involved two stages. In the first stage, 135 high school girls aged 16–19 were rated by their classmates with regard to a trait defined as acting on behalf of others without any external self-interest. Of this group, the 120 girls who received at least average ratings were then administered the Prosocial Motivation Inventory. Two groups were finally selected: an endocentric group ($N = 20$) and an exocentric group ($N = 18$). The groups did not differ with respect to age, socioeconomic status, birth order, and school grades. In order to aid in interpreting differences between both altruistic groups, a third group was also selected, consisting of subjects perceived by their peers as being the least altruistic ($N = 20$).

In the second stage, data concerning socialization techniques was obtained from subjects' mothers in a structured interview. In all cases, the interviewer was blind with respect to the child's type of motivation. During the interview, a mother was given one after another 24 descriptions of hypothetical but common situations in which her child (i.e., daughter) might act in a certain way toward a partner. The descriptions differed as to

1. Her child's age (kindergarten or junior or senior high school)
2. The kind of partner (peer or adult)
3. The effect of behavior upon the partner (positive, e.g., child gives him a snack; or negative, e.g., child refuses to return partner's toy)
4. The intention underlying the behavior that produced negative effects (purposeful, e.g., child refuses partner's request for help; or unpurposeful, e.g., child forgets to fulfill his promise)
5. Presence or lack of previous incitement by the partner to justify negative behavior by child (previous incitement, e.g., child behaves in an aggressive way toward the partner who did harm to him; or no previous incitement, e.g., child behaves in an aggressive way toward an "innocent" partner)

The mother was asked to give a detailed description of how she would typically behave toward her child in each supposed situation. Data obtained during the interviews were rated by two independent judges. The level of agreement between judges ranged from $r = .761$ to $r = .955$, depending on the category being rated. A third judge made the final decision in cases of disagreement. All ratings were "blind."

[7] The study was conducted in collaboration with two students, Anna Szuster and Lena Wojdan.

The main results are presented below. Consistent with our hypotheses, the mothers of endocentric girls scored higher than the mothers of exocentric girls in the reported frequency of

1. Love withdrawal (significant for kindergarten age and the overall index)
2. Indefinite labeling (significant only for the overall index)
3. Persuading a child to apologize (significant for kindergarten age, junior school age, and the overall index)
4. Pointing out inconsistencies appearing between the child's behavior and the demands of his social role (significant for junior school age, senior school age, and the overall index)

For the last result, mothers from both groups did not differ in reported frequency of referring to the social role of the partner (e.g., adult role, teacher role, etc.). Thus, what is critical here is the special stress on the demands associated with the child's own roles rather than the roles other people have.

Another result consistent with our hypotheses was the higher reported frequency of using other-oriented induction by mothers of exocentric girls (significant for kindergarten age, junior school age, and the overall index).

Contrary to our expectation, the mothers of exocentrics did not report more frequent demands for reparation. In fact there was even a tendency for the opposite to occur. Although the mothers of exocentrics reported less frequent use of demands for both apologies and reparations, the first difference is much more pronounced ($t = 3.87$, $p < .001$, and $t = 1.96$, $p < .10$, respectively). The pattern becomes even more distinctive when proportional measures were used. The mean frequency of demands for apologies was over 2.5 times higher for mothers of endocentrics than for mothers of exocentrics; with respect to demands for reparations this ratio was not even 1.2:1. One possible explanation for this pattern of results is that the relative preference of endocentrics' mothers in comparison to exocentrics' mothers for making a child apologize coincides with another difference between the two groups, that is, with respect to the tendency to show respect for a child's autonomy and to avoid direct interference. The pattern of results would become clearer if we assume that both frequent demands for apologies and reparations are cases of interference, and that the tendency to respect a child's autonomy is weaker in mothers of endocentrics. The latter assumption seems to be justified, since mothers of exocentrics tended to report more frequent avoidance of showing any kind of disapproval. This was the case especially when the child's misbehavior was previously instigated by a partner (significant for junior school age and the overall index).

There is striking regularity in the position of nonaltruists with respect to the frequency with which their mothers use the above-mentioned socialization techniques. (Recall that nonaltruists were the third group in our study.) As far as overall indexes are concerned, nonaltruists invariably obtained average scores locating them *between* the two altruistic groups. These results should be interpreted cautiously. However, they seem to support the assumption that certain socialization techniques promote development of some sources of altruistic motivation but not others. These techniques focus a child's attention either on the moral aspect of the self or on external reality.

What Difference Does It Make?: Endocentric versus Exocentric Helping

Some comments seem appropriate concerning differences in the functioning of endocentric and exocentric helpers. Activation of endocentric sources of altruism may be accompanied by relatively low sensitivity to the needs of others, since attention is focused on the self (its moral aspect, but on the self, nevertheless). Some preliminary evidence supporting this view derives from a study by Jarymowicz (1977), who found that individuals with low or inconsistent self-esteem (who are presumably more endocentric), although equally willing to offer help, were significantly less adequate in their perception of the others' needs than individuals with consistent medium-high self-esteem (who are presumably more exocentric).

Because perception of other's needs in the case of endocentric altruism can easily be distorted, helping may depend here more on the extent to which such a behavior can restore (or maintain) equilibrium in the helper's self-concept (e.g., reducing a sense of guilt for refusing help to somebody else) than on the requirements of the external situation. Such helping is often inadequate, at least from the point of view of a helper, and might even be less appreciated. In fact, Nerwinska (1979) has found that among classmates indicated by their peers as "acting on behalf of others, without external self-interests," those scoring high on our Prosocial Motivation Inventory (endocentrics) were liked less than those scoring low (exocentrics).

Endocentrically motivated altruists are often not particularly liked by those whom they help, but often these altruists do not like their helpees either. In one study (Karylowski, 1977b) we manipulated predominance of endocentric over exocentric sources of altruism by a typical self-focused attention manipulation. Half of the subjects either were or were not confronted with their own mirror image when having to decide how hard they were willing to work for a partner (the self-focus and non-self-focus groups, respectively). In the self-focusing group, but not in the non-self-focus group, the harder the subject worked for a highly dependent partner the less favorable was the attitude he or she expressed toward that partner later. Apparently, those self-focusing (and presumably endocentrically motivated) subjects worked for a partner because they felt they ought to rather than because they wanted to.

Such feeling of "ought to" rather than "want to" may have other important consequences. Being spontaneous and free of different obligations has become a central value of contemporary culture in Europe and North America (cf. Jawlowska, 1975; Kohlberg, 1976). This value, when internalized, assumes the form of specific self-expectations dealing with personal freedom. When activated, these self-expectations may neutralize "ought to" feelings resulting from activation of *altruistic* self-expectations. As a result, inhibition of endocentric altruistic behavior will occur. There are two reasons why we expect such a reactance process to take place in the case of endocentric altruism rather than in the case of exocentric altruism:

1. Self-focused attention tends to shift from one aspect of the self to other aspects (Wicklund, 1975). As a result, previous activation of self-expectations of any kind (including altruistic ones) will make activation of self-expectations of personal freedom more likely.

2. Although reactance processes might be activated by experience of any strong preference (cf. Wicklund's, 1974, notion of self-imposed threat to freedom), at least intuitively, preferences experienced as "ought to" seem to be much more directly threatening to our sense of personal freedom than those experienced as "want to" (even if they are very strong).

In a related study (Karylowski, 1979) actual altruistic behavior of those scoring high (endocentrics) and those scoring low (exocentrics) on the Prosocial Motivation Inventory was measured on the basis of peer ratings, while personal freedom and altruistic self-expectations were measured by paper-and-pencil techniques. Results confirmed our predictions: In the case of the endocentric group, but not in the case of the exocentric group, self-expectations of personal freedom were inversely related to the consistency between actual altruistic behavior and altruistic self-expectations.

Concluding Remarks

In this chapter we have argued that it is possible, both theoretically and empirically, to distinguish between two kinds of mechanisms underlying altruism and that one-factor theories are insufficient. We have presented some empirical data indicating that mechanisms of each kind have different antecedents and that their activation may have different behavioral consequences. But, as the reader may have observed, we haven't said much about interrelationships between the two systems. How do they work together? To what extent are they independent from each other or even antagonistic and to what extent and under what conditions do they support each other? Much more theoretical development and research needs to be conducted on the two-factor theory of altruism.

References

Aronfreed, J. The socialization of altruistic and sympathetic behavior: Some theoretical and experimental analyses. In J. R. Macaulay & L. Berkowitz (Eds.), *Altruism and helping behavior*. New York: Academic Press, 1970.

Berkowitz, L. Social norms, feelings, and other factors affecting helping and altruism. In L. Berkowitz (Ed.), *Advances in experimental social psychology* (Vol. 6). New York: Academic Press, 1972.

Berkowitz, L., & Daniels, L. R. Responsibility and dependency. *Journal of Abnormal and Social Psychology*, 1963, *66*, 429–437.

Burton, R. V., Maccoby, R. R., & Allinsmith, W. Antecedents of resistance to temptation in four-year-old children. *Child Development*, 1961, *32*, 689–710.

Coke, J. S., Batson, S. D., & McDavis, K. Empathic mediation of helping: A two stage model. *Journal of Personality and Social Psychology*, 1978, *36*, 752–766.

Gouldner, A. W. The norm of reciprocity: A preliminary statement. *American Sociological Review*, 1960, *25*, 161–178.

Hebb, D. O. Comment on altruism: The comparative evidence. *Psychological Bulletin*, 1971, *76*, 409.

Hoffman, M. L. Parent discipline and the child's consideration for others. *Child Development*, 1963, *34*, 573–588.

Hoffman, M. L. Conscience, personality, and socialization techniques. *Human Development*, 1970, *13*, 90–120.

Hoffman, M. L. Developmental synthesis of affect and cognition and its implications for altruistic motivation. *Developmental Psychology*, 1975, *11*, 607–622.

Hoffman, M. L. Empathy, its development and prosocial implications. In D. Levine (Ed.), *Nebraska Symposium on Motivation* (Vol. 25). Lincoln: University of Nebraska Press, 1977.

Hoffman, M. L., & Saltzstein, H. D. Parent discipline and the child's moral development. *Journal of Personality and Social Psychology*, 1967, *5*, 45–57.

Hornstein, H. A. Promotive tension: The basis of prosocial behavior from a Lewinian perspective. *Journal of Social Issues*, 1972, *28* (2), 191–218.

Hornstein, H. A. *Cruelty and kindness: A new look at aggression and altruism*. Englewood Cliffs, N.J.: Prentice-Hall, 1976.

Jarymowicz, M. Modification of self-worth and increment of prosocial sensitivity. *Polish Psychological Bulletin*, 1977, *8*, 45–53.

Jawlowska, A. *Drogi kontrkultury*. (*The roads of the counterculture*.) Warsaw: PIW, 1975.

Karylowski, J. Explaining altruistic behavior: A review. *Polish Psychological Bulletin*, 1977, *8*, 27–34. (a)

Karylowski, J. Koncentracja na sobie i zawartość "Ja" idealnego a bezinteresowne dzialanie na rzecz innych ludzi. (Objective self-awareness, the contents of ideal-self, and altruism.) *Studia Psychologiczne*, 1977, *15*, 19–36. (b)

Karylowski, J. Prosocial norms, self-focused attention and prosocial behavior. *Polish Psychological Bulletin*, 1979, *10*, 57–66.

Kohlberg, L. Children's perception of contemporary value system. In L. B. Talbot (Ed.), *Raising children in modern America*, Boston: Little, Brown, 1976.

Leeds, R. Altruism and the norm of giving. *Merrill-Palmer Quarterly*, 1963, *9*, 229–240.

Lerner, M. J. The justice motive in social behaviour: Some hypotheses to its origins and forms. *Journal of Personality*, 1977, *45*, 1–52.

Lerner, M. J., Miller, D. T., & Holmes, J. C. Deserving and the emergence of forms of justice. In L. Berkowitz (Ed.), *Advances in experimental social psychology* (Vol. 9). New York: Academic Press, 1976.

MacLean, P. D. *A triune concept of the brain and behavior.* Toronto: University of Toronto Press, 1973.

Nerwinska, E. *Endo-/egzocentrycznie motywowana gotowość do zachowań prospolecznych a atrakcyjność interpersonalna.* (*Endo-/exocentric prosocial behavior and interpersonal attraction.*) Unpublished master's thesis. University of Warsaw, 1979.

Pavlov, I. P. *Conditioned reflexes: An investigation of the physiological activity of the cerebral cortex.* New York: Dover Publications, 1960.

Piliavin, J. A., Dovidio, J. F., Gaertner, S. C., & Clark, R. D., III. *Emergency intervention.* New York: Academic Press, 1981.

Piliavin, J. A., & Piliavin, I. M. *The good samaritan: Why does he help?* Unpublished manuscript. University of Wisconsin, 1973.

Reykowski, J. Position of self-structure in a cognitive system and prosocial orientation. *Dialectic and Humanism*, 1976, *5*, 19–30.

Reykowski, J. Cognitive development and prosocial behavior. *Polish Psychological Bulletin*, 1977, *8*, 35–43.

Reykowski, J. *Motywacja, postawy prospoleczne a osobowość* (*Prosocial motivation, prosocial attitudes and personality.*) Warsaw: Państwowe Wydawnictwo Naukowe, 1979.

Rosenhan, D. L. Learning theory and prosocial behavior. *Journal of Social Issues*, 1972, *28*, 151–163.

Schwartz, S. H. Moral decision making and behavior. In J. R. Macaulay & L. Berkowitz (Eds.), *Altruism and helping behavior.* New York: Academic Press, 1970.

Schwartz, S. H. Normative influences on altruism. In L. Berkowitz (Ed.), *Advances in experimental social psychology* (Vol. 10). New York: Academic Press, 1977.

Schwartz, S. H., & Howard, J. A. A normative decision-making model of altruism. In J. P. Rushton & R. M. Sorrentino (Eds.), *Altruism and helping behavior.* Hillsdale, N.J.: Lawrence Erlbaum, 1981.

Sears, R. R., Maccoby, E. E., & Levin, H. *Patterns of child rearing.* Evanston, Ill.: Row, Peterson, 1957.

Sole, K., Marton, J., & Hornstein, A. H. Opinion similarity and helping: Three field experiments investigating the basis of promotive tension. *Journal of Experimental Social Psychology*, 1975, *11*, 1–13.

Staub, E. *Positive social behavior and morality.* New York: Academic Press, 1978.

Trivers, R. L. The revolution of reciprocal altruism. *Quarterly Review of Biology*, 1971, *46*, 35–37.

Walster, E., Walster, G. W., & Berscheid, E. *Equity: Theory and research.* Boston: Allyn & Bacon, 1978.

Wicklund, R. A. *Freedom and reactance.* Potomac, Maryland: Erlbaum, 1974.

Wicklund, R. A. Objective self-awareness. In L. Berkowitz (Ed.), *Advances in experimental social psychology* (Vol. 7). New York: Academic Press, 1975.

Wynne-Edwards, V. C. *Animal dispersion in relation to social behavior.* Edinburgh: Oliver & Boyd, 1962.

Postscript

Chapter 18

Altruism, Envy,

Competitiveness, and

the Common Good

R. B. ZAJONC

This postscript is written by an unbiased observer—unbiased, however, only by knowledge of the field and of its research literature. For it is the absence of this knowledge that qualified me to take part in this undertaking. The editors of this volume invited me, as a sort of token ignoramus, to put together an outsider's postscript apparently because they wanted someone naive to comment on the subject matter of prosocial behavior. Their reasons appeared to be entirely clear to them. But they remain obscure to me. It is not without recklessness, therefore, that I view my assignment, delighted to share with the editors the responsibility for my irresponsible approach to the problem.

What does research on prosocial behavior look like "from the outside"? It appeared to me that the fruitful and difficult questions being asked in this volume dealt generally with three major research topics:

1. Intention for self versus others' benefit
2. Attributes of the target
3. Internal and external constraints on behavior

Of these three, the first is by far the most significant. It is to the topic of intention that the main thrust of the research is directed, and it is the

417

COOPERATION AND HELPING BEHAVIOR
Theories and Research

concept of intention that affords considerable ambiguity in the formulation of significant and fruitful research questions. I shall, therefore, deal here with the problem of intention, on the assumption that if it is ignorance of the field that qualifies me to comment on its research, then the more difficult the problem the more I should qualify.

Intention is surely a very complex psychological phenomenon, covert and not readily accessible to observation. Psychological knowledge of intentions entails knowledge about the elaborate cognitive structures that are surely involved and about their motivational and affective properties. Concepts like commitment, plans, goals, values, task tension, *Aufgabe*, *Einstellung*, set, purpose, aspiration, and many others are linked with intention in a variety of ways, and although they overlap with intention, none of these captures the full meaning of the concept. Intention is a sphere of behavior in which the psychologist and the philosopher alike need to clarify their conceptual network and the method of inquiry. There is no very satisfactory conceptual language to deal with most of these covert states of the person.

Above all, intention implies that some future states are being anticipated and desired. This feature in itself is fraught with ambiguity. The problem of intention in the case of prosocial behavior is even more complicated because not only one's own future states (that may be brought about by one's own actions) are anticipated and desired, but the states of others as well.

How can the social psychologist make inferences about intentions in the case of prosocial behavior? It is clearly insufficient to make these inferences from the helper's behavior alone because it is the helper's behavior that needs to be explained in the first place. The worker bee is equipped with a barbed sting that can be employed in the defense of the hive only once because its use inevitably results in the death of the worker. Surely, such an action must be defined as prosocial for it involves the highest level of harm, or self-sacrifice, for the benefit of the community. The individual pays the highest price for a small reduction in the danger to the hive. However, it would be awkward to talk about intention in this case, unless the hard-wired program that prompts the worker bee to behave in this manner is arbitrarily categorized in this way by the social psychological theory of prosocial behavior. In fact, Hamilton (1963) suggested a "motive" for altruistic behavior that requires the individual to make discriminations among those to whom such harm is directed. If harms and benefits are not distributed randomly, but if harms are moderated when directed at like genotypes and if benefits are increased, selection will favor the species. Hamilton's model of inclusive fitness postulates that organisms are "motivated" to reproduce their own genes. For example, since we have 1/8 of our genes in common with our cousins, if we were to save the lives of eight of our cousins or help them in such a way that each of them would produce one offspring, then we would be instrumental in the production of eight individuals all of whom are 1/16 like us. This would be equivalent to adding one sibling to our own family because $8 \times 1/16 = 1/2$, which is the proportion of genes that we share with our brothers and sisters. But it is somewhat problematic to equate with intention inclusive fitness forces that lead to nepotistic behavior. Or is it?

Nor is it sufficient in conceptualizing intention to draw on the consequences for the recipient of help, because often these consequences may be fairly independent of the helper's actions and of the helper's intentions. Few people thought that the Aswan Dam would cause erosion of the coastline, kill the sardine industry, deprive the area of the flood silt that made Egypt's soil one of the most fertile agricultural regions of the world, invite the dangerous bilharzia parasite, clog sewer drains, and increase the saline content of the land, reducing agricultural yields by 50% (*The Economist*, 1975). It must be, therefore, that we need four types of information: (*a*) We need to observe the helper's behavior, (*b*) we need to know how to make accurate inferences about the goal structure of that behavior, (*c*) we need to observe the true consequences of the helper's behavior for the target, and (*d*) we need the knowledge of the helper's reaction on learning the consequences suffered or enjoyed by the target. Of these four types of information, the second cannot be obtained by direct observations and relies in part on the other three.

It would be a tedious task to try to gather all this information in every experiment on prosocial behavior. There are, however, several shortcuts, such as the decomposition of mixed motive games, for example. A useful experimental paradigm involves a series of prisoners' dilemma (PD) games, with one trial on each, or similar contrived situations (e.g., bystander intervention, helping with exams, etc.) where the costs and benefits to the helper and to the recipient of help are systematically varied. The typical way to vary this situation is, of course, to make helping more and more difficult for the helper. We also vary the consequences of the helper's action. Thus, for example, a given helping action may on the surface appear to promise benefits to the target, yet after it is carried out, it turns out to be actually harmful. Do helpers adjust their behavior so as to maximize target's benefits? Do they do so independently of what is happening to their own costs and benefits? This approach might yield measures that would resemble psychophysical functions—something like helping thresholds, for example, that would be represented by a family of helping likelihood curves plotted against the helper's costs, with the benefit reaped by the target as the parameter of those functions.

One theme that recurs in the present volume is the question of how best to describe intentions for outcomes. At the risk of repeating something that may have been said elsewhere, I might suggest one other way of describing what is happening in such situations. Consider a typical PD situation, such as the one shown in Figure 18.1. Conventionally, the typical PD game must satisfy two inequalities: $2a > b + c$ and $b > a > d > c$, where a, b, c, and d are cell outcomes[1] as in Figure 18.2. Given that self-interest dominates choice behavior, there is a strong temptation for both players to choose Y which is ultimately less profitable than choosing X. But we know that players often choose X and that they must do so for a number of reasons. If they choose X because they somehow derive pleasure or benefit from the good fortune of their opponents (partners), then perhaps the matrix of payoffs may be rewritten. Suppose that on each move the players not only enjoy the reward that they themselves receive directly but also derive some pleasure from the reward received by their partner. Of course, this form of decomposition has been considered previously very often, but it was viewed in terms that were somewhat different, I believe, from those I am proposing here. Kelley and Thibaut (1978) have described a form of matrix transformation that reflects various types of control (reflexive, fate, and behavioral) in interdependent two-person situations. MacCrimmon and Messick (1976), on the other hand, outlined a categorization of a variety of social motives, such as self-interest, self-sacrifice, altruism, etc., based on people's preferences for their own and others' outcomes.

Altruism

The notion that I am proposing here is that such social motives as altruism or competitiveness can be represented by transforming the given matrix into a subjective form. Suppose that player A enjoys his or her own winnings and that his or her enjoyment that derives from the winnings of his or her opponent is equivalent to 50% of the opponent's take. Thus, if both A and B choose X, both win $a' = a + 1/2a$ instead of simply a. The transformed cell entries will be generally designated as a', b', c', and d'. Thus, each player gets $8 + 4 = 12$ points because each derives 50% benefit from the other's take. Of course, the 4 points are hypothetical and must be estimated from the choice behavior of the subjects. These subjective outcomes are shown in Figure 18.3.

Note that whereas the original game as given by the experimenter had Y as the preferred choice, now the preferred choice is X. The second set

---

[1] If the first inequality were not satisfied it would be to the advantage of the players to choose either cell X,Y or Y,X each of which has a greater joint payoff than the X,X cell.

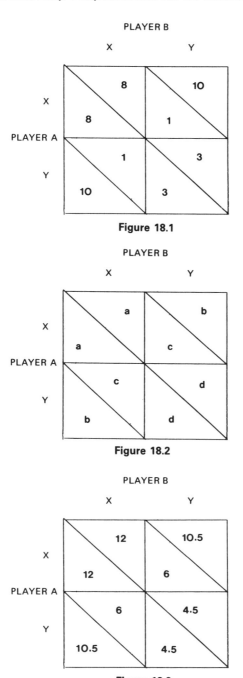

Figure 18.1

Figure 18.2

Figure 18.3

of inequalities is violated at two junctions, and we now have $b' < a' > d' < c'$.

It will *not* suffice to shift the preference from Y to X if each player derives pleasure from the winnings of the other only at the level of 25%, as shown in Figure 18.4. In this instance Y is still favored, albeit only by .25 points. So, it appears that for the typical PD game, subjective rewards derived from the benefits of the partner increase preference for the X choice.

The altruism factor, which we may wish to designate α, that is, the hypothetical weight that must be applied to the opponent's payoffs so as to make the X choice subjectively more attractive than the Y choice, can be readily calculated. We have as given $b > a$ and $d > c$. But if we wish the choice preference to be reversed, such that $b' < a'$ and $d' < c'$ we must have $(b + \alpha c) < (a + \alpha a)$ and $(d + \alpha d) < (c + \alpha b)$. Therefore, $(b - a)/(a - c) < \alpha > (d - c)/(b - d)$. If a is given, the larger the difference $b - c$, the smaller α need be. And given the difference $b - c$, the larger a is, the larger α must be to effect a change in preference from Y to X. Thus, we noted above that $\alpha = .25$ was insufficient to alter the choice preference in the first matrix given. We needed $(10 - 8)/(8 - 1) = .29$. Note that if $a = 101$, $b = 102$, $c = 1$, and $d = 2$, we shall require an altruism factor α equal only to .01, if we wish to reverse the choice preference. But if $a = 2$, $b = 102$, $c = 1$, and $d = 101$, α must be greater than 100. Note finally, that α is clearly not affected by adding a constant to the a, b, c, and d values or by multiplying them by a constant.

The Common Good

A significant variant of prosocial motivation is that in which the *common good* is maximized by the players. Within the context of the present rep-

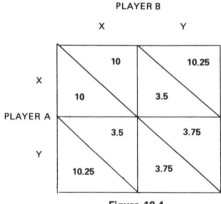

PLAYER B

Figure 18.4

resentation this would amount to having a common good factor, γ, which operates on the *sum* of the partners' outcomes. Thus, given $2a > b + c$, and $b > a > d > c$, we wish to have $a'' > b''$ and $c'' > d''$, where $b'' = b + \gamma(b + c)$, $a'' = 2\gamma a + a$, $c'' = c + \gamma(b + c)$ and $d'' = 2\gamma d + d$. Since we must have $a + 2\gamma a > b + \gamma (b + c)$ and $c + \gamma (b + c) > d + 2\gamma d$, the common good factor must satisfy the two inequalities $(b - a)/(2a - b - c) < \gamma > (d - c)/(b + c - 2d)$. For the game in Figure 18.1, the subjective payoffs, given $\gamma = .5$, would be as in Figure 18.5. The preference for Y is abandoned in favor of X.

How can the motivation for the common good be distinguished from the altruistic motivation considered above? Can we determine whether in a given situation individuals will value their joint outcomes more than simply those of their partners?

Consider the matrix in Figure 18.6. Suppose that altruism is the motive and that each player enjoys the other's winnings at the level of $\alpha = 1$, that is, the partner's win in its entirety is added to one's own take. The subjective payoffs, given $\alpha = 1$, are as shown in Figure 18.7, and we would expect a shift from Y to X. But if the players are motivated by the common good at the same level, that is, $\gamma = 1$, then there will be no shift from Y to X because the subjective matrix is as in Figure 18.8. In fact, the common good must be subjectively valued at six times its objective value for a shift to occur $[(14 - 8)/(2 \times 8 - 14 - 1) < \gamma > (7 - 1)/(14 + 1 - 2 \times 7)]$.

In order to produce a difference between Y and X equivalent to the one produced by $\gamma = 1$ for the above matrix, we need $a'' = c'' - b'' - d'' = 1$, and therefore $\gamma = (1 - a + b)/(2a - b - c)$. Thus we need a γ-factor equal to 7. Given such a value for γ, the matrix of subjective payoffs is as in Figure 18.9.

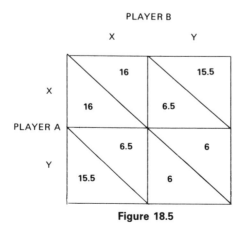

Figure 18.5

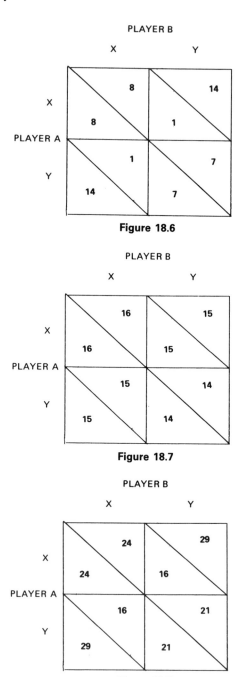

PLAYER B

Figure 18.6

PLAYER B

Figure 18.7

PLAYER B

Figure 18.8

PLAYER B

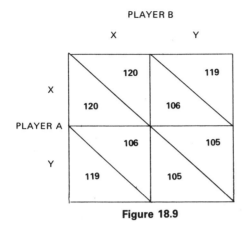

Figure 18.9

It is readily seen that in a matrix where $2a > b + c$ and $b > a > d$ $> c$, the common good factor γ must always be greater than α for a shift from Y to X to occur. Otherwise, if $\alpha > \gamma$, then $(b - a)/(a - c) < (b - a)/(2a - b - c)$, which implies that $a > b$, and $(d - c)/(b - d)$ $> (d - c)/(b + c - 2d)$, which implies $c > d$, contradicting the second inequality of the original PD matrix that must be satisfied.

Envy

If the individual suffers pains of jealousy because of the good luck of his opponent, the Y choice that in Figure 18.1 is preferred over X will be even more favored. Clearly, the above representation may also be used for discovering the extent of envy among the players. But now it is best to set up a benign game situation, such as was employed by McClintock and McNeel (1966). Thus if the players are given the game matrix shown in Figure 18.10, self-interest will predict that they will choose X quite heavily: Note that the inequality $2a > b + c$ still holds. However, we now must have $a > b > c > d$.

But if the players are motivated by envy at the level of 50%, given the above payoffs their choices should favor Y. These subjective values are shown in Figure 18.11.

The envy factor ε can be calculated for the benign matrix in a way similar to that in which α and γ were obtained. Since now $a > b$ and $c > d$, a change of preference from X to Y requires $a^* < b^*$ and $c^* < d^*$ or $(a - \varepsilon a) < (b - \varepsilon c)$ and $(c - \varepsilon b) < (d - \varepsilon d)$. Thus, the envy factor must be greater than the two ratios $(a - b)/(a - c) < \varepsilon > (c - d)/(b - d)$. Note that for the matrix of payoffs in Figure 18.10 we need $\varepsilon > .4$.

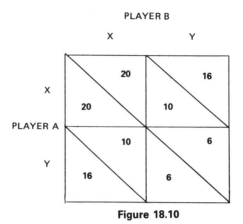

Figure 18.10

Competitiveness

Given payoffs as in Figure 18.10, if the players are motivated by competitiveness and enjoy (and suffer) the *differences* between their payoffs at the 50% level, than a preference for X should emerge, but a very slight one (Figure 18.12).

The competitiveness factor, δ, must satisfy the following inequalities: $b + \delta (b - c) > a$ and $d > c - \delta(b - c)$. Thus, $(a - b)/(b - c) < \delta > (c - d)/(b - c)$. In the above case we have $\delta > .667$. With $\delta = .8$, for example, the transformed matrix would be as in Figure 18.13.

In contrast to a situation dominated by competitiveness, the situation dominated by envy generates a matrix of decreased payoffs. Under these circumstances, the players may well want to leave the game altogether.

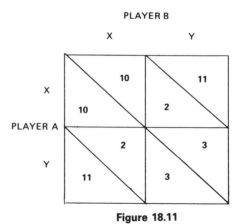

Figure 18.11

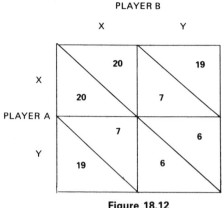

Figure 18.12

Thus, an additional method presents itself in this context. Subjects participating in these experiments could be given alternative games that maximize their competitive desires but have higher payoffs. Choosing to play on another matrix of payoffs that is similar in these critical respects but has generally higher payoffs would indicate that considerations deriving from envy led to the reduction in the payoffs.

Mixed Motives

It is probably rare in a typical experimental situation that both players exhibit the same prosocial or antisocial tendencies in a PD game. And even if they do have the same kind of motivation, say altruism, they might differ

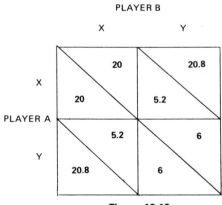

Figure 18.13

in the degree to which they enjoy each other's good fortune. Thus, for example, if A is motivated altruistically at $\alpha = .5$ and B at $\alpha = .25$, and if they are given the payoff matrix in Figure 18.1, then the transformed matrix is as in Figure 18.14. Note that under these circumstances, the players will end up in the upper right-hand cell of the matrix because A's altruism factor (α_A) is above the cross-over threshold (.29), whereas B's altruism factor (α_B) is below that threshold. The values of α_A and α_B can be calculated separately in the same way as the overall α's are calculated.

Another form of mixed motives is for A to be motivated positively and B negatively. For example, A has an altruism factor $\alpha = .5$, whereas B has an envy factor $\varepsilon = .5$. The matrix that emerges is as in Figure 18.15. Again the two players end up with different preferences: A has a 1.5 point preference for X over Y, and B averages 6.5 preference for Y over X. Note that the two players will end up in the upper right hand cell again.

It is also possible, of course, as has been repeatedly noted, for a single player to be influenced in his choices by more than one motive. A likely possibility, for example, is the combination of altruism and competitiveness. Thus, A may delight in the fact that B is winning as long as B is not winning much more than A. Given that both players have an altruism factor $\alpha = .5$ and a competitiveness factor of $\delta = .5$ as well, the objective matrix in Figure 18.1 would be transformed into the one shown in Figure 18.16. Note that a shift from Y to X would not take place given the combination of α and δ both at .5. These combined motives of altruism and competitiveness transform the a, b, c, and d values as follows:

$$a\dagger = a + \alpha a$$
$$b\dagger = b + \alpha c + \delta(b - c)$$
$$c\dagger = c + \alpha b + \delta(c - b)$$
$$d\dagger = d + \delta d.$$

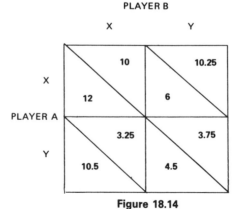

PLAYER B

Figure 18.14

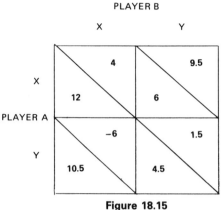

Figure 18.15

It is readily shown that no shift from a preference for Y to a preference for X can take place given $\alpha = \delta = \phi$. We have that $a\dagger$ must be greater than $b\dagger$ and thus, $a + \phi a > b + \phi c + \phi (b - c)$, which implies both $\phi > (b - a)/(a - b)$ and $\phi < (a - b)/(b - a)$. Since the two ratios are both equal to -1, we have the contradiction that ϕ must be both larger and smaller than -1. Of course, if α and δ have different values, a shift to X can occur if α is larger than δ.

The identical contradiction emerges when common good is combined with envy and no values $\gamma = \varepsilon$ can be found for which a shift from Y to X will occur.

Given $\alpha > \delta$ or $\gamma > \varepsilon$, a change in choice preference from Y to X may well take place. Consider, for example, that the players' choices are dominated by altruism and competitiveness. Given $\alpha > \delta$ we can calculate, for a given α, how much larger α must be than δ if a shift from Y to X is to

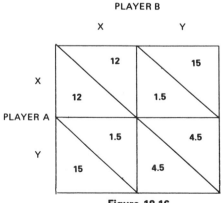

Figure 18.16

take place. In the case of mixed motives of competitiveness and altruism, and given that the values of $a\dagger$, $b\dagger$, $c\dagger$ and $d\dagger$ are as shown in the Figure 18.14, we may treat δ as a proportion of α such that $\delta = p\alpha$. Take a given value of α, say $\alpha = 1$. Then for a shift we require $2a > b + c + p(b - c)$ and $c + b + p(c - b) > 2d$. Therefore, $(2a - b - c)/(b - c) > p < (c + b - 2d)/(b - c)$. For the matrix in Figure 18.1, $p = 5/9$ and $\delta = 5/9$. If $\alpha = .5$, then for the entries in Figure 18.1, $p = 1/3$ and $\delta = 1/6$. Thus, for example, given the values in Figure 18.1, and given the mixed motives of $\alpha = 1$ and $\delta = .5$ (which is less than 5/9), the transformed subjective matrix is as in Figure 18.17, in which there is a preference for X over Y. Given $\alpha = .5$ and $\delta = .15$ (which is less than 1/6), the matrix of transformed subjective values is shown in Figure 18.18.

As α decreases, δ must be an increasingly smaller proportion of α. In fact, there is a lower limit on α for a given matrix of PD objective values. For example, for the matrix in Figure 18.1 the lowest value of α is .286. At $\alpha = .286$, δ must be nearly zero. Below that value the competitiveness factor must be less than zero; thus it loses its character and becomes a form of a self-denial factor under which each player wishes the other to win more.

Successive Trials

The above illustrations apply principally to the first trial. We may wish to extrapolate the scenario further. The question arises, of course, whether on the subsequent trials the same subjective matrix holds that the participants construed for themselves on the first trial. The possibility exists that the subjective feelings that are aroused at Trial 2 take as a starting point not the matrix given by the experimenter but the matrix that existed sub-

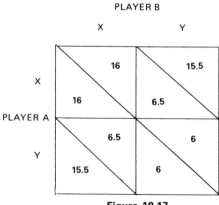

Figure 18.17

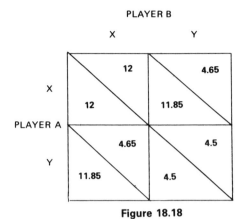

Figure 18.18

jectively for the players at Trial 1. Thus, it is entirely possible that on Trial 2, player A may begrudge B the satisfaction B derived from seeing A get a smaller reward. Or A may be delighted with the outcome that favors him much more than B. On Trial 3 the subjective matrix construed for Trial 2 may be taken as a reference point, etc.

Interesting consequences result if the subjective matrix of payoffs changes with each trial and if the change is based on Trial $n - 1$, keeping the same motivation. In the case of altruism, $\alpha = .5$, we can imagine the succession of trials shown in Figure 18.19, given that the players start with the values such as in Figure 18.10.

Two phenomena appear over trials in the case of altruistic motivation. On the one hand, preference for X increases. But at the same time, the asymmetrical cells b' and c' decrease in their payoff difference such that A and B receive more and more equal rewards.

For the common good, $\gamma = .5$, a similar pattern emerges over trials (see Figure 18.20). However, now the preference for X over Y increases more rapidly over the successive trials and it appears to be systematic. For the example shown in Figure 18.20, the rate of increase in preference for X over Y in case $\gamma = .5$ can be expressed as $a''_{t_n} - b''_{t_n} = (a''_{t_{n-1}} - b''_{t_{n-1}}) + 3$.

If the players are motivated by envy, $\varepsilon = .5$, the succession of trials generates an increasing preference for Y over X (see Figure 18.21).

Finally, competitiveness, given $\delta = .5$, also generates a rise in preference for Y over X. These trials are shown in Figure 18.22. On Trial 1 there is still a preference for X, preserving the pattern of the payoff matrix given by the experimenter. However, already on Trial 2 a preference for Y emerges—a preference that rises with trials quite steeply, more steeply in fact than in the case of envy.

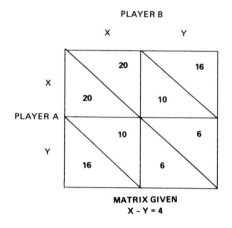

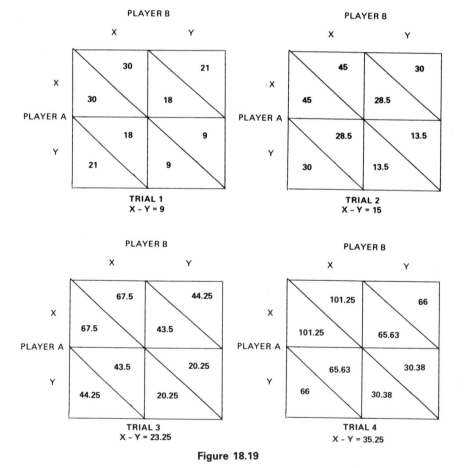

Figure 18.19

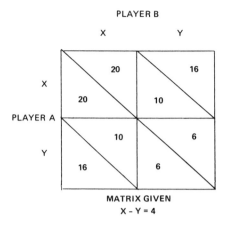

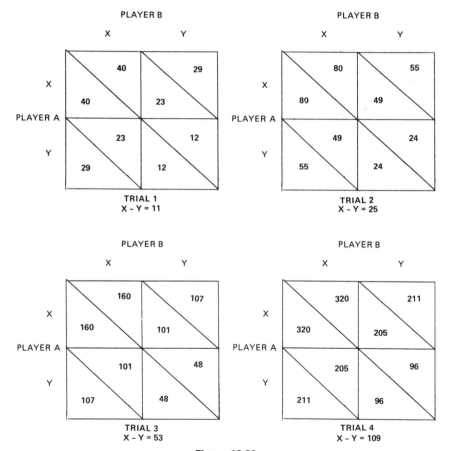

Figure 18.20

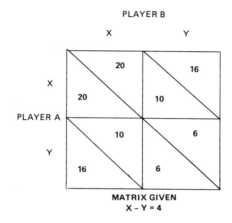

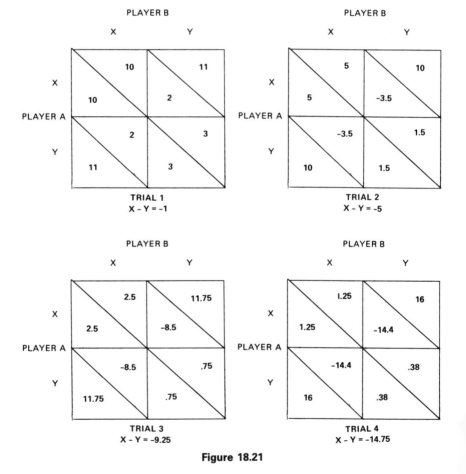

Figure 18.21

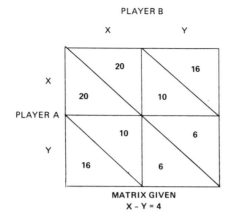

MATRIX GIVEN
X – Y = 4

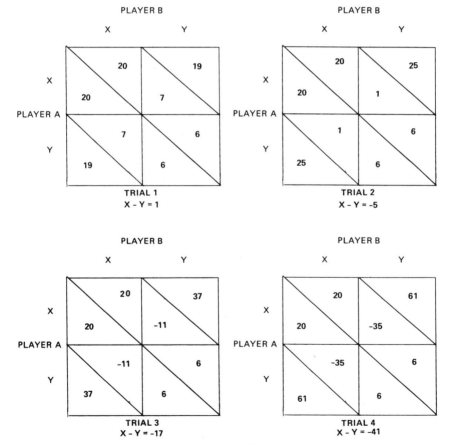

TRIAL 1
X – Y = 1

TRIAL 2
X – Y = –5

TRIAL 3
X – Y = –17

TRIAL 4
X – Y = –41

Figure 18.22

Conclusion

For the above representation to be useful, of course, one needs to translate the likelihood of choosing one response over another into the subjective values of a', b', c' and d' of the matrix, by estimating the factors α, γ, δ, and ε. That will not be an easy psychophysical task, but it is a task that is in fact required in one form or another of all approaches to the study of cooperative and competitive behavior that rely on payoffs and utilities.

Note that the above discussion is entirely dominated by the assumption of self-interest. All motives were transformed into a local self-interest. To be sure, it is self-interest that sometimes benefits others, but it is self-interest nevertheless. I have rewritten the payoff matrices by translating the opponents' rewards and losses into the players' own pleasures and pains. Thus, in Figure 18.1 each player derives satisfaction from the other player's winnings, and it is this satisfaction that directs their choices, changing them from Y to X.

I believe that I have been caught by the spirit of this volume which except for Lerner's chapter (Chapter 11) relies very much on either proximal or distal self-interest for the account of various forms of prosocial behavior. Lerner's concept of justice focuses on social elements that at the first glance appear to be free of self-interest influences. However, the justice theory of prosocial behavior *also* involves some forms of self-interest. If people's prosocial behavior is motivated by considerations of justice, equity, or fairness, the question immediately arises about their motives for the attainment of these values. Justice, equity, and fairness are judgmental criteria under the control of social norms. And defying social norms may be costly. So it is in one's self-interest after all to be just and fair. The notion of inclusive fitness might be the only one, I believe, that does not involve some form of self-interest, unless again the impulse of the worker bee to sting a perceived enemy is unbearable, and thus the ugly head of self-interest looms again in the study of altruism.

References

The Economist, March 22–28, 1975.

Hamilton, W. D. The evolution of altruistic behavior. *American Naturalist*, 1963, 97, 354–356.

Kelley, H. H., & Thibaut, J. W. *Interpersonal relations: A theory of interdependence.* New York: John Wiley & Sons, 1978.

McClintock, C. G., & McNeel, S. P. Reward level and game playing behavior. *Journal of Conflict Resolution*, 1966, 10, 98–102.

MacCrimmon, K. R., & Messick, D. M. A framework for social motives. *Behavioral Science*, 1976, 21, 86–100.

Author Index

Subject Index